Dictionary of Counseling and Human Services

An Essential Resource for Students and Professional Helpers

Edward Neukrug, Michael Kalkbrenner, and Kevin Snow
Old Dominion University New Mexico State University Marywood University

cognella
SAN DIEGO

Bassim Hamadeh, CEO and Publisher
Amy Smith, Senior Project Editor
Alia Bales, Production Editor
Jess Estrella, Senior Graphic Designer
Stephanie Kohl, Licensing Coordinator
Natalie Piccotti, Director of Marketing
Kassie Graves, Vice President of Editorial
Jamie Giganti, Director of Academic Publishing

Printed in the United States of America.

cognella® ACADEMIC PUBLISHING
3970 Sorrento Valley Blvd., Ste. 500, San Diego, CA 92121

Dedicated To All The Hard Working

Counseling and Human Service Professionals

ABOUT THE AUTHORS

Ed Neukrug

Raised in New York City, Dr. Ed Neukrug obtained his bachelor's degree from Binghamton University in psychology, his master's degree in counseling from Miami University of Ohio, and his doctoral degree in counselor education from the University of Cincinnati. After teaching and directing a graduate program in counseling at Notre Dame College in New Hampshire, he accepted a position at Old Dominion University, in Norfolk, Virginia where he is currently a Professor of Counseling and Human Services.

In addition to teaching, Dr. Neukrug has worked as a crisis counselor, substance abuse counselor, an outpatient therapist, an associate school psychologist, a school counselor, and as a private practice psychologist and licensed professional counselor. Dr. Neukrug has held a variety of leadership positions in national professional associations and is currently lead editor of the *Journal of Human Services.*

Dr. Neukrug has written dozens of articles and 10 books. In addition to his books, he has been developing an interactive and animated website entitled *Great Therapists of the Twentieth Century*. If you get a chance, visit the site which can be found on his web page at www.odu.edu/~eneukrug.

Dr. Neukrug is married to Kristina, a former school counselor who is currently developing counseling-related workbooks and activities for mental health professionals. They have two children, Hannah and Emma. If you are interested in their books and materials, visit www.counselingbooksetc.com.

Mike Kalkbrenner

Mike Kalkbrenner, Ph.D., M.S., NCC, is Assistant Professor of Counseling and Educational Psychology at New Mexico State University. He was born and raised in upstate New York where he earned his B.A. in psychology from SUNY Geneseo and his M.S. in counseling from The College at Brockport, State University of New York. Mike was a dissertation fellow and received his doctorate in counselor education from Old Dominion University.

Mike has published numerous articles in both state and national peer-reviewed journals, written encyclopedia entries, and revised sections of textbooks. He has a passion for teaching and conducting quantitative research methodology in psychometrics and multivariate statistics. In addition to research and teaching, Mike has experience providing counseling to a variety of populations in an array of different settings, including a residential treatment facility, college counseling center, Department of Veteran's Affairs, and a medical center. Mike is married to Kristen Hirsch, who is a park ranger.

Kevin C. Snow

Kevin C. Snow, Ph.D., M.A., NCC, ACS, is an assistant professor of counseling at Texas A&M University-Commerce. He was born in Chambersburg, PA and is proud of his deep roots there. He has an interdisciplinary educational background earning a B.A. in sociology with a minor in anthropology and an M.S. in community counseling from Shippensburg University of Pennsylvania, an M.A. in American studies from Penn State Harrisburg, a certificate in school counseling from Indiana University of Pennsylvania, and a Ph.D. in counselor education and supervision from Old Dominion University.

Dr. Snow's research includes spirituality and spiritual inclusion, qualitative research methodology, and advocacy in social justice/multicultural issues in counseling and counselor education. He is active with several professional associations including ACA, ACES, ASERVIC, ALGBTIC, and NOHS, among others. He is currently co-editor of the *Journal of Human Services*, on the editorial review boards of *Counselor Education and Supervision*, *Journal of Counselor Leadership and Advocacy*, and the *Canadian Journal of Counselling and Psychotherapy,* and is active in other service roles at the regional and national level.

Dr. Snow has extensive counseling experience in diverse community-based and clinical settings, including correctional addictions, mobile therapy, and outpatient counseling, and is a skilled educator of a variety of courses. He specializes in teaching, scholarship, and service connected to his passions for social justice advocacy and diversity issues in counseling and counselor education. He is active in writing and editing via articles in several national journals, book chapters, encyclopedia entries, and other works, including having served as managing editor for the two-volume *Sage Encyclopedia of Theory in Counseling and Psychotherapy*.

Other Books by Ed Neukrug

In addition to the *Dictionary of Counseling and Human Services*, Dr. Neukrug has written:

- *The World of the Counselor*
- *Counseling Theory and Practice*
- *A Brief Orientation to Counseling*
- *Experiencing the World of the Counselor*
- *Skills and Techniques for Human Service Professionals*
- *Theory, Practice and Trends in Human Services: An Introduction*
- *Skills and Tools for Today's Counselors and Psychotherapists*
- *The Sage Encyclopedia of Theory in Counseling and Psychotherapy* (Editor)
- *Essentials of Testing and Assessment for Counselors, Social Workers, and Psychologists*
- *Contemporary Theories in Counseling and Psychotherapy*

Contents

Introduction

Welcome to the *Dictionary of Counseling and Human Services*. There are a vast number of concepts and terms in the fields of counseling and human services, and this book provides students, educators, and practitioners with concise and straightforward definitions. The book grew out of years of Ed Neukrug's work and scholarship in the fields of human services and counseling, where he collected many of the definitions found in this dictionary. In fact, a good number of the items can be found in the various glossaries of Ed Neukrug's books. However, despite this "head start," when realizing the enormity of the project he invited two colleagues, Mike Kalkbrenner and Kevin Snow, to join him. Both of these educators had taught, worked, and conducted research in the fields of counseling and human services, and having developed collegial relationships and friendships with them over the years, Neukrug was convinced they would be thorough in developing the dictionary with him.

After combining the words and terms from Neukrug' s glossaries, the authors reviewed other well-known books and texts in counseling and human services, and along with their existing knowledge of the fields, added additional items. The dictionary grew. They also decided to include a rating system based on their knowledge of the credentialing exams in counseling and human services. Each item was ranked for its likelihood to be on a credentialing exam in counseling and separately ranked for its likelihood to be on a credentialing exam in human services. Each word or term was rated from "10" (very likely to be on a credentialing exam) to "1" (fairly unlikely to be on a credentialing exam). First, Ed ranked each item, and then Mike and Kevin followed with their ratings. If either Mike or Kevin's ratings were dramatically different than Ed's, the team discussed the item and come up with a consensus.

Although the authors have no way of knowing exactly which items will appear on any particular credentialing exam, they are familiar with the general content of the exams, have taken many of the exams themselves, and are extremely knowledgeable about the fields of counseling and human services. Thus, they were well equipped to choose those words and terms most likely to appear on such an exam, and believe the dictionary is an excellent resource for a credentialing exam.

The final version of the *Dictionary of Counseling and Human Services* includes definitions of roughly 3,000 words and terms. The dictionary is thorough, comprehensive, readable, and a vital resource for credentialing exams, as well as an important reference book for your professional library. The authors invite additions to the book, and if you believe important items are missing, send them to Counseling Books Etc. (www.counselingbooksetc.com), and the authors will review them for possible inclusion in future additions.

How to Use This Book

If you purchased this book as a basic dictionary for the helping professions, simply look up any word or term you would like to know about, and read its definition. If you picked up the book as a study tool for a credentialing exam, the following is recommended. First, choose the index of most interest to you: counseling or human services. These can be found directly following the definitions. Then starting with the those items ranked as a "10," identify all items that you need to learn thoroughly. Then, work your way down the rankings from 10 toward 1. Initially, concentrate your learning on all items that have a rating between 10 and 7, as they are more likely to appear on a credentialing exam. However, if you have mastered all of those words and terms, then go further down the list.

In addition to the indexes, there are six appendices. Appendix A gives names and web addresses of the American Counseling Association and its twenty divisions. Appendix B gives names and web addresses of the National Organization of Human Services and its six regions, while Appendix C highlights some additional professional organizations within the mental health field and gives their web addresses. Appendix D lists a number of professional associations that offer ethics codes and provides web addresses so you can access the code online. This appendix also provides names and addresses of a number of important competencies (LGBQQIA competencies, multicultural and social justice counseling competencies, spiritual counseling competencies, and best practice guidelines for group work), and concludes with the names and web addresses of important credentialing bodies in counseling and human services. Appendix E provides a number of resources you can use to discover more about a wide range of graduate programs in the mental health professions. Appendix F provides a listing of sources where you can find information about undergraduate programs in human services. Finally, Appendix G provides an overview of the major diagnostic categories found in the DSM-5.

It is hoped that the *Dictionary of Counseling and Human Services* will be an important addition to your personal library and that you will find it a useful and critical tool in your career. Enjoy the book, and send the authors feedback. Good luck on your future career endeavors, and Ed, Mike, and Kevin look forward to hearing from you.

Acknowledgments

A number of people have worked hard to develop the *Dictionary of Counseling and Human Services*. First, let me thank Morgan Bywaters and Sarah Kalafsky who worked diligently on developing the indexes. Also, five doctoral students from Old Dominion University reviewed all of the definitions and suggested additions to the dictionary. These include T'airra Belcher, Cory Gerwe, Sonja Lund, Sonia Ramrakhiani, and Nicole Snyder. Thanks to all of you for your reviews! In addition, I'd like to thank Carole Borstein Weisner for her legal assistance and Ray Weisner for his marketing consultation. Finally, a very special thanks to Kristina Williams-Neukrug whose meticulous and conscientious copy-editing of the book was critical to its publication. We couldn't have done this without her.

Dictionary of Counseling and Human Services

The dictionary lists about 3,000 words and terms in alphabetical order. Following each item, is the letter "C" (for "Counseling) followed by a number and then the letters "HS" (for "Human Services") followed by a number. The numbers represent the subjective rankings of each item for its likelihood to be on a credentialing exam as determined by a consensus from the 3 authors. A ranking of 10 means that in our opinion, the word or term has a very good chance of finding its way on a credentialing exam. A ranking of 1 means we believe the item is somewhat unlikely to be found on a credentialing exam. If you are studying for such an exam, we encourage you to focus on the higher numbered items (perhaps 7 through 10), and if you have time, then review the items that are rated below 7. We hope that the dictionary is a vital source of knowledge for you, whether or not you are studying for a credentialing exam.

Likelihood of Appearing on a Credentialing Exam

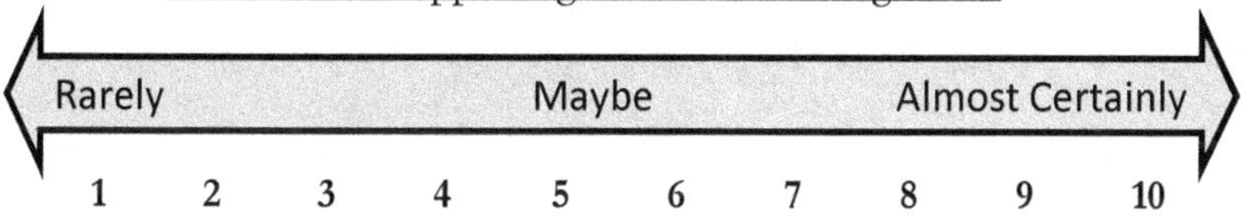

A, B, and Cs (C-10; HS-6). Based on *Albert Ellis's* theory called *rational emotive behavior therapy*, A is the *activating event*, B is the *belief about the event*, and C is the *consequential feelings and behavior.*

***A Mind That Found Itself* (C-6; HS-6).** Written in the early 1900s by *Clifford Beers*, this book helped to establish the *National Committee for Mental Hygiene*, which lobbied the U.S. Congress to pass laws that would improve the deplorable conditions of mental institutions.

AA (C-10; HS-10). See *Alcoholics Anonymous.*

AACD (C-8: HS-1). See *American Association for Counseling and Development.*

AACN (C-3; HS-3). See *American Association of Colleges of Nursing.*

AADA (C-8; HS-3). See *Association for Adult Development and Aging.* A division of the *American Counseling Association.*

AAMFT (C-8; HS-6). See *American Association for Marriage and Family Therapy.*

AAPC (C-6; HS-6). See *American Association of Pastoral Counselors.*

AARC (C-8; HS-3). See *Association for Assessment and Research in Counseling*. A division of the *American Counseling Association.*

AASCB (C-8; HS-3). See *American Association of State Counseling Boards.*

AASECT (C-6; HS-3). See *American Association of Sexuality Educators, Counselors, and Therapists.*

AATA (C-6; HS-6). See *American Art Therapy Association.*

ABA Design (C-8; HS-3). A type of *single-subject experimental design.*

ABAP (C-3; HS-3). See *American Board for Accreditation in Psychoanalysis.*

ABCDEFGH (C-6; HS-3). Based on *Robert Wubbolding*'s contributions to *reality therapy* and *choice theory*, this acronym stands for the eight toxins counselors should avoid when working with clients, where A is argue, attack, accuse; B is boss manage, blame, belittle; C is criticize, coerce, condemn; D is demean, demand; E is encourage excuses; F is instill fear, find fault; G is give up easily, take for granted; and H is hold grudges.

Ability Testing (C-8; HS-3). Testing that assesses an individual's cognitive capabilities. Includes *achievement testing*, which measures what one has learned, and *aptitude testing*, which measures what one is capable of learning.

Ability to Deliver One's Theoretical Approach (C-8; HS-3). Along with the *working alliance*, one of the *common factors* to effective helping relationships. May include such things as *compatibility with and belief in your theory*, *competence*, and *cognitive complexity*. See also *Common Factors.*

Abnormal (C-8; HS-8). A construct that assumes that individuals exhibiting extreme behaviors are not normative, or not like most individuals in society.

Abreaction (C-6; HS-3). Derived from Freudian *psychoanalysis*, the releasing, through therapy, of repressed *emotions*. See also *Catharsis.*

Absent but Implicit Responses (C-6; HS-3). Within *narrative therapy*, where the expression of one experience from a client is obvious, but that expression may be related to other, less obvious or implicit experiences in the individual's life. This can also be viewed by understanding that the *problem-saturated story* is in contrast to other, preferred stories that are in the background (the absent but implicit stories). Concept developed by *Michael White*. See also *Double Listening.*

Absolutistic Musts and Shoulds (C-8; HS-6). The idea, within *rational emotive behavior therapy*, that clients will present certain rigid and inflexible positions of how life must or should be, rather than accepting and coping with the realities of their lives or the world around them.

Abstract (C-10; HS-8). A short description, or summary, of the content of a publication usually found at the beginning of a journal article or other piece of written scholarship.

Abuse (C-10; HS-10). Emotional and/or physical harm that involves the abuser exerting power or undue influence over another through acts of aggression, cohesion, assault, battery, rape, or other forms of mistreatment.

ACA (C-10; HS-6). See *American Counseling Association.*

ACA Code of Ethics (C-10; HS-3). The ethical code of the *American Counseling Association*, which guides the ethical practice of counselors.

ACAC (C-8: HS-3). See *Association for Child and Adolescent Counseling.* A division of the *American Counseling Association.*

Academic Support Services (C-6; HS-2). One area in higher education that individuals with a master's degree in *student affairs and college counseling* sometimes work.

Academy of Certified Social Workers (ACSW) (C-6; HS-6). Established in 1960 by the *National Association of Social Workers*, this association sets standards of practice in the field for master's-level social workers. Experienced social workers can hold a credential as an *ACSW* and a *DCSW.*

ACAF (C-6; HS-1). See *American Counseling Association Foundation.*

ACC (C-8; HS-3). See *Association for Creativity in Counseling.* A division of the *American Counseling Association.*

ACCA (C-8; HS-3). See *American College Counseling Association.* A division of the *American Counseling Association.*

Acceptance (C-10; HS-10). Showing clients, or others, that you respect and accept them as they are and how they express their thoughts and *emotions.* Being *nonjudgmental.* One of the *common factors.* See also *Unconditional Positive Regard.*

Acceptance and Commitment Therapy (ACT) (C-8; HS-3). A therapeutic approach that views behaviors and cognitions as a complex web of relational associations and uses a mixture of *cognitive therapy*, *behavioral therapy* techniques, and Eastern philosophy to help people increase psychological flexibility. Six core principles include acceptance and willingness, defusion, contact with the present moment, self and perspective taking, values, and committed action.

Accommodation (C-8; HS-6). The process of adapting new knowledge and experiences in such a way that one's understanding of the world is altered. See also *Piaget.*

Accountability (C-8; HS-8). Being truthful and honest and taking responsibility for one's behaviors, choices, and reactions to experiences in life. In programs, agencies, and organizations, it is often related to showing efficacy of work-related activities. Accountability is important for clients, professionals, and organizations and is an ethical concern for helpers.

Accreditation (C-10; HS-8). The process that a program or organization goes through to show that it has complied with specific guidelines set by the accrediting body. In counseling and human service programs, attainment of accreditation implies high quality in training. See also *Council for Standards in Human Service Education (CSHSE)* and *Council for the Accreditation of Counseling and Related Educational Programs (CACREP).*

Accreditation Council for Genetic Counseling (C-3; HS-3). Accredits programs in *genetic counseling.*

Accreditation Standards (C-10; HS-8). The written guidelines that underlie the curriculum and training of a counseling or human service program in an effort to ensure quality and maintain high standards. See *Accreditation*, *Council for Standards in Human Service Education* (*CSHSE*), and *Council for the Accreditation of Counseling and Related Educational Programs* (*CACREP*).

Accreditation, Benefits of (C-10; HS-8). Advantages of training programs that have obtained *accreditation* include more rigorous programs, more qualified faculty, better students, a stronger professional identity, more field experiences, an easier time becoming credentialed, the maintenance of high standards, the possibility of having an easier time getting third-party reimbursements, and an easier time getting a job or getting into advanced training programs.

Accredited Programs (C-10; HS-8). Accredited training programs have been determined to meet minimal standards in addressing important competencies in a professional field. The *Council for Standards in Human Service Education* (*CSHE*) accredits human service programs and the *Council for the Accreditation of Counseling and Related Educational Programs* (*CACREP*) accredits counselor training programs.

Acculturation (C-5; HS-6). The process of change that occurs when two or more *cultures* interact with one another as seen by psychological and behavioral changes of those involved. Change can occur either on the individual, group, or larger cultural levels. Usually, the dominant culture is impacted less than the non-dominant one. See also *Assimilation.*

Accurate Empathy Scale (C-8; HS-6). A 5-point scale developed by *Robert Carkhuff* used to measure a helper's ability to make an empathic response with a client. Level 3 responses are seen as accurately reflecting the client's *affect* and content. Responses below Level 3 are seen as detracting, while responses above Level 3 are seen as adding deeper reflection and meaning.

ACES (C-8; HS-3). See *Association for Counselor Education and Supervision.* A division of the *American Counseling Association.*

ACGPA (C-6; HS-1). See *American Council of Guidance and Personnel Associations.*

Achievement Testing (C-8; HS-3). A type of *ability test* that assesses what one has learned. Includes *survey battery tests* that measure achievement based on what has been learned in schools, *diagnostic achievement tests* that are used to delve more deeply into areas of suspected learning problems, and *readiness tests* that are used to assess an individual's ability to move on to the next educational level.

Acid (C-10; HS-10). The non-medical term for *lysergic acid diethylamide* (*LSD*), a potent hallucinogenic drug.

Ackerman, Nathan (1908 - 1971) (C-8; HS-6). An American *psychiatrist* who was one of the pioneers of *family therapy* and developed a *psychodynamic approach* to working with couples and families.

ACOA (C-10; HS-10). See *Adult Children of Alcoholics.*

ACPA (C-8; HS-1). See *American College Personnel Association.* See also *College Student Educators International.*

Acquired Immune Deficiency Syndrome (AIDS) (C-10; HS-10). The last, and most potentially lethal, stage of *human immunodeficiency virus* in which the immune system can be seriously damaged.

ACSW (C-6; HS-6). See *Academy of Certified Social Workers.*

***ACT* Score (C-6; HS-3).** See *American College Test.*

Acting "As If" (C-8; HS-3). A technique, in *Adlerian counseling*, that has the client acting in a manner that is healthier than his or her usual behavior so that the client can practice more positive ways of being in the world. Sometimes called "Fake it till you make it."

Action Plans (C-8; HS-3). Strategies *school counselors* use for meeting *Comprehensive School Counseling Program* (*CSCP*) activities.

Action Research (C-10; HS-6). An approach to research that aims to identify and address a specific problem or challenge and produces recommendations to remedy or improve the problematic circumstances for individuals and groups. Includes selecting a focus, identifying research questions, collecting and analyzing data, reporting results, and taking informed action to resolve problematic situations.

Activating Event (C-8; HS-6). A *stimulus* or incident that leads to one's *belief about the event.* Such beliefs result in feelings or behavioral consequences. A component of *Albert Ellis's* theory called *Rational Emotive Behavior Therapy*. See also *A, B, and Cs.*

Active Imagination (C-8; HS-3). Developed by *Carl Jung*, the process of bringing the *unconscious* to the *conscious* by engaging the imagination by using visualizing, meditative, *narrative*, or creative techniques.

Active Listening (C-10; HS-10). A deliberate and focused process where the helper attempts to establish *empathy* with a client by *reflecting feelings* and *reflecting content* of a client's statements. Good listening is an active process, where the helper talks minimally, concentrates on what is being said, does not interrupt or give advice, hears the speaker's content and *affect*, and uses good non-verbals to show that he or she is understanding the client.

Actualization (C-10; HS-8). The ability to actualize (i.e., realize or bring into being) something in life. Most often refers to the concept of *self-actualization.*

Actualizing Tendency (C-8; HS-8). The inborn, positive inner qualities and inherent traits that arise in a person when placed in a nurturing and facilitative environment. See also *Humanistic Counseling and Education.*

Acute Psychotic Episode (C-10; HS-8). Short-term loss of reality.

***ADA* (C-10; HS-10).** See *Americans with Disabilities Act.*

ADD (C-10; HS-8). See *Attention Deficit Hyperactivity Disorder* (*ADHD*).

Addams, Jane (1860 - 1935) (C-6; HS-10). A social activist who established *Hull House* in Chicago in 1899 and who organized group discussions to help people who were poor with daily living skills. These groups are viewed as early group treatment.

Adderall (C-8, HS-8). A *stimulant* often used in the treatment of *attention deficit hyperactivity disorder* (*ADHD*), this medication tends to have a *paradoxical effect* with individuals who are ADHD in that it calms them down and helps them to focus.

Addiction Counseling (C-10; HS-10). A specialty area that focuses on working with individuals who are struggling with *addictions* (e.g., *substance abuse*, *eating disorders*, and sexual addiction). A *Council for the Accreditation of Counseling and Related Educational Programs* specialty area. See also *Substance Abuse* and *Process Addiction(s)*.

Addiction Counselor (C-10; HS-10). A helper who works with individuals who have *addictions*. Although not all addiction counselors have their master's degree, in reference to *Council for the Accreditation of Counseling and Related Educational Programs*, this refers to a person who has obtained his or her master's degree in *addiction counseling*. See also *Substance Abuse* and *Process Addiction(s)*.

Addiction(s) (C-10; HS-10). A category of *mental disorders* where one's dependency on a substance or activity becomes severe enough to impair a person's ability to function. See also *Substance Abuse* and *Process Addiction(s)*.

Additive Empathic Response (C-10; HS-8). Responses by helpers that reflect feelings slightly beyond what the client is currently aware of and which the client is able to embrace, or when the helper reflects content that results in the client understanding *self* in new and profound ways. Sometimes called an *advanced empathic response*.

ADHD (C-10; HS-8). See *Attention Deficit Hyperactivity Disorder*.

Adjourning (C-7; HS-6). The last *stage of group development* as defined by *Tuckman*.

Adler School of Professional Psychology (C-6; HS-3). Now named Adler University, this non-profit graduate school based in Chicago, IL and Vancouver, B.C. is named in honor of *Alfred Adler* and his principles of therapy.

Adler, Alfred (1870 - 1937) (C-10; HS-6). A student of *Freud* who developed a humanistically oriented *psychodynamic theory* known as *Adlerian therapy* or *individual psychology*.

Adlerian Therapy (C-10; HS-6). See *Individual Psychology*.

Administrative Supervision (C-8; HS-8). Administrative supervision is concerned with survivability of the agency and administrative supervisors' focus on such things as managing costs, developing evaluation techniques, defining roles and functions of employees, encouraging or eliminating services, developing better ways of *case management*, and insisting on some forms of professional development (e.g., mandated reporting of abuse, *affirmative action*).

Administrator (C-6; HS-6). In the context of helping, a person who supervises community service programs. One of the original 13 roles or functions of human service professionals as defined by the *Southern Regional Education Board*.

Admissions Office (C-6; HS-3). One area in higher education that individuals with a master's degree in *student affairs and college counseling* sometimes work.

ADTA (C-6; HS-3). See *American Dance Therapy Association*.

Adult Children of Alcoholics (ACOA) (C-8; HS-8). A *non-profit organization* dedicated to helping people cope with issues stemming from growing up in *substance* *abuse*, or relatedly dysfunctional households by offering *support groups* and other informal services. In some contexts, *ACOA* may refer generically to the people raised within these households, as in "I am an adult child of an alcoholic (ACOA)."

Adultspan (C-6; HS-3). Journal of the *Association for Adult Development and Aging* (*AADA*).

Advanced Empathic Responses (C-10; HS-6). Empathic responses in which clients gain increased self-awareness by the helper reflecting deeper feelings that were not directly stated by the client or by helping a client see a situation in a new way. Includes *reflecting deeper feelings*, *pointing out conflicting feelings or thoughts*, use of *metaphors and analogies*, *self-disclosure*, *tactile responses*, *discursive empathy*, and more.

Advanced Practice Registered Nurse (APRN) (C-8; HS-6). A nurse or nurse-practitioner who has received specialized and advanced training as a human service professional. See also *Psychiatric-Mental Health Nurse.*

Advice Giving (C-10; HS-10). The process by which the helper offers his or her expert opinion in hopes that the client will follow up on the suggestions. Advice giving should be used sparingly as there is the potential that the client will develop a dependent relationship on the helper and could end up relying on the helper for problem-solving. Contrast with *Information Giving* and *Offering Alternatives.*

Advisory Council (C-8; HS-8). A group of experts from outside sources that advise programs and organizations. Advisory councils are critical to agency and educational settings as they offer feedback to programs about their functioning.

Advocacy (C-10; HS-10). One aspect of *social justice* work which involves a helper directly or indirectly taking active steps to heal a societal wound and promote the *welfare* of his or her client. See also *Advocating Directly for Clients*, *Advocating for Societal Change*, *Advocating for Community Change*, and *Empowering Clients to Advocate for Themselves.*

Advocacy Competencies (C-10; HS-8). Competencies endorsed by the *American Counseling Association* that describe *advocacy* in terms of three domains: the client/student, community, and public. Each of these domains is divided into two levels that include a focus on whether the helper is "acting on behalf of" or "acting with" the client, community, or system. The competencies run from the *micro level* (focus on client or student) to the *macro level* (focus on system).

Advocate (C-10; HS-10). A helper who champions and defends clients' causes and rights. One of the original 13 roles or functions of human service professionals as defined by the *Southern Regional Education Board.*

Advocating Directly for Clients (C-10; HS-8). When the helper engages in direct *advocacy* for the benefit of a client.

Advocating for Community Change (C-10; HS-8). When the helper engages in *advocacy* for making positive community change for the benefit of his or her clients.

Advocating for Societal Change (C-10; HS-8). When the helper engages in *advocacy* for broader social issues for the benefit of his or her clients.

AFDC (C-6; HS-6). See *Temporary Assistance for Needy Families.*

Affect (C-8; HS-8). The experience of feeling or *emotion.*

Affective/Impulsive (C-6; HS-3). The first stage of *stages of racism* where a professional may respond impulsively and in a hostile fashion when discussing issues of *diversity*. Developmental theory formulated by *D'Andrea and Daniels*. See also *Dualistic Rational*, *Liberal*, and *Principled Activist* stages.

Affirmation (C-8; HS-8). The process by which a helper reinforces a client's actions, feelings, or behaviors with the intention of giving a positive response to a client's way of being in the world. Contrast with *Encouragement*.

Affirmative Action (C-8; HS-8). Policies, usually in the areas of education and employment, which support members of *marginalized groups* who have suffered *discrimination*.

***Affordable Care Act* (*ACA*) (C-10; HS-8).** Also known as Obamacare, relative to mental health services, ensures that mental health coverage is on par with medical coverage.

African Americans (C-10; HS-10). Making up about 13% of the population of the U.S., 90% of African Americans are descendants of slaves. African Americans and other minorities typically seek out helping relationships at lower rates, are misdiagnosed at higher rates than Whites, and find helping relationships less satisfactory than Whites.

Age Comparison Scoring (C-10; HS-3). A type of *standard score* calculated by comparing an individual score to the average score of others who are the same age.

Ageism (C-10; HS-10). Engaging in *prejudice* or *discrimination* against individuals based on their status as older persons.

Agency Atmosphere (C-8; HS-8). The permeating mood or feeling of an agency, office, or institution including, but not limited to soft lighting, comfortable furniture, arrangement of the waiting room, and placement of the furniture.

AGPA (C-6; HS-3). See *American Group Psychotherapy Association*.

AHC (C-8; HS-3). See *Association for Humanistic Counseling*. A division of the *American Counseling Association*.

AIDS (C-10; HS-10). See *Acquired Immune Deficiency Syndrome* (*AIDS*).

AIDS Epidemic (C-10; HS-10). *Acquired Immune Deficiency Syndrome* (*AIDS*) continues to spread in this country, and worldwide an estimated 34 million children and adults are living with AIDS. Today, human service professionals work in a variety of prevention, helping, and educational programs that support *HIV*-positive individuals and their families.

Al-Anon (C-10; HS-10). A type of *support group* for family members and friends who have loved ones that are living with *addictions* to alcohol.

Alateen (C-10; HS-10). A type of *support group* specifically for teenagers who have loved ones that are living with *addictions* to alcohol.

Albert Ellis Institute (C-8; HS-3). The *psychotherapy* education and research institute based in New York City dedicated to promoting *Albert Ellis's rational emotive behavior therapy*. Ellis, the founder of the institute, was its president during most of his life.

Alchemy (C-6; HS-3). An ancient mystical and philosophical "science" whose purpose was to transmute base matter into noble matter (e.g., lead into gold), develop panaceas for disease, locate the Philosopher's Stone (or an elixir of immortality), and develop other transformations of objects for fantastic purposes. *Carl Jung* saw alchemy as symbolic for how the individual's *psyche* could be transformed as the client became *individuated.*

Alcohol (C-9; HS-9). The intoxicating aspect of wine, beer, or other related "spirits." Alcohol is highly addictive with upwards of 7% of adults being addicted to it.

Alcohol Abuse (C-10; HS-8). Now called *Alcohol Use Disorder* (*AUD*).

Alcohol Dependence (C-10; HS-8). Now called *Alcohol Use Disorder* (*AUD*).

Alcohol Use Disorder (AUD) (C-10; HS-8). The current *Diagnostic and Statistical Manual-5* clinical term used to describe problem drinking, or *alcoholism*, and the attending dysfunctional behaviors and physical symptoms connected to this mental health condition. Severity of alcohol use disorder is either mild, moderate, or severe based on the number of the 11 criteria met. Alcohol use disorder has replaced the former DSM-IV diagnoses of *alcohol abuse* and *alcohol dependence.*

Alcohol Withdrawal (C-10; HS-10). The presence of physical symptoms occurring after one has stopped consuming *alcohol*, including but not limited to headaches, nausea, vomiting, seizures, agitation, shaking, confusion, and death in the most severe cases.

Alcoholics Anonymous (AA) (C-10; HS-10). *Support groups* for individuals who are living with *addictions* to alcohol.

Alcoholism (C-10; HS-10). The common term used for the condition of problematic drinking. See also *Alcohol Use Disorder.*

ALGBTIC (C-8; HS-3). See *Association for Lesbian, Gay, Bisexual, and Transgender Issues in Counseling*. A division of the *American Counseling Association.*

Al-Hajj Malik El-Shabaz (1925 - 1965) (C-4; HS-4). Originally called Malcolm X (Malcom Little at birth), and later in his life taking on a traditional Muslim name, he was a well-known *African American* civil rights leader who embodied many of the characteristics of a *self-actualized person.*

All-or-Nothing Thinking (C-8; HS-6). Seeing the world categorically, rather than in a more complex fashion. See also *Cognitive Distortion.*

Ally (C-8; HS-8). A term that is used generically for anyone advocating or supporting a community, group, or *culture* of which they are not members. Most often, the term is used for a person who is a supporter and advocate for *Lesbian, Gay, Bisexual, Transgender, and Queer* individuals and their equal rights within society.

Almshouses (C-6; HS-8). Established by the *poor laws of 1601*, these were shelters for individuals who could not care for themselves.

Alpha Error (C-8; HS-3). See *Type I Error.*

Alpha Level (C-10; HS-6). The numerical threshold that is used to determine whether or not there are statistically significant differences between groups. Alpha levels, also represented as *p-values*, are typically set at less than .05 and .01. Alpha level is based on probability, for example, at the less than .05 level, there is less than a 5% chance that the differences between the *control group* and the *experimental group* have occurred by random chance. This allows one to conclude that there are statistically significant differences between groups.

Alter Ego (C-8; HS-3). The other, or second, *self* that is uniquely different from the personality one normally presents to the world.

Alternate Form Reliability (C-8; HS-3). A method for determining *reliability* by creating two or more alternate, parallel, or equivalent forms of the same test. These alternate forms mimic one another yet are different enough to eliminate some of the problems found in *test-retest reliability* (e.g., looking up an answer). In this case, rather than giving the same test twice, the examiner gives the alternate form the second time. Also called *equivalent form reliability* and *parallel form reliability*.

Alternative Hypothesis (C-8; HS-4). In *quantitative research*, a *hypothesis* that researchers hope to confirm; that is, the researchers want to show that the *intervention* or treatment has caused statistically significant differences between groups. See also *Alpha Level*, *Statistical Significance*, and *Null Hypothesis*.

Alternative Therapy (C-8; HS-4). The use of alternative approaches (such as *holistic* health or practices such as Reiki) are used instead of conventional methods in counseling.

Alternatives (C-8; HS-8). See *Offering Alternatives* and *Suggesting Alternatives*.

Altruism (C-4; HS-4). The practice of unselfish concern for the wellbeing of another. This includes actions that are not directly beneficial or self-serving to the person acting on behalf of another, but may have indirect benefit through the act of helping.

Alzheimer's Disease (C-8; HS-3). A progressive brain disease resulting in memory loss, changes in personality and thinking, and loss of function that eventually leads to death and generally occurs in older individuals. Alzheimer's disease is the primary cause of *dementia*.

Ambassador (SFBT) (C-8; HS-6). A position taken early in counseling sessions using *solution-focused brief therapy* (*SFBT*) in which the counselor is accepting, interested, and respectful when working with the client.

AMCD (C-8; HS-3). See *Association for Multicultural Counseling and Development*. A division of the *American Counseling Association*.

American Art Therapy Association (AATA) (C-6; HS-6). An association that approves programs that offer curricula in *creative and expressive therapies*.

American Association for Counseling and Development (AACD) (C-6; HS-3). Formerly referred to as the *American Personnel and Guidance Association* (*APGA*), and currently the *American Counseling Association*.

American Association of Colleges of Nursing (AACN) (C-3; HS-3). Along with the *National League for Nursing*, an *accreditation* organization for *psychiatric-mental health nurses.*

American Association for Marriage and Family Therapy (AAMFT) (C-8; HS-8). A professional association for marriage and family therapy, it assists in the development of standards of training and practice for marriage and family therapists. See *Commission on Accreditation for Marriage and Family Therapy Education* (*COAMFTE*).

American Association of Pastoral Counselors (AAPC) (C-8; HS-8). A *professional association* for *pastoral counselors.* Offers a *certification* process for those who are interested in becoming *Certified Pastoral Counselors* (CPCs).

American Association of Sexuality Educators, Counselors, and Therapists (AASECT). (C-6; HS-3). A national organization that is dedicated to promoting sexuality and sexual health counseling, therapy, and education by professionals in various disciplines (e.g., ministry, medicine, therapy, family planning). AASECT offers *certification* programs in various aspects of their mission including sex education, sex therapy, sex counseling, and certified *supervisors* in these areas.

American Association of State Counseling Boards (AASCB) (C-8; HS-3). An association that is a resource for accessing counselor licensing information, and more recently has been helping in designing initiatives that would allow for the *reciprocity* and *portability* of counselors' licenses.

American Board for Accreditation in Psychoanalysis (ABAP) (C-6; HS-3). An organization that *accredits* institutes for training in *psychoanalysis.*

American Board of Genetic Counseling (ABGC) (C-6; HS-3). Offers a *credential* as a *Certified Genetic Counselor* (CGC) to any individual who has gone through a program *accredited* by the *Accreditation Council for Genetic Counseling.*

American Board of Professional Psychology (ABPP) (C-6; HS-3). Established in 1947, today ABPP offers *certifications* in 14 specialty areas for *psychologists.*

American College Counseling Association (ACCA) (C-8; HS-3). A division of the *American Counseling Association* that focuses on counseling issues in college settings.

American College Personnel Association (ACPA) (C-6; HS-1). One of the *American Counseling Association's* founding divisions, disaffiliated from the *American Counseling Association* in 1992. See also *College Student Educators International.*

***American College Test (ACT)* (C-7; HS-3).** An *aptitude test* that was developed as an alternative college entrance exams to the *Scholastic Aptitude Test.* See also *SAT* and/or *PSAT.* The *ACT* test is used to predict success in college and as part of the admission criteria for many colleges. The scores generally have a *mean* of 21 and a *standard deviation* of 5 for college-bound students. The mean score for all students, including those who are not college-bound, tends to be about 18.

American Council of Guidance and Personnel Associations (ACGPA) (C-6; HS-1). An association that was active from 1935 to 1952 which focused on educational and *vocational guidance* and was the forerunner to the *American Personnel and Guidance Association*, the *American Association of Counseling and Development*, and the *American Counseling Association.*

American Counseling Association (ACA) (C-10; HS-1). The main *professional association* for counselors that provides a wide range of benefits for them and offers twenty divisions, or specialty areas, in counseling.

American Counseling Association Foundation (ACAF) (C6; HS-1). An affiliated association to *ACA* that supports counselors, offers graduate student scholarships, provides a fund to assist counselors affected by natural disasters, recognizes outstanding counselors, publishes important counseling-related materials, and more.

American Dance Therapy Association (ADTA) (C-6; HS-1). A *professional association* for *creative and expressive therapists* and helpers who focus on dance and movement when helping.

American Distance Counseling Association (ADCA) (C-6; HS-3). A *professional association* that is focused on supporting the training and practice of *online counseling.*

American Group Psychotherapy Association (AGPA) (C-6; HS-3). A *professional association* for *group therapy* experts including *certification* of professional group therapists through the *International Board for the Certification of Group Psychotherapists* (*IBGCP*).

American Mental Health Counselors Association (AMHCA) (C-8; HS-3). A division of the *American Counseling Association* for *clinical mental health counselo*rs.

American Music Therapy Association (AMTA) (C-6; HS-3). A *professional association* for *creative and expressive therapists* that focuses on music when helping.

American Personnel and Guidance Association (APGA) (C-6; HS-1). A *professional association* for counselors formed out of the *National Vocational Guidance Association* and other associations and established in the 1950s. A forerunner of the *American Counseling Association*

American Psychiatric Association (APA) (C-8; HS-8). The *professional association* for *psychiatrists.*

American Psychiatric Nurses Association (APNA) (C-3; HS-3). *The professional associatio*n for *psychiatric-mental health nurses.*

American Psychoanalytic Association (APsaA) (C-6; HS-3). The primary *professional association* for *psychoanalysis* and *psychoanalysts.*

American Psychological Association (APA) (C-8; HS-8). The *professional association* for *psychologists.*

American Public Human Services Association (APHSA) (C-2; HS-6). A professional association that supports local and state agencies and works on policy issues to develop healthier lives for children, adults, families, and communities.

American Rehabilitation Counseling Association (ARCA) (C-8; HS-3). A division of the *American Counseling Association* that focuses on issues related to disabilities and rehabilitation. See also *Rehabilitation Counselor.*

American School Counselor Association (ASCA) (C-8; HS-3). A division of the *American Counseling Association* for *school counselors.*

***Americans with Disabilities Act* (*PL 101-336*) (C-8; HS-8).** A federal law stating that to assure proper test administration, accommodations must be made for individuals with disabilities who are taking tests for employment and that testing must be shown to be relevant to the job in question.

AMFTRB (C-8; HS-3). See *Association of Marital and Family Therapy Regulatory Boards.*

AMHCA (C-8; HS-3). See *American Mental Health Counselors Association.* A division of the *American Counseling Association.*

Amphetamines (C-6; HS-6). A classification of *stimulant medication* used primarily to treat individuals living with *Attention Deficit Disorder with Hyperactivity* (*ADHD*). Sometimes known as "speed," early on, it was used as an *antidepressant.*

Amplification (C-8; HS-3). A process used in *Jungian therapy* whereby the *analyst* encourages the client to find broader meanings related to his or her experiences, dreams, and symbols. This helps the client to become more in touch with *self* and with *archetypes* that impinge upon him or her.

AMTA (C-3; HS-3). See *American Music Therapy Association.*

Anal Expulsive (C-8; HS-3). Indicating someone stuck at *Freud's anal stage* where the individual exhibits personality characteristics or behaviors that are often aggressive or mean, rebellious, overly emotional, disorganized, negligent, and sometimes generous and artistic. A companion personality, and in some ways opposite, displayed by the *anal retentive personality.* See also *Anal Retentive Personality* and *Anal Stage.*

Anal Retentive Personality (C-8; HS-3). Indicating someone stuck at *Freud's anal stage.* This person is fixated on anal control and exhibits personality characteristics that are focused on order, neatness, control, and obsession. Sometimes this personality is simply referred to as "anal." See also *Anal Expulsive* and *Anal Stage.*

Anal Stage (C-9; HS-4). Sigmund *Freud's* second *psychosexual stage of development*, occurring between ages 1 and 3 years, whereby a child's emotional gratification is derived from bowel movements. See also *Genital Stage*, *Latency Stage*, *Oral Stage*, and *Phallic Stage.*

Analogic Communication (C-6; HS-3). In communication, the meaning about the meaning, often expressed nonverbally. See also *Digital Communication.*

Analogies (C-8; HS-6). See *Metaphors and Analogies.*

Analysis (C-8; HS-6). See *Psychoanalysis.*

Analysis of Covariance (ANCOVA) (C-8; HS-3). A statistical analysis that combines *multiple regression* and *analysis of variance* in which a continuous level *covariate* that might impact the dependent measure is statistically controlled for. Analysis of covariance helps researchers minimize the extent to which *extraneous variables*, or any *variable(s)* besides the *independent variable*, have an effect on the *dependent variable.*

Analysis of the Transference Relationship (C-8; HS-3). Used in *Freudian psychoanalysis*, the process whereby a client projects his or her past relationships onto the *analyst*, and, at the appropriate and opportune moment, the analyst interprets this projection to the client.

Analysis of Variance (ANOVA) (C-8; HS-3). A statistical measure that is used in *quantitative research* to examine differences or relationships between groups.

Analyst (C-8; HS-6). A person trained in *psychoanalysis* techniques. See also *Psychoanalyst.*

Analytic Neutrality (C-8; HS-3). Used in *psychoanalysis*, it includes taking a *nonjudgmental* disposition and not expressing one's values, beliefs, or biases during a helping relationship.

Analytical Psychology (C-8; HS-3). Also called *Jungian Therapy*, this approach was developed by *Carl Jung*. Analytical therapists believe that early child-rearing practices result in a tendency for one to focus on one trait within each of two pairs of *mental functions*: *sensing* or *intuiting*, and *thinking* or *feeling*. They also believe we are born with an innate tendency to have an *extroverted attitude* or *introverted attitude*. One's predominate attitude, matched with one's predominate mental functions, becomes an individual's *psychological type*. The complementary type (the psychological types you are not) resides in one's *personal unconscious* and longs to be "heard." Analytical therapists also believe we all inherit an immeasurable number of primordial images called *archetypes* that are housed in the *collective unconscious* (e.g., mother archetype, father archetype, the shadow, God archetype). They provide the *psyche* with its tendency to perceive the world in certain ways and can sometimes interact with repressed material in the *personal unconscious* and cause *complexes*. See also *Psychodynamic Approaches*.

ANCOVA (C-8; HS-3). See *Analysis of Covariance.*

Anecdotal Information (C-6; HS-6). A record of an individual that generally includes those behaviors that are atypical or typical for that individual. A type of *Record and Personal Document.*

Angst (C-6; HS-3). An *emotion* connected to feelings of dread or high anxiety often connected to existential crises regarding the condition of being human (e.g., death, suffering) or apprehension about the world and its fate in general.

Anima (C-8; HS-6). In *analytical psychology*, the female aspects of self. An *archetype*.

Animal Assisted Therapy (C-6; HS-6). A type of therapy focused on building attachment with animals, often dogs and horses, to promote the social, emotional, and cognitive functioning of the client. Attachment starts with the animal and can later be generalized to people.

Animus (C-8; HS-6). In *analytical psychology*, the male aspects of self. An *archetype.*

Anna O (C-6; HS-3). The pseudonym of Bertha Pappenheim, which was used by *Josef Breuer* in writings with *Freud* in a famous case study about *hysteria* (called "Studies in Hysteria").

Annihilation (C-6; HS-3). In *psychoanalysis*, the child's *unconscious* fear of destruction by a parent.

Annual Agreement (C-6; HS-1). An important tool to working with stakeholders to ensure *consultation* with key people who are working on a *comprehensive school counseling program.*

Anorexia Nervosa (C-8; HS-6). A severe eating disorder whereby an individual fears and obsesses over gaining weight, refrains from or greatly restricts eating food, and often has a very low body weight. Usually, this disorder is due to problems in self-perception whereby the person sees oneself as overweight even when he or she is medically underweight. In extreme cases, this condition can be fatal.

ANOVA (C-8; HS-6). See *Analysis of Variance.*

Antabuse (aka Disulfiram) (C-6; HS-6). A drug used in the treatment of *alcoholism* that causes mental discomfort and unpleasant physical symptoms (e.g., nausea, vomiting, physical pain) if *alcohol* is ingested while using the drug. A wide range of symptoms are experienced immediately after ingestion of alcohol, akin to hangover effects, when taking this drug. The intention of this type of drug therapy is to prevent drinking and/or create an aversion to alcohol use.

Antianxiety Agents (C-8; HS-8). A classification of medications used primarily to treat individuals living with *Generalized Anxiety Disorder* (*GAD*). See also *Psychotropic Medications.*

Anticholinergic Drugs (C-6; HS-6). Drugs used to counter side effects of other drugs.

Anticonvulsant Medication (C-8; HS-6). Medication used to prevent seizures.

Anti-Counselor (C-6; HS-1). See *Triad Model.*

Antidepressants (C-8; HS-8). A classification of medications used primarily to treat individuals living with *depressive disorders* and sometimes used for *anxiety disorders.* See also *Selective Serotonin Reuptake Inhibitors* (*SSRIs*) and *Psychotropic Medications.*

Anti-Deterministic View of Human Nature (C-10; HS-8). The view that rejects the notion that early childhood development and biological factors cause psychological problems and stresses the ability of the individual to change. This view is in opposition to the *deterministic view of human nature.*

Anti-Objectivist (C-6; HS-1). In *narrative therapy*, the opposition to those approaches that develop a theoretical model that explains reality and then use that hypothetical model to define the experience of others.

Antipsychotic Drugs (C-7; HS-7). Sometimes called *neuroleptics*, are generally used for the treatment of *schizophrenia*, as well as schizoaffective disorders, and the manic phase of *bipolar and related disorders.* There are three broad classes of antipsychotic drugs that include the *conventional antipsychotics*, the *atypical antipsychotics*, and the new, *second-generation antipsychotics.* See also *Psychotropic Medications.*

Antithetical Schema of Apperception (C-6; HS-1). A term from *individual psychology* that refers to *schemas* constructed by individuals who lack the skills to build healthy relationships and results in a *subjective final goal* that leads to a dysfunctional *lifestyle.*

Anxiety (C-10; HS-10). Feelings of nervousness, self-doubt, compulsiveness, obsession on certain thoughts or experiences, and related symptoms due to these feelings (e.g., pacing, nail biting). Clinically, this is a reference to *anxiety disorders* or *anxiety attacks.*

Anxiety Attack (C-10; HS-10). Often called a *panic attack*, a condition of mental and physical symptoms (e.g., dizziness, heart palpitations, fear, breathlessness) connected to feelings of *anxiety* and dread. The attack, or episode, can last from a few minutes to several hours and experiencing an attack, or the fear of an attack, can dramatically hinder someone's participation in life events and alter behavior (e.g., seclusion, avoidance of certain social settings or places). Some people confuse these symptoms for heart conditions and seek medical attention not realizing they are experiencing a mental condition.

Anxiety Disorders (C-10; HS-8). A wide range of disorders related to a general or specific cause of unease or fear. This *anxiety*, or fear, is considered clinically significant when it is excessive and persistent over time. Examples of anxiety disorders that typically manifest earlier in development include separation anxiety and selective mutism. Other examples of anxiety disorders are specific phobia, social anxiety disorder (also known as social phobia), *panic disorder*, and *generalized anxiety disorder.*

Anxiolytics (C-5; HS-5). A type of drug that is used to inhibit anxiety. *Barbiturates* and *benzodiazepines* are two types of anxiolytics.

APA (C-8; HS-8). See *American Psychiatric Association and the American Psychological Association.*

APA Commission on Accreditation (APA-CoA) (C-5; HS-4). An affiliate of the *American Psychological Association*, this commission accredits psychology programs.

APGA (C-6; HS-1). See *American Personnel and Guidance Association.*

APHSA (C-2; HS-6). See *American Public Human Services Association.*

APNA (C-3; HS-3). See *American Psychiatric Nurses Association.*

Applied Behavior Analysis (C-8; HS-3). Applying the principles of learning theory to systematically make changes in behavior to improve a person's social, cognitive, emotional, and behavioral patterns.

Applied Research (C-8; HS-6). A methodological approach to research that aims to address and find solutions to a practical problem that has impacted an individual, group, or organization.

Appraisal (C-8; HS-6). The process of assessing an individual or situation. See also *Assessment.*

Approved Clinical Supervisor (ACS) (C-8; HS-3). Administered by the *Center for Credentialing and Education* (*CCE*), this credential indicates a counselor has expertise as a clinical *supervisor* and is required in some states for those who supervise counselors wishing to become licensed.

APRN (C-6; HS-6). See *Advanced Practice Registered Nurse.*

APT (C-6; HS-3). See *Association for Play Therapy.*

Aptitude Testing (C-8; HS-3). Types of *ability tests* that measure what one is capable of learning. Includes *tests of intellectual and cognitive functioning* that encompass *intelligence tests* that are given one-to-one to measure general intellectual ability, *neuropsychological tests* to assess for suspected brain damage, *cognitive ability tests* given in groups to determine the potential of a student in school or as a predictor of college ability, *special aptitude tests* that focus on specific segments of ability often used for job success, and *multiple aptitude tests* that measure a number of specific segments of ability as they relate to potential for success at jobs.

Aquinas, Thomas (1225 - 1274) (C-6; HS-3). During the Middle Ages, Aquinas highlighted *consciousness*, self-examination, and inquiry as philosophies that dealt with the human condition.

ARCA (C-8; HS-3). See *American Rehabilitation Counseling Association*. A division of the *American Counseling Association*.

Archetypes (C-8; HS-3). In *analytical psychology*, found in the *collective unconscious*, the numerous aspects of the person which provide the *psyche* with its tendency to perceive the world in certain ways that we identify as "human" (e.g., the mother, father, warrior, or mother earth archetypes).

Aristotle (384 BCE - 322 BCE) (C-8; HS-6). A Greek philosopher who has been termed the first *psychologist* because of his use of objectivity and reason in studying information.

***Armed Services Vocational Aptitude Battery (ASVAB)* (C-8; HS-3).** A type of multiple *aptitude test* developed by the U.S. federal government and given by the military. It is given for recruitment purposes for the military and for career assessment and military recruitment in high schools.

***Army Alpha* (C-6; HS-3).** One of the first large-scale *ability tests*. This instrument was used by the army in 1917 to identify those who are literate to determine placement of recruits. See also *Army Beta*.

***Army Beta* (C-6; HS-3).** One of the first large-scale *ability tests* and the nonverbal equivalent of the *army alpha*. This instrument was used by the army in 1917 for those who are illiterate to determine placement of recruits. See also *Army Alpha*.

Art Therapy (C-8; HS-8). A *creative and expressive therapy* utilizing art (e.g., drawing, painting) as a *psychotherapy* technique. Art therapy is a specialty requiring specific, advanced clinical training, although elements of art therapy are sometimes used informally by unspecialized professionals in many mental health fields (e.g., *rehabilitation counseling*, counseling children).

Art Therapy Credentials Board (C-3; HS-3). Offers a credential as a *Registered Art Therapist* (ATR).

Artifacts (C-6; HS-4). Symbols of a *culture* or group that can provide multiple meanings to assist in understanding the beliefs, values, and behaviors of that group.

ASCA (C-8; HS-3). See *American School Counselor Association*. A division of the *American Counseling Association*.

ASCA Ethical Standards for School Counselors (C-8; HS-3). Code of ethics for *school counselors*. Separate from the *American Counseling Association*'s *Code of Ethics*.

***ASCA Mindsets and Behaviors for Student Success: K-12 College- and Career-Readiness Standards for Every Student* (C-5; HS-1).** Standards for students in academic, career, and personal/social domains as a function of the *ASCA National Model*.

ASCA National Model (C-7; HS-1). A model developed by the *American School Counselors Association* (*ASCA*) that drives the roles and functions of the *school counselor*. A type of *Comprehensive School Counseling Program*. Includes four elements: foundation, management, delivery, and accountability; and four systems: leadership, advocacy, collaboration, and systemic change.

Asceticism (C-6; HS-3). The practice of intentionally denying oneself of worldly pleasures for spiritual or religious reasons.

ASERVIC (C-8; HS-3). See *Association for Spiritual, Ethical & Religious Values in Counseling*. A division of the *American Counseling Association*.

Asexual (C-8; HS-8). A type of *sexual orientation* in which one does not have sexual attraction to anyone or when one has little interest in sexual activity.

ASGW (C-8; HS-3). See *Association for Specialists in Group Work*. A division of the *American Counseling Association*.

Asian and Pacific Islanders (C-6; HS-6). Americans of Asian and Pacific Island origin. Mostly include fairly large numbers of Chinese, Filipinos, Japanese, Koreans, Asian Indians, Vietnamese, and native Hawaiians, and smaller numbers of Laotian, Thai, Samoans, and Guamanians. Asian and Pacific Islanders typically seek out helping relationships at lower rates than others and find them less satisfactory.

Asperger's Disorder (C-7; HS-7). A disorder characterized by social awkwardness and obsessional interest in one or a few interests. Now considered a high functioning type of *autism spectrum disorder*. See also *Neurodevelopmental Disorders*.

Aspirational Ethics (C-10; HS-10). Holding up very high ideals or expectations for clients or citizens towards the best and most efficacious levels of treatment and professional practice in the helping relationship and in society (e.g., not discriminating against clients who are different from the helper, practicing only within areas of clinical competence, not engaging in harmful practices towards clients).

Assertiveness Training (C-6; HS-6). A behavioral technique, based on *modeling*, that helps individuals learn how to be more direct in their communications with others.

Assessment (C-10; HS-10). A broad array of evaluative procedures that yields information about a person. An assessment may consist of many procedures, including a *clinical interview*, *personality tests*, *ability tests*, and *informal assessment*.

Assessment for Treatment Planning (C-5; HS-5). A type of client *assessment* that involves multiple ways of understanding client concerns in which a helper follows a series of systematic steps which can include: (1) conducting a *clinical interview*, (2) administering *tests*, (3) using *informal assessment procedures*, (4) and coming up with a *diagnosis*.

Assessment Instruments/Procedures (C-8; HS-6). Use of *tests*, *informal assessment*, and the *clinical interview* to understand the person. Also includes use of *ability testing* (*achievement and aptitude*) and *personality assessment* (*objective testing*, *projective testing*, and *interest inventories*).

Assigned Sex (C-10; HS-7). The *sex* label given at birth, generally by a medical or birthing professional, based on the infant's external/physical sex characteristics. See also *Biological Sex*.

Assimilation (C-8; HS-6). The absorption of new information into an existing store of knowledge. In *multicultural counseling*, this refers to the absorption of new or different cultural aspects of identity into one's pre-existing cultural identity (or one's birth *culture*). Developed by *Piaget*.

Assistant to Specialist (C-3; HS-8). A helper who works closely with a highly trained professional as an aide and helper in serving clients. One of the original 13 roles or functions of human service professionals as defined by the *Southern Regional Education Board*.

Association for Adult Development and Aging (AADA) (C-8; HS-3). A division of the *American Counseling Association* that is focused on issues of aging and adult lifespan development.

Association for Assessment and Research in Counseling (AARC) (C-8; HS-3). A division of the *American Counseling Association* that focuses on assessment and research.

Association for Child and Adolescent Counseling (ACAC) (C-8; HS-3). A division of *ACA* that focuses on child and adolescent counseling.

Association for Counselor Education and Supervision (ACES) (C-8; HS-3). A division of the *American Counseling Association* focused on issues critical to counselor educators and supervisors.

Association for Creativity in Counseling (ACC) (C-8; HS-3). A division of the *American Counseling Association* focused on creative and expressive counseling. See also *Creative and Expressive Therapy* and *Creative and Expressive Therapists*.

Association for Humanistic Counseling (AHC) (C-8; HS-3). A division of the *American Counseling Association* for those interested in *humanistic counseling and education*.

Association for Lesbian, Gay, Bisexual, and Transgender Issues in Counseling (ALGBTIC) (C-8; HS-3). A division of the *American Counseling Association* focused on a wide range of issues related to gender, sexual orientation, and the *LGBTQ* community.

Association for Multicultural Counseling and Development (AMCD) (C-8; HS-3). A division of the *American Counseling Association* that focuses on *cultural competence* and other *multicultural counseling* issues.

Association for Play Therapy (APT) (C-3; HS-3). A *professional association* for *creative and expressive therapists* who focus on play and related activities. See also *Creative and Expressive Therapy* and *Creative and Expressive Therapists*.

Association for Specialists in Group Work (ASGW) (C-8; HS-3). A division of the *American Counseling Association* that focuses on working in groups by focusing on such things as *group counseling*, *group therapy*, and *psychoeducational groups*.

Association for Spiritual, Ethical, and Religious Values in Counseling (ASERVIC) (C-8; HS-3). A division of the *American Counseling Association* for those interested in values, ethics, *spirituality*, or *religion* in counseling.

Association of Marital and Family Therapy Regulatory Boards (AMFTRB) (C-8; HS-3). Regulatory body that helps states regulate the licensing process for *marriage, couples, and family counselors*.

Association of Social Work Boards (ASWB) (C-6; HS-3). Regulatory body that oversees the licensing process for *social workers.*

Associative Learning (C-8; HS-3). The process whereby something is learned between two stimuli or through association with a *stimulus* and a behavior. Based on *operant* (behavior and stimulus) and *classical conditioning* (*conditioned stimulus* and *unconditioned stimulus*) paradigms.

Asynchronous (C-6; HS-6). Something that can occur at different times or places or something that is not synchronized, particularly in reference to communication and technology related to distance learning and counseling. For instance, email is an asynchronous tool permitting users to respond whenever they choose as opposed to *synchronous* tools, such as a live broadcast or chat, where the learning or communication must occur at the same time.

Atkinson, Donald (1940 - 2008) (C-6; HS-3). Author of some of the seminal works published in the area of *cross-cultural counseling.*

At-Risk (C-8; HS-8). A general term used to denote populations that are likely to face psychological and/or physical problems due to their situations in life (e.g., poverty, lack of education).

Attachment Theory (C-8; HS-3). A *psychoanalytic* theory developed by *John Bowlby* that emphasizes how the attachments or emotional connections that infants make with their early caregivers have a significant impact on their capacities to form relationships with others in the future.

Attending Behaviors (C-8; HS-8). A *micro skill* that involves combination of the helper's verbal and *nonverbal behaviors* to establish a *working alliance* with the client. Examples of attending behaviors include *eye contact*, open *body positioning*, minimal encouragers, leaning forward, *tone of voice*, and other behaviors that communicate a helper's genuine curiosity and interest in connecting with the client.

Attention Deficit Hyperactivity Disorder (ADHD) (C-8; HS-8). A range of disorders in children or adults that includes poor concentration and an inability to focus, hyperactivity, and impulsivity. Formerly referred to as Attention Deficit Disorder (ADD).

Attention Seeking (C-6; HS-3). From *individual psychology*, one manner in which a child deals with *feelings of inferiority.*

Attire or Dress (C-6; HS-3). In reference to helping jobs, the type of clothes one tends to wear on the job are related to the *overt rules* and *covert rules* within an agency or educational setting where helpers work.

Attitudes and Beliefs, Knowledge, Skills, and Actions (C-8; HS-6). See *Multicultural and Social Justice Counseling Competencies.*

Attitudes (Jungian) (C-8; HS-3). In *analytical psychology* (*Jungian therapy*), the attitudes of being *extroverted* (being oriented socially and outwardly) versus being *introverted* (being oriented inwardly toward one's internal thoughts and feelings). *Jung* suggests that one is born more extroverted or introverted. These attitudes are paired with the *mental functions* of *thinking*, *feeling*, *intuiting*, and *sensing* to create eight *possible psychological types.*

Attitudes, Rules and Expectations, and Assumptions (C-8; HS-3). According to *Aaron Beck*, one's attitudes, rules and expectations, and assumptions about life make up one's *intermediate beliefs* which are directly impacted by one's *core beliefs*. For example, a *core belief* that one is capable of overcoming challenges would be reflected in the attitude "what doesn't kill me makes me stronger," with connected rules and expectations and assumptions in line with this belief. On the other hand, a belief that "I am helpless" would negatively impact one's attitudes, rules and expectations, and assumptions and lead to a person behaving accordingly. Attitudes, rules and expectations, and assumptions directly impact one's *automatic thoughts*.

Atypical Antidepressants (C-6; HS-3). *Antidepressant* medications that do not fit within the existing categories.

Auditor (C-8; HS-3). In *qualitative research*, a person who can check on the *validity* (or *trustworthiness*) and bias of one's research.

Audit Trail (C-8; HS-3). In *qualitative research*, an extremely detailed record of every document and aspect of the research so that others might verify or duplicate the research, similar to what would be needed for a tax audit.

Augustine (354 - 430) (C-3; HS-3). During the Middle Ages, Saint Augustine of Hippo highlighted *consciousness*, self-examination, and inquiry as philosophies that dealt with the human condition.

Authentic Relationship (C-8; HS-6). In *existential* and *humanistic* approaches to helping, the genuine, real, open, and honest relationship with a client that facilitates an "*I-Thou*" relationship and fosters growth, understanding, and healing yet still maintains the boundaries necessary within a therapeutic relationship.

Authenticity (C-8; HS-6). The idea that one is real, genuine, and congruent with others. Particularly important in *existential-humanistic approaches*. Sometimes called *congruence*, *genuineness*, *realness*, or *transparency*.

Autism Spectrum Disorder (C-7; HS-7). A series of disorders that generally begins in childhood and is highlighted by having difficulty speaking with and interacting with others. A type of *neurodevelopmental disorder*. It is also highlighted by repetitive behaviors and restrictive social and occupational functioning.

Autobiography (C-6; HS-6). An assessment procedure that asks an individual to write subjective information that stands out in his or her life. In some ways, the information highlighted in an individual's autobiography is a type of *projective test* as the individual chooses certain items to highlight. A type of *record and personal document*.

Automatic Images (C-8; HS-3). Similar to *Aaron Beck's automatic thoughts*, images that frequently appear *unconsciously*, or barely within *consciousness*, that shape how we behave and feel daily. For example, if someone is feeling like a failure in life, that person may imagine himself or herself being frustrated at work, having an argument with his or her spouse, or being an ineffective parent, which discourages the individual even more. See also *Cognitive Therapy* and *Cognitive-Behavior Therapy*.

Automatic Thoughts (C-10; HS-6). Fleeting thoughts that all individuals have, often barely out of *consciousness*, that drive the manner in which we behave and feel, which in turn, impact one's physiological state. Identified by *Aaron Beck*. See also

Cognitive Therapy and *Cognitive-behavior therapy*.

Autonomic Nervous System (C-6; HS-3). The portion of the peripheral nervous system which influences and regulates the functioning of internal organs. It tends to act *unconsciously* and is in control of such things as heart rate, pupil dilation, sexual arousal, and the fight-flight response.

Autonomy (C-8; HS-6). One of *Kitchener*'s moral ethical principles for working with clients that involves empowering the client's sense of self-determination, independence, and self-sufficiency.

Autonomy vs. Shame and Doubt (ages 1-3 years) (C-9; HS-7). *Erikson*'s second stage of *psychosocial development* where the child begins to gain control over his or her body and explore the environment. Significant caretakers either promote or thwart *autonomy* during this stage.

Aversion Therapy (C-10; HS-8). A therapeutic approach where a *stimulus* that is perceived to be highly noxious by a client is associated with a targeted behavior (e.g., a pedophile receives electric shock when aroused by pictures of children).

Avocation (C-8; HS-6). A chosen activity that is pursued by an individual because it gives satisfaction and fulfills an important aspect of the person's life. It may or may not be income-generating.

Awareness (C-10; HS-8). Understanding of *self*. A word most often used by *existential-humanists* (i.e., in contrast to the *psychodynamic* helpers who talk about one's *conscious* and one's *unconscious*).

Awfulizing (C-8; HS-6). A *cognitive distortion* in *rational emotive behavior therapy*.

Baby-Tender (aka Skinner Air Box) (C-3; HS-1). Developed by *B.F. Skinner*, this device was a comfort controlled crib, which included a safety-glass enclosure, created for his daughter and mass marketed. In practice and design, a pleasant and safe environment to place an infant. Frequently, and falsely confused for the *Skinner box*.

Backup Reinforcer (C-7; HS-7). Similar to a *secondary reinforcer*, when an object, such as a token, becomes paired with something that the individual desires (such as a toy or snacks). Often used in *token economies*.

Bandura, Albert (1925 -) (C-8; HS-6). Behavioral researcher who was the originator of *modeling* and *social learning theory*, which was eventually called *social cognitive theory*. In his research, he showed that people have the capacity to repeat behaviors that they have observed, even at a much later time. One of the many theorists that fueled the diversity of counseling therapies during the 1950s and 1960s.

Bar Graph (C-8; HS-6). See *Histograms*.

Barbiturates (C-8; HS-8). A classification of drugs and medications that has a depressive effect on the *central nervous system* and induces sleep and *anxiety* reduction. Barbiturates were originally developed and prescribed to treat anxiety disorders; however, their usage has declined and been replaced by contemporary *benzodiazepines* due to the high risk of *addiction*, injury, and death that can result from their abuse.

Bartering (C-8; HS-6). The process by which a client exchanges a service, or other goods, instead of paying for services from a counselor or human services practitioner.

Some examples include fixing the helper's car or doing construction work on the helper's office. Bartering is generally discouraged under ethics codes, but may be acceptable in unique situations or more common within certain cultural settings.

Basal Age (C-8; HS-3). On many standardized tests, such as the *Stanford-Binet Intelligence Test*, the highest age group or level at which a person answers all items correctly. This is generally where testing should start. Contrast with *Ceiling Age*. See also *Standardized Testing*.

Baseline (C-8; HS-3). In *functional behavior analysis*, the original number of a specific behavior being observed. See also *ABA design*.

Basic Empathic Responses (C-10; HS-10). Any of a number of responses that reflect back the simple feelings and content that a person is saying. A "level 3" response on the *Carkhuff scale*.

BASIC ID (C-6; HS-3). In *multimodal therapy*, the acronym for the seven dimensions, or modalities, in which individuals operate and includes behavior, *affect*, sensation, imagery, cognition, interpersonal relationships, and drugs and biological processes.

Basic Needs (C-8; HS-8). Frequently connected with *Maslow's hierarchy of needs*, including those essential things needed for basic survival including food, water, shelter, and clothing.

Basic Psychiatric-Mental Health Nurses (PMHN) (C-6; HS-6). *Psychiatric nurses* who generally do not have advanced degrees and can work with clients and families doing entry-level psychiatric nursing.

Bateson, Gregory (1904 - 1980) (C-6; HS-3). An influential anthropologist and social scientist who, with his colleagues at the *Palo Alto Mental Research Institute*, developed key concepts of *systems theory* and *cybernetics* as applied to *family counseling*.

Battered Child (C-10; HS-10). A child (i.e., victim) who experiences *abuse* or witnesses abuse or *neglect* within his or her home environment by parents or other parental figures responsible for his or her care. This *child abuse* could be of physical, emotional, verbal, sexual, or related maltreatment. Most states have laws requiring *mandated reporters* (e.g., teachers, counselors, human service professionals, and others) to report *child abuse*.

Battered Partner/Spouse (C-10; HS-10). Any person (i.e., victim) within a marital, romantic, or other dating or sexual relationship who experiences *abuse* or witnesses abuse or *neglect* by their relationship partner. The abuse could be of physical, emotional, verbal, sexual, or related maltreatment. Some states have laws requiring *mandated reporters* (e.g., teachers, counselors, human service professionals, and others) to report partner abuse. See also *Intimate Partner Violence (IPV)*.

Battered Woman (C-10; HS-10). See *Battered Partner/Spouse*.

Batterer (C-10; HS-10). The individual (i.e., abuser) responsible for inflicting *abuse*, *neglect*, and maltreatment toward children, spouses or partners, or older persons.

Batterers Intervention Program (BIP) (C-6; HS-6). Psychoeducational and counseling programs that focus on services for *batterers* (i.e., abusers) in *intimate partner violence (IPV)* to reduce and prevent *IPV* and break the cycle of violence.

Beck Anxiety Inventory **(C-8; HS-6).** A *self-report* inventory, developed by *Aaron Beck*, to measure the severity of *anxiety* symptoms.

Beck Depression Inventory **(C-8; HS-6).** A *self-report* inventory, developed by *Aaron Beck*, to measure the severity of *depression* symptoms.

Beck, Aaron (1921 -) (C-10; HS-6). Developed *cognitive therapy*, sometimes called *cognitive-behavior therapy*, which stresses that our thoughts affect our feelings, physiology, and behavior.

Beck, Judith (1954 -) (C-6; HS-3). The daughter of *Aaron Beck* who has continued her father's work by advancing the field of *cognitive therapy* and *cognitive-behavior therapy*.

Beers, Clifford (1876 – 1953) (C-6; HS-6). A Yale graduate who had been hospitalized for years due to *schizophrenia* and wrote *A Mind That Found Itself.* In 1909, he helped to establish the *National Committee for Mental Hygiene*, which lobbied the U.S. Congress to pass laws that would improve the deplorable conditions of mental institutions.

Behavior Changer (C-4; HS-6). A helper who uses *intervention* strategies and counseling skills to facilitate client change. One of the original 13 roles or functions of human service professionals as defined by the *Southern Regional Education Board.*

Behavior Modification (C-10; HS-10). Implementing the principles and techniques of *behavior therapy* to change, or modify, an individual's behaviors.

Behavior Therapy (C-10; HS-10). Any of a class of theories that rely on *behavioral approaches/theories*, such as *operant conditioning*, *classical conditioning*, or *modeling* (*social learning*). *Behaviorists* believe that all of these approaches are ways that a person can develop a specific personality style. By carefully analyzing how behaviors are conditioned, helpers can develop behavioral techniques to eliminate undesirable behaviors. Some of the many techniques used include *positive reinforcement*, *extinction*, *systematic desensitization*, *relaxation exercises*, *assertiveness training*, *modeling*, and *the token economy*. Well known behavioral theorists include *Albert Bandura*, *John Krumboltz*, *Ivan Pavlov*, *B. F. Skinner*, *John Watson*, *and Joseph Wolpe*.

Behavior Therapy, Modern Day (C-8; HS-6). When helpers base their principles of working with clients on *operant conditioning*, *classical conditioning*, and *modeling* (*social learning*), while, at the same time, demonstrate and use other skills that build the *working alliance*.

Behavioral Approaches (C-10; HS-10). Methods and approaches to professional helping which share the underlying assumption that behaviors are learned from a process of conditioning. Includes principles based on *classical conditioning*, *operant conditioning*, and *modeling*. Some of the major theorists include *Albert Bandura*, *John Krumboltz*, *Ivan Pavlov*, *B. F. Skinner*, *John Watson*, and *Joseph Wolpe*.

Behavioral Emergency (C-4; HS-4). An escalated behavioral crisis (e.g., extreme acting out) that requires immediate *intervention* to avoid injury or death to others or oneself.

Behavioral Family Therapy (C-10; HS-10). *Family therapy* that utilizes the theory and techniques of *behavior therapy*.

Behavioral Principles (C-10; HS-10). *Operant conditioning, classical conditioning, and modeling (or social learning)* paradigms used in *behavior therapy.*

Behavioral Rehearsal (C-8; HS-6). See *Modeling.*

Behavioral Theories (C-10; HS-10). See *Behavioral Approaches.*

Behaviorism (C-10; HS-10). The belief system that animals and humans can be understood via *conditioning*, as evidenced in *behavior therapy*, instead of through emotional and other internal experiences and motivations.

Behaviorist (C-10; HS-10). An individual who practices, researches, or philosophizes about the theory, principles, and techniques of *behaviorism* and *behavior therapy.*

Being Curious (C-6; HS-6). Helpers who have a genuine interest in getting to know their clients and are comfortable inquiring about a client's life while simultaneously honoring and respecting the person. A technique sometimes associated with *solution-focused brief therapy* and other *post-modern approaches.*

Being Tentative (SFBT) (C-6; HS-6). When helpers gently, cautiously, and tentatively try out or test ideas or techniques with the client. A technique sometimes associated with *solution-focused brief therapy* and other *post-modern approaches.* See also *Not-Knowing Posture.*

Belenky, Mary Field (C-6; HS-3). Formulated a theory of women's development of *self* called *Women's Ways of Knowing.*

Belief About The Event (C-8; HS-6). The patterns of rational or irrational cognitions that one has about an *activating event.* Related to *rational-emotive behavior therapy.*

Bell-Shaped Curve (C-8; HS-6). See *Normal/Bell-Shaped Curve.*

Belonging (C-8; HS-6). The feeling of being welcomed, accepted, or fitting in with others. In many counseling theories, belonging is seen as a need or essential component of mental health and stability for individuals. See also *Love and Belonging* and *Maslow's Hierarchy of Needs.*

***Bender Visual Motor Gestalt Test* (C-8; HS-3).** A popular psychological test of *neurodevelopmental disorders* and neurological functioning developed by Lauretta Bender.

Beneficence (C-8; HS-6). One of *Kitchener*'s moral ethical principles that involves protecting the good of others and of society.

Benevolent (C-6; HS-3). A principle from *virtue ethics*, a characteristic of helpers which involves genuine kindness and compassion. See also *Ethical Decision-Making, Moral Models.*

Benzodiazepines (C-8; HS-6). Any of a number of *anti-anxiety medications* often described as *sedatives* and are frequently used for *generalized anxiety disorders* as they have a calming effect on the individual. These drugs tend to have an elevated risk for tolerance, *substance dependence*, and overdose if not taken properly. They include *Valium, Librium, Tranxene, Xanax*, and others.

Berg, Insoo Kim (1934 - 2007) (C-8; HS-6). One of the founders of *solution-focused brief therapy (SFBT)* and the wife of *Steve de Shazer.*

Bernard's Discrimination Model (C-8; HS-3). A *supervision* model that includes the *supervisor* shifting between three different roles (teacher, counselor, and consultant) while focusing on three areas of a *supervisee's* development (intervention, personalization, and conceptualization).

Best Practice Guidelines (C-8; HS-8). Guidelines developed by *professional associations* and others to guide the practice of counseling and helping relationships.

Beta Error (C-8; HS-3). See *Type II Error.*

Beta Hypothesis (C-8; HS-3). See *Type II Error.*

Between Group Design (C-8; HS-3). An experimental testing design that involves two or more subject groups simultaneously being exposed to different treatments to examine differences amongst groups. Also called between subjects design.

B. F. Skinner Foundation (C-6; HS-3). The official organization dedicated to the promotion, training, and research of *B.F. Skinner's* theories, writings, and clinical application of his ideas.

Bias (C-10; HS-10). A researcher's or practitioner's personal attitudes, values, beliefs, or past experiences that influence or interfere with the research or helping process.

Bibliotherapy (C-8; HS-8). A helping technique that utilizes reading books or other written material in the treatment process. Clients engage in reading the selected materials and discuss them with their helper or read them on their own as an adjunct to the helping process. It is often used in *cognitive-behavioral approaches* or *psychoeducation* to reinforce newly learned behaviors or approaches to living.

Big Book (C-8; HS-8). The primary guiding text used within *12 steps groups* detailing the principles of the *12 step* approach to *recovery* from *substance abuse* or *process addictions* and related compulsive behaviors. Originally, this book was written in 1939 by *Bill W.* for *Alcoholics Anonymous* but has been modified for other *12 steps groups.*

Bigotry (C-8; HS-8). The practice or attitude of being *prejudiced*, intolerant, or hateful to people or groups who are perceived to be different from you, such as racially, religiously, culturally, or ethnically different. See also *Discrimination.*

Bill W. (1895 - 1971) (C-6; HS-6). Also known as Bill Wilson, William Griffith Wilson was a businessman and co-founder of *Alcoholics Anonymous.* He is referred to as Bill W. in the anonymous tradition of the *12 steps* approach to *recovery.*

Binet, Alfred (1857 - 1911) (C-8; HS-6). A French *psychologist* who was commissioned by the Ministry of Public Education in Paris in 1904 to develop an intelligence test to assist in the integration of "subnormal" children into the schools. His work with *Theophile Simon* led to the development of the first modern-day intelligence test (Binet-Simon scale) that eventually became known as the *Stanford-Binet Intelligence Scale.*

Binge Eating Disorder (BED) (C-8; HS-6). An *eating disorder* indicated by episodes of binge eating without purging (e.g., vomiting, laxatives). See also *Binging (Eating or Drinking).*

Binging (Eating or Drinking) (C-8; HS-8). The process by which one consumes inordinate amounts of food or beverages usually to cope with unmet emotional needs or another psychological ailment. See also *Binge Eating Disorder (BED).*

Binswanger, Ludwig (1881 - 1966) (C-5; HS-3). This Swiss *psychiatrist* was an early protégé of *Freud* and *Jung* and developed early ideas of *existential psychology* including the notion of *eigenwelt*, *umwelt*, *mitwelt*, and *uberwelt.*

Biochemical Model (C-8; HS-6). A model that suggests there are chemical imbalances that underlie emotional problems and that the helping process can often be assisted through medication and other biological i*nterventions.*

Bioecological Model (C-8; HS-6). Based on *Bronfenbrenner's ecological systems theory*, a model of human development that emphasizes bidirectional influences from a person's environment and from individual aspects of the person (e.g., biological, gene influence) and how those impact overall human development.

Biofeedback (C-8; HS-6). Used within *neuropsychology* and related counseling approaches, various precision tools are utilized to measure such things as brain waves, heart rate, and perception of pain and assist the individual in controlling them in ways that result in more positive feelings and a better outlook on life.

Biographical Inventories (C-8; HS-6). Provides a detailed picture of the individual from birth. Such an inventory can be obtained by conducting an involved, *structured interview*, by having the client answer a series of items on a checklist, or by having the person respond to a series of questions. A type of *Informal Assessment.*

Biological Determinism (C-8; HS-6). The idea that we are determined by our genes and our biology.

Biological Sex (C-10; HS-10). The sex a person was assigned at birth, being either born male, female, or *intersex.* In some places, individuals who have undergone *sex reassignment surgery* have successfully petitioned to change their birth records to indicate their new sex post-surgery. Contrast with *Gender.*

Biopsychosocial Model (BPS) (C-8; HS-6). A developmental model that emphasizes the interaction that biological, psychological, and social influences have on shaping human development.

Biosocial Theory of Personality Development (C-8; HS-6). In *dialectical behavior therapy*, the idea that some people are born with heightened emotional sensitivity.

Biphobia (C-6; HS-6). The fear, hatred, or intolerance of individuals who identify, or are perceived as, *bisexual.* See also *Homophobia* and *Transphobia.*

Bipolar and Related Disorders (C-8; HS-6). The diagnostic category of the *Diagnostic and Statistical Manual-5* comprising disorders that include disturbances in mood in which the client cycles through stages of *mania, depression*, or both mania and depression. Both children and adults can be diagnosed with bipolar disorder, and the *clinician* can work to identify the pattern of mood presentation, such as rapid-cycling, which is more often observed in children. These disorders include bipolar I, bipolar II, cyclothymic disorder, substance/medication-induced mood disorder, bipolar and related disorder due to another medical condition, and other *specified and unspecified* bipolar and related disorders.

Biracial/Multiracial Identity Development (C-6; HS-6). The psychological process and changes that occur as individuals increasingly understand, accept, or reject their mixed racial, cultural, or ethnic identities over their lifespan. See also *Racial*

Identity Development.

Birth Order (C-8; HS-6). A concept tied to *individual psychology* that emphasizes the impact that one's birth order has on the ways in which one feels about himself or herself. For example, first-born children might have a predisposition to be perfectionists and caregivers compared to younger siblings as a function of birth order.

Biserial Correlation (C-8; HS-3). A type of *correlation* that is conducted when one *variable* is dichotomous (*nominal scale*).

Bisexual (C-10; HS-10). A type of *sexual orientation* in which one is attracted to both males and females.

Bivariate Correlational Studies (C-8; HS-6). A type of *experimental research* based on *correlation coefficients*.

Black Box (C-6; HS-3). Used within *behaviorism* and other scientific fields, any object, device, or system whereby the inner workings, such as of the brain, cannot be observed directly, yet have clearly observable inputs (*stimulus*) and outputs (responses). The opposite of this is an object, device, or system where the process (or inner workings) can be visibly observed, called a white box or clear box.

Black Identity Development Models (C-5; HS-6). The psychological process and changes that occur as *African Americans* increasingly understand, accept, or reject their racial identity over the lifespan. One such model was developed by *William Cross*. See also *Racial Identity Development.*

Blackout (C-6; HS-3). A phenomenon, caused by *alcohol*, medication, or other substances, that induces a state of impaired short and long term memory, like a temporary amnesia, wherein the person taking the substances cannot remember, and may be out of control of their behaviors, cognitions, and *emotions* during the blackout period. Very often, blackouts are caused by heavy alcohol consumption, although blackouts may not always be related to amount of substance usage.

Blank Slate (C-8; HS-6). See *Tabula Rasa.*

Blended Family (C-8; HS-8). A family composed of one biological parent and a non-biological step-parent, where one or more of the parents has children from previous relationships not related to the other parent. May be called a step-family.

Block Grants (C-6; HS-8). Originally proposed by President Reagan, grants that are intended to allocate a specific amount of money to each U.S. state so that the state decides where the money should be spent. In some states, it deleteriously affected money for social programs.

Blockages (C-8; HS-6). Also referred to as *resistance*, areas of clinical importance in counseling and in helping where a client has difficulty talking about, is defensive of, or is unable or unwilling to explore further.

Blood Alcohol Concentration/Level (BAC) (C-8; HS-8). The percentage of *alcohol* (ethanol) concentrated in blood for an individual after drinking alcohol. The higher the BAC, the greater the effect and/or damage of the alcohol upon the individual. This is frequently a measure of *intoxication* used in *sobriety* testing by law enforcement and other settings (e.g., employers, doctors).

Board Certification (C-8; HS-6). Generally, a *credential* that indicates a professional has demonstrated experience and has passed a rigorous exam in a specialty area or a field of learning. In human services, one can become a *Human Services—Board Certified Practitioner (HS—BCP)* indicating a credential in human services. In medicine, a board *certification* is obtained to indicate a specialty field beyond the medical license as a physician (e.g., psychiatry, neurology, etc.). In *psychology*, one can become board certified to indicate any of a number of specialty areas beyond the general license as a *psychologist* (e.g., child and adolescent psychology, neuropsychology, etc.).

Board-Certified Coach (C-8; HS-6). A *credential* for a coach. Individuals can become certified in *coaching* from the *Center for Credentialing and Education* if they have a bachelor's degree or higher. See also *Life-Coaching.*

Body Armor (C-6; HS-3). First developed by *Wilhelm Reich*, a term used by *body-oriented therapies*, for the mechanism individuals use when holding feelings within their body.

Body-Oriented Therapies (C-6; HS-3). A group of therapies that emphasizes that repressed memories, feelings, and experiences are held within our body and that they need to be expressed in some fashion. *Wilhelm Reich* was one of the first body-oriented therapists.

Body Positioning (C-7; HS-7). The ways in which a helper positions his or her body while working with a client. One of the most important *nonverbal behaviors* that clients initially observe.

Bogust v. Iverson (C-3; HS-1). Is an important legal case from 1960, setting a precedent for institutional liability of student suicides at colleges and universities in the United States. Due to this, and related cases, higher education institutions are expected/liable to provide crisis screening, treatment, and referral services for students experiencing suicidal thoughts or actions, likely through the campus counseling center and related support and emergency services (e.g., counseling centers, student affairs offices, medical services).

Bonferroni Correction (C-8; HS-3). A statistical procedure that is used to protect against the *familywise error rate* by dividing the *alpha level* by the number of comparisons that are being made.

Boston Civic Service House (CSH) (C-3; HS-3). This was an early *settlement house*, or social service organization, that was founded in 1901 and devoted to assisting the poor and newly arrived immigrants in Boston, MA. It also housed the *Boston Vocation Bureau.*

Boston Process Approach (C-6; HS-1). A type of *Flexible Battery Approach* to *Neuropsychological Assessment.*

Boston Vocation Bureau (C-6; HS-1). Founded by *Frank Parsons* in 1908, this was the earliest organization focusing on *vocational guidance* or *career counseling.*

Boszormenyi-Nagy, Ivan (1920 - 2007) (C-6; HS-3). A Hungarian-American *psychiatrist* who was influential as a founder of *family counseling* and also known for developing *contextual family therapy.*

Boundaries (C-8; HS-6). The manner in which information flow is managed into and out of a system. Used within *family counseling*, boundaries refer to the rules, codes, expectations, or other ways the family system and subsystems (e.g., parental, spousal, sibling) maintain their information flow. See also *Permeable Boundaries*, *Rigid Boundaries*, and *Semipermeable Boundaries*.

Boundaries and Information Flow (C-8; HS-6). The rigidity versus permeability of *boundaries* and the capacity for information to flow into a system (such as a family or organization) based on those boundaries. For example, a system that has very rigid boundaries does not permit information to flow into or out of the system easily, whereas permeable (or diffuse) boundaries permit information to flow too easily into or out of the system. This concept is applied to boundaries within family systems and subsystems in *family counseling*.

Bowen, Murray (1918 - 1990) (C-8; HS-3). An American *psychiatrist* and educator influential in pioneering *family counseling* from a systems perspective and developing *multigenerational family therapy*.

Bowenian Family Therapy (C-8; HS-6). A type of *family counseling* from a systems perspective that utilizes *Bowen's* eight interactive concepts that include: differentiation of self, triangles, nuclear family emotional system, family projection process, emotional cutoff, multigenerational transmission process, sibling position, and societal emotional process.

Bowlby, John (1907 - 1990) (C-8; HS-3). A British *psychologist* and *psychoanalyst* who separated from *Melanie Klein* and other psychoanalysts to develop his own psychoanalytic *attachment theory*.

Bracketing (C-8; HS-3). In *qualitative research*, sectioning off one's biases to reduce the chances that they will affect the research.

Breuer, Josef (1842 - 1925) (C-6; HS-3). An Austrian physician and neurophysiologist who developed the *talking cure* and served as a teacher and early collaborator of *Freud*. Freud built from *Breuer's* work to develop *psychoanalysis*.

Brewer, John (1877 - 1950) (C-6; HS-1). Influential in school counseling, in 1932, he suggested that guidance in the schools be seen in a total educational context.

Brief Family Therapy Center (C-8; HS-3). Founded in *Palo Alto*, *CA*, this organization revolutionized how some were doing family therapy with its focus on short-term solutions to problems.

Brief Treatment (C-8; HS-3). Short-term approach to counseling and helping that involves working on focused problems and aims for practical change to relieve problems.

Broker (C-3; HS-8). A helper who assists clients in finding and accessing services. One of the original 13 roles and functions of human service professionals as defined by the *Southern Regional Education Board*.

Bronfenbrenner, Urie (1917 - 2005) (C-3; HS-4). An influential developmental *psychologist* who created *ecological systems theory*.

***Brown v. Board of Education* (C-10; HS-10).** A historically significant U.S. Supreme Court case that reversed the decision from *Plessy v. Ferguson*, which had permitted the segregation of students of different races in public education.

BSW (C-10; HS-10). Bachelor's degree of *social work*.

Buber, Martin (1878 - 1965) (C-6; HS-3). A philosopher influential in *existential philosophy* and *existential psychology* who originated the focus on the *I-Thou relationship* over the *I-It relationship*.

***Buckley Amendment* (C-3; HS-3).** See *Family Educational Rights and Privacy Act (FERPA) of 1974*.

Bugental, James (1915 – 2008) (C-6; HS-3). An important theorist, advocate, and educator of *existential-humanistic approaches* to counseling and helping.

Bulimia Nervosa (C-8; HS-8). An *eating disorder* highlighted by incidents of binge eating (i.e., uncontrolled eating) and purging (e.g., vomiting, laxatives) connected to *feelings of inferiority*, low self-worth, and distorted views of body weight, size, and shape. See also *Binging (Eating or Drinking)*.

Burnout (C-10; HS-10). Emotional, physical, and psychological *stress* or disenfranchisement that impairs an individual from working effectively as a helper and is highlighted by extreme frustration, cynicism, lack of empathy and/or compassion, and a general disregard for the quality of one's work with clients and consumers. See also *Compassion Fatigue*.

***Buros Mental Measurement Yearbook* (C-8; HS-3).** A sourcebook that includes reviews of more than 2,000 different *assessments*, *tests*, instruments, or screening devices. Most university libraries carry this as a hardbound copy and/or online.

CACREP (C-10; HS-3). See *Council for Accreditation of Counseling and Related Educational Programs*.

***CAI* (C-8; HS-3).** See *Career Assessment Inventory*.

***California Psychological Inventory* (*CPI*) (C-6; HS-3).** A type of *objective personality test* used to measure common personality factors.

Cannabis (C-10; HS-10). A genus of plants also known as *marijuana*, cannabis is a psychoactive *controlled substance* used to obtain a "high," to feel a sense of tranquility, and to ameliorate a variety of medical problems. At times, intake of the substance can lead to cannabis use disorder, and in severe cases, be addictive. Some U.S. states have legalized cannabis for recreational and medical use. Some medical uses include the treatment of glaucoma, anxiety, pain, and to reduce nausea and increase appetite in cancer treatment and other medical conditions.

Canonical Correlation (C-6; HS-3). A type of multivariate *correlational research* that is used to measure the relationship between two vectors (sets of *variables*). Canonical correlations can be computed by taking the square root of an *eigenvalue*.

Caplan, Gerald (1917 - 2008) (C-6; HS-6). Developed a well-known model of mental health *consultation*. See also *Consulting Inward*.

Career (C-8; HS-6). The totality of *work* and life roles through which an individual expresses himself or herself across the lifespan. It may include work, leisure, and *avocational* activities.

Career and Employment Agencies (C-8; HS-6). Setting where *career counseling* takes place and helpers may be employed.

***Career Assessment Inventory* (*CAI*) (C-8; HS-3).** A type of *interest inventory* to help in career and vocational planning.

Career Awareness (C-8; HS-6). One's *consciousness* about *career*-related decisions, which can be facilitated through self-examination of one's values, abilities, preferences, knowledge of *occupations* and life roles, and interests.

Career Counseling (C-8; HS-6). The process of using helping skills, *career development* theories, and *assessment* instruments to help a person in their *vocational* and career process. A *Council for the Accreditation of Counseling and Related Educational Programs* specialty. See also *Career Development.*

Career Counselor (C-8; HS-3). A helper who has expertise in *career counseling.*

***Career Decision-Making System* (*CDM*) (C-8; HS-3).** A type of *interest inventory* used to help people make *career* decisions.

Career Development (C-8; HS-6). All of the psychological, sociological, educational, physical, economic, and other factors that are at play in shaping one's *career* over the lifespan.

Career Development Assessment and Counseling Model (C-DAC) (C-8; HS-3). Developed by *Donald Super*, this model utilizes up-to-date *career development* information and theory to enhance *career counseling* and lifespan issues connected to *vocational guidance* for clients.

***Career Development Quarterly* (C-6; HS-3).** Journal of the *National Career Development Association* (*NCDA*).

Career Development Services (C-8; HS-6). In higher education, the office where *career counseling* is provided. For those with a master's degree or higher in counseling, especially *student affairs and college counseling* or career counseling, a possible area of employment.

Career Development Theories (C-8; HS-6). Any theories that address the *career development* process when working with clients. Includes c*onstructivist career counseling*, *social cognitive career theory*, the *lifespan developmental approach of career counseling* of *Donald Super*, the *personality theory of occupational choice* of *John Holland*, *psychodynamic approaches to career counseling* (e.g., *Anne Roe's*), and the *trait and factor theory* of *Frank Parsons.*

Career Exploration Tools (C-8; HS-6). Various tools, such as *interest inventories*, websites, books, films, and related materials focused on *work* or *career* used to assist individuals to gain knowledge, explore career options, and increase one's *career awareness.*

Career Guidance (C-8; HS-6). A program designed by helpers that offers information concerning *career development* and facilitates *career awareness* for individuals.

Career Information (C-8; HS-6). Any resource about *work* and *career* used to help increase one's *career awareness.*

***Career Occupational Preference System* (C-8; HS-6).** An *interest inventory* containing a series of questions to measure one's *career* interests. Test-takers' scores are then compared to 14 different career clusters.

Career Path (C-8; HS-6). The sequence of positions and jobs that typically signifies potential advancement through one's *career.*

Career Typology (C-8; HS-6). See *Holland Code* and *RIASEC.*

Caregiver (C-6; HS-8). A human service professional who offers direct support, encouragement, and hope to clients. One of the original 13 roles or functions of human service professionals as defined by the *Southern Regional Education Board.*

Caring Habits (CS-8; HS-6). A concept promoted by *William Glasser* who encouraged people and helpers to use language that is supportive, encouraging, listening, accepting, trusting, respectful, and promotes negotiating differences. Contrast with *Deadly Habits.*

Carkhuff, Robert (C-6; HS-3). An American *psychologist* who developed a 5-point scale to measure a helper's ability to make an empathic response. Level 3 responses are seen as accurately reflecting the client's *affect* and content. Responses below Level 3 are seen as a *subtractive* empathic response, while responses above Level 3 are seen as an *additive* empathic response. See also *Carkhuff Scale*, *Accurate Empathy Scale*, and *Empathy.*

Carkhuff Scale (C-8; HS-6). A scaled developed to measure the ability to make empathic responses. Measures empathy from a scale of 1 through 5. Above 3 is an *additive* empathic response, below 3 is a *subtractive* empathic response. A "Level 3" response is when a person accurately reflects back meaning (content) and feelings (*affect*). See also *Carkhuff, Robert*, *Accurate Empathy Scale*, and *Empathy.*

***Carl Perkins Act (PL 98-524)* (C-8; HS-6).** Originally passed in 1984 and subsequently amended, this law assures that adults or special groups in need of *job* training have access to vocational *assessment*, counseling, and placement. These groups include (a) individuals with disabilities; (b) individuals from economically disadvantaged families, including foster children; (c) individuals preparing for nontraditional fields; (d) single parents, including single pregnant women; (e) displaced homemakers; and (f) individuals with limited English proficiency.

Case Conceptualization (C-9; HS-6). A method that allows a helper to understand a client's *presenting problems* and subsequently apply appropriate helping skills and treatment strategies based on the helper's theoretical orientation.

Case Conference (C-8; HS-8). A formal meeting of helpers with their colleagues and supervisors within mental health and social service settings where clients (or cases) are discussed and *treatment planning* is examined.

Case Management (C-8; HS-8). The overall process involved in maintaining the optimal functioning of clients. Includes (1) *treatment planning*, (2) *diagnosis*, (3) *medication management*, (4) writing *case reports* and *case notes;* (5) managing *client contact hours*, (6) monitoring *progress toward client goals*, (7) making *referrals*, (8) *follow-up*, and, (9) *time* *management.*

Case Notes (C-8; HS-8). Ways of documenting and summarizing clients' information, including the *intake interview*, highlights of a clients' goals and objectives, periodic summaries of clients' progress, termination summaries, specialized reports for the courts or other agencies, and more. Also referred to as *case reports.* Generally, clients have a right to access their case notes if they so choose. One aspect of the *case management* process. Contrast with *Process Notes.* See also *SOAP Format.*

Case Reports (C-8; HS-8). See *Case Notes.*

Case Study Method (C-8; HS-8). In *qualitative research*, deeply probing and analyzing events and phenomena in an effort to allow themes and the meaning of the phenomena to emerge.

Caseload (C-8; HS-6). The total number of clients (individual and group) that a mental health professional is providing helping services to at a given time.

Castration Anxiety (C-8; HS-3). In *psychoanalysis*, fear that one's penis will be cut off. Related to *Oedipal Complex.*

Catastrophizing (C-8; HS-6). A *cognitive distortion* in which one irrationally assumes that a present or future situation is or will be substantially worse than it is.

Catchment Area (C-8; HS-8). The primary region from where clients or students come for a particular service to address mental health or educational needs. For example, many counseling agencies will only serve clients within a certain city or county, thus these are the catchment areas for these agencies.

Catharsis (C-8; HS-6). A concept derived from Freudian *psychoanalysis* wherein *emotions* that have been repressed by an individual are expressed and released through therapy. See also *Abreaction.*

Cattell-Horn-Carroll (CHC) (C-7; HS-1). A theory of intelligence that includes 16 broad ability factors, 6 of which are tentative, and over 70 associated tasks that may or may not be related to a *g factor.*

Cattell, James (1860 - 1944) (C-8; HS-3). One of the earliest *psychologists* to use statistical concepts to understand people. His main emphasis became testing mental abilities, and he is known for coining the term *mental test.*

Cattell, Raymond (1905 - 1998) (C-8; HS-1). A British-American *psychologist* who differentiated *fluid intelligence* which is innate, from *crystallized intelligence*, which is learned. He also attempted to remove cultural bias from *intelligence testing.*

Causal-Comparative Research (C-7; HS-2). A kind of *quantitative research* that examines intact groups instead of randomly assigning subjects to groups. Also called *Ex Post Facto Research.*

Causal Relationships (C-9; HS-5). An association between one or more *variables* in which one variable(s) directly impacts one or more other variables, thus causing change in the second set of variables. Causal relationships are inferred in *experimental research.*

CCE (C-8; HS-8). See *Center for Credentialing and Education.*

CCMHC (C-8; HS-3). See *Certified Clinical Mental Health Counselor.*

***CDM* (C-8; HS-3).** See *Career Decision-Making System.*

Ceiling Age (C-8; HS-3). The highest age, or level, where someone can no longer correctly answer *test* items (like on the *Stanford-Binet*), and consequently, further testing can cease. Contrast with *Basal Age.*

Center for Credentialing and Education (CCE) (C-8; HS-8). A *credentialing* body that offers a variety of credentials in the helping professions, including the *approved clinical supervisor* (*ACS*), *Human services—Board-Certified Professional* (*HS—BCP*), and *Board-Certified Coach* (*BCC*).

Center for the Studies of the Person (C-8; HS-3). An organization dedicated to the *person-centered counseling* approach of *Carl Rogers* and to his theories and writings on counseling and life.

Central Nervous System (C-8; HS-3). The division of the nervous system that includes the brain and spinal cord. This portion of the nervous system controls one's thoughts, movement, and sensations.

Cerebral Electric Stimulation (C-6; HS-3). A *neurological therapy* that involves electric stimulation of the brain to improve clients' functioning.

Ceremonies (C-8; HS-3). See *Definitional Ceremonies.*

Certification (C-8; HS-8). A type of *credential* that is more rigorous than *registration* but less rigorous than *licensure.* Guidelines are usually set by states or national organizations, and often provide protection of a "title" (e.g., *national certified counselor*) but generally do not define *scope of practice.* See also *Licensure.*

Certified Clinical Mental Health Counselor (CCMHC) (C-8; HS-3). A specialty *certification* for mental health counselors that is offered through the *National Board for Certified Counselors* (*NBCC*).

Certified Family Therapist (CFT) (C-7; HS-3). A national *certification* developed by the *International Association of Marriage and Family Counselors* and sponsored by the *National Credentialing Academy.* This credential is open to those who have a master's in counseling or a related degree and a specialty in *couples and family counseling.*

Certified Genetic Counselor (CGC) (C-6; HS-3). A credential obtained by individuals who have gone through a program accredited by the *Accreditation Council for Genetic Counseling.* Genetic counselors hold graduate degrees in any number of areas including law, medicine, and counseling.

Certified Pastoral Counselor (CPC) (C-8; HS-3). A professional *certification* for *pastoral counselors* offered by the *American Association for Pastoral Counselors.*

Certified Rehabilitation Counselor (CRC) (C-8; HS-3). A national credential for *rehabilitation counselors* offered by the *Commission on Rehabilitation Counselor Certification* (*CRCC*).

Certified School Counselor (C-8; HS-3). A *school counselor* who is certified by his or her State Board of Education. Sometimes called licensed school counselor. See also *Counselor*.

Certified School Psychologist (C-8; HS-3). Generally, a *certification* that one gains after having successfully graduated from a state-approved school *psychology* program. Sometimes called *Licensed School Psychologist*.

CESNET-L (C-8; HS-1). The Counselor Education and Supervision Network Listserv. It is the *American Counseling Association's* electronic mailing list for *counselor education and supervision* faculty and students.

Chaining (C-6; HS-3). A technique used within *behavior therapy*, when the final behavior in a series of behaviors is reinforced so that every other previous behavior is associated with the final reinforcer.

Challenging Clients (C-6; HS-6). When helpers encourage their clients to deeply examine, question, or explore particular beliefs, values, opinions, or expectations about their lives and the world around them so that they can develop a more rational or realistic perspective.

CHAMPUS (C-6; HS-3). The Civilian Health and Medical Program of the Uniformed Services. A supplemental medical care program provided to United States military personnel.

Change Process Model (C-6; HS-3). One name for *Virginia Satir's* model of *couples and family counseling*. See also *Human Validation Process Model*, *Communication Theory*, and *Virginia Satir*.

Chaos Stage of Integrative Counseling (C-6; HS-3). The first stage of developing an *integrative approach to counseling* in which no theory is used and the *clinician*'s responses are based on moment-to-moment subjective judgments that can be harmful to the client. See also *Eclecticism*.

Chaos Theory Consultation (C-6; HS-3). The application of chaos theory to *consultation*. This approach tries to reduce the unpredictability in a system while realizing there is always a certain amount of chaos.

Character (Jungian) (C-6; HS-3). A person's personality related to how one's *mental functions* and *attitudes* divert experiences into *consciousness* or the *personal unconscious*.

Charcot, Jean Martin (1825 – 1893) (C-6; HS-3). One of the seminal theorists who practiced the then new scientific technique called *hypnosis* during the mid-1800s.

Charity Organization Society (COS) (C-6; HS-8). Arising in the United States in the 1800s, an organization of volunteers who tried to alleviate the conditions of poverty by entering the poorer districts of cities and helping the residents there.

Chi Sigma Iota (CSI) (C-8; HS-1). A counseling honor society that promotes and recognizes scholarly activities, leadership, professionalism, and excellence in the profession of counseling.

Chi Square (C-8; HS-6). In research, used to compare whether the observed frequency of scores differs from the expected frequency of scores.

Chickering, Arthur (1927 -) (C-6; HS-1). An influential educator who formulated a theory of adult development for those who attend college. His ideas are extensively used within *student affairs and college counseling*.

Chickering's Seven Vectors of Student Development (C-6; HS-3). Seven factors that are crucial in the development of college students, including achieving competence, managing *emotions*, developing autonomy, establishing identity, forming interpersonal relationships, developing purpose, and developing integrity. See also *Chickering, Arthur.*

Child Abuse (C-10; HS-10). A type of *abuse* involving an abuser, often the parent or caregiver, who physically, verbally, emotionally, or sexually harms a child or is consistently *neglectful* of the child's needs. All states have laws requiring *mandated reporters* (e.g., teachers, counselors, human service professionals, and others) to report suspected child abuse.

Child Development (C-8; HS-8). *Developmental theories* which emphasize the notion that children face predictable tasks as they pass through the inevitable developmental stages and that knowledge of such tasks could greatly aid helpers in their work with children.

Child Guidance Clinics (C-6; HS-6). Clinics that were organized by the *National Committee for Mental Hygiene*, in the early 1900s, to improve the quality of services for children and their families.

Child Protective Services (C-6; HS-3). Sometimes referred to as children and youth agencies, a variety of government service agencies that are tasked with the protection of children and adolescents from *abuse* and *neglect*. See also *Child Abuse* and *Mandated Reporters*.

Child-Rearing Practices (C-6; HS-3). An important focus of therapy in *psychodynamic* approaches to helping and counseling.

Choice and Free Will (C-8; HS-6). *Carl Rogers* and others believed that healthy individuals can freely make choices; however, many people are limited in their ability to choose because of distortions of thinking and personal defenses. Healthy choices can be made by becoming free of defenses, thought distortions, and past negative influences. For fully aware individuals, healthy choices are clear and nearly automatic, as if there is no actual choice.

Choice Theory (C-6; HS-3). Originally called *control theory*, the theoretical underpinning for *William Glasser's* counseling approach, called *reality therapy*, in which the process of understanding the world through one's unique filters (*quality world*) is examined. Based on this quality world, an individual makes choices, sometimes dysfunctional ones, to meet his or her needs. Clients are helped to make new choices that meet their needs in healthy ways. It is an *anti-deterministic* approach. See also *Reality Therapy*.

Choose Our Actions and Thoughts (C-6; HS-3). Beliefs by *reality therapy* practitioners that we can choose how we act and how we think and thus change our acting, thinking, feeling, and physiological responses.

***Choosing a Career* (C-5; HS-1).** A booklet written by *Eli Weaver* in the early 1900s. Weaver helped to establish *vocational guidance* in New York.

***Choosing a Vocation* (C-5; HS-3).** A book written by *Frank Parsons* that was used to establish *vocational guidance* in schools.

Circular Causality (C-8; HS-6). A phenomenon in which events occur in circles and the effect of one event becomes the cause of the next event which continues the circular effect. Thus, A causes B which also causes A, in a circular loop of causality. An example of this within *family counseling* is when parental violence leads to children growing up to be violent which leads to more parental violence by the now grown children towards their offspring in a loop of causality and effect.

Cisgender (C-8; HS-8). When one's *gender identity* matches or is congruent with the sex that he or she was assigned at birth (i.e., one's biological sex). This is sometimes seen as the "acceptable" or "default" mode of expectations for people within a society, meaning those born male are expected to identify and behave as males within the *culture* of that society, thus to be cisgender. Contrast with *Transgender.*

Civil Liability (C-8; HS-8). The responsibility one has as a result of having violated a legal duty to another. For helpers, clients can file *civil suits* against the helper if they believe they have been aggrieved through the helping process. Contrast with *Criminal Liability*.

Civil Rights Acts (1964 and Amendments) (C-6; HS-3). Relative to *tests* and *assessment*, laws requiring that any test used for employment or promotion be shown to be suitable and valid for the job in question. If this is not done, alternative means of assessment must be provided. Differential test cutoffs are not allowed.

Civil Rights Liability (C-6; HS-3). In postsecondary education, the concerns about how the rights of students may be violated and how the university may be held liable.

Civil Suits (C-6; HS-1). Lawsuits involving *civil liability* when clients make allegations of alleged malpractice by human service professionals.

Class (C-10; HS-10). See *Social Class* and *Socioeconomic Status*.

Class Interval (C-3; HS-1). Grouping scores from a frequency distribution within a predetermined range to create a *histogram*, *frequency polygon*, or other similar graph.

Classical Conditioning (C-9; HS-9). Behavior change brought about by pairing a *conditioned stimulus* (such as the sound of a bell) with an *unconditioned stimulus* (such as the sight of food) until the conditioned stimulus alone evokes a response (such as salivation). Developed by *Ivan Pavlov* and expanded by *John Watson* and *Joseph Wolpe*, among others.

Classification Method (C-6; HS-3). A type of *informal assessment* procedure where information is provided about whether an individual possesses certain attributes or characteristics (asking a person to check off those adjectives that seem to best describe him or her). It includes *behavior checklists* and *feeling word checklists*.

Classifications of Mental Diseases (C-8; HS-6). A mechanism to understand and differentiate *mental disorders*. One of the original classification systems for mental disorders was developed by *Emil Kraepelin* in the mid-1800s. The most recent and widely used classification system is the *Diagnostic and Statistical Manual-5*.

Classroom Guidance (C-8; HS-3). Programs, presentations, and activities used within the classroom by *school counselors* and related human service professionals to teach lessons about anti-bullying, character development, *vocational guidance*, and other relevant *school counseling* curricula.

Cliché Layer (C-8; HS-3). In *Gestalt therapy*, a part of the *structure of neurosis* where individuals behave casually and inauthentically with others on a day-to-day basis.

Client Contact Hours (C-6; HS-6). A measure of time, usually in parts of hours (e.g., 45 minutes), that delineate the amount of time helpers spend providing treatment to their clients. An aspect of *Case Management.*

Client Empowerment (C-8; HS-8). The practice of the helper assisting the client in identifying external barriers that are impeding growth and offering skills to the client, so the client feels inspired and emboldened to make specific changes in his or her life. An aspect of the *Advocacy Competencies.*

Client Strengths (C-7; HS-6). Areas of life that clients are handling effectively or when the helper reframes times and experiences when the client has successfully handled situations (possible exceptions to the current situation or struggle). Emphasized in *Solution-Focused Brief Therapy.*

Client(s) (C-10; HS-8). The preferred term in counseling and many related helping fields for the person(s) on the receiving end of the *therapy* or treatment. Contrast with *Patient(s)*.

Client-Centered (C-10; HS-8). A *nondirective* approach in which helpers allow clients to take the lead in the direction of their session. Contrast with the *Helper-Centered* approach.

Client-Centered Therapy (C-10; HS-8). An approach to helping developed in the 1940s by *Carl Rogers* and part of the *existential-humanistic approach* to counseling. This approach had a humanistic *client-centered* focus that was a major shift from the *psychoanalysis* approach of *Freud.* Later called *Person-Centered Counseling.*

***Client-Centered Therapy: Its Current Practice, Implications, and Theory* (C-6; HS-3).** The second book that was published by *Carl Rogers* in the 1950s that impacted the shift in the counseling field toward a *humanistic* and *nondirective approaches.*

Clinical Assessment (C-7; HS-6). The process of assessing the client through multiple methods, including the *clinical interview*, *informal assessment techniques*, and *objective tests* and *projective tests.*

Clinical Counseling (C-10; HS-6). See *Clinical Mental Health Counseling.*

Clinical Interview (C-9; HS-6). An assessment technique that allows the helper to obtain an in-depth understanding of the client through an *unstructured interview* or *structured interview* process. See also *Structured Interview*, *Unstructured Interview*, and *Semi-Structured Interview.*

Clinical Mental Health Counseling (C-10; HS-6). A *Council for the Accreditation of Counseling and Related Educational Programs* specialty area that focuses on conducting *mental health counseling*, including *diagnosis*, *assessment*, *prevention* and treatment, in agencies or in *private practice settings.*

Clinical Mental Health Counselor (C-10; HS-6). A person who has obtained his or her master's degree in *clinical mental health counseling.*

Clinical Mental Health Counselors, Roles and Functions (C-8; HS-6). Includes the following: *assessment* and *diagnosis*; *case manager*; *counseling* and *therapy*; *consultant*; *cultural competence*; *crisis*, *disaster*, *and trauma helping*; *ethical standards of practice* and legal issues; *evaluation*; maintaining *case reports* and *case notes*; *psychoeducation*; providing *primary*, *secondary*, *and tertiary prevention*; *social justice advocate; supervisee/supervisor;* and *testing.*

Clinical Mental Health Counselors, Settings Where You Find Them (C-8; HS-6). These include: *career and employment agencies*; *community mental health centers*; *correctional facilities*; *family service agencies; gerontological settings; HMOs*, *PPOs*, and *EAPs;* the *military and government; pastoral, religious, and spiritual counseling agencies; private practice settings; rehabilitation agencies; residential treatment centers; substance abuse settings;* and *youth service programs.*

Clinical Psychologist (C-8; HS-8). See *Psychologist.*

Clinical Rehabilitation Counseling (C-8; HS-6). A 60 credit *Council for the Accreditation of Counseling and Related Educational Programs* specialty area that involves helping clients manage the physical, emotional, and social effects of disabilities. See also *Rehabilitation Counseling.*

Clinical Supervision (C-10; HS-8). See *Counseling Supervision.*

Clinician (C-10; HS-6). See *Clinical Mental Health Counselor* and *Counselor.*

Closed Groups (C-8; HS-8). *Counseling groups* or *support groups* in which group members cannot leave and come for treatment as they please, or groups that have a fixed membership that is not added to for the duration of the group. Contrast with *Open Groups.*

Closed Questions (C-10; HS-10). Questions that can be answered with "yes" or "no" or with a limited number of choices being offered to them. Closed questions can delimit *affect* or content and should be used sparingly.

Closeted (C-6; HS-6). Individuals who identify as *lesbian*, *gay*, *bisexual*, *transgender*, *queer*, *questioning*, *intersex*, *ally* (or *asexual*) and other non-*heterosexual* people who choose not to disclose their *sexual identity* and/or *gender identity* (or identities) to others (either to select people or to everyone in general). This choice can be for many reasons including not feeling secure in their orientation or identity or not wanting to face real or perceived *discrimination.*

Closure Stage (C-8; HS-8). The stage of the helping relationship in which the leader summarizes the learning that has occurred and facilitates the separation process. See also *Stages of the Helping Relationship.*

Cluster Sample (C-8; HS-3). A sampling procedure where naturally occurring heterogeneous groups of participants are divided up into sets or clusters that are randomly selected by the researcher.

Coaching (C-8; HS-8). A short-term helping relationship in which the coach uses *solution-focused questions* to identify one or more issues to focus upon, collaboratively sets goals, affirms and encourages the client to work on goals, and helps to ensure maintenance of goals reached through follow-up. The *Center for Credentialing and Education* (*CCE*) offers a *certification* in business, health and *wellness*, *career*, and personal life coaching for those who hold a bachelor's degree or higher.

Coalescence Stage of Integrative Counseling (C-6; HS-3). The second stage of developing an *integrative approach to counseling*, in which the *clinician* becomes comfortable with one approach and begins to integrate techniques from other orientations into his or her theoretical style. See also *Eclecticism*.

COAMFTE (C-6; HS-3). See the *Commission on Accreditation for Marriage and Family Therapy Education.*

Cocaine (C-10; HS-10). A *stimulant*, made from the coca plant, which produces an intense euphoria, hyper-alertness, or arousal, and increased senses of confidence, happiness, and sexual arousal, among other effects. Cocaine is highly addictive, generally illegal, and can produce major health complications such as increased chances of heart attack or stroke. It can be smoked, snorted, or injected. It is a *controlled substance.*

***Code of Fair Testing Practices in Education* (C-8; HS-3).** A code that was created to ensure fairness in testing individuals from all backgrounds.

Codeine (C-7; HS-7). An *opiate* used to treat pain and also used to treat coughing and diarrhea. It is a highly addictive and often abused *controlled substance.*

Codependency (C-8; HS-8). A type of dysfunctional relationship where one member believes he or she cannot function, or relies solely on, the other person for his or her sense of worth or identity, or when one member feels he or she must *enable* the unhealthy behaviors of the other (e.g., *addiction*, irresponsibility).

Coding (C-8; HS-6). In *qualitative research*, the breaking down of large amounts of data into smaller parts that seem to hold some meaning regarding the research question. Usually done by having separate researchers identify patterns and themes of responses by individuals and naming them. Similar patterns by the various researchers are eventually recognized and a common code (e.g., number or name) is placed for that pattern.

Coefficient of Determination (Shared Variance) (C-8; HS-3). An underlying commonality that accounts for the relationship between two sets of *variables.* For instance, a high *correlation* between *SAT* scores and grade point average in high school may be due to common elements driving each of the scores (e.g., intelligence, study habits, *socioeconomic status*). It is calculated by squaring the *correlation coefficient* between the variables.

Coercive Control (C-4; HS-4). A type of *intimate partner violence*, which in its most intense form, strips the *battered partner/spouse* of many of his or her basic human rights. The concept was made prominent by Evan Stark.

Cognitive Abilities Tests (C-8; HS-3). A type of *ability test* that is often based on what one has learned in school, these instruments measure a broad range of cognitive abilities and are useful in making predictions about the future (e.g., whether an individual is likely to succeed in college). When a *cognitive ability test* score is much higher than a *survey battery achievement test* it could indicate problems in learning (e.g., a *learning disability*, motivation, poor teaching). Cognitive abilities tests are a type of *aptitude test*. Some popular cognitive ability tests include the *Otis-Lennon School Ability Test*, the *Scholastic Aptitude Test*, and the *ACTs*.

Cognitive Approach (C-8; HS-6). An approach to helping that stresses the importance of assisting a client to understand his or her thinking process to facilitate change. See also *Cognitive-Behavioral Approaches*.

Cognitive-Behavior Therapy (CBT) (C-8; HS-6). See *Cognitive Therapy*.

Cognitive-Behavioral Therapy (CBT) (C-8; HS-6). See *Cognitive Behavioral Approaches*.

Cognitive-Behavioral Approaches (C-8; HS-8). A conceptual orientation that includes *behavior therapy*, *rational emotive behavior therapy*, *cognitive therapy*, *reality therapy*, and other approaches to the helping relationship. To some degree, all of these approaches rely on learning theory and focus on the changing of behaviors and cognitions when assisting clients in the change process. Sometimes, *behavior therapy* is listed as a separate approach to cognitive-behavioral approaches since in its pure form, it does not focus on cognitions.

Cognitive-Behavioral Consultation (C-8; HS-3). The application of *cognitive behavioral approaches* or principles to the *consultation* process.

Cognitive-Behavioral Counseling (C-8; HS-6). See *Cognitive Therapy*.

Cognitive-Behavioral Family Counseling (C-8; HS-6). The use of *cognitive-behavioral approaches* and techniques in *couples and family counseling*.

Cognitive-Behavioral Group Therapy (C-8; HS-6). The application of *cognitive-behavior therapy* in *group counseling*.

Cognitive-Behavioral Responses (C-8; HS-6). Clients' active reactions to their thoughts and feelings.

Cognitive-Behaviorists (C-8; HS-6). Theorists who believe in *cognitive-behavioral approaches* to counseling.

Cognitive Complexity (C-8; HS-6). The ability to view the world from multiple perspectives, to understand different points of view, and be open to new ways of understanding. One of the *common factors* of counseling/helping.

Cognitive Conceptualization (C-8; HS-6). Within *cognitive therapy*, the process a helper uses to understand which *automatic thoughts*, *intermediate beliefs*, and *core beliefs* are connected to the client's psychological disorder, which are then used to develop *treatment plans* that match the particular disorder and thoughts to effect change.

Cognitive Development (C-8; HS-6). Understanding the natural development of an individual's cognitive growth so that helpers can have a sense of whether individuals may have delays or be gifted.

Cognitive Disputation (C-8; HS-6). A technique used within *rational emotive behavior therapy*, when the helper makes a statement to dispute (e.g., challenges, questions) the illogical, or faulty, cognition of the client. In time, clients can learn to dispute their own faulty cognitions.

Cognitive Dissonance (C-6; HS-5). An unpleasant feeling or mental *stress* experienced by an individual who simultaneously holds contradictory beliefs.

Cognitive Distortions (C-8; HS-6). Identified by *Aaron Beck*, a number of distorted ways of thinking that are related to one's *automatic thoughts*, *intermediate beliefs*, and *core beliefs*, including *all-or-nothing thinking*, *catastrophizing*, *disqualifying or discounting the positive*, *emotional reasoning*, *labeling*, *magnification/minimization*, *mental filer*, *mind reading*, *overgeneralization*, *personalization*, *should and must statements*, and *tunnel vision*.

Cognitive Homework (C-8; HS-6). Homework in therapy that focuses on cognitive processes.

Cognitive Principles (C-8; HS-6). The manner in which people come to understand the world and create their unique *cognitive schemas*. With *cognitive-behaviorists*, the understanding and application of cognitive and thinking processes in therapy.

Cognitive Processes (C-8; HS-6). A generic term that refers to the many systems, or processes, of the mind that result in thinking, feeling, and behaving (e.g., *Skinner's* "mentalistic concepts," *Beck's automatic thoughts*, *intermediate thoughts*, and *core beliefs*, and *Freud's* view on the *conscious* and *unconscious*).

Cognitive Restructuring (C-8; HS-6). The process of learning to recognize and dispute, or correct, *cognitive distortions*.

Cognitive Therapy (C-10; HS-8). Developed by *Aaron Beck* and sometimes called *cognitive behavior therapy*, this approach suggests that individuals may be born with a predisposition toward certain emotional disorders that manifest under stressful conditions (i.e., *diathesis-stress model*). It also proposes that genetics, biological factors, and experiences produce *core beliefs* that are responsible for *intermediate thoughts* which drive *automatic thoughts* (fleeting thoughts about what we perceive and experience). Automatic thoughts result in a set of behaviors, feelings, and physiological responses. By understanding automatic thoughts, *intermediate beliefs*, and core beliefs, one can address and change them and prevent dysfunctional behaviors and distressing feelings. A number of cognitive and behavioral techniques are used to change automatic thoughts, intermediate beliefs, and core beliefs and their resulting dysfunctional behaviors and distressing feelings.

Cohen's d (C-7; HS-6). A commonly reported measure of *effect size* in standardized terms to report the magnitude of the difference between two *means*. This allows one to examine practical differences, as opposed to statistical differences. Cohen's d is frequently used in *meta-analysis*.

Cold Turkey (C-10; HS-10). Used within *substance abuse recovery*, to refer to an individual who abruptly quits using a substance in order to become *sober*. Stopping all usage of the substance can result in intense *withdrawal symptoms*.

Collaboration/Collaborative Process (C-8; HS-6). The joint effort between helper and client that determines what goals would best meet the client's needs.

Collaborative Consultation Model (C-8; HS-6). In this type of *consultation*, a partnership develops in which the *consultant* offers expertise but also relies on the expertise of individuals in the system to offer input into the problems and solutions.

Collection of Documents and Artifacts (C-7; HS-5). Items of interest and popularity used by a group or *culture* that help to define the group or culture. Used in *ethnographic research*, which is a type of *qualitative research*, and also used in *historical research*.

Collective Unconscious (C-8; HS-3). In *analytical psychology*, the aspect of the person that houses the *archetypes* that are ingrained models of ways of behaving or being that are believed to be shared by all individuals.

Collectivistic Perspective (C-10; HS-10). Clients who tend to focus more on a *universal identity* or *group identity* and the impact that the community has on them as opposed to a focus that is mostly on *self*. See also *Individualistic Perspective*.

College Counseling (C-8; HS-6). A specialty area in counseling that focuses on *mental health counseling* within the postsecondary setting of community, technical, private, or public college campuses and other unique issues that are relevant to the college population. See also *College Counselors*.

College Counselors (C-8; HS-3). Generally, counselors who have graduated from a *student affairs and college counseling* master's or doctoral program and who focus on helping students who are attending postsecondary education. See also *College Counseling*.

College Student Educators International (ACPA) (C-6; HS-1). This organization was formerly the *American College Personnel Association* and has kept the acronym *ACPA*. It tends to focus on administration of student services.

Colorblindness (C-6; HS-6). The ideology that equality comes from treating people the same and holding them to the same standards, with the underlying assumption that one does not see *race*. However, such a belief can be detrimental as it negates the experiences of those who have suffered, and continue to suffer, *discrimination* due to their racial, ethnic, and cultural heritage.

Coming Out (C-7; HS-7). The process by which one accepts one's own *sexual identity* and/or *gender identity* (or identities) and feels comfortable disclosing them to others.

Commission on Accreditation (COA) (C-4; HS-3). This commission of the *American Psychological Association* currently sets standards for doctoral-level programs in counseling and *clinical psychology*.

Commission on Accreditation for Marriage and Family Therapy Education (COAMFTE) (C-6; HS-3). This association is affiliated with the *American Association of Marriage and Family Therapy* (*AAMFT*) and sets guidelines for *marriage, couples, and family counselors* and is often contrasted with couples, marriage, and family guidelines set by the *Council for the Accreditation of Counseling and Related Educational Programs*.

Commission on Rehabilitation Counselor Certification (CRCC) (C-6; HS-3). A credentialing body that credentials rehabilitation counselors as *Certified Rehabilitation Counselors* (*CRCs*).

Commitment (court action) (C-8; HS-6). The term used for the legal process of having someone remanded, or committed, to mental health custody (i.e., psychiatric hospitalization) due to potential harm to *self* or others, until psychological stabilization can be achieved.

Commitment in Relativism (C-8; HS-3). Individuals who are more complex thinkers, flexible, empathic, sensitive to the contexts of ethical dilemmas, non-dogmatic, and have personal viewpoints but are open to differing opinions- these people are thus said to have a commitment to relativism. See also *Dualism* and *Relativism.*

Commitment to a Metatheory (C-6; HS-3). The final stage of an *integrative approach to counseling* where the professional begins to wonder about underlying commonalties and themes among theories and begins to integrate these major themes into his or her own, unique approach.

Common-Core Curriculum (C-6; HS-1). Eight areas that the *Council for the Accreditation of Counseling and Related Educational Programs* requires in the curriculum. Includes: professional orientation and ethical practice, social and cultural diversity, human growth and development, career development, helping relationships, group work, assessment, and research and program evaluation.

Common Core State Standards (C-6; HS-3). National academic standards, embraced by most states, that specify what K-12 students should know in math and English language.

Common Factors (C-8; HS-8). Elements in all counseling relationships that have been found to increase the likelihood of positive outcomes when working with clients. Includes: having a *working alliance* (e.g., *empathy*, *acceptance*, *genuineness*, *embracing a wellness perspective*, *cultural competence*, and the *"it" factor*), and *ability to deliver one's theoretical approach* (e.g., *compatibility with and belief in your theory*, *competence*, and *cognitive complexity*).

Common Sense (C-6; HS-3). Used within *individual psychology* and in contrast to *private logic*, to refer to the logic that focuses on benefit to others, or efforts for the common good, such as notions that building a better life requires working well with others.

Common-Theme Groups (C-8; HS-8). Groups that focus on a particular issue or problem.

Communication Patterns (C-8; HS-8). Typical ways that individuals in couples and families tend to communicate and develop their specific *homeostasis.*

Communication Theory (C-6; HS-3). One name for *Virginia Satir's* model of *couples and family counseling.* See also *Human Validation Process Model*, *Change Process Model*, and *Virginia Satir.*

Community-Based Counseling (C-8; HS-8). Refers to various models of providing counseling to clients within their community settings, through either *community-based mental health centers*, *mobile therapy*, *family-based therapy*, or other approaches.

Community-Based Mental Health Centers (C-10; HS-10). Typically, outpatient treatment facilities for clients who are living with a variety of *mental disorders.* Community mental health centers flourished in the 1960s as a result of the *deinstitutionalization* of hundreds of thousands of hospitalized patients who now needed to be seen in community-based clinics. See also *Community Mental Health Centers Act.*

Community Collaboration (C-8; HS-8). The process of helpers working with community members, with agencies, and with organizations to work toward common goals. An aspect of the *Advocacy Competencies.*

Community Feeling (C-6; HS-1). The inherent desire one has to develop a sense of community or belonging with others. In *individual psychology*, this is called *social interest* or social concern and is taken from the German word *gemeinschaftsgefühl.*

Community Mental Health Centers (C-8; HS-8). A setting where *clinical mental health counselors* and human service professionals may be employed, includes generally non-profit or not-for-profit agencies employing many different types of helpers (e.g., *social workers*, *counselors*, *case managers*, *psychiatrists*) with the intent of providing affordable mental health treatment within a community. These agencies usually provide services to recipients of *medical assistance* and/or offer services on income-sensitive sliding-fee scales. Contrast with *Private Practice Settings.*

***Community Mental Health Centers Act* (C-8; HS-8).** A legislative act passed in 1963 that provided U.S. federal funds for the creation of comprehensive mental health centers across the country, which greatly changed the delivery of mental health services.

Community Organizing (C-8; HS-8). During the early 1900s, *social workers* joined together with community members and focused on *social justice* and *advocacy* work in poorer communities in order to improve the lives of those who lived in those communities. This process continues in today's world and is an aspect of *advocacy* for clients.

Community Planner (C-6; HS-8). A helper who designs, implements, and organizes new programs to service client needs. One of the original 13 roles or functions of human service professionals as defined by the *Southern Regional Education Board.*

Community Systems, Affecting Change in (C-6; HS-6). Six steps for implementing change in communities including: accurately defining your problems, collaborating with community members, respecting community members, collaboratively developing strategies for change, implementing change strategies, and assessing the effectiveness of your strategies.

Commuter Services (C-3; HS-1). One area in higher education that individuals with a master's in *student affairs and college counseling* sometimes work focusing on students who commute to campus, as opposed to those who are residential (i.e., live on campus).

Co-Morbidity (C-7; HS-7). The simultaneous occurrence of two *mental disorders* in the same person. This often occurs with individuals experiencing *substance abuse.*

Compassion Fatigue (C-10; HS-10). When a helper becomes emotionally exhausted from the process of hearing client concerns. It can result in ineffective work, *burnout*, and an inability to feel *empathy* with clients and is related to *Vicarious Traumatization.*

Compatibility with and Belief in a Theory (C-8; HS-6). The extent to which a helper is comfortable with his or her theoretical orientation and believes strongly that it works. An aspect of one's *ability to deliver one's theoretical approach*, which, along with the *working alliance*, are critical *common factors* in all helping approaches that positively impact client outcomes.

Compensation (C-8; HS-6). Replacing a behavior that is perceived as weak with one that is perceived as strong, such as when a person purchases a fancy car or large truck to impress people. A *defense mechanism* in *psychoanalysis*, and the process of replacing *feelings of inferiority* in *individual psychology*.

Compensatory Behaviors (C-6, HS-3). In *individual psychology*, behaviors that individuals develop to deter themselves from *feelings of inferiority*.

Compensatory Strategies (C-6; HS-3). See *Coping Strategies*.

Competence (C-8; HS-6). The extent to which a mental health professional is knowledgeable of the most recent professional research and trends in one's field of study or expertise and being able to apply it with clients. An aspect of one's *ability to deliver one's theoretical approach*, which, along with the *working alliance*, are critical *common factors* in all helping approaches that positively impact client outcomes.

Competence and Scope of Knowledge (C-8; HS-8). A crucial ethical concern that involves knowing and practicing within the limits of one's professional knowledge and his or her level of *competence*.

Competence in the Use of Tests (C-8; HS-6). In accordance with most professional codes of ethics, examiners are required to have adequate training and knowledge before using a *test*. Some test publishers have a tiered system to describe the levels of training required to administer their tests. As an example, Level A often requires a bachelor's degree and the individual can give basic tests. Level B requires a master's degree in counseling or a related degree, a course in testing, and the individual can give a number of more refined tests. Level C requires a minimum of a master's degree, a basic testing course, and additional testing courses in areas that require advanced training (e.g., projective testing, intellectual assessments).

Competencies for Counseling LGBQQIA (C-8; HS-6). Competencies endorsed by the *Association for Lesbian, Gay, Bisexual, and Transgender Issues in Counseling* for counseling individuals who identify as *lesbian*, *gay*, *bisexual*, *queer*, *questioning*, *intersex*, and *ally*.

Competencies for Counseling Transgender Individuals (C-6; HS-3). Competencies endorsed by the *Association for Lesbian, Gay, Bisexual, and Transgender Issues in Counseling* for counseling individuals who identify as *transgender*.

Complainant (C-8; HS-3). In *solution-focused brief therapy*, a client who is capable of identifying his or her issues and has come to agreement with the helper on what to focus upon in sessions, however struggles to develop solutions or to implement those solutions. Contrast with *Customers* and with *Visitors*. See also *Readiness, Not Resistance*.

Complementary, Alternative, and Integrative Therapies (C-6; HS-3). Therapeutic approaches which are *holistic* and focus on all aspects of a person's *wellness* by using wellness *assessment* instruments, nutrition, *mindfulness*, body awareness therapy, scented oils, massage, and more ways to help people heal and become whole from this perspective.

Complementary Relationship (C-6; HS-3). Within couples, a relationship style defined by roles that tend to be opposite, such as when one member is dominant and one is submissive. Disruption of these roles leads to an imbalanced relationship.

Complex (C-6; HS-3). In *analytical psychology*, the process by which repressed experiences get pushed into the *personal unconscious* and become bound with one or more *archetypes* leading to a specific personality type that personifies the combination of the archetype and the repressed memory. For instance, a person who was abused by a parent might have repressed memories from that abuse and those memories become bound with the "warrior" archetype which leads to a bully complex (anger and shame from the repressed memory attached with the warrior creates the bully and prevents the person being abused again).

Complimenting (C-6; HS-3). In *solution-focused therapy*, reinforcing client's efforts toward *preferred goals*.

Comprehensive School Counseling Program (C-8; HS-3). A method of ensuring that a wide range of programs are offered by *school counselors* in the schools. See also *ASCA National Model*.

Compulsion (C-6; HS-6). An uncontrollable urge to behave in a certain way.

Computer-Driven Assessment (C-6; HS-3). Allowing a computer program to assist in the *assessment* process and preparation of reports. Some observers believe computer-assisted questioning is at least as reliable as *structured interviews* and can provide an accurate *diagnosis* at a low cost.

Computers and Related Technologies (C-8; HS-8). The use of computers and related technologies in a wide range of human service and counseling activities such as in *case management*, record keeping, *diagnosis*, *case conceptualization*, *testing* and *assessment*, *career counseling*, billing, marketing, assisting clients in the learning of new skills (e.g., parenting skills, assertiveness training), vocational skills training, *online counseling*, online *supervision*, interactive DVDs, and more.

Conant, James Bryant (1893 - 1978) (C-3; HS-1). A Harvard president who conceived the idea of the *SAT* (formerly *Scholastic Aptitude Test*), which was developed by the Educational Testing Service after World War II. Conant thought that such tests could identify the ability of individuals and ultimately help to equalize educational opportunities.

Conceptual Orientation (C-8; HS-8). Categories that theories are placed in based on shared key concepts related to their *view of human nature*. Four classic conceptual orientations include *psychodynamic*, *cognitive-behavioral*, *existential-humanistic*, and *post-modern*.

Concrete-Operational Stage (C-10; HS-8). *Jean Piaget's* third stage of *cognitive development* (ages 7–11 years) when a child starts to develop logical thinking. See also *Formal-Operational Stage*, *Preoperational Stage*, and *Sensorimotor Stage*.

Concurrent Validity (C-8; HS-3). Evidence that *test* scores are related to an external source (e.g., ratings of experts) that can be measured at around the same time the test is being given ("here-and-now" validity). A type of *Criterion-Related Validity*.

Conditioned Response (C-10; HS-10). In *behavior therapy*, any response that is learned when paired with a *stimulus*. Often, this is the desired response, or the outcome, of the behavioral *intervention* developed for an individual. See also *Classical*

Conditioning.

Conditioned Stimulus (C-10; HS-10). When a previously *neutral stimulus* has been paired with an *unconditioned stimulus* so that it now elicits a *conditioned response*. See also *Classical Conditioning.*

Conditioning (C-10; HS-10). The learning process used in *behavior therapy* to develop a *conditioned response*. Two types of conditioning include *operant conditioning* and *classical conditioning.*

Conditions of Worth (C-10; HS-10). *Carl Rogers's* term for how conditions and opinions of significant others may lead to incongruity in an individual because the individual's need to be loved outweighs his or her need to be real or genuine.

Confidentiality (C-10; HS-10). The ethical guideline that emphasizes discretion in retaining client information and knowing when confidentiality should be breached. Keeping a client's personal information private and discreet is an essential component of *competence* in helping and is generally only broken based on written client consent or in cases of concern about harm to *self* or others by the client. See also *Privileged Communication.*

Confidentiality of Records (C-10; HS-10). Keeping clients' information in secured places, such as locked file cabinets and password secured computers. See also *Confidentiality.*

Confirmatory Factor Analysis (C-6; HS-1). A type of *factor analysis* that is based on *structural equation modeling* in which researchers test the degree to which the factor structure from an existing theoretical model has goodness-of-fit or matches the parameters of different population(s). See also *Exploratory Factor Analysis.*

Confluence (C-6; HS-1). In *Gestalt therapy*, when an individual meets the "other" and recognizes very little difference between the other and the *self*, thus showing poor *ego* boundary between one's own identity and the other's identity.

Confounding Variables (C-10; HS-6). *Variables*, or factors, other than the *independent variable*, that have an influence on the *dependent variable* or outcome measure. Also referred to as *Extraneous Variable*s.

Confrontation: Challenge with Support (C-6; HS-6). The process by which a helper assists a client in gaining self-awareness about a discrepancy between the client's values and behaviors, feelings and behaviors, idealized *self* and real self, or expressed feelings and underlying feelings by directly pointing out (or challenging) the discrepancy in the session, but doing so in a supportive manner. Includes *you/but statements*, *inviting the client to justify the discrepancy*, *reframing*, *using satire*, and *using higher level empathy*.

Confrontational Groups (C-6; HS-6). Groups where high levels of hostile confrontation and direct challenges are used to push a person to change. Unlike when *confrontation: challenge with support* techniques are used, this form of confrontation generally excludes supportive measures. In the past, *substance abuse* groups have used this technique, although outcome studies have shown this technique to not be particularly helpful and its use has been much less frequent in recent years.

Congruence (in Career Counseling) (C-10; HS-10). In *career counseling*, the fit of one's personality code (e. g., *Holland Code*) with the work setting in which the individual works. The better the fit, the better the job satisfaction.

Congruence or Congruent (in Person-Centered Counseling) (C-10; HS-8). See *Genuineness.*

Conjoint Family Therapy (C-8; HS-6). A type of *couples and family counseling* where two or more family members are seen together. *Virginia Satir* was influential in the development of this type of counseling and in coining the term.

***Conner's Rating Scales* (C-6; HS-3).** A testing instrument used for the *diagnosis* and *assessment* of child and adolescent disorders, such as *attention deficit hyperactivity disorder* (*ADHD*) or oppositional defiant disorder.

Conscience (C-8; HS-6). The part of one's mind that is responsible for making moral, ethical, or just decisions based on values, beliefs, expectations, or rules of the *self*, *culture*, or society one ascribes to.

Conscious (C-8; HS-6). The part of *self* which is aware of one's inner life and of external objects. Contrast with *Unconscious.*

Consciousness (Freudian) (C-8; HS-6). All of the aspects of *self* (e.g., feelings, cognitions, fantasies, behaviors) that a person is aware of and that motivate the individual in life.

Consciousness-Raising (C-8; HS-6). The process of bringing something into conscious awareness of which the individual was previously unaware

Consensual Qualitative Research (CQR) (C-8; HS-3). A type of *qualitative research* that emphasizes the description of complex experiences and behaviors as they exist in their natural settings. CQR is an inductive reasoning method that uses *open questions*, small samples, an understanding of context, multiple viewpoints, and consensus making with the research team.

Consequential Feelings and Behaviors (C-8; HS-6). A concept from *cognitive-behavioral* approaches that examines how *emotions* and actions are influenced by one's *automatic thoughts* (i.e., *cognitive therapy*) or by an *activating event* (i.e., *rational emotive behavior therapy*).

Conservation (C-8; HS-6). The notion that liquids and solids can be transformed in shape (e.g., into differently sized containers) without changing their volume or mass. Children in early stages of development are not capable of distinguishing these differences in volume or mass according to *Piaget*. Conservation tasks are thus often used in developmental *assessment* of children's abilities.

Constant Comparative Analysis (C-6; HS-3). Used in *qualitative research*, the process of collection of information from the field, analyzing the information, and organizing it into categories or themes, returning to the field to collect more information with refined questions, and comparing new information to themes that emerged from earlier data.

Construct Validity (C-8; HS-3). A type of test for *validity* that attempts to show that a theoretical construct or attribute is being measured by an instrument. Often used with difficult constructs to measure, such as *empathy* or intelligence. Four types of construct validity include *experimental design*, *factor analysis*, *convergent validity*, and *discriminant validity*.

Constructivism (C-8; HS-5). A theory that individuals construct their own reality and knowledge about the world through their unique experiences and how they reflect on those experiences. See also *Social Constructivism (or Constructionism)*.

Constructivist Career Counseling (C-6; HS-2). A *post-modern approach* to *career counseling* that examines how clients construct or make meaning out of their *career development* process.

Constructivist Career Development Theory (C-6; HS-2). See *Constructivist Career Counseling*.

Constructivist Model (C-8; HS-6). The idea that new knowledge about *self* is constantly being constructed and understood through the experiences that one has and his or her ability to reflect on those experiences.

Constructivist Therapy (C-8; HS-3). The idea that people are continually creating and recreating their understanding of reality and how they come to make sense of their world. One main theorist is *Michael Mahoney*.

Consultant (C-8; HS-8). An individual, who is an expert, and can provide services to a *consultee*. These services are usually provided to increase the efficacy of work with clients or organizational and programmatic success and efficiency. One of the original 13 roles or functions of human service professionals as defined by the *Southern Regional Education Board*.

Consultant-Centered (C-8; HS-6). A *consultation style* that can be expert, prescriptive, or trainer/educator focused.

Consultation (C-8; HS-8). When a professional (the *consultant*), who has specialized expertise, meets with one or more other professionals (the *consultees*) to improve their work with current or potential clients.

Consultation Style (C-8; HS-6). Manner of *consultation* represented on a spectrum between *consultant-centered* consultants, who view themselves as experts, prescriptive, or educators and trainers versus those who are *consultee-centered* consultants, and tend to be collaborative, facilitative, and process-oriented. See also *Consultant* and *Consultee*.

Consultation, Stages of (C-6; HS-3). Includes pre-entry, entry, goal setting, implementation, evaluation, and disengagement stages of *consultation*.

Consultee (C-8; HS-8). An individual who is in need of assistance from an expert/colleague (the *consultant*) who can provide services. Usually these services are to increase the efficacy of work with clients or organizational and programmatic success and efficiency.

Consultee-Centered (C-8; HS-6). A *consultation style* that can be collaborative, facilitative, or process-oriented.

Consulting Inward (C-8; HS-6). *Consultation* focused on clients within an agency. *Gerald Caplan* is particularly known for developing a well-known model of inward consultation for mental health settings.

Consulting Outward (C-8; HS-6). When *consultation* is focused outside of the agency, such as when one is collaborating with parents, the family of clients, the community, etc.

Contact (C-6; HS-3). In *Gestalt therapy*, the boundary that one encounters between one's *self* and the other, be it object or person.

Content Self-Disclosure (C-8; HS-8). The helper's revelation of some personal information in an effort to enhance the helping relationship. See also *Self-Disclosure.*

Content Validity (C-8; HS-3). Evidence that the *test* developer adequately surveyed the domain (field) the test is to cover, that test items match that domain, and that test items are accurately weighted for relative importance. Common methods for ensuring construct validity include *pilot testing*, creating a *theoretical blueprint*, and *expert review.*

Contextual Family Therapy (C-6; HS-3). Developed by *Ivan Boszormenyi-Nagy*, a multigenerational approach to understanding family systems. In particular, his approach looked at how one's *loyalties*, *ledger of indebtedness*, and *ways of relating* are passed down through the generations.

Continuing Education (C-8; HS-8). The process of pursuing knowledge by joining *professional associations*, participating in workshops, reading journal articles, taking additional coursework, and being involved in related activities throughout one's *career.*

Continuity Hypothesis (C-6; HS-3). *Aaron Beck's* idea that older, emotional responses from previous generations may be continued into the current lived experience of the client.

Continuous Reinforcement Schedule (C-8; HS-6). Within *operant conditioning*, a *schedule of reinforcement* where every occurrence of a specific behavior is reinforced.

Contract Liability (C-6; HS-1). The responsibility and implied contract that higher education colleges and universities have with their students to ensure their safety.

Control Group (C-8; HS-8). In *quantitative research*, the group in an experiment that does not receive the *intervention* or treatment. Oftentimes, the control group is compared to the *experimental group.*

Control Theory (C-3; HS-1). The former name of *Choice Theory.*

Controlled Response (C-6; HS-3). In *behavior therapy*, this *self-management technique* refers to the targeted behavior to be produced following the *controlling response.*

Controlled Substance (C-8; HS-8). The legal classification of drugs and other substances that are regulated by the government, requiring a prescription to obtain or that are otherwise classified as illegal.

Controlling Response (C-6; HS-3). In *behavior therapy*, *self-management techniques* wherein a behavior is identified and used when one engages in a *controlled response.* For example, one places dots around the house to remind the person to be empathic toward his spouse and children. Being empathic is the *controlled response*, seeing the dots and reminding oneself to be empathic is the controlling response.

Convenience Sample (C-8; HS-3). A nonprobability sampling procedure whereby researchers access a sample of participants who are easily accessible. See also *Random*

Sampling.

Conventional Level (C-8; HS-8). *Lawrence Kohlberg's* second level of *moral development* (ages 9–18 years) when a person makes a moral decision based on peer approval or disapproval (Stage 3) or on established rules of what is right or wrong (Stage 4). See also *Preconventional Level* and *Postconventional Level.*

Convergent Validity (C-6; HS-3). A type of test *validity* in which individuals take a *test* (usually one under development) and the results from that test are correlated with the results of the same individuals on a different, well-known and well-made test, that measures the same attributes (e.g., depression). A high *correlation* indicates good convergent validity.

Conversion Disorder (C-6; HS-3). A former clinical *diagnosis* wherein the individual has physical symptoms (such as neurological symptoms like paralysis, blindness, or emotional outbursts) that are not otherwise accounted for by known medical or mental health causes. In the past, it was also known as *hysteria.*

Conversion Therapy (C-8; HS-8). The idea that a person who is *gay* or *lesbian* can learn new, *heterosexual* behaviors. This approach is in disrepute and nearly all helping *professional associations* warn against, and even have banned, referring to conversion therapists. Today, this is more commonly called *sexual orientation change efforts*. Also called *reparative therapy.*

Converted Scores (C-6; HS-3). See *Standard Scores.*

Cooper's Cube Model (C-3; HS-1). Suggested that *consultation* by *college counselors* addresses one of four audiences: students, faculty, staff, or administrators. It also states that their *interventions* can be focused on the individual, a group, or an organization and the model generally is focused on education or training, offering a program, the "doctor–patient" relationship (diagnosing and prescribing), or is process-oriented.

Coping Mechanisms (C-6; HS-3). The mechanisms (e.g., behaviors, thoughts) that clients have used in the past that have been successful in preventing, ameliorating, or ending problems or that they can use in the future to address problems.

Coping Questions (C-6; HS-3). Used in *solution-focused therapy*, questions that attempt to discover how a person has successfully dealt with similar problems in the past.

Coping Self (C-6; HS-4). One of the five factors of the *indivisible self model* that includes having satisfactory leisure time, being able to deal with *stress*, feeling a sense of self-acceptance, being real with the *self* and others, absence of irrational beliefs, and seeing reality in an accurate way.

Coping Strategies (C-8; HS-3). The behaviors one engages in to avoid negative *core beliefs* about *self*. Also called *compensatory strategies*. See *Cognitive Therapy.*

***COPS* (C-6; HS-3).** See *Career Occupational Preference System.*

CORE (C-6; HS-3). See *Council on Rehabilitation Education.*

Core Belief Worksheet (C-6; HS-3). A worksheet tool used to help clients understand their *core beliefs*. See *Cognitive Therapy.*

Core Beliefs (C-8; HS-6). Deep rooted opinions, values, and judgments that one has about the world and about oneself ("I am worthwhile, I am inadequate"). Core beliefs impact one's *intermediate beliefs*, *automatic thoughts*, feelings, behaviors, and physiology. A concept from *Aaron Beck's cognitive therapy.*

Core Conditions (C-10; HS-10). In *person-centered counseling*, these include *empathy*, *congruence*, and *unconditional positive regard.*

Core Irrational Beliefs (C-7; HS-4). See *Grandiose Irrational Beliefs.*

Correctional Facilities (C-6; HS-6). Settings where *clinical mental health counselors* and human service professionals may be employed including detention centers, jails, and prisons within the criminal justice system. Ostensibly, the goal of these facilities is to "correct" criminal behavior in the inmates.

Correlation (C-8; HS-6). A statistical expression of the relationship between two sets of scores (or *variables*). See also *Correlation Coefficient.*

Correlation Coefficient (C-8; HS-6). A statistical procedure

where the relationships among two or more *variables* are examined. Correlations run, in hundredths, from 0 to minus 1 (*negative correlation* or *inverse relationship*) or from 0 to plus 1 (*positive correlation* or direct relationship). The closer to plus 1 or minus 1, the stronger the relationship.

Correlational Research (C-6; HS-3). Used to explore the relationship between two *variables* (*simple correlational studies*) or to predict scores on a variable from scores obtained from other variables (*predictive correlational research*).

COS (C-6; HS-3). See *Charity Organization Society.*

Council for Accreditation of Counseling and Related Educational Programs (CACREP) (C-10; HS-3). The *accreditation* body for counseling programs that accredits master's programs in *school counseling*; *clinical mental health counseling*; *marriage, couples, and family counseling*; *addiction counseling*; *career counseling*; *clinical rehabilitation counseling*; and *student affairs and college counseling*, as well as doctoral programs in *counselor education and supervision.*

Council for Standards in Human Service Education (CSHSE) (C-1; HS-10). Founded in 1979, this organization focuses on education and training in the human service profession by setting national *accreditation* standards, helping to establish *credentialing*, and providing education-related materials.

Council on Rehabilitation Education (CORE) (C-10; HS-3). The *accreditation* body for *rehabilitation counseling* programs.

Council on Social Work Education (CSWE) (C-10; HS-3). The *accreditation* body for *social work* programs.

Counseling (C-10; HS-4). As per the *20/20 vision*, "Counseling is a professional relationship that empowers diverse individuals, families, and groups to accomplish mental health, *wellness*, education, and career goals." Sometimes seen as the practice of working with a client that is short term, in the here-and-now, developmental, focused more on surface issues, massaging rather than reconstructing personality, dealing more with the *conscious* than the *unconscious*, and dealing with moderate client revelations that can be mildly uncomfortable for the client. However, this definition is debated amongst experts in the field. Contrast with *Psychotherapy.*

Counseling and Values **(C-6; HS-3).** Journal of the *Association for Spiritual, Ethical & Religious Values in Counseling (ASERVIC).*

Counseling Centers (C-6; HS-3). In *student affairs* practice and *college counseling*, a setting where you may find *college counselors* working.

Counseling Environment (C-10; HS-10). The helper's office set up and *nonverbal behaviors.* The counseling environment can have a negative or positive impact on the helping relationship.

Counseling Group (C-8; HS-6). Similar to a *therapy group* but with less *self-disclosure* and personality reconstruction expected; a meeting of individuals whose purpose is to effect behavior change and increase self-awareness.

Counseling Men (C-6; HS-3). A type of *gender aware therapy* that focuses on men's issues in counseling.

Counseling Online (C-8; HS-3). Providing counseling services to clients through Internet access, such as through e-mail, through Skype or other video services, and through the use of related technologies. See also *Cybercounseling.*

Counseling Outcome Research and Evaluation **(C-6; HS-3).** Journal of the *Association for Assessment and Research in Counseling (AARC).*

Counseling Psychologist (C-8; HS-8). See *Psychologist.*

Counseling Skills (C-10; HS-10). Any of a variety of verbal and nonverbal communication skills that are used to enhance the *working alliance* between clients and helpers which support clients as they gain self-awareness while empowering them to make positive changes in their lives.

Counseling Supervision (or Clinical Supervision) (C-10; HS-8). An intensive, extended, and evaluative interpersonal relationship in which a senior member of a profession enhances the professional skills of a junior person, assures quality services to clients, and provides a gatekeeping function for the profession. See also *Supervision, Supervisor*, and *Supervisee.*

Counseling Today **(C-10; HS-3).** The monthly counseling magazine that one receives as a member of the *American Counseling Association.*

Counselor (C-10; HS-8). A person who has a master's degree (or higher) in counseling in one of a number of specialty areas including *school counseling; clinical mental health counseling; marriage, couples, and family counseling; addiction counseling; career counseling; clinical rehabilitation counseling;* and *student affairs and college counseling.*

Counselor Education and Supervision **(C-6; HS-3).** Journal of the *Association for Counselor Education and Supervision (ACES).*

Counselor Preparation Comprehensive Examination (CPCE) (C-8; HS-1). A national exam that some college programs use as part or all of their comprehensive examination process for counselors-in-training. When used, it's taken close to program completion and used as a means to evaluate required skills and knowledge prior to graduation.

Counselors for Social Justice (CSJ) (C-8; HS-3). A division of the *American Counseling Association* for those interested in *advocacy* and other issues related to *social justice.*

COUNSGRADS (C-8; HS-1). The *American Counseling Association's* electronic mailing list for graduate students.

Counterconditioning (C-8; HS-8). The process of applying new *reinforcement contingencies* in an effort to change behaviors.

Countertransference (C-10; HS-8). The process by which a helper's own issues interfere with effectively helping his or her clients through the *unconscious* transferring of thoughts, feelings, and attitudes onto the client. Countertransference is a primary aspect of *psychodynamic approaches* to therapy. Contrast with *Transference.*

Couples and Family Counseling (C-8; HS-8). This area of counseling focuses on conducting counseling with couples and families. This is a specialty area of the *Council for Accreditation of Counseling and Related Educational Programs.* It is also known as *Marriage, Couples, and Family Counseling.*

Couples and Family Counselors (C-8; HS-8). Individuals who have a master's or doctoral degree in counseling or a related field and are specifically trained to conduct counseling with couples and families. See also *Marriage, Couples, and Family Counseling.*

Courage (Adlerian) (C-6; HS-3). When clients take responsibility to identify and address their harmful and unhealthy behaviors. It is shown through their commitment to explore *feelings of inferiority* and to make positive, but sometimes difficult changes in their lives.

Covariate (C-6; HS-3). A *variable* that may be predictive of outcomes in *quantitative research.* The variable may be directly related to the outcomes or may be confounding of the outcomes.

Covert Rehearsal (C-6; HS-3). The use of repetitive mental practice or actual practice in order to better remember something or to be better prepared to engage in identified positive behaviors. For example, repeatedly practicing a speech or a difficult conversation one is anxious about giving.

Covert Rules (C-8; HS-6). *Unconscious* or unspoken rules of behavior created by families that are partially responsible for the ways in which family members interact with one another. Contrast with *Overt Rules.*

CPCE (C-6; HS-3). See *Counselor Preparation Comprehensive Examination.*

CRC (C-8; HS-8). See *Certified Rehabilitation Counselor.*

CRCC (C-6; HS-3). See *Commission on Rehabilitation Counselor Certification.*

Creative and Expressive Therapists (C-8; HS-6). Art therapists, play therapists, dance/movement therapists, poetry therapists, music therapists, and others who use creative tools to work with individuals who experience trauma or emotional problems in their lives. See also *Creative and Expressive Therapy.*

Creative and Expressive Therapy (C-8; HS-6). An umbrella term for many types of counseling that employ creative tools to work with individuals who experience trauma or emotional problems in their lives. See also *Creative and Expressive Therapists.*

Creative Self (C-6; HS-4). One of the five factors of the *indivisible self model.* It is highlighted by our ability to be mentally sharp and open minded (thinking), being in touch with our feelings (*emotions*), being intentional and planful and knowing how to express our needs (control), being effective at work and using our skills successfully (work), and being able to deal with life as it comes at us (positive humor).

Credentialed School Counselor (C-8; HS-6). The credential used to identify those who have successfully passed state-approved requirements for becoming a *school counselor.* Set by *State Boards of Education* who determine what *State-Approved School Counseling Programs* need to offer for individuals to become certified, licensed, or endorsed in each state as a school counselor, with each state determining what standard to use.

Credentialing (C-10; HS-10). The process of becoming registered, certified, or licensed in one's professional field with *licensure* being the most rigorous and *certification* being more rigorous than *registration.* Credentialing offers many benefits including increased professional identity, increased sense of professionalism, demonstrating expertise within a profession, gaining parity, protecting the public, and more.

Credibility (C-8; HS-4). See *Trustworthiness.*

Criminal Liability (C-8; HS-6). The responsibility under the law for a violation of U.S. federal or state criminal statute. For helpers, when the state or federal government prosecutes the helper due to suspicion that the helper acted criminally during the helping process. Contrast with *Civil Liability.*

Crisis, Disaster, and Trauma Helping (C-8; HS-6). An approach to helping that is short term, built on client strengths, non-diagnostically oriented, supportive, and provided at agencies or where the crisis has occurred.

Crisis Hotline (C-10; HS-10). A free (e.g., 800 number), emergency or otherwise designated phone line or online internet chat where an individual in crisis can speak to a trained crisis intervention worker, such as a suicide prevention hotline.

Criterion-Referenced Assessment (C-8; HS-6). Sometimes called mastery learning, these *assessment* techniques are designed to assess specific learning goals of an individual and are not norm based.

Criterion-Related Validity (C-8; HS-3). The relationship between a *test* and a standard (external source) to which the test should be correlated. The external standard may be in the here-and-now (*concurrent validity*) or a predictor of future criteria (*predictive validity*).

Criterion Variable (C-8; HS-3). The *variable* that is being predicted in a *multiple regression analysis.*

Cronbach's Coefficient Alpha (C-8; HS-3). A method of measuring *internal consistency reliability* by calculating *test* reliability using all the possible split-half combinations. This is done by correlating the scores for each item on the test with the total score on the test and finding the average correlation for all of the items.

Cross-Cultural Counseling (C-10; HS-10). See *Culturally Competent Helping.*

Cross-Cultural Counseling Competencies (C-10; HS-8). Competencies endorsed by the *Association for Multicultural Counseling and Development* and the *American Counseling Association* that highlight issues to address in the training of culturally competent counseling and human service professionals. More recently, they have been replaced by the *Multicultural and Social Justice Counseling Competencies.*

Cross-Cultural Fairness (C-8; HS-6). In *assessment*, the extent to which a *test* measures what it is supposed to measure in a consistent manner for all groups for which the test is given. One of the four qualities that make up *test worthiness.*

Cross-Cultural Helping, Nonverbal Behaviors in (C-8; HS-8). A helper's awareness and sensitivity to recognize the cultural context of *nonverbal behaviors.*

Cross-Cultural Sensitivity (C-8; HS-8). Being sensitive to clients from *non-dominant groups* and having the desire to learn about others in an effort to effectively counsel and work with all clients, regardless of age, cultural background, *disability*, *ethnicity*, *gender*, *religion*, *sexual orientation*, and *socioeconomic status*. One of the *common factors* related to building a *working alliance.*

Cross-Cultural Symptomatology, Misunderstanding (C-8; HS-7). A helper's confusing common aspects of a diverse client's *culture* for symptoms of mental illness. For example, many cultures believe in ancestor communication after death. If a client informs the helper that he or she spoke to a dead grandfather or saw his spirit, this could be an aspect of such a culture and is not necessarily an indication of a *hallucination.* Helpers should work to understand diverse client cultures to avoid potential misdiagnoses based on lack of knowledge of cross-cultural symptomatology.

Crossdresser (C-8; HS-8). An individual who enjoys wearing the clothes of the opposite *sex*, formerly called *transvestite*, which is now considered a derogatory term.

Cross-Sectional Research (C-8; HS-3). A type of *observational research* that analyzes data at a specific point in time within a population.

Cross, William (1959 -) (C-6; HS-3). An author of seminal publications in the area of *cross-cultural counseling* during the 1980s.

Crystal Meth (C-8, HS-8). An illegal *stimulant* drug that is highly addictive and can have a number of serious side effects, a few of which include rapid heart rate, mood swings, unpredictable behavior, high blood pressure, tremors and convulsions, and sometimes death. It is a *controlled substance.*

Crystallize (C-8; HS-3). The latter part of the *exploration stage* of *Super's developmental self-concept theory* where individuals choose an *occupation* or further professional training.

Crystallized Intelligence (C-8; HS-3). As identified by *Raymond Cattell*, learned skills, knowledge, and information from experiences that tend to increase over time. Contrast with *Fluid Intelligence.*

CSCORE (C-3; HS-1). See *Center for School Counseling Outcome Research and Evaluation.*

CSCP (C-8; HS-3). See *Comprehensive School Counseling Program.*

CSHSE (C-1; HS-8). See *Council for Standards in Human Service Education.*

CSI (C-8; HS-1). See *Chi Sigma Iota.*

CSJ (C-8; HS-3). See *Counselors for Social Justice.* A division of the *American Counseling Association.*

CSWE (C-6; HS-3). See *Council on Social Work Education.*

Cultural Anthropology (C-8; HS-6). See *Ethnographic Research.*

Cultural Competence (C-8; HS-8). The gaining of the necessary attitudes, skills, and knowledge to be able to work with a wide variety of ethnically and culturally diverse clients. One of the important *common factors* related to building a *working alliance.*

Cultural Fatalism/Fatalismo (C-8; HS-6). The concept, held by some *Latinas/Latinos*, that life is not in our control and that destiny is decided for us.

Cultural Heritage (C-8; HS-6). *Artifacts* and intangible traits that are passed down from previous generations.

Cultural Identity (C-8; HS-8). Individual or group affiliation with a particular *culture* and to that culture's customs, rules, norms, values, beliefs, and practices. Usually, this is an affiliation with a culture one is born into, but can also include affiliation with adopted or different cultures than that shared with one's *family of origin.*

Cultural Mosaic (C-8; HS-8). A society that has many diverse values and customs.

Cultural Sensitivity (C-8; HS-8). The ability and readiness of a helper to understand the cultural identity of a client and to be cognizant of how the client's cultural heritage as well as the helper's attitudes, knowledge, and skills, may impact the helping relationship.

Culturally Competent Helping (C-10; HS-10). The ability and readiness of a helper to understand the cultural identity of a client and to be cognizant of how the client's cultural background may impact the helping relationship. Also, understanding the unique issues of clients (*individual identity*), how *culture* impacts them (*their group identity*), understanding shared human experiences (*the universal identity*), and determining if a client relies more on an *individualistic perspective* (focus more on *self*) or a *collectivistic perspective* (focus more on the group).

Culture (C-8; HS-8). The common values, beliefs, customs, norms of behavior, symbols, language, and life patterns and practices that people share due to belonging to a specific group.

Culture-Specific Skills (C-8; HS-8). Counseling skills and approaches that are unique to working with individuals from specific cultural backgrounds.

Cumulative Distribution (C-6; HS-3). A method of converting a *frequency distribution* of scores into increasing percentages as a function of the percentage of scores counted. A *bar graph* is often generated by placing the *class interval* scores along the *x*-axis and the cumulative percentages along the *y*-axis.

Cumulative Records (C-6; HS-6). File containing information about a client's *test* scores, grades, behavioral problems, family issues, relationships with others, and other matters. School and workplace records are examples of cumulative records that can add vital information to our understanding of clients. A type of *Record and Personal Document*.

Custody (C-8; HS-8). The official legal status that determines place of residence and responsibility for primary care of children. At birth, custody is assumed to belong to the birth parents of children, needing no additional legal intervention. Due to divorce, separation, or other situations where the birth parents, other relatives, or legal guardians are seeking to care for children, custody is determined by the court and may provide one party with primary custody, could provide shared custody between multiple parties, or provide some other variation on custody status for care of the children.

Customer (C-8; HS-3). In *solution-focused brief therapy*, the client that comes to counseling prepared to work on defining clinical goals and on achieving solutions to his or her problems. Contrast with *Complainants* and with *Visitors*. See also *Readiness, Not Resistance*.

Cybercounseling (C-8; HS-6). A variety of Internet-based services that uses *synchronous* and *asynchronous* tools to provide counseling, such as online chats or live counseling using video conferencing technology. See also *Counseling Online*.

Cybernetics (C-8; HS-6). In *family counseling*, control mechanisms used to help understand the dynamics of a system. For example, one type of cybernetic system is a *negative feedback loop* where one member of a couple communicates a disturbing statement to the second, but the second member responds with a statement that defuses the situation, thus returning the system to its usual way of functioning (i.e., its usual *homeostasis*.) A *positive feedback loop* occurs when change in one component in a system leads to a change in another component within the same system, which leads to a change in the first component, and so on. Couples arguing out of control, for example, are in a positive feedback loop.

D'Andrea, Michael and Daniels, Judy (C-4; HS-2). Counselor educators who formulated a developmental theory that addressed *stages of racism* of helpers.

Dance and Movement Therapy (DMT) (C-4; HS-3). A form of *creative and expressive therapy* that utilizes techniques from dance and other movement-based practices to achieve therapeutic goals.

DAT (C-6; HS-3). See *Differential Aptitude Test*.

Data Manager (C-3; HS-7). A human service professional who develops systems to gather facts and statistics as a means of evaluating programs. One of the original 13 roles and functions of human service professionals as defined by the *Southern Regional Education Board*.

Davis, Jesse (1871 - 1955) (C-7; HS-2). Developed one of the first *vocational guidance* curricula in the schools in Grand Rapids, Michigan, and thus is considered the first *school counselor* by some.

DCSW (C-5; HS-4). See *Diplomate in Clinical Social Work*.

De Arevalo, Rodrigo Sanchez (1404 - 1470) (C-5; HS-1). A Catholic bishop who wrote the first *job* classification system in the book *Mirror of Men's Lives*.

de Shazer, Steve (1940 - 2005) (C-9; HS-2). An American *psychotherapist* and one of the founders of *solution-focused brief therapy*. He was the husband of *Insoo Kim Berg*.

Deadly Habits (CS-6; HS-4). A concept promoted by *William Glasser* who encouraged people and helpers not to use language that is criticizing, blaming, complaining, nagging, threatening, punishing, or bribing. Contrast with *Caring Habits*.

Death and Non-Being (C-8; HS-4). Within *existential therapy*, the emphasis on the denial or acceptance that all individuals face of their impending death and the state of non-being. Individuals' fear of death and non-being results in the engagement of a wide range of behaviors or thoughts to avoid *self-awareness* of these states.

Death Instinct (C-8; HS-3). In *psychoanalysis*, the seeking of our own demise which ultimately can lead to hate, self-destructive behavior, and aggression. Also called *Thanatos*.

Debriefing (C-7; HS-7). The process of reviewing, analyzing, discussing, or decompressing from experiences that are frequently emotionally intense, traumatic, or otherwise significant to individuals or groups.

Deceleration/Disengagement Stage (C-8; HS-3). Stage 5 of *Donald Super's lifespan theory of career development*, occurring between age 60 and the time of death, where the individual starts to separate *self* from *job* and focuses more on retirement and *avocations*. See also *Growth*, *Exploration*, *Establishment*, and *Maintenance Stages*

Decentration from Self (C-6; HS-2). In *Fowler's Theory of Faith Development*, the ability to understand fully the views of others and be able to see the world through their eyes. It is considered a true knowing of others.

Decompensation (C-8; HS-8). When an individual is mentally destabilizing and his or her condition and/or mental health is deteriorating to unhealthy levels.

Deconstruct (C-8; HS-6). Taking apart an individual's understanding of his or her *narrative*. Often used in *narrative therapy*.

Deductive Reasoning (C-7; HS-4). A type of logical reasoning where one moves from a general premise, assumed to be true, to a more specific conclusion that is also assumed to be true. For example: "All cats are born with whiskers. Max was born with whiskers. Thus, Max is a cat." Contrast with *Inductive Reasoning*.

De-Emphasizing of Social Forces (C-9; HS-9). The false assumption, by some helpers, that all problems are intrinsically created, and one reason why some clients from *non-dominant groups* are dissatisfied with the helping relationship.

Deepening Understanding and Goal Setting Stage (C-7; HS-7). The third stage of the helping relationship where the client feels free to explore his or her issues at deeper levels (e.g., connect issues to early childhood development). Such exploration leads to the identification of goals to work on. See also *Stages of the Helping Relationship*.

Defamation and Libel (C-7; HS-4). Being falsely accused of a vial act (defamation) and the idea that one can sue due to that fact (libel). Postsecondary schools are particularly vigilant about these issues today.

Defense Mechanisms (C-9; HS-7). An *unconscious* mental process that results in a person acting in ways to avoid *anxiety* and to protect the *ego*. Some of the more common ones are *repression*, pushing out of awareness threatening or painful memories; *denial*, distorting reality to deny perceived threats to the person; *projection*, viewing others as having unacceptable qualities that the individual himself or herself actually has; *rationalization*, explaining away a bruised or hurt ego; and *regression*, reverting to behavior from an earlier stage of development that is a less demanding way of responding to anxiety (e.g., sucking one's thumb).

Deficit Model (C-8; HS-8). A helping model that focuses primarily on a person's destructive behaviors and failures. This model assumes that problems need to be focused upon if one is to fix them or manage them (as opposed to avoiding them or focusing on solutions). It often assumes the problem is inherent within the person. Contrast with a *Strengths-Based Model.*

Definitional Ceremonies (C-8; HS-2). Also called *outsider witness groups* or *ceremonies*, a technique used in *narrative therapy* after a client has started to develop new, healthier *narratives* and shares these new narratives with a group of witnesses in a ceremony, often close friends or others that have experienced similar difficulties. Individuals who witness the telling of new narratives are encouraged not to applaud, interpret, or congratulate, but instead ask questions to help to understand and deepen the new narrative.

Deflection (C-7; HS-2). In *Gestalt therapy*, the process of avoiding contact with another individual by modifying or diverting attention to something or someone else, such as by changing the subject, laughing, talking over someone, looking away, or engaging in other behaviors designed to avoid the contact.

Deinstitutionalization (C-7; HS-7). A social change occurring in the mid-1970s, highlighted by the U.S. Supreme Court decision of *Donaldson v. O'Connor*, whereby patients who had been held against their will and were not in danger of harming themselves or others were released from psychiatric hospitals.

Delimiting Power and Developing an Equal Relationship (C-6; HS-6). The process by which a professional helper shows his or her client respect, shows humility, and treats the client fairly and caringly. Often used in *Post-Modern Approaches.*

Delirium Tremens (DTs) (C-7; HS-7). A series of physical and neurological symptoms individuals may experience during *withdrawal* from heavy alcohol use. These symptoms often include *hallucinations*, shaking (especially in the extremities), excessive sweating, mental confusion, nightmares, high blood pressure, and elevated heart rate, among other symptoms.

Delivering a Theoretical Approach (C-4; HS-3). Having the knowledge and skills of a theory so that one is capable of being effective with clients. Shown to be important in client outcomes, regardless of the theory. Encompasses three characteristics: *belief in one's theory*, *competence*, and *cognitive complexity*, and along with building a *working alliance*, is a major *common factor* to positive client outcomes.

Delusions (C-5; HS-4). A belief in a reality that is not accepted by the public at large and for which there seems to be no rational argument to support it (e.g., Aliens have landed and have taken over the higher ranks of the government). Contrast with *Hallucinations.*

Delusive Perceptions (C-3; HS-2). Misinformed thoughts and ideas that lead to problematic and negative consequences.

Demands (C-5; HS-4). A *cognitive distortion* in *rational emotive behavior therapy* in which the person assumes that he or she can make requests and suggestions to others that they must or should follow.

Dementia (C-9; HS-8). Describes a large group of brain disorders resulting in loss of memory, of thinking abilities, and of behavioral functionality. Also referred to as *senility*. See also *Alzheimer's Disease.*

Demisexual (C-6; HS-6). Sexual attraction to another individual only due to strong emotional connections or bonds.

Democratically Held Discussion Groups (C-3; HS-7). An important process in *individual psychology* where clients are asked to decide issues and concerns in a manner that builds consensus and/or uses voting. Helps to build *empathy* and understanding of other points of view.

Demonstrating the 3 C's (C-3; HS-4). A helper who is committed (follows-up on promises made to clients) courteous (continually treats clients respectfully, with appropriate politeness, and is aware of clients' customs), and caring (shows concern to others, has regard for others, and is there for them in times of need).

Denial (C-9; HS-6). See *Defense Mechanisms.*

Dependent Variable (C-10; HS-7). In *true experimental research*, an *outcome measure* or a quantity that is measured following manipulation of the *independent variable.* Also referred to as *endogenous variable.*

Depotentiated (C-7; HS-4). Reduction of traumatic memories in *eye movement desensitization response therapy* (EMDR).

Depression (C-10; HS-9). A popular term used for the various *depressive disorders* or symptoms or behaviors of these disorders (e.g., sadness, isolation, lack of interest).

Depressive Disorders (C-9; HS-5). Previously grouped into the broader category of "mood disorders" in the 4th edition of the *Diagnostic and Statistical Manual*, in *Diagnostic and Statistical Manual-5* these disorders describe conditions where depressed mood is the overarching concern. They include disruptive mood, dysregulation disorder, major depressive disorder, persistent depressive disorder (also known as dysthymia), and premenstrual dysphoric disorder.

Depth Psychology (C-8; HS-5). Used most frequently to describe *psychodynamic approaches*, the psychological exploration of mental drives, motivations, and processes that are *unconscious.*

De-Reflection (C-5; HS-2). Also called *refocusing*, in *existential therapy*, the process of redirecting one's thoughts away from a problem instead of overly worrying or obsessing about it.

Derived Score (C-7; HS-2). See *Standard Score.*

Descartes, René (1596 - 1650) (C-4; HS-4). An influential scientist, philosopher, and mathematician who believed that knowledge and truth come through *deductive* *reasoning.* He most famously said, "I think, therefore I am."

Descriptive Statistics (C-8; HS-6). Used in the reporting of *quantitative research* to describe characteristics of a *sample* and often include *measures of central tendency*, *measures of variability*, *percentages*, and *frequencies.*

Designer Drugs (C-7; HS-7). See *Synthetic Drugs.*

Determinism (C-9; HS-7). The philosophical view that behavior is influenced by reasons outside of an individual's control, and thus, people have little, if any, free will.

Deterministic View of Human Nature (C-9; HS-6). The view that instincts, genetics, and early childhood development are so influential that there is little ability for the person to change. This view is in opposition to the *anti-deterministic view of human nature.*

Detox (Detoxification) (C-10; HS-10). In *recovery* from *substance abuse*, the process of the substance physically leaving the body after stopping usage. *Withdrawal symptoms* may be present when someone is detoxing.

Developing an Understanding of Self and Others (DUSO) (C-3; HS-1). An *individual psychology* counseling technique developed by *Don Dinkmeyer* that utilizes hand puppets to promote communication with children.

Developmental Counseling and Therapy (C-7; HS-3). Developed by *Allen Ivey*, an integrated theory of counseling based on five themes: (1) knowledge and relationships are constructed over time; (2) *cognitive development*, as understood by *Piaget*, is critical to how one works with clients; (3) *cultural competence* is critical in the counseling relationship; (4) counseling changes the neurological makeup of the brain; (5) and, treatment should be matched to the client. It recognizes four cognitive/emotional styles: sensorimotor, concrete, formal operational, and dialectic/systemic.

Developmental Crisis (C-7; HS-7). A predictable lifespan problem with which an individual or family must deal.

Developmental Models (C-9; HS-7). Theoretical models that identify predictable stages of development to which the helper can apply helping skills.

Developmental Models of Cultural/Racial Identity (C-9; HS-7). A variety of models that examine how individuals from various cultural/racial groups pass through unique stages of development as they become increasingly aware of their cultural selves.

Developmental Models of Ethical Decision-Making (C-7; HS-6). Approaches to making ethical decisions that emphasize how one's cognitive ability impacts a professional helper's *ethical decision-making* process. See also *Dualism* and *Relativism.*

Developmental Norms (C-3; HS-7). Direct comparison of an individual's score to the average scores of others at the same age or grade level. Examples include *age comparison* and *grade equivalent scoring.*

Developmental Readiness (C-8; HS-5). The state where the client is ready to advance to a higher developmental stage.

Developmental Self-Concept Theory (C-8; HS-3). Developed by *Donald Super*, a theory in *career counseling* that assumes that individuals develop their sense of *self* as they pass through predictable career developmental stages in which individuals have specific tasks to face. See also *Lifespan Developmental Theory of Career Development.*

Developmental Stress (C-7; HS-7). *Stress* that is related to predicted developmental life stages in families (e.g., having your first child, puberty, children leaving home). Contrast with *Situational Stress.*

Developmental Tasks (C-6; HS-6). Expected actions that individuals need to take as they pass through predictable age-related milestones. Sometimes these milestones and tasks are a painful part of the life process (e.g., learning how to accept differences when one becomes a couple).

Developmental Theories (C-9; HS-8). Theories that emphasize the notion that individuals will face predictable tasks as they pass through the inevitable developmental stages of life and that knowledge of such tasks could greatly aid helpers in their work with clients.

Deviation IQ (DIQ) (C-9; HS-3). *Standard score* with a *mean* of 100 and a *standard deviation* of 15. As the name implies, these scores are generally used in *intelligence testing.*

Dewey, John (1859 - 1952) (C-7; HS-4). An educational reformer who advocated for *humanistic* teaching methods. Dewey emphasized the value of infusing experiential learning into pedagogy.

Diagnoses (C-10; HS-9). The plural of *diagnosis*, referring to multiple specific *mental disorders.*

Diagnosis (C-10; HS-9). The process of identifying a *mental disorder*, which is typically done through counselors using the *Diagnostic and Statistical Manual of Mental Disorders.* Also refers to the specific mental disorder under discussion, as in one has a diagnosis of *depression.* See also *Diagnostic and Statistical Manual-5.*

Diagnosis, Making an Accurate (C-7; HS-6). Due to the delicate nature of *diagnoses*, *ethical codes* stress that professionals should be particularly careful when deciding which *assessment* techniques to use in forming a diagnosis for a *mental disorder.*

Diagnostic Achievement Test (C-8; HS-3). An *achievement test* used to identify learning problems. Diagnostic tests assess suspected learning, neurological, or psychological problem areas and are usually given one-on-one by a highly trained, experienced examiner.

***Diagnostic and Statistical Manual of Mental Disorders* (*DSM*) (C-10; HS-8).** Developed by the *American Psychiatric Association*, a manual that details the different types of mental disorders and emotional problems. Currently, in its fifth edition. See also *Diagnostic and Statistical Manual-5.*

***Diagnostic and Statistical Manual-5* (*DSM-5*) (C-9; HS-8).** The fifth edition of the *Diagnostic and Statistical Manual of Mental Disorders.*

Dialectical Behavior Therapy (DBT) (C-7; HS-3). Developed by *Marsha Linehan*, this theory assumes some people are born with heightened emotional sensitivity. The helper needs to be empathic, caring, warm, and teach *mindfulness* and offer problem solving skills. At the same time, the helper needs to be committed to the client while having an ongoing dialogue. One of the leading approaches to treating individuals who are living with borderline *personality disorder.*

Dialectical Process (C-8; HS-4). A process of discussing the client's issues in an atmosphere of open exchange (i.e., a dialectic).

Diaries/Journals (C-7; HS-7). A type of *informal assessment* where the author writes down his or her candid personal responses, ideas, and thoughts. In *qualitative research*, methods of ensuring researcher subjectivity and our *trustworthiness* strategies.

Diathesis-Stress Model (C-7; HS-2). In *cognitive therapy*, the idea that a combination of genetics, biological factors, and experiences combine to produce specific *core beliefs.*

Dictionary of Holland Occupational Codes (C-6; HS-3). A listing of thousands of *jobs* by their *Holland code.* Written by *John Holland.*

Dictionary of Occupational Titles (DOT) (C-8; HS-4). A comprehensive classification system for thousands of *jobs* that is published by the U.S. federal government. Currently being replaced by *O*NET.*

Differential Analysis (C-6; HS-2). A type of *Multivariate Correlational Research.*

Differential Aptitude Test (DAT) (C-6; HS-3). A type of *aptitude test* that is used in the *career counseling* process to determine one's *aptitude* in a variety of domains related to the world of *work.* The *test* is somewhat predictive of ability at certain *jobs.*

Differential Diagnosis (C-8; HS-5). The process of distinguishing the symptomatology of similar disorders to identify a particular *diagnosis.*

Differentiation of Self (C-7; HS-4). In *Bowen*'s therapy, the ability of a person to separate thinking and feeling states and make mature decisions. This is considered a move toward *individuation.*

Diffuse Boundaries (C-7; HS-6). As pertains to *general systems theory*, a framework that allows information to flow too easily into and out of the system, thus causing difficulty in the system's sense of identity. In *couples and family counseling*, loose *boundaries* that make it difficult to maintain a sense of identity.

Digital Communication (C-4; HS-2). In communication, the exact meaning of the words. Contrast with *Analogic Communication.*

Dimensional Diagnosis (C-6; HS-3). Used in the *DSM* for some *diagnoses*, it presents the diagnosis on different dimensions. For example, the severity of levels of *autism spectrum disorder* can be requiring support, requiring substantial support, and requiring very substantial support.

Dinkmeyer, Don (1924 - 2001) (C-3; HS-1). A *psychologist* and educator who adapted *Adler*'s *individual psychology* principles to work with children.

Diplomate in Clinical Social Work (DCSW) (C-4; HS-3). One of the most advanced national credentials an individual with a master's in *social work* can obtain. See also *ACSW* and *QCSW.*

DIQ (C-9; HS-3). See *Deviation IQ.*

Direct Observation (C-5; HS-4). A type of environmental *assessment* in which the examiner visits the classroom, workplace, or other setting in an effort to view the client, organization, or system and obtain additional information not usually retrieved in the office.

Direct-Service Approach (C-5; HS-3). In *consultation*, during the 1940s and 1950s, when "the expert" *consultant* would solve an existing problem after coming to the setting.

Direction and Doing (C-7; HS-4). In *Robert Wubbolding's WDEP* system of *reality therapy*, the "D" stands for what clients are doing in their life's direction.

Directive Approach (C-8; HS-7). Aimed at guiding clients through the change process by teaching them about and steering them toward healthier ways of living. This view is in opposition to the *nondirective approach*.

Directive Theories (C-8; HS-7). Theories that take on a *directive approach* to professional helping which emphasize that clients require guidance from helpers to make changes in their lives.

Directives (C-6; HS-4). The process by which a helper tells a client specific tasks to accomplish in order to reach goals. Used in *strategic therapy* and other approaches to helping. See also *Problem-Solving Therapy*.

Disability/Disabilities (C-10; HS-10). Intellectual, physical, psychological, neurological, developmental, or other related conditions or maladies that impair normal/typical functioning in human behavior.

Disability Services (C-8; HS-6). An office in higher education settings were individuals with degrees in *student affairs and college counseling* sometimes work focusing on helping students with *disabilities*, such as students with learning disorders or test *anxiety*.

Disaster Counseling (C-10; HS-7). See *Crisis, Disaster, and Trauma Helping*.

DISCOVER (C-6; HS-2). A comprehensive computer-based *career* awareness program.

Discrepancies, Pointing Out (C-5; HS-4). A way of gently confronting a client by highlighting incongruence in the client's life between client's values and behaviors. See also *Confrontation*.

Discrepancy Between a Client's Values and Behavior (C-5; HS-4). When a client expresses a certain value and then his or her actions do not match that expressed value, there is incongruence in the client's life, which can cause *stress* and lead to problem issues.

Discrepancy Between Expressed Feelings and Underlying Behavior (C-5; HS-4). When a client expresses certain feelings and then acts in a manner that seems to be inconsistent or indicates otherwise, which can cause *stress* and lead to problem issues.

Discrepancy Between Idealized Self and Real Self (C-5; HS-4). When clients have lofty thoughts and fantasies about how they want to act (*ideal self*), but in reality, fall short from these self-imposed ideals (*real self*), which can cause *stress* and lead to problem issues. See also *Idealized Self*.

Discriminant Analysis (DA) (C-4; HS-2). A type of regression analysis that is used for placing continuous level *predictor variables* into categories of a *dependent variable.* For example, suppose a researcher is trying to identify the most influential factors that predict *relapse prevention* for clients who are in *recovery.* The categorical level dependent variable would be *relapse* (yes or no). The continuous level predictor variables might be the number of *group therapy* sessions, number of days in treatment, and clients' net income. A DA would allow the researcher to predict which clients would be likely to maintain *sobriety* and which clients would be likely to relapse. The DA analysis would also allow the researcher to identify (or to discriminate) the comparative significance of each predictor variable(s) on the dependent variable (e.g., the number of group therapy sessions is a more accurate predictor of relapse prevention than income). DA is also referred to as a "discriminant function analysis" and is commonly used *post hoc analysis* for *MANOVA.*

Discriminant Validity (C-7; HS-3). A type of *validity* in which a *test* is shown not to be related to another test, thus showing that it can accurately discriminate between traits or attributes. This is particularly important when one wants to discriminate between two competing *diagnoses* that might lead to different treatment options (e.g., *depression*, *anxiety*).

Discrimination (in Diversity Issues) (C-10; HS-10). An active behavior that negatively affects individuals of ethnic, cultural, and racial groups and is frequently based on *stereotypes.* Can include *microaggressions.*

Discrimination (in Learning Theory) (C-7; HS-6). In *operant conditioning*, the ability of a person to respond selectively to one *stimulus*, but not respond to a similar stimulus.

Discursive Empathy (C-5; HS-3). A type of *advanced empathic response* in which direct knowledge about the cultural and historical antecedents of a client are used to make assumptions about the ongoing experience of the client. For instance, to a client who is upset about how she was treated at a supermarket, the helper might say, "Sounds like your experience with *discrimination* has permeated many aspects of your life."

Discussion, Implications, and Conclusions (C-8; HS-7). The last sections of a *manuscript* where, after the *literature review*, *methods*, and the *results* sections, thoughts are presented about the meaningfulness of the research and applications of it in various ways. Lastly, a concluding summary is provided of the entire manuscript.

Disease Model of Alcoholism (C-9; HS-9). This model views *alcoholism* as a medical disease with specific genetic, biological, and neurological sources, as well as environmental exposure, which leads to the brain disease of alcohol *addiction.* This model assumes that exposure to *alcohol* begins the process of disease and that alcoholism is technically incurable, requiring lifelong abstinence and routine reliance on *support groups* for *recovery* and seeing alcoholism as a progressive disease with distinct stages of impaired development and connected medical problems. E. Morton Jellinek originated this model. Contrast with *Harm Reduction Theory.* See also *Jellinek's Alcoholism Model.*

Disequilibration (C-7; HS-4). Breaking up the existing ways of relating in couples and families.

Disequilibrium (C-7; HS-6). Transition points from one developmental level to another, earmarked by a shakeup in the person's understanding of the world as the individual accommodates to a new way of living in the world. See also *Accommodation.*

Displacement (C-8; HS-4). A *defense mechanism* where a person feeling a strong *emotion* or impulse toward another person fears the consequences of sharing that emotion or impulse and instead redirects it onto a third, and safer, individual. For example, a child who is angry with his father, but fears the consequences of yelling at him, instead takes out his anger on his innocent little brother.

Disputations (Cognitive, Behavioral, and Emotional) (C-8; HS-3). Within *rational emotive behavior therapy*, when the counselor helps the client dispute or challenge illogical, or faulty, cognitions, behaviors, or *emotions*. See also *Cognitive Disputation.*

Disqualifying or Discounting the Positive (C-7; HS-2). A type of *cognitive distortion* in which a person assumes that a positive event means very little.

Disruptive, Impulse Control, and Conduct Disorders (C-9; HS-6). A group of *mental disorders* that are characterized by socially unacceptable or otherwise disruptive and harmful behaviors that are outside of the individual's control. Generally, more common in males than in females, and often first seen in childhood, they include the *diagnoses* oppositional defiant disorder, conduct disorder, intermittent explosive disorder, antisocial personality disorder (which is also coded in the category of *personality disorders*), kleptomania, and pyromania.

Dissociation (C-9; HS-5). A *defense mechanism* that involves detaching oneself from the reality of experiencing something harmful. It can exist on a continuum of severity and is frequently seen in victims of trauma, such as sexual abuse.

Dissociative Disorders (C-9; HS-6). These disorders indicate a temporary or prolonged disruption to *consciousness* that can cause an individual to misinterpret identity, surroundings, and memories. *Diagnoses* include dissociative identity disorder (formerly known as multiple personality disorder), dissociative amnesia, depersonalization/derealization disorder, and other specified and unspecified dissociative disorders.

Distance Learning Sites (and Directors of) (C-8; HS-2). Areas in higher education that individuals with a master's degree or higher in *student affairs and college counseling* sometimes work focusing on services for distance learning students and education (e.g., fully online learning).

Distortion (C-8; HS-5). A type of *defense mechanism* where the individual bends reality to ignore a painful aspect of *self.*

Distortion of Situations (Rogers) (C-7; HS-5). Within *person-centered counseling*, a mechanism that individuals use to shape, or warp, their view of a situation that threatens their *self-concept* so that the situation instead matches their self-concept. For instance, a parent who is constantly telling a child to act more "feminine" ends up believing that her identity should be more feminine and this results in a child who acts in that manner, but does not really feel that way. This is intimately related to *conditions of worth* placed on individuals by others.

Diverse Populations Human Service Professionals Work With (C-6; HS-9). Human service professionals work with a variety of different populations, a portion of which include *different ethnic and racial groups*, *individuals from diverse religious backgrounds*, *individuals using and abusing substances*, *individuals with disabilities*, *individuals with mental illness*, *lesbian*, *gay*, *bisexual*, and *transgender individuals*, *men*, *women*, *older persons*, *the homeless*, *the poor*, and more. See also *Multicultural and Social Justice Counseling Competencies.*

Diversegrad-L (C-5; HS-1). The electronic mailing list of the *American Counseling Association* for those who are interested in *cross-cultural* and *multicultural counseling* and *diversity* issues.

Diversity (C-10; HS-10). Referring to issues and interest pertaining to *cross-cultural counseling competencies*, *multicultural counseling*, and other issues promoting a diverse society in terms of *culture*, *race*, *religion*, *ethnicity*, and other categories.

Division 5 of the APA (C-5; HS-4). A professional organization of the *American Psychological Association* for *psychologists* that promotes "research and practical application of psychological *assessment*, evaluation, measurement, and statistics."

Division 12 of the APA (the Society of Clinical Psychology) (C-5; HS-4). A division of the *American Psychological Association* for clinical *psychologists.*

Division 16 of the APA (School Psychology) (C-5; HS-4). A division of the *American Psychological Association* for *school psychologists.*

Division 17 of the APA (Counseling Psychologist) (C-7; HS-4). A division of the *American Psychological Association* for *counseling psychologists.* The division that most closely aligns itself with the goals and ideals of counselors and the *American Counseling Association.*

Division Expansion and Autonomy (C-7; HS-1). Some of the *American Counseling Association's* (*ACA*) 20 divisions, such as *ASCA* and *AMHCA*, have become increasingly autonomous and no longer require membership in ACA to be a member of their division.

Divisions of ACA (C-10; HS-4). The *American Counseling Association* currently sponsors 20 divisions, all of which maintain newsletters and journals and provide a wide variety of professional development activities.

Dix, Dorothea (1802 - 1887) (C-7; HS-7). An early American activist who fought for humane treatment of the mentally ill and helped to establish "modern" mental institutions in the mid-1800s.

Doctor of Social Work (DSW) (C-7; HS-4). The most advanced degree in *social work* that typically prepares *social workers* for faculty positions in social worker training programs and leadership positions in agencies or private practice. Sometimes, this is a Ph.D. in social work.

Doctoral Degree in Counselor Education and Supervision (C-10; HS-4). An advanced degree in *counseling* that typically prepares counselors for faculty positions in counselor training programs and leadership positions in counseling practice. See also *Counselor Education and Supervision.*

Documentation (C-8; HS-8). The process of writing *process notes*, *case notes*, *case reports*, and identifying the number of contact hours conducted with each client to ensure local, state, and federal U.S. government funding regulations. One aspect of the *case management* process.

Documents (C-8; HS-4). Often used in *ethnographic research* and *historical research*, documents are symbols of a *culture* or group that provide the researcher an understanding of the beliefs, values, and behaviors of the group. May include such things as *diaries*, personal letters, *anecdotal records*, official documents, communications, records, and personnel files. See also *Artifacts* and *Relics*.

Doing (C-7; HS-4). In *reality therapy*, those aspects of ourselves which we can change, which only include our actions and our thoughts. See also *Total Behavior*.

Domestic Violence (C-8; HS-8). See *Intimate Partner Violence* or *Interpersonal Violence (IPV)*.

Dominant Narratives (C-5; HS-4). In *narrative therapy*, stories that predominate one's understanding of the world.

***Donaldson v. O'Connor* (C-6; HS-6).** The 1975 U.S. Supreme Court Decision that led to the *deinstitutionalization* of the mentally ill. The decision stated that a person who is not dangerous to *self* or others could not be confined to a psychiatric hospital against his or her will.

DOT (C-8; HS-4). See *Dictionary of Occupational Titles*.

Double-Barreled Questions (C-6; HS-6). A type of *open question* that increases the chances of inducing biases in the respondent by addressing two or more items in the same question. For example, asking a respondent "do you think that the revised curriculum covers math and English effectively?" This question asks about the effectiveness of both math and English simultaneously which makes it difficult to determine how the respondent feels about math and English independently. These should be avoided in interviewing.

Double Blind Research (C-9; HS-5). See *Double Blind Study*.

Double Blind Study (C-9; HS-5). A type of *experimental*, *research design* where both the researcher and participants are unaware which participants have been randomly assigned to the *control group* and the *experimental group*.

Double-Bind Theory (C-7; HS-4). A theory of communication that attempts to explain how people are caught in a web of mixed, or conflicted, messages from family members or other significant people in a person's life. Often messages given are opposite, or conflicting, with other given messages. A parent telling a child to "be spontaneous" is a double message. A child cannot be spontaneous when one tells him or her to be so.

Double Listening (C-7; HS-4). In *narrative therapy*, when a helper hears a client's story and also listens for deeper, hidden, or less obvious meanings than were implied by the surface story. See also *Absent but Implicit*.

Downers (C-8; HS-8). A generic term for various drugs/medications that produce a less aroused, less stimulated, or depressant state (i.e., down) in individuals such as *alcohol, cannabis, opioids, barbiturates, or benzodiazepines.*

Drama Therapy (C-7; HS-6). A creative therapy that uses drama and related theater techniques in counseling. See also *Creative and Expressive Therapists* and the *North American Drama Therapy Association.*

Dream Analysis (C-9; HS-5). In *psychoanalysis*, this technique is used to understand the *psyche* and *unconscious* motivations and desires. Often dreams are broken down into the *manifest meanings* (obvious) and *latent meanings* (hidden).

Dreikurs, Rudolf (1897 - 1972) (C-4; HS-2). A *psychiatrist* and educator from Austria, who emigrated to the U.S. and developed techniques for applying *individual psychology* to children. In particular, he focused on misbehavior and gaining cooperation from children without emphasizing rewards or *punishments.*

Drive for Completion and Wholeness (C-7; HS-5). In *individual psychology*, the individual's inherent desire to achieve completion and *wholeness* as one moves through life. It is reflected in one's *lifestyle.* See also *Striving for Perfection.*

Drives (C-5; HS-4). The often unconscious processes, or *instincts*, that motivate, encourage, or compel an individual's behaviors. This concept is primarily used in *psychodynamic approaches* to counseling.

Drug Abuse (C-10; HS-10). Harmful or addictive use of drugs, medications, or related *controlled substances.* See also *Substance Abuse.*

***DSM* (C-10; HS-8).** See *Diagnostic and Statistical Manual.*

***DSM-5* (C-10; HS-8).** See *Diagnostic and Statistical Manual-5.*

DSW (C-7; HS-6). See *Doctor of Social Work.*

Dual and Multiple Relationships (C-10; HS-10). Those potential and actual professional helping relationships in which there exists potential ethical conflicts because there are multiple roles between the helper and the client, such as when a potential or actual client is also a neighbor, colleague, or when a helper goes to a personal celebration or activity sponsored by a client (wedding, funeral, etc.).

Dualism/Dualistic (C-7; HS-5). The first stage in *William Perry's* theory of adult *cognitive development*, where a person views the world in terms of black or white, or right or wrong, and has little tolerance for ambiguity. See also *Relativism* and *Commitment to Relativism.*

Dualistic Rational Stage (C-6; HS-3). The second *stage of racism* in which professionals learn to monitor their prejudices but still feel them. Developmental theory formulated by *D'Andrea and Daniels.* See also *Affective/Impulsive*, *Liberal*, and *Principled Activist Stages.*

Duhka (C-3; HS-2). In Buddhism, suffering, which is an aspect of all life and a key focus of the *religion* (in terms of accepting suffering).

Dummy Coding (C-6; HS-2). A statistical coding procedure where researchers convert continuous level data (*interval* or *ratio*) into categorical level data (*nominal* or *ordinal*) for statistical analysis. See also *Nominal, Ordinal, Interval,* and *Ratio Scales.*

Duty to Protect or Duty to Warn (C-10; HS-10). Sometimes referred to as *foreseeable danger*, the ethical and sometimes legal obligations for a professional helper to take action and breach *confidentiality* if a client is in danger of harming himself or herself or someone else. See also *Tarasoff Case.*

Dynamic (C-7; HS-4). The idea that in some theories, particularly those that are *psychodynamic*, there is an interaction between early child-rearing practices and the development of the *psyche.*

Dysfunctional Couples and Families (C-9; HS-8). The term used to describe families that have relational problems. Usually, such problems are the result of *unfinished business* that husbands and wives bring into the marriage that effects their marriage and, in turn, the family. In such families, you often see blaming, *boundaries* that are too rigid or too permeable, and *scapegoating.*

Dystonic (C-5; HS-4). *Erik Erikson* suggested that as individuals pass through his eight stages of *psychosocial development*, they are faced with a *task*, sometimes called a *crisis.* Portrayed as a pair of opposing forces, Erikson described the first opposing task in each stage as *syntonic*, or positive emotional quality, and the second task as *dystonic*, or negative emotional quality. He suggested that individuals needed to experience both syntonic and dystonic qualities. See also *Psychosocial Development, Stages of.*

EAP (C-7; HS-4). See *Employee Assistance Program.*

Early Recollections (C-7; HS-4). Memories, feelings, or thoughts recalled from early childhood or adolescence. A term often used by those who practice *individual psychology* (*Adlerian therapy*).

Eating Disorder (C-9; HS-8). Mental health conditions that center on disturbed eating behaviors and may be frequently motivated by *feelings of inferiority*, low self-worth, and/or distorted views of self, connected to body weight, shape, size, or other emotional or psychological distress. *Eating disorders* can have significant adverse physical symptoms due to the disturbed eating behaviors including death, in the extreme. Examples include avoidant/restrictive food intake disorder, *anorexia nervosa, bulimia nervosa*, *binge eating disorder*, pica, and rumination disorder.

EBP (C-9; HS-6). See *Evidenced-Based Practice.*

EBSCO (C-7; HS-6). An *electronic database* that can assist with conducting research in education, counseling, and human services literature. See also *ERIC*, *Gale*, and *PsychINFO.*

Eclecticism (C-7; HS-4). The selection of what appears to be the best of several methods, approaches, or styles and their integration into one approach to professional helping. Whereas eclecticism has come to imply a pick and choose method whenever one thinks something will work, the term *integrative approach* is more grounded in that it integrates one or more approaches into a solid framework. See also *Integrative Approach to Counseling.*

Ecological Counseling (C-7; HS-4). See *Ecological Systems Theory.*

Ecological Systems Theory (C-7; HS-4). Developed by *Bronfenbrenner*, this model of human development explores the interaction of a person's environmental contexts within his or her individual contexts. It includes the following five systems of interactional context: microsystem, mesosystem, exosystem, macrosystem, and chronosystem.

***Economic Opportunity Act* (C-6; HS-6).** One of a number of legislative acts during the 1960s that provided opportunities for minorities and the poor, which helped to reshape attitudes toward social problems. Resulted in increased job opportunities for human service professionals and counselors.

Ecosystemic Crisis (C-5; HS-5). When a traumatic crisis, disaster, or negative event impacts a whole community or system.

ECT (C-8; HS-7). See *Electroconvulsive Therapy.*

***Education for All Handicapped Children Act* (*PL94-142*) (C-6; HS-6).** Enacted in 1975, a federal law that guarantees an education in the least restrictive environment to individuals who are living with a disability that are between the ages of 3 and 21 years old. This act mandates U.S. states to fund the services.

Education Trust (C-7; HS-1). During the turn of the 21st century, the Education Trust was instrumental in suggesting new ways of implementing *school counseling*, which eventually influenced the development of the *ASCA National Model.*

Educational Resources Information Center (ERIC) (C-7; HS-6). An *electronic database* that can assist when you are conducting research in education, human services, and counseling-related literature. See also *EBSCO*, *Gale*, and *PsychINFO.*

Effect Size (C-7; HS-6). In research, the practical significance of one's findings as opposed to the *statistical significance.* Effect size is a measure of the magnitude of the differences between groups. Research findings can reach *statistical significance* without being practically significant.

Ego (C-7; HS-5). According to *Freudian* theory, the *conscious* portion of the *psyche* that is the mediator between the person and reality, especially in the functioning of the person's perception of and adaptation to reality. Ruled by the *reality principle.* See also *Id*, *Superego*, and *Structures of Personality.*

Ego Boundary (C-7; HS-6). The recognition, or reference point, one has that distinguishes identity of the *self* from identity of the "other" within *Gestalt therapy.* This boundary between self and the other is always shifting based on interactions with people or objects in life.

Ego Identity (Adolescents) (C-9; HS-7). Related to *Erikson's* fifth stage of *psychosocial development*, this is when a child or juvenile has successfully incorporated all aspects of the previous roles into a unified concept of self. This stage's *virtue* is fidelity.

Ego Integrity vs. Despair (Later Life) (C-7; HS-6). *Erik Erikson's* last stage of *psychosocial development* where the older person examines whether or not he or she has successfully mastered the preceding developmental tasks. Such mastery will lead to a sense of integrity, whereas lack of mastery will lead to despair. This stage's *virtue* is wisdom.

Ego States (C-7; HS-6). The various behaviors, feelings, and ideas that characterize individuals' personalities. See also *Ego.*

Ego Strength (C-7; HS-6). The state of having a stable, healthy, mature *ego* or sense of self, and thus, one is capable of successfully handling the challenges of life. See also *Ego.*

Eigenvalue (C-6; HS-2). A statistical value that is used in *factor analysis* to identify the proportion of *variance* in the total model that a particular factor accounts for. See also *Scree Plot.*

Eigenwelt (C-7; HS-5). In *existential* terms, our psychological world, or how we come to understand ourselves. See also *Mitwelt*, *Uberwelt*, and *Umwelt.*

Einfiihlung (C-4; HS-2). A German word meaning, "to feel within," from which the word *empathy* was derived.

Elavil (C-6; HS-4). A *psychotropic medication* that is an *antidepressant* and a *controlled substance.*

Elder Abuse (C-9; HS-9). *Intimate partner or interpersonal violence (IPV)* that focuses on older persons. Elder abuse is usually perpetrated by children, relatives, or unrelated caretakers of the older persons. Older persons are frequently incapable of protecting themselves due to diminished physical, mental, or emotional capacity or feel conflicted about seeking protection from the loved ones causing the abuse.

Electra Complex (C-7; HS-3). In *psychoanalysis*, this developmental process is characterized by the girl's realization that she lacks a penis and her *unconscious* belief that she must have been castrated. Thus, she sees her genitals as wounded and inferior. She subsequently desires a penis of her own, and when she realizes she will not have one, her *penis envy* is eroticized through a desire for her father and the wish for a child by him. In essence, she wants to "take in" his penis so she has one of her own. Feeling rebuffed by her father, the young women has no choice but to identify with her mother and replace her erotic desire for her father for other, more appropriate men, still hoping to have a child to substitute for the missing penis. *Freud* believed that women go through life feeling lacking, which manifests itself in passive role-taking and feelings of competitiveness with men due to not having a penis and what comes with being male. This concept is highly criticized by feminists and not a theory that is popular today.

Electroconvulsive Therapy (ECT) (C-8; HS-7). A treatment approach that involves stimulating the brain with electric shock in an effort to provide relief from certain *mental disorders*, particularly major *depression.* Also known as *shock therapy* or other variations on this theme. More recent advances have made it more amenable to severe cases of *depression* as compared to the past, when it was seen as particularly harmful to a person's emotional state and cognitive functioning.

Electroencephalograph (EEG) (C-6; HS-4). A procedure used to test the brain's electrical activity, where electrodes are attached to specific points on the scalp of the individual under testing. Usually conducted to locate abnormalities in brain functioning,

Electronic Databases (C-7; HS-5). Online collections of articles and other scholarly sources through which one can search. Examples include *Educational Resources Information Center (ERIC)*, *PsycINFO*, *Gale*, and *EBSCO.* These databases are valuable tools for research.

***Elementary and Secondary Education Act* (C-7; HS-5).** An act passed in the late 1960s that allocated funding to improve the quality of elementary and secondary education, partly by increasing job opportunities for *school counselors*. One of a number of legislative acts during the 1960s that provided opportunities for minorities and the poor and helped to reshape attitudes toward social problems.

Elementary School Counselor (C-9; HS-8). One of three levels of *school counseling*. States sometimes credential across K-12 grades, or sometimes credential at specific grade levels.

Eligibility Worker (C-6; HS-8). In the field of human services, a professional who determines which benefits an individual client is eligible to receive.

Elimination Disorders (C-7; HS-5). A group of *mental disorders*, which include *enuresis* (the inappropriate elimination of urine) and *encopresis* (the inappropriate elimination of feces), and can manifest at any point in a person's life, although they are typically diagnosed in early childhood or adolescence. The behaviors may or may not be intentional.

Elizabethan Poor Laws (C-5; HS-8). During the 1500s, England established legislation for the Church to help the destitute. They set the stage for government sponsored social services and were, to some degree, used as models in the United States.

Ellis, Albert (1913 – 2007) (C-10; HS- 5). An influential American *psychologist* and author who developed a *cognitive approach* to therapy called *rational emotive behavior therapy* that highlighted the *A*, *B*, *and C's* and *irrational thoughts*.

Ellis, Debbie Joffe (C-2; HS-1). The widow of *Albert Ellis*, is a *licensed mental health counselor* in New York and a committed writer, lecturer, and practitioner of Ellis's ideas of therapy.

EMDR (C-7; HS-4). See *Eye Movement Desensitization Response Therapy*.

Emic Counseling (C-7; HS-5). Within the area of *multicultural counseling*, the perspective from within the social group, or relating to the internal elements of the social group. Contrast with *Etic*.

Emotional Cutoff (C-7; HS-4). Within *Bowenian family therapy*, the process of individuals dealing with dysfunction in the family system by distancing, emotionally and physically, from other members of the family.

Emotional Intelligence (C-7; HS-6). The ability to monitor one's *emotions*. In a helping relationship, emotional intelligence seems to be related to knowing the appropriate time to share one's feelings and thoughts (or be genuine) with the client.

Emotional Reasoning (C-4; HS-3). A type of *cognitive distortion*, in which one assumes that feelings are always correct, even when there is evidence to the contrary.

Emotions (C-5; HS-5). A natural and instinctive response to behavior changes, subjective perceptions, and physiological changes that includes any of a number of feeling stages.

Emotive Techniques (C-8; HS-5). Feeling oriented techniques often identified with their use in *rational emotive behavior therapy*.

Empathic Understanding (C-10; HS-10). When an individual has a deep understanding of another person's point of view. See also *Empathy* and the *Carkhuff Scale.*

Empathy (C-10; HS-10). Originally derived from the German word *Einfühlung*, empathy has become a core *counseling skill.* Popularized by *Carl Rogers* and listed as one of his three *core conditions* of helping along with *genuineness* (*congruence*) and *unconditional positive regard*, it is viewed today as the ability to understand another person's feelings and thoughts or to put oneself in the other's shoes. High-level empathic responses help a client see hidden parts of himself or herself. One of the nine *Common Factors.*

Empiricism (C-7; HS-6). In the sciences, the idea that knowledge can be uncovered by experiments and is the basis for the scientific method and the development of *hypotheses.* Much social science research is empirical research.

Employee Assistance Program (EAP) (C-7; HS-4). A program run by businesses or industry that provides primary prevention and early referral for mental health or *substance abuse* treatment. Often used in addition to or instead of full insurance programs.

Empowering Clients to Advocate for Themselves (C-8; HS-8). The process by which a helper supports and encourages clients to *advocate* for themselves.

Empty Chair Technique (C-8; HS-4). A *Gestalt therapy* technique whereby a client has a conversation with an important part of *self*, or an important person in his or her life, by talking to an empty chair and imaging that part of self, or the person, is seated in the chair. This technique assumes that all parts of self, and pieces of others that we find significant, are projections of an important aspect of self, which can be examined in this *role-play.*

Enable (C-7; HS-7). To offer emotional, financial, psychological or other support for unhealthy behaviors within a relationship, such as addictive, irresponsible, or dangerous behaviors. The result of enabling is that the unhealthy member's behavior continues freely and often without challenge or change. See also *Enabler.*

Enabler (C-7; HS-7). The person within a relationship who provides support to the unhealthy member of the relationship being enabled. See also *Enable.*

Encopresis (C-7; HS-6). Refers to fecal soiling or stool holding, most often seen with children. See also *Elimination Disorders.*

Encounter Group (C-7; HS-7). A *group therapy* setting in which expressions of feelings are encouraged, which leads to new *self-awareness* and growth. Became popular during the 1960s.

Encounters with Self (C-2; HS-1). An important focus in *Gestalt therapy* encouraging individuals to focus on *self.*

Encouragement (Adlerian) (C-4; HS-3). From an *individual psychology* perspective, encouragement encompasses a large variety of skills, such as *active listening*, *empathy*, being *strength-based*, being accepting, being non-judging, and using other related techniques that focus on building a client's self-worth.

Encouragement (C-8; HS-8). Expressing a positive attitude toward your client by reinforcing his or her ability to perform a task. See also *Affirmations.*

End-of-Life Care (C-8; HS-7). Providing services to clients who are living with terminal illness or other end-of-life health concerns, including possible discussion of end-of-life suicide (aka doctor assisted suicide). In recent years, some ethics codes have suggested that it is important to work with clients who are in this situation. However, helpers are generally warned to examine state laws concerning end-of-life helping and counseling to ensure they are practicing within their state guidelines.

Endogenous Variable (C-5; HS-2). See *Dependent Variable.*

Endorsement (C-6; HS-5). One way a professional can be acknowledged as authentic is through an endorsement by a *professional association* or other professional body. An endorsement generally does little more than acknowledge that the professional has met basic standards.

Enjoyment Need (in Reality Therapy) (C-5; HS-3). See *Fun Need.*

Enmeshment (C-8; HS-7). Within *Bowenian family therapy*, a dynamic where individual members of the family are overly entangled or dependent within each other's lives.

Enneagram (C-5; HS-2). Based on the work of psychiatrist Claudio Naranjo and philosopher/mystic G.I. Gurdjief, among others, a typology of human personality based on nine different types (e.g., reformer, helper, achiever, individualist, investigator, loyalist, enthusiast, challenger, and peacemaker).

Entropy (C-3; HS-2). The amount of change from order to disorder that occurs over time in a closed system, such as a family.

Enuresis (C-7; HS-7). The inability to control urination, or the involuntary act of peeing, most often seen within children. See also *Elimination Disorders.*

Environmental Assessment (C-7; HS-7). A naturalistic and systems approach to *assessment* in which practitioners collect information about clients from their home, work, or school environments. It includes *direct observation*, conducting a *situational assessment*, applying a *sociometric assessment*, or using an *environmental assessment instrument.* A type of *Informal Assessment.*

Environmental Assessment Instrument (C-6; HS-4). A type of *environmental assessment* in which any of a number of instruments are used, in conjunction with simple observation, to obtain additional information about a client.

Environmental Contexts (C-5; HS-7). Examining one's surroundings in an effort to obtain a full picture of a person's functioning. Similar to *Environmental Assessment.*

Epictetus (55AD – 135AD) (C-5; HS-3). An ancient philosopher whose ideas included the notion that having true opinions would lead to faring well, while having false opinions would lead to faring poorly. *Albert Ellis* used this philosophy as a basis of his ideas about *rational emotive behavior therapy.*

Epistemological Reflection (C-5; HS-2). Reflecting on knowledge and theory creation.

Epistemology (C-7; HS-7). In *qualitative research*, the philosophical way of knowing, or the methods of understanding something, and the tools researchers use to achieve this understanding.

Epston, David (1944 -) (C-7; HS-3). Along with *Michael White*, one of the developers of *narrative therapy*. He is a New Zealand *psychotherapist.*

Equal Employment Opportunity Commission (EEOC) (C-5; HS-6). An independent U.S. federal agency, formed under the Civil Rights Act of 1964, to eliminate *discrimination* in employment based on *race*, *ethnicity*, *gender*, age, *religion*, and other categories.

Equivalent Form Reliability (C-8; HS-3). See *Alternate Form Reliability*.

Eras (C-5; HS-2). In *Levinson's* theory, the phases people pass through including pre-adulthood, early adulthood, middle adulthood, late adulthood, and late, late adulthood. See also *Levinson's Seasons of a Man's Life and Seasons of a Woman's life.*

ERIC (C-7; HS-3). See *Educational Resources Information Center.*

Erickson, Milton H. (1901 - 1980) (C-7; HS-6). An influential American *psychiatrist* and author who used unconventional techniques with clients and influenced the development of *family counseling*, clinical *hypnosis*, and brief therapy approaches to counseling like *solution-focused brief therapy*.

Erikson, Erik (C-9; HS-7) (1902 - 1994). An influential German *psychologist* and founder of *Erikson's psychosocial theory of development.*

Erikson's Psychosocial Theory of Development (C-8; HS-7). One of the *post-psychoanalytic models* that moved significantly away from stressing the role *instincts* play in the formation of the *ego* and toward the importance of relationships in *ego* formation. *Erikson's* theory focuses on eight developmental stages that individuals pass through from birth to death. In each stage, one must resolve a conflict before progressing to the subsequent stage. See also *Psychosocial Development, Stages of.*

Erogenous Zones (C-8; HS-6). The *psychoanalytic* term used to describe places on the body from which sexual satisfaction is derived as a result of the individual's *psychosexual stage of development*. See also *Oral, Anal, Phallic, Latency*, and *Genital Stages.*

Eros (C-7; HS-5). In *psychoanalysis*, the *life instinct* that includes the sex instinct and the drive to live.

Error (C-7; HS-4). The inherent flaws and inaccuracies that all *tests* have, and thus, test scores should be examined tentatively and one should statistically measure the amount of error in a test. See also *Standard Error of Measurement* and *Error Variance.*

Error Variance (C-8; HS-4). Any *variance* in a statistical model that is uncontrolled for or unaccounted for. For example, suppose a researcher was administering an *achievement test* to high school students in different locations during different times of day. Distractions in the *test* taking environment (e.g., noise level in the room and hunger) that impacted students' test scores would represent error variance.

Esalen (C-7; HS-5). A retreat center in California where well-known *existential-humanists*, and others, led workshops and conferences. Became popular in the 1960s by Michael Murphy and is still active today.

Esquirol, Jean (1772 - 1840) (C-3; HS-1). An early *psychiatrist*, who used language to identify different levels of intelligence while working in French mental asylums; his work led to the concept of verbal intelligence.

Essential Self (C-6; HS-4). One of the five factors of the *indivisible self model.* It is recognizing the part of us that is beyond our mind and body (*spirituality*), feeling comfortable in the way we identify with our *gender* (*gender identity*) and with our *culture* (*cultural identity*), and being able to care for ourselves by minimizing harm in our environment (self-care).

Establishment Stage (C-8; HS-3). Stage 3 of *Donald Super's lifespan theory of career development*, occurring between ages 24 and 44 years, where the individual stabilizes *career* choice and advances in the chosen field. See also *Growth*, *Exploration*, *Maintenance*, and *Deceleration/Disengagement Stages*

Ethical Code (C-10; HS-10). Professional guidelines for appropriate behavior and guidance on how to respond under certain conditions. Each professional group has its own ethical code, including guidelines for *human service professionals*, *counselors*, *psychologists*, *social workers*, *marriage and family therapists*, *psychiatrists*, and others. Generally, ethical codes are not legal documents unless they have been adopted as such by a state legislature; however, they can be used in a court of law if a professional is sued and has abided by the code, thus showing the court adherence to professional standards.

Ethical Codes, Limitations of (C-7; HS-7). Instances where the *ethical codes* can be problematic including (a) some issues cannot be handled with a code, (b) difficulties in enforcing codes, (c) lack of public involvement in the code construction process, (d) issues addressed by codes being handled in other ways (e.g., the courts), (e) conflicts within a code or between related codes, (f) and, conflicts between a code and the values of the professional.

Ethical Codes, Purposes of (C-9; HS-8). Including but not limited to (a) protecting consumers, (b) furthering professionalism, (c) denoting a body of knowledge, (c) asserting a professional identity, (d) reflecting a profession's underlying values and suggested behavior, (e) offering a framework for ethical decision-making, (f) and, offering a measure of defense in case one is sued.

Ethical Decision-Making Models (C-9; HS-8). Models that assist helpers in making difficult ethical decisions, including *developmental models*, *moral models*, *problem-solving models*, and the *social constructivist perspective*.

Ethical Decision-Making, Moral Models of (C-6; HS-5). In ethical decision making, models that rely on *moral principles*. Such models generally include *principled ethics* and *virtue ethics*. *See* also *Kitchener*, *Principle Ethics Model*, *Rest*, and *Virtue Ethics Model.*

Ethical Hot Spots (C-7; HS-7). Issues that continue to surface within counseling ethics research as being important and are frequently highlighted in *ethical codes*. A limited number of these include *boundary* issues, *cultural competence*, *duty to warn*, not placing one's *values* onto clients, *online counseling* and *supervision*, and limiting *dual and multiple relationships* with clients.

Ethical Standards of Human Service Professionals (C-1; HS-10). Ethical guidelines adopted by the *National Organization of Human Services* in 2014 that reflect the unique perspective of the human service professional. The sections include the following: The preamble; Responsibility to Clients; Responsibility to the Public and Society; Responsibility to Colleagues; Responsibility to Employers; Responsibility to the Profession; Responsibility to Self; and Responsibility to Students.

Ethical Standards of Practice (C-7; HS-6). See *Ethical Codes.*

Ethical Violations, Reporting of (C-10; HS-10). Refers to a helper's obligation to follow a series of procedures for reporting an ethical violation of a colleague. Often, it is suggested that the helper first speak to the individual who is suspected of making an ethical violation. If the situation is not resolved, then further reporting to the proper sources (e.g., credentialing board, *professional association*) would be called for.

Ethics (C-9; HS-9). Principles and guidelines that specify how professionals should act. See also *Ethical Codes.*

Ethics Code of the American Counseling Association (C-10; HS-2). A code that helps guide counselors toward the appropriate ways of responding when making ethical decisions. The sections of the 2014 edition (the most recent) include the following: The preamble; Section A: The Counseling Relationship; Section B: Confidentiality and Privacy; Section C: Professional Responsibility; Section D: Relationships with Other Professionals; Section E: Evaluation, Assessment, and Interpretation; Section F: Supervision, Training, and Teaching; Section G: Research and Publications; Section H: Distance Counseling, Technology, and Social Media; and Section I: Resolving Ethical Issues.

Ethnicity (C-9; HS-9). Shared long-term patterns of behavior among a group of people that include specific cultural and social patterns such as a similar language, values, *religion*, foods, and artistic expressions.

Ethnocentric Worldview (C-8; HS-8). Those who view the world through the lens of their own *culture* and falsely assume clients view the world in a similar manner or believe that when clients present a differing view, they are emotionally disturbed, culturally brainwashed, or just simply wrong.

Ethnographic Interviews (C-8; HS-6). A common method used in *ethnographic research*, which includes asking *open questions* to ascertain information about how the interviewees construct meaning and make sense of their world.

Ethnographic Research (C-9; HS-6). Involves the description and understanding of human *culture* through *immersion* within the cultures. Sometimes called *cultural anthropology.*

Ethnography (C-7; HS-6). The description (graphy) of human *culture* (ethno).

Etic Counseling (C-7; HS-5). Within *multicultural counseling*, cultural aspects of the group that are noticed or highlighted from an objective perspective, usually from one who is not in the group. Contrast with *Emic.*

Etiology (C-7; HS-6). The study of the cause(s) and origin(s) of a disorder, disease, condition, or syndrome.

Evaluation (in Program Evaluation) (C-7; HS-6). Measuring whether a program has achieved its goals and objectives and has been shown to have worth and value.

See also *Formative Evaluation* and *Summative Evaluation.*

Evaluation of the Program (C-3; HS-1). The fourth area that the *Council for the Accreditation of Counseling and Related Educational Programs* evaluates in master's-level training programs; this includes *assessment* of the following: program mission and objectives, curricular offerings, and characteristics of program students and applicants. See also *Master's-Level Standards.*

Evaluative Questions (C-6; HS-6). Used in *solution-focused brief therapy*, questions that help clients identify behaviors that have led *to preferred goals.*

Evaluator (C-5; HS-6). One who assesses client programs and shows that agencies are accountable for services provided. One of the original 13 roles and functions of human service professionals as defined by the *Southern Regional Education Board.*

Event and Time Sampling (C-5; HS-3). Observing a targeted behavior for a set amount of time. A type of *Observation.*

Event Sampling. (C-5; HS-3). A type of *observation* in which one is observing a specific behavior with no regard to time.

Evidence-Based Practice (EBP) (C-8; HS-6). Research-supported treatments for specific *mental disorders.* A mental health professional uses his or her clinical expertise to understand the client's situation and chooses the most effective treatments for it, and when client's personal preferences, values, and cultural backgrounds for such treatment are considered. Sometimes, simply referred to as when the practitioner matches the best-known researched treatments to the client's presenting problems. However, this is seen as a somewhat limited definition.

Ex Post Facto Research (C-8; HS-5). A kind of *quantitative research* that examines intact pre-existing groups instead of *randomly assigning* subjects to groups. Also called *Causal-Comparative Research.*

Exaggeration Technique (C-8; HS-4). A *Gestalt therapy* technique where the client is asked to exaggerate or repeat a word, phrase, or sentence to help him or her connect with feelings on a deeper level.

Examining Early Recollections (C-7; HS-4). Process used in *individual psychology* to help determine how *early recollections* have influenced a person's *style of life.*

Exception-Seeking Questions (C-9; HS-8). Questions that identify times in the clients' lives when they did not have the problem. One type of *solution-focused question.* See also *Exceptions to the Problem.*

Exceptions to the Problem (C-9; HS-8). Often used in *narrative therapy* and *solution-focused brief therapy*, in which the helper invites clients to talk about times in their lives when they did not have their problems. Used to examine different *narratives* in clients' lives and other resources the clients have had to keep problems at bay.

Existential Anxiety (C-9; HS-6). Also known as *angst*, and refers to *anxiety* that develops due to awareness of one's death, the meaninglessness of life, and knowledge of avoidance of living life fully and genuinely.

Existential Crisis (C-7; HS-7). The point in a person's life when one questions his or her meaning or purpose in life as well as the meaning and purpose of existence. See also *Existential Angst.*

Existential Guilt (C-7; HS-6). Guilt that is derived from the knowledge that one has not lived his or her life to the fullest of one's potential due to avoidance of essential issues in life and the connected *existential anxiety* one experiences.

Existential-Humanistic Approaches (C-9; HS-7). A conceptual orientation that includes *existential therapy*, *person-centered counseling*, *Gestalt therapy*, and other approaches to the helping relationship. Based loosely on *existential philosophy* and *humanistic theory*, all of these approaches focus on struggles of living, how individuals construct meaning, the subjective reality of the client's understanding of their own existence (*phenomenological psychology*), and the ability of clients to change, fulfill their potential, and move toward *self-actualization*. They all tend to deemphasize the role of the *unconscious* and focus on *consciousness* and/or *self-awareness*. They are more optimistic than many other approaches and all are *anti-deterministic.*

Existential Isolation (C-7; HS-6). In *existential therapy*, one's awareness that all people are born alone, live alone (except for brief moments of contact with others), and will ultimately die alone. See also *Isolation.*

Existential Philosophy (C-8; HS-5). The philosophical belief centering on the individual's existence in an incomprehensible universe and on the plight of the individual to assume full responsibility for his or her acts without certainty of what is moral or immoral.

Existential Psychology (C-8; HS-5). A subspecialty of *psychology* that is based loosely on some of the early *existential philosophers* and *humanistic theorists*, it focuses on struggles of living, how individuals construct meaning, and the subjective reality of the client.

Existential Therapy (C-9; HS-5). An *existential-humanistic approach* to counseling that suggests we are born into a world that has no inherent meaning, that we all struggle with the basic questions about life, and that we alone can create meaning and purpose. Existential therapists believe we all have the ability to live authentically and experience fully, but sometimes avoid doing so because we are fearful of looking at our existence, including our ultimate demise, which is death or nonbeing. They suggest that *anxiety* and struggles are a natural part of living and are messages about how we live and relate to others. They also believe we can choose to live meaningfully and experience a limited sense of freedom. Two well-known theorists are *Viktor Frankl* and *Rollo May.* An *anti-deterministic approach.*

Existential Vacuum (C-8; HS-5). The empty, internal void or hole, individuals feel in their lives (and seek ways to fill). It is connected to the meaninglessness and purposelessness of life acknowledged in *existential therapy.*

Existential Void (C-8; HS-5). A similar term to *existential vacuum*, describing the emptiness one feels when realizing that life is utterly meaningless. One can only create meaning after one has experienced the *existential vacuum* or existential void.

Experiential Family Therapy (C-6; HS-3). A type of *family therapy* that primarily emphasizes the relationship between counselor and clients for change, sees families as having natural tendencies for growth, and draws on self, family members, and therapist experiences to achieve that growth within sessions. One well-known experiential family therapist was *Carl Whitaker.*

Experimental Design Validity (C-5; HS-1). Using experimentation to show that a *test* measures a specific concept or construct. A type of *Construct Validity.*

Experimental Group (C-9; HS-7). In *quantitative research*, the group that receives the treatment or *intervention.* See also *Control Group.*

Experimental Psychologists (C-8; HS-7). *Psychologists* who typically work in laboratories and conduct research to attempt to understand the psychophysiological causes of behavior.

Experimental Research (C-9; HS-6). A type of *quantitative research* where the researcher is manipulating the treatment and hopes to show a cause-and-effect relationship between the experimenter's manipulation and specific *outcome measures.* Experimental research includes *True Experimental, Quasi-Experimental, Pre-Experimental,* and *Single-Subject Experimental Designs.*

Experimenter Bias (C-9; HS-6). Also known as *researcher bias*, or simply *bias*, when the outcome of an experiment is potentially altered due to influence from the researcher, oftentimes towards a desired result.

Expert Review (C-3; HS-1). A process by which experts (typically at least three) who have a wealth of experience in a certain area, review a measurement instrument to ensure the *content validity* of the measure. For example, if one was developing a measure to assess clinical *depression*, he or she might seek three expert *clinicians* who have many years of experience, researching, working with, and treating clients with *depression.*

Expert Witness (C-9; HS-8). In a courtroom, a witness who is called to testify based on having a particular expertise, or area of professional specialty, to the case in question. Human service professionals, counselors, or other mental health professionals could be called to court as expert witnesses to speak on behalf of, or in defense of, their clients or to provide objective *assessments* to plaintiffs or defendants.

Explanatory Correlation (C-5; HS-2). The relationship between variables in an effort to explain a phenomenon. A type of *Nonexperimental Research.*

Exploration Stage (C-8; HS-3). Stage 2 of *Donald Super's lifespan theory of career development*, occurring between ages 14 and 24 years, where the individual tentatively tests occupational fantasies through work, school, and leisure activities and later chooses an *occupation* or additional professional training. See also *Deceleration/Disengagement Stage, Establishment Stage, Growth Stage,* and *Maintenance Stage.*

Exploratory Factor Analysis (C-6; HS-2). A type of *factor analysis* in which the researchers attempt to uncover the underlying factor structure in a data set. See also *Confirmatory Factor Analysis.*

Exploratory Research (C-4; HS-2). A type of research that is conducted when there is little known about the problem or cause of something, so that a theory or hypothesis cannot yet be formulated about the phenomenon under study. Frequently, it is undertaken to determine the best *research design* and methods for such a phenomenon.

Explosive/Authentic Layer (C-4; HS-2). In Gestalt *therapy*, a part of the *structure of neurosis* (and the therapeutic process) when a client must choose to live authentically and to be real in all his or her experiences.

Ex-Post Facto Research (C-7; HS-2). See *Causal-Comparative Research.*

Exposure Therapy (C-8; HS-4). A broad range of approaches in which a client is repeatedly exposed to an *anxiety* or fear inducing *stimulus* until it stops eliciting the distressful response and is *extinguished.* Exposure to the situation (the stimulus) can be conducted live ("*in vivo*"), through one's imagination or mental images ("*imaginal exposure*"), or, more recently, through computer-simulations or virtual reality apparatuses ("*in virtuo exposure*"). Three classic exposure therapy techniques are *systematic desensitization, flooding therapy*, and *implosion therapy.*

Expression of Feeling (C-9; HS-8). When a professional helper encourages a client to express his or her *emotions;* a goal of a number of therapies in order to release underlying tension and to get at the heart of a problem. See also *Catharsis* and *Abreaction.*

External Control Language (C-7; HS-5). Identified by *reality therapists*, as blaming language used by individuals in dysfunctional relationships.

External Locus of Control (C-9; HS-8). A belief that things outside of oneself are in control of one's behavior and the result of that behavior. For example, one might believe that fate determines whether one will get a *job*, rather than having good qualifications, a well-done resume, and performing well in the interview.

External Validity (C-9; HS-6). The extent to which the results of a research study can be generalized and applied to situations and individuals outside of the setting in which the research was conducted.

Externalization (C-7; HS-6). A type of *defense mechanism* in which one acts out, projects onto others, or blames others or things outside of oneself, for one's problems.

Externalizing the Problem (C-9; HS-4). In *narrative therapy*, the client gives a name to his or her problem(s) so the problem can be placed outside of, or external to, the client to assist with objectively focusing on the problem and finding solutions to it. For example, a client might name his or her social *anxiety* "the nervous Nellie," helping to openly talk about it outside of his or her self. It also assists the client in not assuming that there is something inherently wrong "inside" of the client.

Extinction (C-9; HS-8). A principle of *operant conditioning* that states a behavior will cease if it is not reinforced.

Extinguished (C-8; HS-7). In *operant conditioning*, when a behavior is not reinforced and consequently is no longer present.

Extraneous Variables (C-10; HS-6). See *Confounding Variables.*

Extroverted Attitude (C-7; HS-5). According to *Jung*, a personal *attitude* that is socially outgoing, people loving, conversational, and more focused on people and things than on personal ideas and *emotions.* These people can be said to derive energy from being social with people. Contrast with *Introverted Attitude.*

Eye Contact (C-10; HS-10). A *nonverbal behavior* related to the degree to which a helper is able to appropriately engage a person by looking in a person's eyes. Norms of eye contact can vary from *culture* to culture and helpers should consider this when using it.

Eye Movement Desensitization Response Therapy (EMDR) (C-8; HS-4). A type of therapy that focuses on how rhythmic stimulation (e.g., rapid eye movements, tapping) can lessen symptoms associated with traumatic events.

Eye Movement Integration Therapy (EMIT) (C-7; HS-3). Similar to *eye movement desensitization response therapy*, this neurophysiological approach attempts to help individuals adapt new neuropathways through eye movement techniques.

Eysenck, Hans (1916 – 1997) (C-7; HS-3). A researcher who conducted a controversial and flawed study suggesting counseling and therapy were not effective. However, subsequent research has demonstrated overwhelming evidence that counseling is helpful. See also *Common Factors.*

F2M or FTM (Female-to-Male) (C-5; HS-5). Individuals who were assigned the female *gender* at birth and currently identify as male. Includes those who are at different stages of their transition or gender affirmation process. See also *M2F or MTF* and *Sex Reassignment Surgery.*

Face Validity (C-8; HS-2). In testing and *assessment*, the extent to which an instrument seems superficially *valid* due to its appearance, title, or because the questions seem to match with what is being measured. However, this does not necessarily mean that the instrument has *test validity*, only that it appears to be related to what is being measured.

Facial Expressions (C-8; HS-8). A *nonverbal behavior* related to a wide range of facial gestures made by a helper and intended to foster the helping relationship.

Facilitative Consultation Model (C-7; HS-3). When the *consultant* plays a facilitative role by helping individuals within the system communicate with one another, understand each other, and resolve conflicts.

Factor Analysis (C-7; HS-3). A method of demonstrating *construct validity* by statistically examining the relationship between subscales and the larger construct (*test*). Factor analysis helps to identify and/or verify subscales of an instrument by showing their relative statistical independence from one another. It is frequently used in *multiple aptitude tests* to help developers determine the purity of subtests. See also *Exploratory Factor Analysis* and *Confirmatory Factor Analysis.*

Factor Loading (C-5; HS-2). The extent to which items on a measurement instrument group together statistically to form factors or subscales. For example, items on a *test* of *depression* might group together to form the following three subscales or dimensions of depression: hopelessness, low *self-esteem*, and despondency. Factor loadings are a measure of how well the items "load" or fit into those three scales. See also *Factor Analysis.*

Factor Rotation (C-7; HS-3). A procedure that is used in *factor analysis* to make the factors easier to recognize. Rotation helps researchers to identify which test items group together to form the factors (i.e. how the test questions clump together to form the instrument's subscales). Factor rotations can be oblique, or rotated at less than 90 degree angles. An *oblique rotation* is appropriate when researchers expect that the factors will be correlated (i.e. participants' scores on the subscales will be related). If, for example, researchers were measuring a client's symptomatology of *mental disorders* by administering an instrument with a *depression* inventory subscale and an *anxiety* inventory subscale, it is reasonable to expect that there will be a relationship between participants' scores on the depression subscale and anxiety subscale, thus an oblique rotation is appropriate. Factor rotations can also be rotated at 90 degree angles called *orthogonal rotation.* An orthogonal rotation (commonly called *varimax*) should be used when one would not expect the factors to be correlated (i.e. participants' scores on the subscales will not be related).

Factorial Analysis of Variance (C-7; HS-3). A type of *quantitative research* that is used with more than one *independent variable* and a single *dependent variable* when the researcher is interested in examining the potential main effects and interaction effects between the independent variables and the dependent variable.

Failure Identity (C-6; HS-5). In *reality therapy*, where individuals develop a sense that they are not successful in life.

Fairbarn, W. R. D. (1889 – 1964) (C-5; HS-2). A Scottish *psychiatrist* and *psychoanalyst* who was a key *object relations therapy* theorist.

Faith Development, Fowler's Theory of (C-4; HS-2). A *developmental model* of faith development, which moves from a *dualistic* understanding of God, values, and meaning-making to a more complex, *relativistic* understanding. The stages include: primal faith, intuitive-projective faith, mythic-literal faith, synthetic-conventional faith, individuative-reflective faith, conjunctive faith, and universalizing faith.

Fallible Human Beings (C-7; HS-6). The view of human nature, in *rational emotive behavior therapy*, that humans make errors of thinking in life (i.e., irrational thinking and choices), and at the same time can make rational decisions based on rational thoughts.

False Connection (C-6; HS-2). A term originally coined by *psychoanalysts*, it is when clients project feelings, thoughts, and attitudes onto a helper as if that helper were another person (like a mother or father). Also called *transference.*

False Positives and Negatives (C-7; HS-4). When an *assessment* instrument incorrectly classifies someone as having an attribute they do not have (false positive), or not having an attribute they do have (false negative).

Family-Based Helping/Counseling (C-7; HS-7). Various models of family helping and counseling where the treatment services are primarily provided within the home setting as opposed to an office or elsewhere in the community.

Family Constellation (Adlerian) (C-8; HS-3). Within *individual psychology*, an individual's placement within a family, such as *birth order*, and/or mediating factors (e.g., illnesses, years apart from siblings) affecting his or her placement within the family. Individual personality characteristics are, thus, a function of the interaction of one's placement and mediating factors within the family.

Family Counseling (C-9; HS-8). Using any of a number of advanced training techniques to counsel and help families change. May include such approaches as *strategic family therapy*, family therapy from a communication perspective, *structural family therapy*, *multigenerational family therapy*, *experiential family therapy*, *psychodynamic family therapy*, *cognitive-behavioral family therapy*, and *narrative family therapy*. Whereas human service professionals tend to be trained to do *family guidance*, counselors and other master's level or higher professionals may be trained to do *family counseling*. Also called *Family Therapy*.

Family Counselor (C-9; HS-8). A person specifically trained in couples and/or family counseling work. Generally, has a master's or above in *family counseling* or a related degree with specialty coursework in family work.

Family Dynamics (C-8; HS-8). The different communication and behavioral patterns that occur in families. See also *General Systems Theory*.

***Family Educational Rights and Privacy Act* (*FERPA*) (C-8; HS-8).** Also called the *Buckley Amendment*, this 1974 U.S. federal act ensures the privacy of student records and grants parents access to their children's educational records and adults access to their past educational records.

Family Guidance (C-5; HS-7). The process of offering support and advice concerning appropriate parenting methods and assisting families in how to communicate with one another. Not as intensive as *family counseling*, this type of work is usually performed by human service professionals whereas counselors and related professionals may conduct *family counseling*.

Family Life Cycle (C-8; HS-8). A series of developmental stages families go through as they change over time and circumstances. Life events, such as birth of a new child or graduation of another, can lead to expected changes and *stress* within family dynamics.

Family Life Fact Chronology (C-7; HS-5). Similar to a *genogram*. Used by *Virginia Satir*.

Family of Origin (C-9; HS-9). The family one is born into and is primarily raised within as a child. Most often, this will be a family of blood relationship, but for adopted children or blended families this may include non-blood related family members.

Family Projection Process (C-7; HS-3). In *Bowenian family therapy*, this occurs when parents unconsciously *triangulate* with their children or project their own issues onto the children.

Family Sculpting (C-7; HS-4). Used by *Virginia Satir* and similar to *psychodrama*, the therapist would physically position people in a family based on how they acted in the family to assess and work with *family dynamics* (e.g., a depressed family member might look down, an autocratic and blaming family member might have a stern look and be pointing at someone).

Family Service Agencies (C-8; HS-8). Settings where human service professionals or *clinical mental health counselors* may be employed where the focus is on working with families and family issues.

Family Therapy (C-5; HS-8). See *Family Counseling*.

Familywise Error Rate (C-8; HS-3). A statistical phenomenon in which the probability of a *type 1 error* increases as more statistical procedures are included in an analysis. The familywise error rate can be protected against by using a *Bonferroni correction* or other related statistical measures.

Faulty Logic (C-7; HS-4). *Cognitive distortions* that impact one's understanding of the world in negative ways. In *Adlerian therapy*, they affect one's *private logic.*

Federal Emergency Management Agency (FEMA) (C-8; HS-8). The federal agency charged with addressing crises and disasters in the United States. FEMA has developed some key principles for crisis counseling. See *Crisis, Disaster, and Trauma Helping.*

Fee for Service (C-8; HS-7). The out-of-pocket, or cash, price a client would pay for an individual service by a professional helper.

Feedback Loops (C-7; HS-4). In *cybernetics* and systems views of *family therapy*, the processes families employ to regulate themselves, either through *positive feedback loops* or *negative feedback loops.*

Feeding and Eating Disorders (C-8; HS-7). This group of *mental disorders* describes clients who have severe concerns about the amount or type of food they eat to the point that serious health problems, or even death, can result from their eating behaviors. Examples include avoidant/restrictive food intake disorder, *anorexia nervosa*, *bulimia nervosa*, and *binge eating disorders*. See also *Eating Disorders.*

Feeling Mental Function (C-7; HS-4). In *analytical psychology* (*Jungian therapy*) one of the four *mental functions* that make up one's *psychological type*. Individuals who primarily use their feeling mental function evaluate situations through empathy and by understanding relationships and considering people's needs. See also *Thinking Mental Function*, *Sensing Mental Function*, and *Intuiting Mental Function.*

Feeling Word Checklist (C-8; HS-7). A type of *classification method* that allows an individual to identify those words that best describe the kinds of feelings an individual might typically or atypically exhibit.

Feelings of Inferiority (C-8; HS-6). A major focus in *individual psychology*, personal feelings of being inadequate or inferior to others.

Feminism (C-9; HS-8). A variety of social, political, cultural, psychological, and related movements, theories, research, and professional practices that emphasize women's rights and roles and the unique aspects of being a woman within society. See also *Relational-Cultural Theory*, *Gender Aware Therapy*, *Karen Horney* and *Jean Baker Miller.*

Feminist Counseling/Therapy (C-9; HS-7). A form of *therapy*, based in *feminism*, that emphasizes *gender* awareness, *gender roles*, oppression of women, and gender equality within therapy. See also *Relational-Cultural Theory*, *Gender Aware Therapy*, *Karen Horney* and *Jean Baker Miller.*

Fentanyl (C-7; HS-7). A synthetic *opiate* and *controlled substance* that is used to treat pain. It is generally taken orally and is highly addictive.

***FERPA* (C-8; HS-8).** See *Family Education Rights and Privacy Act.*

Fetal Alcohol Syndrome (FAS) (C-9; HS-9). A series of conditions that can result from a mother's *alcohol* consumption during pregnancy. Children with FAS may experience severe symptoms including cognitive deficiencies, small stature or low body weight, altered facial features, and various behavioral problems, among other symptoms.

Fictional Final Goal (C-6; HS-3). The goal to which one strives in the attempt to seek perfection and wholeness, but which is distorted due to *feelings of inferiority*. The original name for the *subjective final goal* to which a person strives to achieve in *individual psychology*.

Fictions (C-6; HS-3). In *individual psychology*, the lies individuals create about the reality of life and then view and respond to as truth.

Fidelity (C-8; HS-6). One quality of *Kitchener's* model, and related to *principle ethics*, this has to do with maintaining trust (e.g., keeping conversations *confidential*) in the counseling relationship and being committed to the client within that relationship.

Fifth Force (C-8; HS-7). *Social justice* and *advocacy* are widely referred to as the fifth force in *psychology* and counseling after *psychoanalysis*, *behaviorism*, *existential-humanism*, *and multicultural counseling*.

Fight or Flight Response (C-8; HS-7). The physiological process that occur in humans and animals when there is a real or perceived threat to survival, such as a traumatic experience or attack, charging the body for action or reaction. In this process, the body prepares to fight or to flee from danger by sending certain hormones throughout the nervous system.

Figure-Ground (C-7; HS-5). Within *Gestalt psychology*, the tendency of people to emphasize what is in the *foreground* of experience and to ignore what is in the background. One can learn to reverse or flip experience to focus on the experience/needs in the background instead of those at the foreground.

Financial Aid Office (C-8; HS-2). One area in higher education, dealing with student finances, grants, and scholarships, that individuals with a master's in *student affairs and college counseling* sometimes work.

First Comprehensive Theory of Counseling (C-9; HS-2). Developed by *E.G. Williamson*, one of the first comprehensive approaches to counseling that is known as the *Minnesota point of view* or *trait and factor theory*. Williamson's approach grew out of the ideas of *Frank Parsons*.

Fisch, Dick (1926 - 2011) (C-4; HS-2). An American *psychiatrist* associated with the *Mental Research Institute* who was influential in *Solution-Focused Brief Therapy*.

Fixated (C-9; HS-7). In *Freudian psychoanalysis*, being stuck in a *psychosexual stage of development*.

Fixed Battery Approach to Neuropsychological Assessment (C-5; HS-1). Using a uniform (standard) set of instruments for clients who require a *neuropsychological evaluation*.

Fixed Interval Schedule of Reinforcement (C-7; HS-5). The process by which a behavior is reinforced after a predetermined amount of time has elapsed (e.g., every two minutes).

Fixed Ratio Schedule of Reinforcement (C-7; HS-5). The process by which a behavior is reinforced based on the number of specific times that have been identified (e.g., every two times the behavior is exhibited).

Flexible Battery Approach to Neuropsychological Assessment (C-5; HS-1). Tailoring techniques, or aspects of standardized instruments, specific to each client who requires a *neuropsychological evaluation.*

Fliess, Wilhem (1858 - 1928) (C-6; HS-2). An ear, nose, and throat physician and an early colleague of *Sigmund Freud*, whose relationship with Freud was influential in the development of *psychoanalysis.* He believed the similarity between nose and genital tissue meant that you could work on psychological issues through surgery on the nose. His theory was known as "nasal reflex neurosis."

Flooding Therapy (C-7; HS-4). A type of *behavior therapy* where clients are increasingly exposed to a feared *stimulus* until the stimulus no longer induces the fear response. Often used in combination with *systematic desensitization.* A type of *Exposure Therapy.*

Fluid Intelligence (C-7; HS-2). As identified by *Raymond Cattell*, a type of innate intelligence that permits applying new solutions to situations and identifying patterns without relying on previous learning. Contrast with *Crystallized Intelligence.*

Follow-Up (C-9; HS-9). The process of ensuring that clients are managing well after the helping relationship has ended by contacting or meeting with them. One aspect of the *case management* process.

Food Stamps (C-6; HS-8). See *Supplemental Nutritional Assistance Program.*

Forced Choice Closed Question (C-8; HS-7). Questions that give the client a minimum of two options when responding (e.g., "yes" or "no;" "bad" or "good"). See also *Closed Questions.*

Foreground (C-7; HS-4). In *Gestalt therapy*, the need that is most present in one's *consciousness.*

Forensic Evaluations (C-7; HS-4). A specialized type of *assessment* often used in a court of law. The assessing examiner frequently collects information from *interviews*, *testing*, and the reviewing of supplemental records and may be called as an expert witness. Professional organizations offer specific endorsements for this.

Foreseeable Danger/Harm (C-10; HS-10). The ethical and sometimes legal obligation for a professional to take action if a client is in danger of harming himself or herself or someone else. See also *Duty to Protect or Duty to Warn* and *Tarasoff case.*

Formal Operational Stage (C-9; HS-8). *Jean Piaget's* fourth stage of *cognitive development* (ages 11-16 years) when a child can think abstractly, consider more than one aspect of a problem at one time, and understand more complex meanings. See also *Concrete-Operational Stage*, *Preoperational Stage*, and *Sensorimotor Stage.*

Formal Operational Thinking (C-9; HS-8). See *Formal Operational Stage.*

Formative Evaluation (C-7; HS-6). A type of *program evaluation*; an *assessment* of a program activity prior to it being fully implemented or of an existing program that has been adapted. These types of evaluations are done while the program is running and are in contrast to *summative evaluations*. Contrasts with *Summative Evaluation*.

Forming (C-8; HS-7). The beginning stage of *group therapy* following Bruce *Tuckman's stages of group development*, wherein the group meets each other and begins to develop goals and addresses them together.

Formula Responses (C-6; HS-5). A structured *basic empathic response* that is typically made by beginning helpers and uses a "You feel (enter feeling word) because (enter content)" structure or related formulaic phrasing.

Foucault, Michel (1926 - 1984) (C-7; HS-3). A French philosopher and author who influenced the development of *narrative therapy* concerning how language is created and used by privileged people to bolster their belief in truth and reality and thus prop up their privileged *status* and *oppression* of other people.

Foundation, Delivery, Management, and Accountability (C-6; HS-1). The four systems of the *ASCA national model.*

Foundational Rules (C-3; HS-3). Guidelines and regulations for practicing counseling or when making ethical decisions (e.g., protecting the *autonomy* of the client, promoting the good of society).

Foundational Skills (C-6; HS-6). The basic skills used in developing a helping relationship such as the ability to listen, show *empathy*, and use *silence* effectively.

Founder of the Counseling Field (C-10; HS-2). See *Parsons, Frank.*

Founder of Vocational Guidance (C-10; HS-2). See *Parsons, Frank.*

Fourth and Fifth Forces (C-9; HS-5). *Multicultural counseling* and *social justice advocacy* are sometimes called the fourth and *fifth forces* of counseling, as their importance follows that of *psychoanalysis*, *behaviorism*, and *existential-humanism.*

Fowler, James (1940 - 2015) (C-7; HS-5). An American theologian who formulated an important, stage-based theory of faith development. See also *Faith Development, Fowler's Theory of.*

Frankl, Viktor (1905 - 1997) (C-9; HS-6). An influential Austrian *psychiatrist* and neurologist who became an *existential-humanistic* theorist and who is considered one of the founders of *existential therapy*, which he called *logotherapy.* One of the many theorists that fueled the diversity of counseling theories during the 1950s and 1960s.

Free Association (C-9; HS-5). In *psychoanalysis*, a technique that encourages clients to talk about anything that comes to mind on a given topic, idea, image, or word. For example, a therapist might ask the client to free associate on the word "mother" and the client responds "absent." This technique can be used to explore *unconscious* thoughts or feelings.

Freedom (C-7; HS-4). In *existential therapy*, freedom, or the condition of being free, is an important concept that can be examined within many contexts such as whether one experiences a sense of internal freedom, even when external forces prevent freedom via slavery, imprisonment, poverty, *oppression*, etc. *Viktor Frankl* argued the freedom to choose one's attitude or responses to circumstances cannot be taken away by external limiting forces.

Freedom Need (in Reality Therapy) (C-5; HS-3). One of the five needs that makes up one's *need-strength profile* in *reality therapy*. Also called *independence*.

***Freedom of Information Act* (C-8; HS-6).** Enacted in 1974, this U.S. federal law allows individuals to have access to any records maintained by a federal agency that contain personal information about the individual. States have enacted their own freedom of information act laws.

Frequency Distribution (C-8; HS-6). A method of understanding *test* scores by ordering a set of scores from high to low and listing the corresponding *frequency* of each score across from it.

Frequency/Frequencies (C-8; HS-6). The number of times each number, in a series of numbers, occurs. One way of reporting results in *descriptive statistics*.

Frequency Polygon (C-7; HS-5). A method of converting a *frequency distribution* of scores into a line graph. After combining scores by *class interval*, the intervals are placed along the *x*-axis and the frequency of scores along the *y*-axis.

Freud, Anna (1895 - 1982) (C-7; HS-3). The daughter of *Sigmund Freud*, she continued his work and developed many of her own ideas as an influential *psychoanalyst* in her own right. In particular, she expanded the definition and types of *defense mechanisms*.

Freud, Sigmund (1856 - 1939) (C-10; HS-8). Founder of *psychoanalysis*, the first comprehensive approach to *psychotherapy*. Freud developed his theory in the late 1800s to mid-1900s after dabbling with *hypnosis* at which point he realized that many of his patients' symptoms had psychological, not physical origins. His *psychosexual stages of development* offered one perspective on how personality is formed.

Freudian Slip (C-9; HS-5). Also known as *parapraxis*, when *unconscious* desires or internalized thoughts make themselves known in external speech, thought, memory, or other human behaviors. Most commonly refers to slips of the tongue although the *psychoanalytic* meaning of the concept goes deeper.

Friendly Visitors (C-5; HS-7). Volunteers in the late 1800s and early 1900s who worked with the poor and socially deprived for *charity organization societies*. They frequently stressed moral judgment and religious values while helping these individuals.

Fry, William (1924 - 2014) (C-3; HS-1). An influential *family therapist* and *psychiatrist* who was a member of the *Palo Alto Mental Research Institute*.

Full Potential (Rogers) (C-8; HS-7). Connected to an individual's *actualizing tendency*, the ability one has to achieve his or her best, or fullest, in life that *Carl Rogers* believed was inherent in all infants/children and the growing person. If left to grow unhindered in children, one's actualizing tendency will lead to healthy relationships, high *self-esteem*, and the attainment of one's full potential.

Fun Need (in Reality Therapy) (C-5; HS-4). One of the five needs that make up one's *need strength profile* in *reality therapy*. Also called *Enjoyment Need*.

Functional Behavior Analysis (FBA) (C-7; HS-6). In *behavior therapy*, a way of assessing and monitoring a person's behaviors using a systematic tool to chart those behaviors, the settings in which they occur, how often they occur, and other influences on the behavior. Used to develop comprehensive *treatment plans* to decrease certain behaviors.

Future Oriented (SFBT) (C-7; HS-6). In *solution-focused brief therapy*, helping that is focused on the future and to finding solutions, rather than on the past and problems.

G Factor (C-8; HS-6). See *General (g) Factor of Intelligence.*

"GAF" Scale (C-6; HS-4). See *Global Assessment of Functioning Scale.*

Gale Database (C-7; HS-6). A type of *electronic database* search engine that can be of assistance when one is conducting research in education, counseling, and human services literature. See also *EBSCO*, *ERIC* and *PsychINFO.*

Galt, John Minson, II (1819 - 1862) (C-4; HS-4). A physician and mental asylum administrator who employed humane methods of treating the mentally ill in the public mental hospitals of the 1800s in the U.S.

Galton, Sir Francis (1822 - 1911) (C-6; HS-2). An English scientist in many fields, he examined the relationship of sensorimotor responses to intelligence and hypothesized that individuals who had a quicker reaction time and stronger grip strength were superior intellectually. One of the first *experimental psychologists.*

Galton's Board (C-4; HS-2). See *Quincunx.*

Gamblers Anonymous (GA) (C-8; HS-8). An international *twelve step* program providing *support groups* and related assistance for individuals desiring to quit gambling.

Gardner, Howard (1943 -) (C-9; HS-6). An American *psychologist* who vehemently opposed current constructs of intelligence measurement and developed his own theory of multiple intelligences asserting that there are eight or nine intelligences, including verbal-linguistic, mathematical-logical, musical, visual-spatial, bodily-kinesthetic, interpersonal, intrapersonal, naturalist, and potentially, existential intelligence.

Gatekeeping (C-8; HS-7). The ethical role and duty practitioners, educators, *supervisors*, and licensed therapists have to protect their clients from harm by unfit or impaired professionals or who are in training or are working in the mental health field.

Gaussian Curve/Distribution (C-8; HS-6). See *Normal/Bell-Shaped Curve.*

Gay (C-9; HS-9). A *sexual orientation* usually referring to men who have a same-sex attraction. Sometimes used to refer to *lesbians*, *bisexual*, *transgender*, *queer*, *questioning*, *intersex*, and *ally* individuals.

Gemeinschaftsgefühl (C-7; HS-3). A term from *individual psychology* that refers to an innate evolutionary desire among individuals to relate to one another and to establish a sense of belonging.

Gender (C-9; HS-9). Whether one is masculine, feminine, or another gender (e.g., *third gender*, Two Spirit). Frequently confused with and assumed to mean biological sex (especially on surveys and many government forms), but in reality it is separate and based on socially constructed cultural norms. For example, one can be biologically female but have a masculine (or male) *gender identity*, which is a closely related term.

See also *Gender Expression*, *Gender Identity*, and *Gender Non-Conforming.*

Gender Affirmation Surgery (C-9; HS-9). See *Sex Reassignment Surgery.*

Gender Aware Therapy (C-9; HS-5). Approaches to counseling that focus on the ways that men and women are impacted by cultural stereotypes and how each gender can develop new, more adaptive roles.

Gender Binary (C-8; HS-7). The belief that there are only two *genders* and that every person is one of those two. This undermines those who do not identify as a traditional male or a traditional female. See also *Gender*, *Gender Identity*, *Gender Expression*, and *Gender Non-Conforming.*

Gender Dysphoria (C-7; HS-4). Formerly termed, "gender identity disorder," this category includes those individuals who experience significant distress with the *sex* of which they were born and with associated *gender roles.* This *diagnosis* has been separated from the category of *sexual disorders*, as it is now accepted that gender dysphoria does not relate to a person's sexual attractions.

Gender Expression (C-8; HS-7). A person's external, or outward, display of their internal *gender identity* (masculinity to femininity) through choices in fashion, hair styles, adornments (e.g., make-up, jewelry), behaviors, or other observable expressions. See also *Gender*, *Gender Identity*, and *Gender Non-Conforming.*

Gender Identity (C-8; HS-7). A person's internal, self-identity and experience of being on the masculine to feminine *gender* spectrum (or *third gender* and other gender identities) but is separate from *gender expression.* For example, some individuals are born female and have a feminine *gender identity*, although others are born female and have a masculine *gender identity.* In another example, someone born a male may have a *transgender* identity (feeling inside their identity is feminine or female) but choose a masculine *gender expression* in clothing. See also *Gender*, *Gender Expression*, and *Gender Non-Conforming.*

Gender Neutral (C-7; HS-7). A unisex or inclusive policy, space, language (e.g., pronouns), or other social construct, such as a gender neutral bathroom, that is open to people of all *gender identities* and expressions. See also *Gender.*

Gender Non-Conforming (GNC) (C-8; HS-7). A person who identifies with a *gender identity* outside of the *gender binary* of masculine vs. feminine. Some gender non-conforming individuals feel that they are a mix of the two traditional *genders.* See also *Gender*, *Gender Expression*, and *Gender Identity.*

Gender Reassignment Surgery (C-9; HS-9). See *Sex Reassignment Surgery.*

Gender Role (C-6; HS-6). The cultural norms which dictate *gender* behaviors, attitudes, values, and beliefs appropriate for individuals based on their *assigned sex* at birth. See also *Gender.*

Gender Splitting (C-5; HS-4). The notion, by *Daniel Levinson*, that traditional *stereotypes* were the center point for the struggles of men and women culturally, socially, institutionally, and within one's individual *psyche.* Although gender splitting is much less today, such differences, and the stereotypes that they yield, highlight struggles within *self*, at work, and in society (e.g., how much time should a dad spend parenting vs. working).

Gender Transition (C-8; HS-8). See *Transition.*

Gender Variant (C-6; HS-6). Individuals whose *gender identity* and expression are different from societal *norms* or commonly accepted *gender roles.*

Genderqueer (C-6; HS-6). A term used to describe individuals whose *gender identity* does not fit the *gender binary.* Usually, this is a self-applied term.

***General Aptitude Test Battery* (*GATB*) (C-6; HS-3).** One of the first *tests* to measure multiple aptitudes. It was developed by the U.S. Employment Service. See also *Multiple Aptitude Test.*

General (*g*) Factor of Intelligence (C-8; HS-6). A belief that there is an underlying, overall, factor that mediates intelligence and is separate from *specific (s) factors* that are responsible for certain areas of ability (e.g., musical ability, kinesthetic ability, etc.). It was popularized by *Charles Edward Spearman.*

General Systems Theory (C-7; HS-5). Originally proposed by the biologist Ludwig von Bertalanffy, this theory postulates that any system (e.g., individual, family, community, institution) has regulatory mechanisms that maintain its unique *homeostasis* while it interacts with other systems. See also *Cybernetics.*

General, Typical, Variant (C-5; HS-2). In *consensual qualitative research* (*CQR*), determining if a category is general (meaning that it is common), typical (meaning that it occurs in half the cases), or variant (meaning that it is unusual).

Generalist (C-3; HS-10). The term used to describe the general interdisciplinary knowledge and work of the human service professional or someone who practices human service work without having a particular specialty.

Generalizability (C-9; HS-7). The ability to apply research findings to other settings or populations.

Generalization (C-8; HS-7). In *operant conditioning*, the tendency for *stimuli* that are similar to a *conditioned stimulus* to take on the power of the conditioned stimulus.

Generativity vs. Stagnation (Middle/Late Adulthood) (C-9; HS-7). *Erikson's* seventh stage of *psychosocial development*, where the healthy adult becomes concerned about the meaningfulness of his or her life through such activities as work, volunteering, parenting, and community activities.

Generosity Error (C-6; HS-3). Error that occurs when an individual rates another person inaccurately because he or she identifies with the person being rated.

Genetic Counseling (C-8; HS-7). Counseling individuals for problems associated with having, or potentially having, a genetic disorder.

Genital Stage (C-9; HS-4). *Sigmund Freud's* fifth and final *psychosexual stage of development*, occurring at puberty and continuing through the lifespan, where sexual energy is focused on social activities and love relationships and where unresolved issues of earlier stages emerge. See also *Anal Stage*, *Latency Stage*, *Oral Stage*, and *Phallic Stage.*

Genogram (C-8; HS-7). A map of an individual's family tree that includes relationship histories over a few generations, and may also include history of medical illnesses, *mental disorders*, substance use, family expectations, significant relationships, cultural issues, and other concerns relevant to counseling. Special symbols may be used to assist in creating this map. A type of *Record and Personal Document.* See also *Family Life Fact Chronology.*

Genuineness (C-10; HS-8). The quality of expressing one's true feelings and being *congruent* or "in sync" with one's feelings, thoughts, and behaviors. Popularized by *Carl Rogers* and listed as one of his three *core conditions* of helping along with *empathy* and *unconditional positive regard.* One of the *common factors.* Sometimes called *congruence*, *realness*, *authenticity*, or *transparency.*

Geriatrics (C-8; HS-8). The focus on health care of older adults.

Gerontological Counseling (C-9; HS-8). A specialized area of counseling focusing on the *holistic* health needs of older adults and older persons.

Gerontological Settings (C-7; HS-7). Settings where *clinical mental health counselors* and human service professionals may be employed that focuses on the aging or older adults, such as a nursing home.

Gerontology (C-9; HS-9). The professional field dedicated to the study of aging and older adults connected to their biopsychosocial and *cognitive development.* It can be found as a standalone field or a sub-field of other professions such as *psychology*, sociology, *social work*, human services, etc.

Gestalt (C-8; HS-4). In *Gestalt therapy*, the idea that one tends to view the whole, as opposed to its component parts. In reference to *therapy*, it suggests that one cannot *deconstruct* a person into his or her component parts (i.e., the whole is greater than the sum of its parts). It also suggests that our most immediate needs float into *consciousness* and that all other parts of *self*, fall into the background.

Gestalt Consultation (C-4; HS-2). *Consultation* that applies *Gestalt therapy* principles.

Gestalt Group Counseling (C-6; HS-3). A type of *group counseling* based on *Gestalt therapy.*

Gestalt Psychology (C-6; HS-4). Developed by psychologist Kurt Goldstein, this *experimental psychology* paradigm suggests that an organized whole is more than the sum of its parts. This concept was integrated into *Gestalt therapy* by its developer *Fritz Perls.*

Gestalt Therapy (C-8; HS-3). Founded by *Fritz Perls*, who postulated that we are born with the capacity to embrace an infinite number of personality dimensions. With the mind, body, and soul operating in unison, the individual is in a constant state of *need identification* and *need fulfillment.* However, parental dictates, social mores, and peer norms prevent a person from attaining needs which results in *resistances* or *blockages* to the experiencing of the person's needs. Needs therefore get pushed out of *awareness.* Gestalt therapy suggests that our experience = awareness = reality. One of the philosophies that anchors Gestalt therapy is related to the *figure-ground* in a person's life and suggests that one's current needs come to the foreground. Gestalt therapy emphasizes a *holistic* view of humans. See also *Gestalt Psychology.*

Gestalt Therapy Techniques (C-8; HS-4). A wide range of techniques that are used to help the client understand his or her *unfinished business* and move the client to the satisfaction of unmet needs based in *Gestalt therapy.* Some include: the dialogue game, *empty chair technique*, feeding the client a sentence, "I have a secret," "I take responsibility for…," making the rounds, making statements out of questions, playing the projection, and using "I" language."

G.I. Bill (C-5; HS-2). Providing support to many American military veterans, it enabled many individuals who fought during World War II to go to college and was one of the reasons for the revival of student personnel services in higher education. It is still used today by veterans.

Giftedness (C-8; HS-6). Defined differently by school systems, an *assessment* of the intellectual, and sometimes creative, ability of a child that may result in special services in the schools.

Gilligan, Carol (1936 -) (C-9; HS-7). A *feminist psychologist* who questioned some of the work of *Lawrence Kohlberg*. See also *Gilligan's Theory of Women's Moral Development*.

Gilligan's Theory of Women's Moral Development (C-9; HS-7). In contrast to men's *moral development*, which tends to be *individualistically oriented* and focused on *autonomy* and independence, *Gilligan* suggested that women's *moral development* is focused on a standard of care that is concerned with how choices affect others. Gilligan also found that adolescent girls would often lose their voice, but as grown women, find it again.

Ginzberg, Eli (1911 - 2002) (C-7; HS-3). An American economist who formulated an early developmental model of *career development*.

Giving Advice (C-10; HS-10). A technique in *counseling* that involves the helper dictating what the client should do. Giving advice should be used cautiously, or avoided entirely, as it can create dependency and defensiveness in the client.

Glasser, William (1925 - 2013) (C-10; HS-7). An American *psychiatrist*, author, and counselor who founded *reality therapy* which he eventually based on *choice theory*. Throughout his *career*, he wrote numerous publications on his ideas, in some cases applying them to school and business settings, and founded the William Glasser Institute for training and research into his methods. One of the many theorists that fueled the diversity of counseling theories during the 1960s.

GLBT (C-10; HS-10). An acronym that stands for *gay*, *lesbian*, *bisexual*, and *transgender*. See also *Lesbian*, *Gay*, *Bisexual*, *Transgender*, *Queer*, *Questioning*, *Intersex*, and *Ally* and *LGBTQQIA*.

Globalization (C-9; HS-9). The process of internationalization, and in counseling and human services, the expansion and integration of counseling and human services around the globe. See also *International Registry of Counselor Education Programs* (*IRCEP*).

Gnosticism (C-4; HS-2). A general term that encompasses many early religious and philosophical perspectives. It deemphasized the material world and emphasized the importance of gnosis (e.g. wisdom, knowledge, enlightenment, unity with God) instead. Followers of Gnosticism generally encourage restraint from physical and personal needs, such as taking vows of poverty or abstaining from *sex*, in order to seek wisdom through aiding others in need and engaging in other ascetic practices.

***GOE* (C-7; HS-4).** See *Guide for Occupational Exploration*.

Going Around (C-6; HS-2). A process in *psychoanalytic group therapy* where all group members participate, one at a time, in expressing their thoughts and feelings.

Good Enough Mothering (C-6; HS-3). See *Good Enough Parenting.*

Good Enough Parenting (C-6; HS-3). Developed from the ideas of *D. W. Winnicott* and *object relations theory*, the idea that to be a quality parent one does not have to be a perfect parent and that all parents make errors or mistakes. A good parent provides stable, normal, healthy, attentive, reasonable, understanding parenting to their children and has similar expectations for their children as they grow. See also *Good Enough Mothering.*

Good Girl-Nice Boy Orientation (C-7; HS-5). In *Kohlberg*'s *conventional level*, when moral decisions are based on social conformity and mutualism ("I scratch your back and you scratch mine"). Stage 3 in the *conventional level.*

Goodness-of-Fit (C-6; HS-2). A statistical *test* used in *confirmatory factor analysis* to determine the extent to which a model or data set matches a pre-established theoretical construct.

Gould, Roger (1935 -) (C-4; HS-2). An American *psychiatrist* who formulated a theory of adult psychological development that suggested that in childhood we have illusions of safety, and these are slowly dismantled as we develop through life. His ideas were largely used in the bestselling book "Passages," by Gail Sheehy.

Grade Equivalent Scoring (C-7; HS-4). A type of *standard score* calculated by comparing an individual's score to the average score of others at the same grade level. It is important to note that generally, an individual who is performing much better than this or her grade level is not doing so at the grade level noted, but is performing better than his or her own grade level. Similarly, a person performing much worse than his or her grade level, is not performing at the grade level noted, but is performing worse than his or her grade level.

***Graduate Record Exam* (*GRE*) (C-7; HS-5).** A c*ognitive ability* test used for admission into graduate college.

Grandiose Irrational Beliefs (C-8; HS-5). Also called *mustabatory irrational beliefs*, in *rational emotive behavior therapy* which include the *three core irrational beliefs Ellis* focused on in his later writings. These include the idea that: (1) one must, all the time, do important tasks well and be approved by significant others or else one is inadequate and unlovable; (2) that other people absolutely must treat others fairly and justly or else they are rotten, damnable people, and; (3) that conditions under which one lives must absolutely always be the way one wants them to be, give one almost immediate gratification, and not require one to work too hard to change or improve them, or else it is awful and impossible for one to be happy at all.

Grandma's Law (C-6; HS-4). See *Premack's Principle.*

Graphic Scale (C-7; HS-4). See *Likert-Type Scale.*

***GRE* (C-7; HS-5).** See *Graduate Record Exam.*

Great Society (C-7; HS-7). The term given to the numerous social programs (e.g., in civil rights, *social welfare*, education) generated by President Lyndon Johnson.

Grief, Stages of (C-9; HS-7). Popularized by *Elisabeth Kübler-Ross*, five experiences individuals who are grieving may go through or become stuck within during the grieving process. They are denial, anger, bargaining, *depression*, and acceptance. Originally developed in connection to terminally ill people and their significant others, and seen as common experiences rather than a linear progression through the stages, they have been generalized for any form of grief or loss, including loss of relationships, *jobs*, pets, freedom, etc.

Griggs v. Duke Power Company **(C-3; HS-3).** A U.S. Supreme Court decision asserting that *tests* used for hiring and advancement at work must show that they can predict *job* performance for all groups.

Grounded Theory (C-7; HS-4). A research process in which a broad research question is examined in a multitude of ways that eventually leads to the emergence of a theory. Process elements include preparing, data collection, note taking, coding, and writing and involves *saturation* of data sources. A type of *Qualitative Research.*

Group Cohesion (C-7; HS-7). The connection that individuals feel with each other as part of their group experience.

Group Counseling (C-8; HS-7). *Groups* that are usually focused on prevention and *wellness*, self-enhancement, increased *insight*, *self-actualization*, and *conscious* as opposed to *unconscious* motivations. See also *Group Therapy.*

Group Dynamics (C-8; HS-7). The ongoing interactions and interrelationships among the group members and between the leader and group members.

Group Identity (C-6; HS-6). Relative to a cross-cultural understanding of the person, along with *individual identity* and *universal identity*, one of three identities that make up the person. The group identity has to do with shared values and customs that individuals have with specific cultural groups with which they identify.

Group Leadership Styles (C-6; HS-4). Various techniques adopted by group leaders that are based on the personality of the leader, their theory of group leadership, and on the *stage of group development.*

Group Level (C-6; HS-4). In the *tripartite model of personal identity*, the group level relates to aspects of the person that can vary based on the cultural and ethnic groups to which the client belongs. See also *Culturally Competent Helping.*

Group Membership Behavior (C-6; HS-6). Behaviors taken on by group members that are a function of the personality of the member and the *stage of group development.* Behaviors often mimic those in one's "real" life.

Group Process (C-8; HS-7). The changes that occur in a group as a function of the developmental stages through which the group will pass.

Group Supervision (C-7; HS-6). A type of *consultation* in which a practitioner meets with other practitioners in a group setting and receives *clinical supervision* from a more experienced *clinician* who can give feedback to all of the members of the group. Advantages include being exposed to multiple perspectives about an issue, viewing multiple ways that helpers may respond to clients, hearing about different kinds of *interventions* and educational opportunities, being able to learn how to do *supervision* by watching others undergo it, obtaining feedback from more than one individual, and normalizing experiences by seeing others that are dealing with similar issues

Group Therapy (C-8; HS-7). Usually, such groups are focused upon deep-seated, long-term issues, remediation of severe pathology, and personality reconstruction. See also *Group Counseling.*

Group Work (C-8; HS-8). A wide range of *group counseling* and related activities that assist in personal growth, and include *self-help groups*, *psychoeducational groups*, and *counseling* and *therapy groups.* Group work was an early focus of *social workers* that came out of the work of those in *charity organization societies* and the *settlement movement.*

Groups (C-9; HS-8). Whenever individuals function together in a systematic manner, they are considered a group. All groups are affected by *systems theory* and can be understood by examining the dynamic interaction of their members and how that interaction results in specific communication patterns, power dynamics, hierarchies, and the system's unique *homeostasis.* Groups that assist in personal growth include *self-help groups*, *psychoeducational groups*, and *counseling* and *therapy groups.*

Growth Stage (C-8; HS-3). Stage 1 of *Donald Super's lifespan theory of career development*, occurring between birth and age 14 years, where the individual becomes aware of interests and abilities related to the world of *work* and begins to compare his or her abilities with those of peers. See also *Exploration*, *Establishment*, *Maintenance*, and *Deceleration/Disengagement Stages*

Guidance (C-7; HS-7). A term that first appeared around the 1600s and was defined as "the process of guiding an individual." See also *Vocational Guidance* and *Guidance Counselor.*

Guidance Counselor (C-8; HS-7). The former and outdated term used for *school counselors.* See also *School Counselor.*

Guidance Groups (C-8; HS-8). See *Psychoeducational Groups.*

***Guide for Occupational Exploration* (*GOE*) (C-7; HS-5).** A sourcebook, and now also a website, to examine interests in relation to potential *jobs* and *occupations.*

Guided Imagery Exercises (C-8; HS-7). Within *individual psychology*, mental exercises that helpers lead their clients through to imagine being or behaving in new ways in life and relationships. Helpers from many theoretical approaches employ similar guided imagery techniques.

Guidelines for Psychological Practice with Girls and Women (C-6; HS-5). Guidelines developed by the *American Psychological Association* for clinical practice with girls and women.

Guidelines for Psychologists Conducting Growth Groups (C-7; HS-6). Ethical guidelines for leading groups developed in response to the mishandling of some groups during the 1960s and 1970s.

Guilford, J. P. (1897 - 1987) (C-6; HS-1). An American *psychologist* who developed a multifactor/multidimensional model of intelligence based on 180 factors. His three-dimensional model can be represented as a cube and involves the interaction of three kinds of cognitive ability: operations, contents, and products.

Guntrip, Harry (1901 - 1975) (C-3; HS-1). A British *psychologist* and a key *object relations therapy* theorist.

Habituation (C-7; HS-6). Needing more of something in order to experience the same results. A common concept within *substance abuse*, *medication management*, or *behavior modification* programs. For example, a frequent *heroin* user may require more and more of the drug to approach a similar experience each time the drug is used. Sometimes also referred to as "tolerance."

Haldol (C-5; HS-4). A *psychotropic medication* and *controlled substance* that is an *antipsychotic*.

Haley, Jay (1923 - 2007) (C-7; HS-5). An influential American *family counselor* who was one of the prime researchers at the *Mental Research Institute* and developed a problem-solving approach to therapy called *strategic therapy* and *strategic family therapy.*

Halfway House (C-7; HS-8). Temporary living establishments where people coping with *addictions*, incarceration, psychiatric hospitalization, or related issues begin a reintroduction into living in a community after a period of intensive, often inpatient, treatment or confinement. The resident is seen as being halfway back to living on one's own. These living situations may provide a safe place to live, often have strict rules of conduct (e.g., curfews, finding employment), and may also provide other services to support transitioning to healthy living.

Hall, G. S. (1846 - 1924) (C-5; HS-3). A prolific *psychologist* who worked with *Wundt* and eventually set up his own experimental lab at John Hopkins University. Hall became a mentor to other great American psychologists and was the founder and first president of the *American Psychological Association* in 1892.

Hallucinations (C-5; HS-4). Having sensations that seem to be based in reality, but actually do not exist outside of the person. Hallucinations can be auditory, visual, or sensing (e.g., feeling things crawling up one's skin, smelling odors that do not exist). Visual hallucinations tend to be the most serious, although all hallucinations can represent a *decompensating* mental state, often are associated with *psychosis*, and should be treated quickly and thoughtfully. Contrast with *Delusions*.

Halo Effect (C-7; HS-5). When the overall impression of an individual clouds the rating of that person in one or more select areas.

***Halstead-Reitan Battery* (C-5; HS-1).** Developed by Halstead and modified by his graduate student Reitan, a method of *neuropsychological assessment* that provides cutoff scores or indexes of impairment to identify individuals who have suffered brain-damage. This *assessment* takes 5-6 hours to administer and includes eight core *tests.* There is not strong *psychometric* support regarding the *validity*, *reliability*, and norming of this measure.

Handicap (C-9; HS-9). An outmoded term for someone with a *disability.*

Happenstance Learning Theory (C-6; HS-1). Developed by *John Krumboltz*, a *career counseling* theory that suggests being involved in a wide variety of interests and activities makes one more likely to benefit from unplanned events.

Harm Reduction Theory (C-8; HS-8). Practices that seek to reduce the harm associated with the use of *alcohol*, psychoactive drugs, or other problematic behaviors in people unable or unwilling to stop the problematic behavior. It seeks to prevent or reduce harm from the behavior by developing plans to reduce, but not eliminate the behavior. With alcohol use, it contrasts with the *disease model of alcoholism*.

Hate Crime (C-8; HS-8). Any derogatory, harassing, violent, or discriminatory acts committed against legally protected classes of individuals who are seen to be different from the perceived majority members of a community, such as violent acts committed against someone for being of a different *race*, *religion*, or *sexual orientation*. Different groups are protected under hate crime laws in different jurisdictions. See also *Discrimination*.

Hawthorne Effect (C-7; HS-5). Also known as the *observer effect*, a phenomenon related to how individuals under observation (e.g., those in a research study) may alter their behavior due to being aware of the fact that they are under observation.

Hayes, Steven (1948 -) (C-3; HS-1). A scientist, author, educator and major contributor to *acceptance and commitment therapy* (*ACT*).

Head Start (C-7; HS-7). A U.S. federally funded program, started in the 1970s, which provides an intellectually stimulating and nurturing environment to disadvantaged preschool children. One of a number of legislative acts during the 1960s that provided opportunities for minorities and the poor and helped to reshape attitudes toward social problems.

Health Care Management (C-5; HS-4). The overarching administration of health care issues. Human service professionals and counselors will increasingly be dealing with a wide variety of health care issues related to the *Affordable Care Act*, and their ability to be providers for a wide range of insurance and health care management systems will likely increase (e.g., *HMO*s, TRICARE, Veterans Administration hospitals).

***Health Insurance Portability and Accountability Act* (*HIPAA*) (C-10; HS-10).** Relative to client rights, an act that ensures the privacy of client records and limits sharing of such information by restricting the amount of personal information that can be shared without the client's consent and allows clients to have access to their records.

Health Maintenance Organization (HMO) (C-6; HS-4). A *managed health care* system that offers subscribers a pool of designated helping providers (e.g., doctors) from which they can choose.

Health Services (C-3; HS-1). One area in higher education that individuals with a master's degree in *student affairs and college counseling* sometimes work, including doctors' offices, hospitals, and related medical settings.

Heidegger, Martin (1889 – 1976) (C-5; HS-2). A philosopher whose ideas were influential to the development of *existential therapy* and the field of *phenomenology*.

Heinz Dilemma, The (C-7; HS-5). A *moral dilemma* given to adolescent boys that helped *Lawrence Kohlberg* formulate his theory of moral development. The dilemma had to do with the ethics of a man breaking into a lab to obtain medicine for his wife who was dying.

Helms's White Identity Model (C-5; HS-4). A model for increasing helpers' *competence* for working with clients from diverse *cultures*. Includes the following stages: contact, disintegration, reintegration, pseudoindependence, *immersion*, emersion, and *autonomy*.

Helper-Centered (C-9; HS-9). In contrast to being *client-centered*, when the helper directs the content and flow of the session and focuses on problem's s/he identifies needing change.

Herd Instinct (C-4; HS-3). See *Mob Instinct*.

Here-and-Now (C-8; HS-6). When the mental health professional has the client focus on what is happening in the moment (or present reality) of counseling, such as exploring *emotions*, as opposed to the *there and then*, which is focusing on the past. Often used in *existential-humanistic* approaches (e.g., *Gestalt therapy*).

Heritability (C-8; HS-7). The probability of passing down an inheritable trait.

Hermaphrodite (C-6; HS-5). Colloquially, a person born with a combination of male and female genitalia, mixed chromosomes, gonads, etc. This term has been falsely used for *intersex* persons. The term is outdated and seen as derogatory. The actual biological meaning of hermaphrodite is an organism that is both fully male and fully female and is capable of self-reproduction or changing sex to reproduce, which is impossible for humans but common in the many plants and animals. See also *Intersex*.

Hermeneutical Psychology (C-4; HS-2). An early name *Jung* used for his theoretical approach before settling on *analytical psychology*. Hermeneutic implies a branch of *psychology* that has to do with interpretation.

Heroin (C-7; HS-7). An *opioid* and *controlled substance* originally used to treat pain. It can be given orally, injected intravenously, or smoked and is highly addictive. Its illegal sale and use has grown exponentially in many countries recently.

Herr, Edwin L. (1933 - 2016) (C-6; HS-1). An influential counselor educator and leader in the field of *school counseling* and *guidance*, having held many higher education positions and counseling leadership posts. Among other achievements, he is a past-president of the *American Cocounseling Association*, *Association for Counselor Education and Supervision*, and *Chi Sigma Iota* and was the first director of the Pennsylvania Department of Education's Bureau of Guidance Services and the Bureau of Pupil Personnel Services.

Heteronormativity (C-7; HS-4). A social construct that assumes that *heterosexuality* is the only *sexual orientation*. Often, seen in the form of *microaggressions*, which reinforce the marginalization of the *LGBT* community. See also *Heterosexual* and *Heterosexism/Heterosexist*.

Heterosexism/Heterosexist (C-9; HS-8). The conscious *discrimination*, denigration, or stigmatizing of a person for non-*heterosexual* behaviors. Preferred over the word *homophobia*.

Heterosexual (C-9; HS-9). Sexual attraction to the opposite sex.

Heterosexual-Homosexual Rating Scale (C-4; HS-2). See *Kinsey Scale*.

Heuristic (C-7; HS-3). The process of gathering information that can be used in an investigation. Something that is researchable and testable.

Hierarchy/Hierarchies (C-8; HS-7). In families and in systems, the ways in which individuals interact that supports the power dynamics within the system. For example, usually in families, parents are at the top of a hierarchy because they yield the most power.

Hierarchy of Needs (C-8; HS-8). In *Abraham Maslow's hierarchical theory*, the postulation that lower-order needs must be fulfilled before higher-order needs. The needs are (1) physiological needs, (2) safety needs, (3) *love and belonging*, (4) *self-esteem*, and (5) *self-actualization* in ascending order.

High School Counselor (C-8; HS-5). One of three levels of *school counseling*. U.S. states sometimes credential K-12, or sometimes credential at specific grade levels.

Higher-Level Empathy (C-7; HS-7). On the *Carkhuff scale*, above a "level 3." See also *Advanced Empathic Responses.*

High-Level Distancing Tasks (C-7; HS-2). In *narrative therapy* tasks assigned to clients to help distance them from their problem stories. For example, after having accomplished a *low-level distancing task* (a person discusses changing by developing a new loving identity), a high-level distancing task is eventually completed, such as a ceremony to celebrate the development of the new loving identity with caring friends and family.

High-Stakes Testing (C-7; HS-4). The term used to describe the pressure placed on examinees, teachers, administrators, and others as a result of the major decisions that are made from the use of tests, usually national standardized tests such as the *SATs* and those used as the result of *No Child Left Behind.*

***HIPAA* (C-10; HS-10).** See *Health Insurance Portability and Accountability Act.*

Hippocrates (460 BCE - 370 BCE) (C-5; HS-4). A renowned Greek philosopher who was one of the first individuals in recorded history to reflect on the human condition and is considered the father of medicine. See also *Hippocratic Oath.*

Hippocratic Oath (C-8; HS-6). Allegedly developed by *Hippocrates*, it is the medical and ethical principle which states "do no harm" to clients or patients. See also *Non-maleficence.*

Hispanic (C-8; HS-7). An individual having an ethnic heritage, and who identifies with that heritage, from Spain or countries of Spanish historical and cultural heritage (e.g., Hispaniola, Cuba). Contrast with *Latinos/Latinas.* For example, Brazil is not a Hispanic country, as the primary cultural and historical influence comes from Portugal, not Spain, and most citizens speak Portuguese rather than Spanish. Some people are both *Hispanic* and *Latino/Latina* and others are one or the other.

Histogram (C-6; HS-2). A *bar graph. Frequency distributions* can easily be converted to histograms, or other similar graphs, by combining scores into *class intervals* and plotting the intervals on a graph with the intervals on the *x*-axis and the frequency of scores along the *y*-axis.

Historical Research (C-8; HS-5). A type of *qualitative research* which relies on the systematic collection of information through a literature review to describe and analyze conditions and events from the past in an effort to answer research questions.

HIV (C-9; HS-9). Stands for *Human Immunodeficiency Virus*. The virus attacks one's immune system, eventually leading to the onset of *AIDS*. It is estimated that in the United States, about 45,000 new cases of HIV arise each year, and about 1.2 million Americans are living with HIV.

HMO (C-6; HS-4). See *Health Maintenance Organization.*

Holism (C-8; HS-6). The concept that mind, body, and spirit, and even the *conscious* and *unconscious*, cannot be separated, and that individuals are made of many aspects deserving full expression to become healthy. In contrast, those who follow a philosophy of *reductionism*, include *Freud*, who dissected the person into the *id*, *ego*, and *superego*, and *experimental psychologists*, who attempted to understand the individual relative to isolated aspects of behavior. The counseling field is considered to embrace holism. See also *Holistic Process.*

Holistic Process (C-4; HS-2). The idea that it is important to use multiple measures of assessment or to take into account the vast different aspects of a person if one is to draw adequate conclusions about a person. See also *Holism.*

Holland Code (C-8; HS-3). Six codes used to describe one's personality type that can be matched to specific *jobs*. The codes include: *realistic types*, who are individuals who are practical and have good physical skills; *investigative types*, who are *introverted* individuals interested in problem solving; *artistic types*, who are individuals who can skillfully express their imaginations; *social types*, who are verbally skilled individuals who enjoy social situations and care for others; *enterprising types*, who are persuasive people who like to lead; and *conventional types*, who are individuals who think in concrete terms and prefer clerical tasks. When individuals' personality types are accurately matched to job types, there is a greater likelihood of job satisfaction. See also *Holland's Personality Theory of Occupational Choice.*

Holland's Personality Theory of Occupational Choice (C-8; HS-3). *John Holland* proposed that genetic predispositions and environmental influences lead people to develop a preferred method of living in the world, that some might call their personality. Holland suggested that if individuals could identify their unique personality styles, they could find *jobs* that best fit their personalities and ultimately find satisfaction in their *careers*. He thus created the *Holland code* which, for years, has been used in the *career counseling* process as it is predictive of satisfaction in jobs.

Holocaust, The (C-10; HS-10). The mass murder of 6 million Jewish people, and countless others, as a result of Adolf Hitler's Nazi Germany and collaborators.

Home Visit (C-7; HS-9). Meeting with a client in his or her home to check on his or her status and to ensure consistency in treatment.

Homeostasis (C-7; HS-5). The tendency for a system to maintain *equilibrium* and its usual way of functioning. A concept often used in understanding families.

Homework Assignments (C-8; HS-7). Assignments given to clients to complete outside of the helping sessions to reinforce new behaviors and new ways of thinking.

Often used in *cognitive-behavioral approaches.*

Homicidal Ideation (C-10; HS-10). Thoughts of causing physical harm, including death, to someone. One can have homicidal ideation, without homicidal intent, and clients need to be assessed for *homicidality*. See also *Homicidality, Assessment for Lethality.*

Homicidal Intent (C-10; HS-10). Making intended actions or threated actions to cause physical harm, including death, to someone. One can have *homicidal ideation*, without homicidal intent, and clients need to be assessed for *homicidality*. See also *Homicidality, Assessment for Lethality.*

Homicidality, Assessment for Lethality (C-7; HS-7). The process of evaluating if a client is posing an imminent danger to others, including but not limited to the degree to which the client has developed a plan to harm others, has the means to carry out the plan, is prepared to implement the plan, has rehearsed the plan, and has acted on the plan. See also *Risk Factors*, *Protective Factors*, *Homicidal Ideation* and *Homicidal Intent.*

Homophobia (C-7; HS-7). The implication that there is a fear/disorder within a person which makes that person *discriminate*, denigrate, or stigmatize another due to his or her non-*heterosexual* orientation. Today, the word *heterosexism* is preferred by many to describe such actions, as it removes the notion that such actions are the result of a disorder (*phobia*) and stresses the *conscious* decision to discriminate.

Homosexuality (C-7; HS-7). An outdated, and sometimes seen as a derogatory, *sexual orientation* term used to describe same-sex or same *gender* attraction. See also *Gay* and *Lesbian.*

Hormone Therapy (C-6, HS-6). Intake of hormones to enhance one's secondary *sex* characteristics to align with one's *gender identity*. For example, a male who is *transgender* may take Estrogen, a female hormone, to develop his breasts and other female sex characteristics.

Horney, Karen (1885 - 1952) (C-7; HS-3). An influential German *psychoanalyst* who was instrumental in developing *feminist psychology* and other ideas in *psychoanalysis.*

Hospice (C-8; HS-8). A care setting and type of treatment that focuses on terminally ill individuals where different helping professionals are employed.

Hotline (C-10; HS-10). See *Crisis Hotline.*

House Tree Person (HTP) (C-7; HS-3). A *projective personality test* in which the test-taker is instructed to draw a picture of a house, tree, and a person. Qualified test administrators ask a series of questions about the images the test-taker has drawn to make inferences about his or her personality and other mental abilities.

HS--BCP (C-3; HS-10). See *Human services--Board Certified Practitioner.*

Hull House (C-5; HS-9). A *settlement house* established in 1889 by *Jane Addams* in Chicago.

Human Resources (Field of) (C-3; HS-3). The professional field that deals with hiring, firing, training, payroll, benefits, and related employment and personnel management areas. May refer to the human resources department of an organization that handles these professional areas.

Human Service Professionals (C-7; HS-10). Persons who have earned an associate's or bachelor's degree, and less commonly a master's or doctoral degree, in human services or a closely related field and who work in a wide variety of human service agencies within the social services and whose practices are based on the guidelines of the *Council for Standards in Human Services Education* (*CSHSE*) and the *National Organization of Human Services* (*NOHS*).

Human Service Professionals, Roles and Functions (C-1; HS-9). A classification system developed in the 1960s for human service work, and sometimes still used in today's understanding of human service work. It includes *outreach worker*, *broker*, *advocate*, *evaluator*, *teacher/educator*, *behavior changer*, *mobilizer*, *consultant*, *community planner*, *caregiver*, *data manager*, *administrator*, and *assistant to specialist.*

Human Service Worker (C-5; HS-7). See *Human Service Professionals.*

Human Services (C-7; HS-10). A professional field with an emphasis on helping people, or meeting human needs, through interdisciplinary education that explores problem *prevention*, problem alleviation, and improving overall physical and mental health well-being. Today, degrees exist at all level of human service education.

Human Services—Board Certified Practitioner (HS-BCP) (C-3; HS-10). The credential that has been developed by the *Center for Credentialing and Education* (*CCE*) that human service professionals can obtain if they have adequate education, training, and have passed the *credentialing* exam.

Human Services Practitioner (C-7; HS-10). See *Human Service Professionals.*

Human Validation Process Model (C-6; HS-3). One name for *Virginia Satir's* model of *couples and family counseling*. See also *Change Process Model* and *Communication Theory.*

Humanistic Approach (C-9; HS-8). Developed by *Carl Rogers*, *Abraham Maslow*, and others, an approach to counseling that tends to be *nondirective*, facilitative, and present-centered in comparison with the more *directive* and past-focused approach of *psychoanalysis* and the more goal-oriented approach of *cognitive-behaviorists.*

Humanistic Counseling and Education (C-9; HS-8). Founded by *Carl Rogers*, *Abraham Maslow*, and others, this philosophy asserts that individuals are born with positive qualities that can flourish if the individual is provided a loving, caring, and nurturing environment. If such an environment was not present in early childhood, such qualities could be developed later in life if a nurturing environment is provided, such as those that can be produced in counseling and educational settings. See also *Actualizing Tendency.*

Humanistic Theory (C-7; HS-6). Theory based on *humanistic counseling and education* and the *humanistic approach.*

Humanistically Oriented Therapies (C-9; HS-8). Classification of helping therapies that emphasize the importance of focusing on the present, free will, and creating egalitarian relationships with clients. See also *Humanistic Approach.*

Husserl, Edmund (1859 - 1938) (C-6; HS-4). The German philosopher who created the school of thought of *phenomenology* and whose ideas have heavily influenced *existential therapy.*

Hydrocodone (C-8; HS-8). A synthetic *opiate* and *controlled substance* that is used to treat pain. It is generally taken orally and is highly addictive.

Hypnosis (C-9; HS-8). A trancelike state of *consciousness* induced by a person whose suggestions are voluntarily accepted by the client. See also *Hypnotherapy.*

Hypnotherapy (C-8; HS-6). A counseling technique where the counselor induces his or her client into a trancelike, or hypnotic, state of *consciousness.* In this state, it is believed that clients can gain *self-awareness*, make progress, and develop new neuropathways. See also *Hypnosis.*

Hypnotics (C-6; HS-5). Often called "sleeping pills" a class of *controlled substances* that are similar to sedatives and are generally *benzodiazepines* or *nonbenzodiazepines.*

Hypothesis (C-10; HS-8). An assumption or prediction that is derived from prior research and allows one to examine phenomena. See also *Null Hypothesis*, *Alternative Hypothesis*, and *Research Question.*

Hysteria (C-7; HS-4). See *Conversion Disorder.*

IAAOC (C-8; HS-3). See *International Association of Addictions and Offender Counselors.* A division of the *American Counseling Association.*

IAMFC (CHS-8; HS-3). See *International Association of Marriage and Family Counselors.* A division of the *American Counseling Association.*

Iatrogenic Disorder (C-3; HS-2). A disease, psychological disorder, or condition created through adverse exposure to medical or mental health treatment.

I-Can't-Stand-It-Itis (C-6; HS-4). A *cognitive distortion* in *rational emotive behavior therapy* that implies one constantly is complaining about the state of the world and their lives.

ICD (C-8; HS-4). See *International Classification of Diseases (ICD).*

Id (C-9; HS-5). According to *Freudian theory*, the *unconscious* portion of the *psyche* that is the source of instinctual drives and needs. See also *Ego* and *Superego.*

***IDEA* (C-8; HS-6).** See *Individuals with Disabilities Education Act.*

Ideal Self (C-8; HS-4). In *person-centered counseling*, the *self* we strive to be. Contrast with *Real Self.* See also *Idealized Self.*

Idealization (C-6; HS-3). A *defense mechanism* that involves the over exaggeration or over valuing of someone or something in order to avoid negative thoughts and feelings towards the object or person.

Idealized Self (C-8; HS-4). Related to the *person-centered counseling* idea of *ideal self*, the person that we wish we were, strive to be, or fantasize we are. See also *Ideal Self* and *Real Self.*

Ideation (C-8; HS-6). Of or relating to the creation of thoughts or ideas. Often used when discussing *suicidal ideation* or *homicidal ideation.*

Identification (C-6; HS-4). A *defense mechanism* that involves affiliating or associating with certain individuals or groups with unique beliefs or values to avoid negative or unwanted personal feelings. For example, some individuals who have been taken as hostages, have identified with the hostage takers plight as a mechanism to reduce their *anxiety.*

Identified Patient (IP) (C-8; HS-7). In a family or system (e.g., organization), the individual who is blamed for a behavioral problem, when actually, the family or system, "owns" the problem.

Identify Resources and Strengths (C-6; HS-5). A counseling approach used in *solution-focused brief therapy* and *solution-focused family therapy* to help clients identify potential areas of strength (as opposed to the client's tendency to focus on weak areas) in their lives and resources for helping them change.

Identifying and Challenging (C-6; HS-5). In *cognitive therapy*, the counseling approach of selecting and examining clients' *automatic thoughts.*

Identity (C-8; HS-7). All of the various roles or parts of *self* that form the person, and include such aspects as one's cultural affiliation, *career* focus, *sexual orientation, gender identity*, personality style, and more.

Identity vs. Role Confusion (Adolescence) (C-9; HS-7). *Erikson's* fifth stage of *psychosocial* development, in which adolescents begin to identify the temperament, values, interests, and abilities they hold. Self-understanding can lead to a strong sense of *identity*, whereas lack of self-understanding can lead to role confusion.

Idiosyncratic Rules (C-4; HS-3). Rules specific to each family that impact its functioning.

Idiosyncratic Stress (C-6; HS-5). According to *Minuchin*, unexpected interpersonal *stress* that impacts a family, such as a sudden illness or getting fired from a *job.*

IEP (C-8; HS-7). See *Individualized Education Plan.*

Ignorance of One's Own Racist Attitudes and Prejudices (C-8; HS-8). A person who has not spent time examining his or her own *racist* attitudes and *prejudices* and will *unconsciously* project negative and harmful attitudes onto others.

I–It Relationship (C-7; HS-4). In *existential therapy*, this type of relationship is characterized by helpers objectifying, diagnosing, emotionally distancing from, and using techniques "on" clients and is seen as detrimental to developing a successful therapeutic relationship. Contrast with *I-Thou Relationship.*

Illogical and Irrational Ways of Thinking (C-8; HS-7). Mechanisms clients use to cause *dysfunctional behaviors* and negative feelings in *cognitive-behavioral approaches.*

Imagery-Changing (C-7; HS-5). In *cognitive therapy*, the process by which clients change images to positively impact behaviors, thoughts, feelings, and physiological responses.

Imagery Exercises (C-7; HS-5). In *rational emotive behavior therapy*, a variety of exercises that help clients practice imaging healthier ways of acting.

Imaginal Exposure (C-5; HS-3). Using one's imagination in the helping process, such as imagining a fearful situation that causes *anxiety* in an effort to expose oneself to the fearful situation and eventually *extinguish* the fear. See also *Exposure Therapy.*

Imago (C-6; HS-3). In *psychoanalysis*, the *unconscious* idealized image of another person, such as a beloved mother or father, which impacts a person's behaviors.

Imitation (C-6; HS-3). See *Modeling.*

Immediacy (C-7; HS-5). A type of *self-disclosure* in which the counselor shares moment-to-moment thoughts or feelings with the client, usually about the helping relationship and appropriate to the ethical boundaries of the helping relationship.

Immersion (C-6; HS-6). The experiential and affective understanding of another *culture* by placing oneself within that culture, usually through some common activity with members of that culture. Also, the fifth stage of *Helm's White Identity Development Model.* It is an activity often used in the training of mental health professionals.

Impaired Helper/Counselor (C-9; HS-9). When a helping professional has become unable to ethically or effectively treat clients due to professional *burnout*, personal issues, or other issues that may cause the helper to negatively influence the helping relationship. See also *Compassion Fatigue* and *Vicarious Traumatization.*

Impasse Layer (C-6; HS-2). In *Gestalt therapy*, a part of the *structure of neurosis* (and the therapeutic process) when a client realizes he or she is playing a role in life rather than being *authentic.*

Impasses/Blockages (C-7; HS-4). In *Gestalt therapy*, unsatisfied needs from the past that prevent satisfaction of current needs.

Imperial Stage (C-6; HS-4). Stage 2 of *Robert Kegan's subject/object theory*, where a person can begin to control impulses and where needs, interests, and wishes become primary. See also *Incorporative Stage*, *Impulsive Stage*, *Interpersonal Stage*, *Institutional Stage*, and *Interindividual Stage*.

Impersonal Unconscious (C-6; HS-2). In *analytical psychology*, another term for what *Jung* called the *collective unconscious*.

Implosion Therapy (Implosive Therapy) (C-7; HS-4). A type of *behavior therapy* where clients are increasingly exposed to a *stimulus* which elicits a fear response until the fear response is *extinguished.* In implosion therapy, the stimulus is often imagined and the stimulus may be exaggerated (e.g., if one has a fear of snakes, one imagines oneself in a den of snakes). A type of *Exposure Therapy.*

Implosive Layer (C-6; HS-2). In *Gestalt therapy*, a part of the *structure of neurosis* (and the therapeutic process) when a client must choose who he or she really wants to be-that is, to live authentically as opposed to continually living in a made up role.

Impulsive Stage (C-6; HS-4). Stage 1 of *Robert Kegan*'s *subject/object theory*, where a person has limited control over his or her actions and acts spontaneously to have needs met. See also *Incorporative Stage*, *Imperial Stage*, *Interpersonal Stage*, *Institutional Stage*, and *Interindividual Stage*.

Impulsivity (C-7; HS-7). When an individual has trouble managing his or her *emotions* and and/or controlling behaviors.

Impulsivity (as per Erikson) (C-3; HS-2). In *Erikson's psychosocial theory of development*, the idea that unhealthy expressions of *autonomy* could lead to *impulsivity.*

In Loco Parentis (C-8; HS-3). The concept that elementary and secondary schools, colleges, and universities are the parents, in absentia, when students are at school.

In Virtuo Exposure (C-5; HS-3). Using computer-simulations or virtual reality apparatuses in the helping process to expose oneself to a fearful situation that causes *anxiety* in an effort to eventually *extinguish* the fear. See also *Exposure Therapy.*

In Vivo (C-6; HS-4). Referring to something happening or being studied in the real world or in a real-life situation. Latin for "in the living organism."

Inadequacy (C-6; HS-2). From *individual psychology*, one manner in which a child deals with *feelings of inferiority.*

Inadvertent Modeling (C-6; HS-5). A type of *modeling* in which new behaviors are learned from the helper in a passive way through the helper just being his or her natural self. For example, a helper who demonstrates good *empathy* is modeling good empathy for the client. Contrast with *Intentional Modeling.*

Incongruent Expectations about Counseling (C-7; HS-7). When expectations about the helping relationship differ between the helper and the client. This is more likely to occur with minority clients, especially those who are not American born, because the helping relationship tends to be based on Western values and consequently stresses the expression of feelings, self-disclosure, cause-and-effect thinking, open-mindedness, and internal locus of control, attributes not embraced by all *cultures.*

Incongruent/Nongenuine (C-8; HS-7). Having one's thoughts, feelings, and actions out of sync. In *person-centered counseling*, usually a result of *conditions of worth* that lead to a person not living out his or her true *self.* Also called *Nongenuineness.* See also *Congruence* and *Genuineness.*

Incorporative Stage (C-6; HS-4). Stage 0 of *Robert Kegan's subject/object theory*, where a person is self-absorbed and has no sense of being separate from the outside world. See also *Imperial Stage*, *Impulsive Stage*, *Interpersonal Stage*, *Institutional Stage*, and *Interindividual Stage.*

Indebtedness (C-6; HS-2). See *Ledger of Indebtedness and Entitlements.*

Independence Need (in Reality Therapy) (C-5; HS-3). See *Freedom Need.*

Independent Providers (C-9; HS-5). Professionals who are able to provide services on their own, independently. In counseling, it generally refers to being in *private practice* and usually entails having a license (e.g., *Licensed Professional Counselor*) and being able to obtain *third-party reimbursements.*

Independent Variable (C-9; HS-7). In a research study, the *variable* that is being manipulated to examine its effect on some outcome measure. See also *Dependent Variable.*

Indigenous People (C-7; HS-7). Also called first people, first nations, aboriginal people, tribal people, or native people, these individuals have historical claims to their land and *culture* that predates colonization.

Individual Counseling (C-10; HS-10). Counseling provided by a *therapist* to one person, typically in an office setting, as opposed to *group* or *family therapy.*

Individual Identity (C-7; HS-6). Relative to a cross-cultural understanding of the person, along with *group identity* and *universal identity*, one of three identities that make up the person. This identity has to do with an individual's unique ways of being in the world.

Individual Level (C-5; HS-3). In the *tripartite model of personal identity*, the level that represents the client's uniqueness.

Individual Psychology (C-9; HS-5). Developed by *Alfred Adler*, individual psychology suggests that memories of early childhood experiences result in our character or personality. Believing that as children we all experience *feelings of inferiority*, Adler suggested that if we learn how to respond to such feelings in healthy ways, we will move towards *wholeness*, completion, and perfection. Feelings of inferiority, can, however, develop negative *private logic*, which results in *compensatory behaviors* that are maladaptive and/or neurotic. Although a *psychodynamic approach*, individual psychology is seen as less *deterministic* and more optimistic in that a person can change through education and *therapy*. Sometimes placed in the *humanistic* or *constructivist* theoretical schools.

Individualistic Perspective (C-8; HS-6). Clients who tend to focus on *individual identity* with a focus on *self* for answers to problems as opposed to outside groups, such as the family or *culture*, from which they come. See also *Collectivist Perspective*.

Individualized Education Plan (IEP) (C-9; HS-3). This aspect of *PL94-142* and the *IDEA*, states that children who are identified as having a *learning disability* will be provided a school team that will create a specific plan or program that will assist the students with their learning problem(s).

Individuals from Diverse Religious Backgrounds (C-7; HS-7). One type of *diverse populations human service professionals work with.*

Individuals Using and Abusing Substances (C-7; HS-7). One type of *diverse population human service professionals work with.*

Individuals with Disabilities (C-7; HS-7). One type of *diverse population human service professionals work with.*

***Individuals with Disabilities Education Act* (*IDEA*) (C-8; HS-6).** A legislative act that assures the right of students to be tested, at the school system's expense, if they are suspected of having a *disability* that interferes with learning. These students must be given accommodations for their disability and taught within the "least restrictive environment," which often is a regular classroom. See also *Education for All Handicapped Children Act* (*PL94-142*).

Individuals with Mental Illness (C-7; HS-7). One type of *diverse population human service professionals work with.*

Individuation (C-8; HS-6). In *analytical psychology*, although also referenced in other approaches, the lifelong process of bringing the *unconscious* and *conscious* parts of the *self* into integrated unity together.

Indivisible Self Model (C-7; HS-5). One model that views *wellness* as the conglomeration of five factors: *creative self*, *coping self*, *social self*, *essential self*, and *physical self* as well as the individual's context.

Indoctrinate (C-7; HS-5). To ingrain or program a thought or belief system, as in *irrational beliefs* in *rational emotive behavior therapy*.

Inductive Analysis (C-7; HS-3). Used in *qualitative research*, data collection to determine the patterns and categories that emerge from data. See also *Inductive Reasoning*.

Inductive Reasoning (C-5; HS-4). A type of logical reasoning where one starts with particular information or data and then determines which conclusions (or theories) can logically be drawn from (or explain) that information. An example of inductive reasoning (in this case, one that is false) is: Ernest Hemingway owned cats. All of Ernest Hemingway's cats were polydactyl (had more than 18 toes total). Thus, all cats are polydactyl. Contrasts with *deductive reasoning*.

Industrial Revolution (C-6; HS-3). Beginning after the Civil War, this economic and social revolution resulted in individuals relocating to urban settings and set the stage for the need for *vocational guidance*. It is an early marker of the beginning of the counseling profession.

Industry vs. Inferiority (ages 6–12 years) (C-9; HS-7). *Erikson's* fourth stage of *psychosocial development* where the child begins to examine what he or she does well. High self-worth or feelings of inferiority can be formed in this stage.

Infantile Sexuality (C-7; HS-3). The *psychoanalytic* perspective of infants experiencing sexual arousal and pleasure and a reference to the different stages of *Freud's psychosexual stages of development*.

Inferential Statistics (C-8; HS-4). A variety of statistical procedures that are used to make inferences about a larger population from the sample being studied.

Inferiority Complex (C-8; HS-6). In *analytical psychology* (*Adlerian therapy*), although used by many other counseling approaches, when a person believes he or she is unworthy or inferior to others and behaves accordingly.

Informal Assessment Instruments (C-7; HS-6). *Assessment* instruments that are often developed by the user and are specific to the testing situation. All of these instruments can be used to assess broad areas of ability and personality attributes in a variety of settings. Types of informal assessment instruments include: *observation*, *rating scales*, *classification methods*, *environmental assessment*, *records and personal documents*, and *performance-based assessment*.

Informant (C-7; HS-3). In *ethnographic research*, individuals within the *culture* who can provide entrance into the group and can explain phenomena. See also *Key Informants*.

Information Flow (C-6; HS-4). The manner in which information flows into and out of systems. Affected by *boundaries*, *hierarchies*, and *system rules*.

Information Gathering Questions (C-7; HS-7). Questions that are intended to gather information that the helper believes will assist in solving the client's problems or address the client's concerns. These questions tend to be *helper-centered*. Includes *open questions*, *closed questions*, *tentative questions*, and *why questions*.

Information Giving (C-7; HS-7). The process by which a helper offers the client important, "objective" information of which the client is likely unaware. Contrast with

Advice Giving and *Offering Alternatives*.

Informational Interviews (C-5; HS-5). Meeting with potential employers or others that may advance one's career to gain valuable information about *jobs* and related *career* goals.

Informed Consent (C-9; HS-9). The principle that individuals being counseled, interviewed, or assessed should give their permission for the procedure after they are provided basic information about what is about to occur, such as philosophy of counseling, procedures to be used, length of treatment, costs involved, limits of *confidentiality*, and more. Informed consent documents should generally be signed by the client acknowledging that he or she understands the procedures involved.

Initial Email and Phone Contact with Agency (C-7; HS-7). Refers to a client's first point of contact with the agency during which it is essential for helpers to be kind and courteous while they begin to establish a positive helping relationship.

Initial Stage (C-8; HS-8). The beginning *stage of group development* where trust is just starting to be built.

Initiative vs. Guilt (ages 3–5 years) (C-9; HS-7). *Erikson*'s third stage of development where the child explores the environment and gains an increased sense of independence. Caretakers either encourage or thwart exploration during this stage.

Ink Blot Test (C-7; HS-4). See *Rorschach Inkblot Test* and *Rorschach, Herman.*

Innate (C-8; HS-8). Born with or inherent in an individual, such as some talents or skills. For instance, some may have an innate (inherent) talent for singing.

Inner Control Need (in Reality Therapy) (C-5; HS-3). See *Power Need.*

Inpatient Facilities (C-10; HS-10). Also referred to as *inpatient treatment* and *inpatient hospitalization*, settings where *clinical mental health counselors* and other helping professionals (e.g., *psychiatrists*, *social workers*) may work and whose focus is on stabilization of severe psychological and psychiatric issues (e.g., suicidal ideation, alcohol withdrawal). Frequently, these settings are housed within hospitals (and may be referred to as hospitalization or other related terms) and focus on short-term (1-3 weeks) stabilization of severe mental health issues and any attending physical or medical symptoms. In the past, these settings provided long-term treatment and warehousing of mentally ill individuals but following *deinstitutionalization* and changes in *managed care* their role changed in American society. See also *Involuntary Hospitalization.*

Inpatient Hospitalization (C-10; HS-10). See *inpatient facilities.*

Inpatient Treatment (C-10; HS-10). See *inpatient facilities.*

Insight (C-9; HS-9). Possessing degrees of personal perception, *self-awareness*, and self-understanding.

Insight and Interpretation (C-4; HS-2). The third stage of *individual psychology*, where the client is encouraged to develop personal *insight* and explore therapist interpretation about the client's problems/life.

Instersubjectivity Theories (C-4; HS-1). *Psychodynamic* theories that emphasize early child-rearing, the *conscious*, and the *unconscious*, but more actively use the relationship between the *analyst* and the client to highlight issues. Thus, the analyst may be more likely to use *self-disclosure* in an effort to raise client's issues as the client responds to the analyst as he or she might have to an early *caregiver*.

Instincts (C-8; HS-5). In *psychoanalysis*, the *life instinct* (*Eros*) and *death instinct* (*Thanatos*) that drive behavior. In general, instincts imply that there are inherent drives that motivate certain behaviors, such as the instinct of survival or procreation.

Institute for Sex Research (C-3; HS-2). See *Kinsey Institute* (*for Research in Sex, Gender, and Reproduction*).

Institutional Racism (C-9; HS-9). On a systems level, policies or behaviors that are inherently racist and discriminatory to individuals based on their *race* or *ethnicity* (generally, non-White races are targeted).

Institutional Review Board (IRB) (C-9; HS-5). A regulatory body required by any institution that receives U.S. federal funds, with its purpose being to assure the ethical nature of research being conducted. All individuals who conduct research at such an institution must submit their research to the IRB and receive permission to move forward after the IRB has examined the ethics of the research and ensured that little or no harm will come to individuals, or animals, who participate in the research.

Institutional Stage (C-6; HS-4). Stage 4 of *Robert Kegan's subject/object theory*, where a person has separated his or her values from others' values and has a strong sense of personal *autonomy* and self-reliance. See also *Incorporative Stage*, *Imperial Stage*, *Impulsive Stage*, *Interpersonal Stage*, and *Interindividual Stage*,

Instrumental-Hedonism Orientation (C-7; HS-5). *Kohlberg's* Stage 2 of the *preconventional level*, where decisions are made with an egocentric/hedonistic desire to satisfy one's own needs.

Intake Interview (C-9; HS-9). The client's initial contact *interview* with the agency or individual helper which must be completed in a manner that will allow the client to be open and honest with the helper so that understanding of client issues are clear and comprehensive. See also *Clinical Interview*.

Integrated Developmental Model (IDM) (C-7; HS-3). A *supervision* model that primarily focuses on how counselors and helpers will predictably grow and change in three areas: self- and other-awareness, motivation, and autonomy.

Integrative Approach to Counseling (C-9; HS-7). Formerly called *eclecticism*, an integrative approach implies that the helper has drawn his or her approach to helping from a number of different theoretical orientations. The development of an integrative approach can be seen as moving from *chaos*, in which the helper is new to the field and has no firm theory from which he or she works- to *coalescence*, where there is movement toward the adherence of one theoretical approach- to *multiplicity*, where helpers have thoroughly learned one theory and are beginning to gain knowledge and use of other theories- to *metatheory*, where the professional begins to wonder about underlying commonalties and themes among theories and begins to integrate these major themes into his or her own, unique approach.

Integrative Models of Supervision (C-6; HS-2). In *supervision*, models that are not theory specific and can be used regardless of the theoretical approach of the supervisee. Includes: *Bernard's discrimination model*, the *integrative developmental model*, and *interpersonal process recall.*

Integrity (C-5; HS-4). In a *moral model* of ethical decision-making that focuses on *virtue ethics*, one way a helper's individual character may be important. In this case, it refers to whether the helper/person shows uprightness in his or her decision-making.

Integrity vs. Despair (Later Life) (C-9; HS-7). *Erikson's* last stage of *psychosocial development* where the older person examines whether or not he or she has successfully mastered the preceding developmental tasks. Such mastery will lead to a sense of *integrity*, whereas lack of mastery will lead to despair.

Intellectual and Cognitive Functioning, Assessment of (C-8; HS-4). *Tests* that measure a broad range of cognitive functioning in the following domains: general intelligence (overall *IQ*), *intellectual disabilities*, *giftedness*, and changes in overall cognitive functioning. It includes *intelligence testing* and *neuropsychological assessment*, both of which are types of *aptitude tests.*

Intellectual Disability (C-10; HS-10). Formerly referred to as *mental retardation*, but has been renamed *intellectual disability* due to the negative connotations of the term mental retardation. These are people who are intellectually disabled and have *IQ*s that tend to be lower than 70 (although there is no specific cut-off) and also have daily living difficulties.

Intellectualization (C-8; HS-7). A *defense mechanism* where the individual overly focuses on the intellectual aspects of situations or experiences to avoid negative *emotions* or *anxiety*.

Intelligence Quotient (IQ) (C-8; HS-4). The original concept was developed by *Lewis Terman*, who divided mental age by chronological age and multiplied the quotient by 100 to derive a score that he called "IQ." Today, intelligence is measured by determining a *z-score* and then converting the *z*-score to a scale that has a mean of 100 and a *standard deviation* of 15.

Intelligence Testing (C-8; HS-5). Individual tests that assess a broad range of cognitive capabilities that generally results in an *IQ* score (*Deviation IQ*). Often used to identify individuals with *intellectual disabilities*, *giftedness*, *learning disabilities*, and general *intellectual and cognitive functioning*. A type of *aptitude test* that measures general intellectual ability and is usually given one-to-one by a highly trained, experienced examiner.

Intentional Modeling (C-7; HS-6). A type of *modeling* in which the helper deliberately demonstrates a behavior for the client so the client will view, practice, learn, and adopt the new behavior. Clients can also choose behaviors of others with the intention of viewing, practicing, learning, and adopting those behaviors. Contrast with *Inadvertent Modeling*.

Interactional Rules (C-6; HS-4). According to *Salvador Minuchin*, *rules* and *boundaries* defined by the family for interacting with each other.

Interdisciplinary Approach (Interdisciplinary Team) (C-7; HS-6). A team approach to helping people that relies on professionals from many disciplines such as *psychologists*, *psychiatrists*, physicians, nurses, *counselors*, and *social workers* working together to develop treatment approaches for clients. This approach is frequently seen in settings such as *inpatient facilities*, *correctional facilitates*, or large *community-based* agencies although it is beginning to become more common in other settings also.

Interest Areas (C-7; HS-5). In *career counseling*, *jobs*, *avocations*, and *leisure* activities to which individuals are drawn to. They are not necessarily related to ability.

Interest Inventories (C-8; HS-6). Types of *personality tests* that measure individuals' likes, dislikes, and orientation to occupational choices. Often these tests compare an individual's interests or personal characteristics with those of people in varying *occupations* to gain a sense of which occupations best fit that person.

Interindividual Stage (C-6; HS-4). Stage 5 of *Robert Kegan's subject/object theory*, where a person maintains a separate sense of *self* while accepting feedback from others in order to grow and change. See also *Incorporative Stage*, *Imperial Stage*, *Impulsive Stage*, *Interpersonal Stage*, and *Institutional Stage*.

Intermediate Beliefs (C-6; HS-3). Attitudes, rules and assumptions individuals make based on *core beliefs* that impact the development of our *automatic thoughts*. Based on *Aaron Beck's* approach to *cognitive therapy*.

Intermittent Reinforcement (C-8; HS-6). A *schedule of reinforcement* in *behavior therapy* and research where the reward is given intermittently, or occasionally, for the expected response. Intermittent reinforcement tends to be more powerful than continual reinforcement in that it increases resistance to *extinction*.

Internal Consistency Reliability (C-8; HS-2). A type of *reliability* estimate of *test* scores that is based on a single administration of a test. The reliability estimate found, more or less, reflects the average of all *split-half reliabilities*. Includes *Kuder-Richardson* and *Coefficient Alpha* reliabilities.

Internal Control Language (C-6; HS-4). In *reality therapy*, when individuals demonstrate they are responsible for their language, behavior, and feelings and use positive language when interacting with others.

Internal Locus of Control (C-7; HS-6). When an individual focuses on *self* and listens to his or her inner voices and feelings to make decisions.

Internal Validity, Threats To (C-7; HS-4). Ways in which researchers may come to false conclusions because the study was not fully controlled for certain things. Some common types of internal validity include selection, history, maturation, regression, attrition, testing, instrumentation, and additive and interactive effects. See also *External Validity*.

Internalize/Internalization (C-8; HS-7). To incorporate or *assimilate* certain attitudes, feelings, or behaviors into one's preexisting beliefs.

Internalized Racism (C-6; HS-6). The *conscious* or *unconscious* acceptance of the dominant *culture's* racist views, biases, *stereotypes*, and attitudes towards members of one's own racial or ethnic group.

Internally Oriented (C-7; HS-6). See *Internal Locus of Control.*

International Association of Addictions and Offender Counselors (IAAOC) (C-

8; HS-3). A division of the *American Counseling Association* that focuses on *substance abuse* and use and counselors who tend to work in the *correctional facilities* and the broader criminal justice system.

International Association of Counseling (C-8; HS-3). An association that is dedicated to the global practice of counseling and international unity for the profession.

International Association of Marriage and Family Counselors (IAMFC) (C-8; HS-3). A *professional association* for marriage and family counselors. A division of the *American Counseling Association.*

International Board for the Certification of Group Psychotherapists (IBCGP) (C-4; HS-2). An affiliate of the *American Group Psychotherapy Association* (*AGPA*) that is responsible for the *certification* of group counselors and *therapists.*

International Classification of Diseases (ICD) (C-8; HS-6). A diagnostic manual used by health care providers in many countries, currently in its 10th edition (ICD-10), that identifies medical and mental health *diagnoses* and includes most classifications from the *Diagnostic and Statistical Manual-5*, although it does not describe diagnoses in as much detail as the *Diagnostic and Statistical Manual-5*.

International General Medical Society for Psychotherapy (C-2; HS-1). An organization that was headed by *Jung* following Nazi purge of Jews from the German National Society of Psychotherapy. He attempted to mitigate the national purge by permitting Jews to join this larger organization.

International Psychoanalytic Association (C-5; HS-3). The international association for *psychoanalysts.*

International Registry of Counselor Education Programs (IRCEP) (C-5; HS-2). An organization that was created by the *Council for Accreditation of Counseling and Related Educational Programs* to assist in the creation of standards for and the approval of international counseling programs.

Interpersonal Process Recall (IPR) (C-6; HS-3). Developed by Norm Kagan, a type of *supervision* that views the *supervisor's* role as one in which he or she attends to the feelings and thoughts of the *supervisee* and, when appropriate, asks leading questions and uses reflections to deepen the supervision session.

Interpersonal Stage (C-6; HS-4). Stage 3 in *Robert Kegan*'s *subject/object theory*, where a person cannot separate his or her own sense of being from family, friends, or community groups. See also *Incorporative Stage*, *Imperial Stage*, *Impulsive Stage*, *Institutional Stage*, and *Interindividual Stage.*

Interpretation (C-8; HS-6). A helper's assumptions about human behavior external to the client's understanding of reality and usually based on some external model (e.g., *psychoanalysis*).

Interpretation of Client Resistance (C-7; HS-4). Making assumptions about why a client is acting defensively or resisting in counseling. An important technique in *psychoanalysis* and related therapies.

Interpretation of Defense Mechanisms (C-7; HS-4). Making assumptions about the development of a person's psychic structure based on his or her use of specific *defense mechanisms*. An important technique in *psychoanalysis* and related therapies.

Interpretation of Parapraxes (C-7; HS-4). Making assumptions concerning the meaning of errors of speech, slips of tongue, and misspeaks. An important technique in *psychoanalysis* and related therapies. See also *Parapraxis.*

Interquartile Range (C-6; HS-2). Provides the range of the middle 50% of scores around the *median*. Because it eliminates the top and bottom quartiles, the interquartile range is mostly useful with *skewed curves* because it offers a more representative picture of where a large percentage of the scores fall.

Inter-Rater Reliability (C-8; HS-3). A type of *reliability* involving two or more raters who observe or rank order a behavior, instrument construct, or study code in order to find the level of agreement between the raters. The higher the agreement, the higher the reliability.

Intersex (C-7; HS-7). A person who is born with a combination of male and female genitalia, mixed chromosomes, gonads, and other *biological sex* variations outside the *gender binary*. Formerly called and falsely called *hermaphrodite.*

Interval Scale (C-8; HS-4). A *scale of measurement* in which there are equal distances between measurements with no absolute zero reference point.

Interval Schedule (C-7; HS-5). In *behavior therapy*, a *schedule of reinforcement* that is based on time periods, such as providing a reward for students staying on task every 10 minutes, or on average every 10 minutes. Interval schedules can be given on a *fixed schedule of reinforcement* or a *variable schedule of reinforcement.*

Intervention (C-7; HS-7). Within a therapeutic context, synonymous with treatments that mental health professionals may implement with clients. More recently, in lay terms, this word has become associated with active involvement by family and/or friends in intervening (i.e., having an intervention) with a person to help him or her with some type *of mental disorder*, such as a *substance abuse.*

Interview (C-8; HS-8). The process by which human service professionals interact with clients, often in the attempt to gather information or assist them with a problem.

Intimacy vs. Isolation (early adulthood/adulthood) (C-9; HS-7). *Erikson's* sixth stage of *psychosocial development* where, if the young adult has achieved a sense of *self*, he or she is ready to develop intimate relationships. Lack of self-understanding in this stage leads to isolation.

Intimate Partner Violence or Interpersonal Violence (IPV) (C-8; HS-8). Violence of an emotional, sexual, verbal, physical, or financial nature, or other related maltreatment, that occurs within intimate relationships (e.g., marriage, dating, sexual). The term *domestic violence* is used synonymously, although IPV has become the preferred term describing violent situations not solely confined to the home, or domestic, sphere.

Intoxication (C-9; HS-9). A substance induced altered stage of *consciousness*. Also referred to as buzzed, drunk, high, smashed, and many other terms, the state of being intoxicated by a substance such as *alcohol*, *marijuana*, *cocaine*, or other substances.

Intrapsychic (C-9; HS-8). Internal, often *unconscious* mental processes and anything processed through them.

Introjection (C-8; HS-5). *Unconsciously* adopting, or "swallowing whole," significant others' beliefs and values.

Introspective/Introspection (C-9; HS-8). An individual who is open to his or her deeper feelings and is willing to be self-critical and receive feedback from others. See also *Self-Awareness.*

Introverted Attitude (C-7; HS-6). According to *Jung*, a personal *attitude* that is socially inhibited, preferring to be alone, and being more focused on personal ideas and *emotions* than on people and things. These people can be said to derive energy from spending time alone. Part of what makes up one's *psychological type.* See also *Extroverted Attitude.*

Intuiting Mental Function (C-7; HS-6). In *analytical psychology* (*Jungian therapy*), one of the four *mental functions* that make up one's *psychological type.* Individuals who primarily use their intuiting mental functions rely on their gut feelings, innate sensing, or *unconscious* knowing in trying to understand the world. See also *Sensing Mental Function*, *Feeling Mental Function*, and *Thinking Mental Function.*

Invasion of Privacy (C-9; HS-9). The idea that any kind of helping and *assessment* is an infringement on a person's private world and that helpers should be sensitive and attuned when invading one's privacy. This process can be softened if the client has given *informed consent*, has the ability to accept or refuse helping or an assessment, and knows the limits of *confidentiality.*

Inverse Correlation (C-8; HS-5). See *Negative Correlation.*

Inverted Pyramid Method (IPM) (C-5; HS-2). A model used in *case conceptualization* that includes four steps: broadly identifying client concerns and symptomatic behavior, organizing client difficulties into logical groupings or constellations, tying symptom groups to one's theoretical orientation, narrowing these symptom groups to the client's most basic difficulties in development, or adjustment based on one's theoretical orientation.

Involuntary Discharge (C-8; HS-8). When an individual in an *inpatient treatment* (or hospitalization) setting removes himself or herself from the setting, or treatment, against the advice of medical or human service professionals (i.e., "against doctors' orders").

Involuntary Hospitalization (C-9; HS-9). When individuals who are at risk of harming others or themselves are placed in an *inpatient treatment* (or hospitalization) setting against their will to prevent harm. Outside of emergency situations, it takes a court order to hospitalize someone in this way.

Iowa Test of Basic Skills (C-6; HS-2). A national *survey battery achievement test.*

IRB (C-9; HS-5). See *Institutional Review Board.*

IRCEP (C-7; HS-2). *International Registry of Counselor Education Programs.* Established by the *Council for Accreditation of Counseling and Related Educational Programs.*

Irrational Beliefs or Thoughts (C-8; HS-6). Patterns of thought, or cognitions, which are illogical and are often related to the subsequent development of negative *emotions*, dysfunctional behaviors, and erratic physiological responses. Based on *Albert Ellis's* theory of *rational emotive behavior therapy*.

Irrational Functions (Jungian) (C-5; HS-1). According to *Jung*, the *mental functions* of *intuiting* and *sensing*, called irrational due to people collecting information via their perceptions, rather than being based on collected evidence. See also *Rational Functions*.

Isolation (C-6; HS-3). An important concept in *existential therapy*, also recognized and interpreted by many other counseling approaches, and describes the emotional or physical separation and aloneness one can experience from oneself or others. See also *Existential Isolation*.

I-Statements (C-8; HS-7). An interpersonal communication technique in which an individual takes responsibility for his or her thoughts and feelings when communicating with another person. For example, rather than saying "You made me feel nervous when you clenched your fist and hit the table" a client says, "I felt nervous when you clenched your fist and hit the table." Often attributed as a technique originating with *Gestalt therapy*.

It-Factor (C-4; HS-4). The unique characteristics of a counselor that contribute to special ways of working with, and ultimately building alliances with, their clients. One of the *Common Factors*.

Item Response Theory (C-5; HS-1). An extension of *classical test theory* that allows for a detailed analyses of individual *test* items. Using what is called the item characteristic curve, the validity and difficulty of each item on a test are determined. Based on this determination, items are used accordingly on a test.

I–Thou Relationship (C-8; HS-5). In *existential therapy*, a type of relationship that is characterized by a free-flowing, back-and-forth between client and counselor, *authenticity*, *genuineness*, and treating each other *realistically*. It is seen as the basis for the successful therapeutic relationship. Contrast with *I-It Relationship*.

Ivey, Allen (1933 -) (C-6; HS-4). One of the instrumental educators and researchers who developed *microcounseling skills training*. Also, came up with *developmental counseling and therapy*.

Jackson, Don (1920 - 1968) (C-4; HS-1). An influential American *psychiatrist* and *family therapist* connected to the *Palo Alto Mental Research Institute*.

Jacobson, Edmund (1888 - 1983) (C-7; HS-5). An American *psychiatrist* and physician influential for developing *progressive muscle relaxation* and founder of *biofeedback* techniques.

***Jaffee v. Redmond* (C-9; HS-5).** A 1996 U.S. Supreme Court case that upheld the right of a licensed *social worker* to keep her case records *confidential*. Describing the social worker as a "therapist" and "psychotherapist," the ruling is seen as protecting all licensed therapists in U.S. federal courts and may affect all licensed therapists who have *privileged communication*.

James, William (1842 - 1910) (C-4; HS-4). An American *psychologist* and philosopher who originated the idea of philosophical pragmatism, which states reality is continually constructed as a function of its utility or practical purpose.

Janet, Pierre (1859 - 1947) (C-3; HS-3). A French philosopher and *psychologist* who saw a relationship between certain psychological states and organic disorders.

Jellinek's Alcoholism Model (C-7; HS-7). Also known as the *disease model of alcoholism*, the view that *alcoholism* is a progressive medical disease/condition having distinct stages of impaired development and attending health problems. Developed by E. Morton Jellinek.

Jim Crow Laws (C-8; HS-8). Laws which promulgated "separate but equal" status for African Americans as well as laws that clearly *discriminated* against African Americans and others, such as those preventing African Americans from voting or requiring them to use separate drinking fountains. These laws were officially repealed in the *Civil Rights Act* of 1964, but their influence lasted beyond that era.

Job (C-7; HS-4). Specific work tasks which one is responsible to accomplish.

Job Corps (C-4; HS-4). One of a number of legislative acts during the 1960s that provided opportunities for minorities and the poor and helped to reshape attitudes toward social problems. Resulted in increased *job* opportunities for counselors.

Johari Window (C-5; HS-4). A model that is used to help individuals gain *self-awareness* through investigating four quadrants in their lives: (1) open, or areas of one's life that the individual and others are aware of; (2) blind, or areas of one's life that the individual is not aware of but others are aware; (3) hidden, or areas of one's life that the individual is aware of but are unknown to others; and (4) unknown, or areas of one's life that the individual and others are unaware of.

Joining (C-7; HS-5). A term that *Salvador Minuchin* used to describe the manner in which helpers build relationships with clients. See also *Relationship Building*.

Joint Commission on Mental Illness and Health (C-5; HS-4). Established by the 1955 *Mental Health Study Act*, this commission made a number of far-reaching recommendations around increased funding and services for mental health and mental illness.

***Journal for Individual Psychology* (C-4; HS-2).** The professional journal of the North American Society of Adlerian Psychology.

***Journal for Social Action in Counseling and Psychology* (C-4; HS-2).** Journal of *Counselors for Social Justice (CSJ)*.

***Journal for Specialists in Group Work* (C-4; HS-2).** Journal of the *Association for Specialists in Group Work (ASGW)*.

***Journal of Addictions and Offender Counseling* (C-6; HS-3).** Journal of the *International Association of Addictions and Offender Counselors (IAAOC)*.

***Journal of College Counseling* (C-4; HS-2).** Journal of the *American College Counseling Association (ACCA)*.

***Journal of Counseling and Development* (C-9; HS-3).** The professional journal of the *American Counseling Association*. Free subscriptions are available to members of the *American Counseling Association*.

***Journal of Creativity in Mental Health* (C-4; HS-2).** Journal of the *Association for Creativity in Counseling* (*ACC*).

***Journal of Employment Counseling* (C-4; HS-2).** Journal of the *National Employment Counseling Association* (*NECA*).

***Journal of Human Services* (C-3; HS-10).** Journal of the *National Organization of Human services* (*NOHS*).

***Journal of Humanistic Counseling* (C-4; HS-2).** Journal of the *Association for Humanistic Counseling* (*AHC*).

***Journal of LGBT Issues in Counseling* (C-4; HS-2).** Journal of the *Association for Lesbian, Gay, Bisexual, and Transgender Issues in Counseling* (*ALGBTIC*).

***Journal of Mental Health Counseling* (C-6; HS-4).** Journal of the *American Mental Health Counselors Association* (*AMHCA*).

***Journal of Multicultural Counseling and Development* (C-8; HS-7).** Journal of the *Association for Multicultural Counseling and Development* (*AMCD*).

Journals and Diaries (C-7; HS-6). Written personal documents that allow individuals to describe themselves and can provide valuable insight into *self*, or to a *clinician*, by revealing *unconscious* drives and desires and by uncovering patterns that highlight issues in a client's life. Types of *Records and Personal Documents*. Also used as methods of *subjectivity* and for *trustworthiness* in *qualitative research*.

Journals of ACA Divisions (C-8; HS-4). Professional journals that are available based on membership in the *American Counseling Association* and its divisions.

Judging Mental Function (C-7; HS-6). A *mental function*, along with the *perceiving mental function*, that was added by *Katherine Cook Briggs* and *Elizabeth Myers* to *Jung's* other *mental functions* (*sensing-intuiting* and *feeling-thinking*). The *mental functions*, and the *attitudes* of being an *introvert* or *extrovert*, make up one's *psychological type* and are used in the *Myers-Briggs Type Indicator*. Judging types see the world in a routine, planned and ordered fashion and like to obtain closure on issues.

Jung, Carl (1875 - 1961) (C-10; HS-6). Founder of *Jungian therapy*, often called *analytical psychology*, which proposed a *conscious*, *personal unconscious*, and *collective unconscious*. He also was one of the first to develop a word association *projective test*, which included a list of 156 words to which subjects were asked to respond to as quickly as possible. Depending on the response and the answer time, *Jung* believed that he could identify *complexes*. He also created the personality type construct that includes *mental functions* (*sensing-intuiting* and *thinking-feeling*) and *attitudes* (*extroverted* and *introverted*) that are partly used in the *Myers-Briggs Type Inventory*.

Jungian Therapy (C-8, HS-4). See *Analytical Psychology*.

Justice (C-8; HS-6). One of *Kitchener'* moral ethical principles that involves treating clients fairly and equally.

Kaiser Criterion. A method used in *factor analysis* for determining the appropriate numbers of factors to extract and involves selecting factors with *eigenvalues* greater than or equal to one.

Kegan, Robert (1946 -) (C-7; HS-5). An adult developmental *psychologist* and theorist whose *subject/object theory* suggests that all individuals can pass through as many as six stages in life, although most do not reach the higher ones. They include the following stages: *Incorporative*, *Impulsive*, *Imperial*, *Interpersonal*, *Institutional*, and *Interindividual.*

Kernberg, Otto (1928 -) (C-4; HS-2). An Austrian-Chilean American *psychoanalyst*, *psychiatrist*, and a key *object relations therapy* theorist.

Key Informants (C-7; HS-4). In *ethnographic research*, special or essential individuals within the *culture* who can provide entrance into the group and can explain phenomena. See also *Informants.*

Kierkegaard, Søren (1813 - 1855) (C-7; HS-5). An influential Danish philosopher, poet, theologian, and critical thinker who is sometimes known as the first *existential* philosopher, and thus, his ideas had great influence on *existential therapy.*

***Kinetic Family Drawing* (C-5; HS-3).** A *projective technique* in which a client is instructed to draw his or her entire family, including himself or herself, "all doing something together" in an effort to obtain a picture of the family. Based on the drawing, interpretations can be made about the individual and about family dynamics.

Kinsey, Alfred (1894 - 1956) (C-7; HS-4). An American zoologist and sexologist, responsible for landmark studies of human sexual behavior in the 1940s and 1950s. See also *Kinsey Institute (for Research in Sex, Gender, and Reproduction)*, *Kinsey Study/Reports*, and *Kinsey Scale.*

Kinsey Institute (for Research in Sex, Gender, and Reproduction) (C-7; HS-4). The research center founded in 1947 at Indiana University by sexologist *Alfred Kinsey* that carries on his work in the study of human sexual behavior and related topics. Formerly called the *Institute for Sex Research.*

Kinsey Scale (C-7; HS-4). Also known as the Heterosexual-Homosexual Rating Scale, this scale of human sexual attraction was developed by *Alfred Kinsey* and assessed individuals on a spectrum ranging from exclusively *heterosexual* (score of 0) to exclusively *homosexual* (score of 6). Although some have questioned his results, *Kinsey* found that large numbers of people identify somewhere in the middle of this scale, having a mixture of same and opposite sex attractions.

Kinsey Study/Reports (C-6; HS-4). A historic and influential human sexual behavior study developed by *Alfred Kinsey* and his team at Indiana University. It was published in two parts in 1948 and 1953.

Kitchener, Karen (1943 - 2016) (C-7; HS-6). An influential American *psychologist* and educator, who examined the role of moral principles in the making of ethical decisions. Her moral principles included *Autonomy*, *Nonmaleficence*, *Beneficence*, *Justice*, *Fidelity*, and *Veracity.*

Klein, Melanie (1882 - 1960) (C-5; HS-3). A British-Austrian *psychoanalyst* and a key *object relations therapy* theorist who was also influential in developing important techniques for counseling children.

Kohlberg, Lawrence (1927 - 1987) (C-8; HS-7). An influential American *psychologist* most known for examining *moral development* throughout the lifespan. See also *Kohlberg's*

Theory of Moral Development.

Kohlberg's Theory of Moral Development (C-8; HS-7). *Kohlberg* discovered that moral reasoning developed in a predictable pattern that spanned three levels of development, each containing two stages. See also *Preconventional*, *Conventional*, and *Postconventional* levels.

Köhler, Wolfgang (1998 - 1967) (C-4; HS-3). A German *psychologist* whose ideas about *phenomenology* contributed to the field of *Gestalt psychology*.

Kohut, Heinz (1913 - 1981) (C-4; HS-3). An Austrian-American *psychoanalyst* who adopted a *psychodynamic approach* to counseling that highlights the way people attach and separate from important others in their lives. Also a key *self-psychology* theorist.

Kraepelin, Emil (1856 - 1926) (C-4; HS-2). A German *psychiatrist* who developed one of the first classifications of mental diseases around the year 1900. See also *Classifications of Mental Diseases.*

Krumboltz, John (1928 -) (C-7; HS-7). A *behaviorist* who had many of his ideas adapted to the *career counseling* process, most notably, his *social learning theory* of *career counseling*, and more recently his *happenstance learning theory* which suggests that being involved in a wide variety of interests and activities makes you more likely to benefit from unplanned events. One of the many theorists that fueled the diversity of counseling theories during the 1950s and 1960s. See also *modeling*.

Kruskal-Wallis Test (C-6; HS-3). The *nonparametric* equivalent to a *one-way ANOVA* used to measure if samples originate within the same distribution. This *test* is an extension of the *Wilcoxon Ranked Sum* and the *Mann-Whitney U* test because it can be used with three or more independent samples. The Kruskal-Wallis Test is especially useful when researchers are working with independent samples of differing sizes.

Kübler-Ross, Elisabeth (1926 - 2004) (C-7; HS-7). A Swiss born *psychiatrist* who popularized the stages of grief in her famous book "On Death and Dying." See also *Grief, Stages of.*

Kübler-Ross Stages of Grief (C-9; HS-7). See *Grief, Stages of.*

Kuder-Richardson (C-7; HS-3). A type of *internal consistency reliability* measure used with dichotomous data which is calculated by using all the possible split-half combinations. This is done by correlating the scores for each item on the *test* with the total score on the test and finding the average correlation for all of the items.

Kuhn, T. S. (1922 - 1996) (C-6; HS-4). An American scientist and writer who developed the concept of the *paradigm shift.*

Kurtosis (C-5; HS-3). A descriptive statistical measure of the extent to which a data distribution is similar to a *normal distribution.* Kurtosis values represent the "peakedness" of a distribution.

Labeling (C-8; HS-7). When a person is given a *diagnosis*, or some other label, which tends to define his or her usual way of functioning. Labeling can be helpful, such as when the label leads to effective *treatment planning*. However, labeling can be harmful, such as when a person tends to *dualistically* label other people instead of seeing them in more complex ways (see *cognitive distortion*), or when the label leads to bullying or stigmatizing.

Labile (C-7; HS-5). In the mental health field, this usually refers to emotional lability, or when a person's expressed *emotions* seem to fluctuate greatly.

Lack of Understanding of Social Forces (C-8; HS-8). When the helper is unaware of the social influences that have impacted the manifestation of a client's presenting concern.

Laing, R. D. (1927 - 1989) (C-6; HS-3). He was a Scottish *psychiatrist* who viewed *abnormal* behavior as a normal response to a stressful situation.

Latency Stage (C-9; HS-4). *Sigmund Freud's* fourth *psychosexual stage of development*, occurring between age 5 years and the onset of puberty, where the child replaces sexual feelings with socialization. See also *Anal Stage*, *Genital Stage*, *Oral Stage*, and *Phallic Stage*.

Latent Meanings (C-8; HS-5). Refers to meanings about something that are inherent but not yet known, developed, or revealed. In other words, meanings that are hidden or obscured. Often used to describe the hidden meaning of dreams in *psychoanalysis* or other *psychodynamic* approaches to counseling.

Latent Variables (C-5; HS-3). *Variables* that cannot be directly observed or measured. Latent variables (sometimes referred to as *factors*) are oftentimes theoretical constructs that are only identified through mathematical and statistical procedure such as *factor analysis*.

Latino/Latina (C-7; HS-7). An individual having heritage, and who identifies with that heritage, from one or more Latin American countries (e.g., Mexico, Central America, South America) on one or more sides of his or her family. For example, Brazilians are considered to be *Latinos/Latinas*, by nature of the country being in Latin America, but not *Hispanic*, as their primary cultural and historical influences come from Portugal and not Spain. Some people are both *Hispanic* and *Latino/Latina* and others are one or the other. Contrast with *Hispanic*.

Law and Order Orientation (C-7; HS-5). *Kohlberg's* stage 4 of the *conventional level*, where behaviors are based on rule-governed behavior.

Layers of Neurosis (C-5; HS-2). Another term for *Perls'* five *structures of neurosis*.

Lazarus, Arnold (1932 - 2013) (C-7; HS-5). A South African *psychologist* who eventually settled in the United States, who specialized in *cognitive-behavioral therapy*, and developed *multimodal therapy*.

LCPC (C-10; HS-9). See *Licensed Clinical Professional Counselor.*

LCSW (C-10; HS-10). See *Licensed Clinical Social Worker.*

Leading Questions (C-9; HS-9). A type of question that is worded in a way that directs or influences the respondent to answer in a certain way. For example, a helper who asks a client "Do you and your partner have any problems?" Since there are problems in all relationships, it is likely the client would then discuss the problems, which could bias the session to focus on the problems and not give a broader sense of the relationship. Leading questions should be used sparingly and appropriately because they increase the chances of respondent bias.

Learned Helplessness (C-8; HS-7). A sense of victimhood, powerlessness, and helplessness following exposure to repeated *trauma* or *abuse*. Developed by *Martin Seligman*. Contrast with *Learned Optimism*.

Learned Optimism (C-5; HS-4). As opposed to *learned helplessness*, a sense of being optimistic, joyful, and having power within the world. An aspect of *positive counseling* and *positive psychology* and developed by *Martin Seligman*.

Learning Disability/Disorder (C-9; HS-9). A cognitive *disability* connected to learning, such as in reading, math, or related areas of scholastic development.

Learning Environment (C-3; HS-1). One of the four primary areas that the *Council for Accreditation of Counseling and Related Educational Programs* examines when accrediting master's and doctoral programs. This aspect of the *accreditation* process sets minimal standards for the institution as a whole (the college or university), the academic unit (the counseling program), and for faculty and staff.

Learning Styles (C-5; HS-5). An individual's approach to learning based on various preferences, strengths and weaknesses. According to Neil Fleming's VARK model, these include visual, auditory, kinesthetic, and reading/ writing.

Learning Theorists (C-6; HS-6). Any theorist who believes that *learning theory* is the basis for personality development.

Learning Theory (C-7; HS-7). Theories that propose behaviors and/or cognitions are reinforced and become the basis for the development of personality. See also *Behaviorism*, *Operant Conditioning*, *Classical Conditioning*, *Modeling* (*Social Learning*), and *Cognitive Theories*.

Least Restrictive Environment (C-8; HS-5). Related to *PL 94-142* and the *IDEA*, it ensures the right of a child with a disability to be given an education within the public schools in the least restrictive manner; that is, "mainstreamed" as much as possible.

Ledger of Indebtedness and Entitlements (C-6; HS-3). In *multigenerational family therapy*, this represents the aspects of what couples carry over from their *families of origin* (e.g., one member felt unloved growing up and the other member felt smothered). The ledger is often imbalanced and couples will attempt to balance it within their relationship, normally unsuccessfully, causing relational problems for the couples. See also *Ivan Boszomenyi-Nagy* and *Contextual Family Therapy*.

Leisure (C-5; HS-3). Time taken from required effort (e.g., *work*) to pursue self-chosen activities that express one's abilities and interests, like reading, camping, or cooking.

Lesbian (C-10; HS-10). A female who has same-sex attractions. See also *Homosexual*.

Lesbian, Gay, Bisexual, and Transgender Individuals (C-10; HS-10). Some of the many *diverse populations human service professionals work with*.

Lesson Plans (C-6; HS-3). Used in the management system of the *ASCA National Model*, their purpose is to thoughtfully develop and evaluate classroom activities, such as *psychoeducational groups*.

Letting Down of Boundaries (C-2; HS-1). To allow others to see who you really are. One goal in *Gestalt* consultation.

Levinson, Daniel (1920 - 1994) and Judy (C-7; HS-5). Formulated theories of male and female adult development over the lifespan. Daniel was a noted *psychologist* whose wife, Judy, was his co-author and research collaborator. See also *Levinson's Seasons of a Man's Life and Seasons of a Woman's Life.*

Levinson's Seasons of a Man's Life and Seasons of a Woman's Life (C-7; HS-4). An adult development theory proposed by *Daniel Levinson* who identified four comparable eras through which men and women pass, including: pre-adulthood, early adulthood, middle adulthood, and late adulthood, but focused on the last three eras. Eras reflect unique issues or life structures that all individuals face in the areas of career, love relationships, marriage and family, relationships with *self*, uses of solitude, roles in social contexts, and relationships with individuals, groups, and institutions. Eras are preceded by transition periods whose purpose is to help ease the person into the next era.

Lewin, Kurt (1890 - 1947) (C-7; HS-4). A German-American *psychologist* who developed the *National Training Laboratory* (*NTL*) to examine group dynamics, or the ways in which groups tend to interact.

LGBTQ Affirmative Counseling (C-7; HS-7). An approach to counseling that positively embraces *Lesbian, Gay, Bisexual, Transgender, and Queer* (*LGBTQ*) identities and relationships in the therapeutic dynamic. Additionally, this approach aims to address the negative effect that *transphobia*, *heterosexism*, and *heteronormativity* have on the lives of LGBTQ clients.

LGBTQQIA (also LGBTQ) (C-9; HS-9). An acronym *for lesbian, gay, bisexual, transgender, queer, questioning, intersex,* and *ally* (or *asexual*) individuals. Common abbreviated versions of this acronym include *LGBTQ* or other variations.

Liability Insurance (C-9; HS-7). Insurance offered to mental health or medical professionals (e.g., *human service professionals, counselors, psychologists*) to protect against professional liability for harmful treatment, impaired work, unethical behavior, etc. See also *Malpractice Insurance.*

Liberal Stage (C-5; HS-2). The third stage of *D'Andrea and Daniels'* developmental theory of *stages of racism* where professionals can understand different viewpoints when working with clients from *non-dominant cultures.* See also *Affective/Impulsive, Dualistic Rational,* and *Principled Activist* stages.

Libido (C-9; HS-6). *Freud* postulated that *psychic energy* was made up of *eros* (*life instincts*) and *thanatos* (*death instincts*). Most commonly associated with the *sex* drive or sexual desires, but *Freud* used the term for all *psychic energy* that drives us, not just sex.

Librium (C-6; HS-6). A type of *antianxiety medication* and *controlled substance.*

Licensed Clinical Professional Counselor (LCPC) (C-10; HS-9). See *Licensed Professional Counselor (LPC).*

Licensed Clinical Social Worker (LCSW) (C-9; HS-9). A U.S. state-sponsored credential for licensed *social workers.* Two other, more advanced, credentials that generally require a license in social work include the *Qualified Clinical Social Worker* and the *Diplomate in Clinical Social Work*.

Licensed Marriage and Family Therapist (LMFT) (C-9; HS-9). A U.S. state-sponsored credential for licensed marriage and family *therapists* that generally follows the curriculum standards of the *Commission on Accreditation for Marriage and Family Therapy Education* or the *Council for the Accreditation of Counseling and Related Educational Programs*.

Licensed Mental Health Counselor (LMHC) (C-10; HS-7). See *Licensed Professional Counselor* (*LPC*).

Licensed Physician (C-9; HS-9). An individual who has earned a medical degree and has met specific state requirements to obtain licensure as a physician, i.e., a doctor.

Licensed Professional Clinical Counselor (LPCC) (C-10; HS-9). See *Licensed Professional Counselor* (*LPC*).

Licensed Professional Counselor (LPC) (C-10; HS-9). An individual who has earned at least a master's degree in *counseling* and has met specific state requirements to obtain *licensure*. In 1976, Virginia passed the first law that granted licensure for counselors, and other states soon followed suit. Now, all 50 states have licensure. Sometimes called *a Licensed Mental Health Counselor* (*LMHC*), *Licensed Clinical Professional Counselor* (*LCPC*), or *Licensed Professional Clinical Counselor* (*LPCC*).

Licensed Psychologist (C-9; HS-9). An individual who has earned a doctoral degree in *counseling* or *clinical psychology* and has met specific U.S. state requirements to obtain *licensure*.

Licensure (C-9; HS-9). This most rigorous form of *credentialing* is generally set by each U.S. state and requires a minimum educational level, usually a state or national exam, and additional documentation of expertise such as evidence of post-education *supervision*. See also *Certification*, *Registration*, and *Credentialing*.

Licensure Committee (C-3 HS-1). The original committee, established in 1974 by the *American Counseling Association*, to assist in state *licensure* of counselors.

LICSW (C-9; HS-9). See *Licensed Independent Clinical Social Worker*.

Life Instinct (C-9; HS-5). Sometimes called *eros* in *psychoanalysis*, this *instinct* meets our basic need for love and intimacy, *sex*, and survival for the individual and the species. The *libido* holds the *life instincts* and *death instincts*.

Life Structures (C-5; HS-3). In *Levinson's* theory of men and women, areas of *career*, love relationships, marriage and family, relationships with *self*, uses of solitude, roles in social contexts, and relationships with individuals, groups, and institutions.

Life-Coaching (C-8; HS-8). See *Coaching*.

Lifespan Development Theories (C-9; HS-7). Models of understanding the development of the person that stress that individuals continue to grow throughout their lives. Some examples include *Erikson's* stages of *psychosocial development*, *Kegan's subject/object theory*, and *Levinson's seasons of a man's and seasons of a woman's life*.

Lifespan Developmental Approach to Career Counseling (C-8; HS-3). An approach developed by *Donald Super* that states *career development* is a lifespan process that involves a series of predictable stages through which people pass as they develop their *self* through their life roles. See also *Growth, Exploration, Establishment, Maintenance, and Deceleration/Disengagement Stages*

Lifestyle (C-7; HS-6). A person's or group's style, or way, of living or how people or groups routinely or typically respond to life experiences. This term was first used by *Alfred Adler* to describe an individual's way of living in the world which reflected his or her *subjective final goal* which was fueled by the individual's *private logic*. Today, however, it has application in many counseling approaches.

Lifestyle Assessment (C-6; HS-5). An *assessment* tool used to gather information about a person's *family constellation, birth order*, and/or group's *lifestyle*. See also *Lifestyle.*

Likert-Type Scale (C-7; HS-4). Sometimes called *graphic scales*, this kind of *rating scale* contains a number of items that are being rated on the same theme and are anchored by both numbers and a statement that corresponds to the numbers.

Limit Setting (C-6; HS-7). An important technique in *Adlerian therapy* (*individual psychology*) that involves setting behavioral *boundaries* or rules of conduct in counseling (such as in *Adlerian* play therapy). Limit setting has become a common tool used in many helping and parenting approaches.

Linehann, Marsha (1943 -) (C-7; HS-4). An American *psychologist* who created *Dialectical Behavior Therapy* (*DBT*).

Link, The (C-1; HS-6). The newsletter of the *National Organization of Human Services.*

Listening (C-8; HS-8). An active process when the helper talks minimally, concentrates on what is being said, does not interrupt or give advice, hears the speaker's content and *affect*, and uses good non-verbals to show that he or she is understanding the client.

Listening, Hindrances to Effective (C-5; HS-5). Factors that prevent or interfere with one's ability to listen effectively such as preconceived notions, anticipatory reaction, cognitive distractions, personal issues, emotional responses, and distractions.

Listening Skills (C-8; HS-8). A counseling technique that stresses being able to hear the client and enable the establishment of a trusting, open relationship. See also *Listening.*

Lithium (C-7; HS-7). A *psychotropic* drug and controlled substance sometimes used to treat *bipolar and related disorders.*

Little Albert (C-7; HS-5). The pseudonym used in a famous *case study* validating the effectiveness of *classical conditioning* in humans. Published in 1920 by *John B. Watson* and Rosalie Rayner, this experiment involved striking two steel bars near the head of an 11-month-old baby named Albert while he held a white rat. The loud noise created a fear response in "little Albert that generalized to a white rabbit, cotton, wool, a fur coat, a dog, a Santa Claus mask, and the experimenter's hair."

Little Hans (C-6; HS-3). The pseudonym used in a famous *case study* published by *Freud* in 1909, concerning the sexual behavior of children and connected to his ideas of *infantile sexuality*, and related ideas. One of the few case studies *Freud* ever published.

LMFT (C-9; HS-9). See *Licensed Marriage and Family Therapist.*

LMHC (C-10; HS-9). See *Licensed Mental Health Counselor.*

Lobbying (C-8; HS-8). *Advocacy* efforts that *professional associations* take to introduce and/or defeat legislation. Lobbying has become crucial to the survival of mental health professions, through such efforts as the establishment of *credentialing* laws and other laws that protect mental health workers' jobs.

Locke, John (1632 - 1704) (C-6; HS-3). An influential English Enlightenment philosopher and physician who believed the mind is a *blank slate* upon which ideas are generated. See also *Tabula Rasa.*

Loevinger, Jane (1918 - 2008) (C-7; HS-4). An American developmental *psychologist* who formulated a theory of *ego* development and examined how individuals develop interpersonally, cognitively, and morally over the lifespan.

Logical Analysis (C-7; HS-3). The process used in *qualitative research* to understand the information collected. It involves reviewing the data, synthesizing results, and drawing conclusions and generalizations.

Logical Consequences (C-6; HS-6). Similar to *natural consequences*, this involves the intervention by another person, usually one who is in a position of authority, who enacts a "logical" or "commonsense" consequence to a behavior. For instance, the child who talks excessively during class is asked by the teacher to leave so he or she won't distract others. Later, this child is asked by the teacher to make up the work during recess, when the student can't distract others. Or, the child who acts aggressively toward the counselor loses "play time" with the toys in the counselor's office. Originally used in *Adlerian therapy.*

Logotherapy (C-7; HS-3). The *existential therapy* developed by *Viktor Frankl.*

Longitudinal Research (C-8; HS-6). Research that is conducted over long periods of time (months and sometimes years).

Love and Belonging (C-8; HS-8). One of the primary needs based on *Maslow's Hierarchy of Needs.*

Love and Belonging (in Reality Therapy) (C-8; HS-7). One of the five needs of *reality therapy* that make up one's *need-strength profile.*

Low-Level Distancing Tasks (C-6; HS-2). In *narrative therapy*, beginning tasks assigned to a client to help create distance from his or her problem stories, such as finding exceptions to a client story in which the client consistently sees himself or herself as failing.

Loyalties (C-4; HS-2). In *multigenerational couples and family counseling*, how our sense of loyalty to others is passed down through the generations.

LPC (C-10; HS-9). See *Licensed Professional Counselor.*

LPCC (C-10; HS-9). See *Licensed Professional Clinical Counselor.*

LSD (C-9; HS-9). See *Lysergic Acid Diethylamide (LSD).*

Lysergic Acid Diethylamide (LSD) (C-9; HS-9). Commonly referred to as *acid*, a non-addictive psychedelic drug used recreationally or ritualistically to produce hallucinogenic experiences called "trips" or "tripping." It can also lead to intense feelings of paranoia, *anxiety*, and *delusions* resulting in unusual behavior in users. LSD is isolated from the fungus ergot and is a *controlled substance* in the United States. Although, it has been researched for various medical uses, including the reduction of *existential anxiety* in terminally ill people, these uses are controversial and not officially endorsed by the medical community.

M2F or MTF (Male-to-Female) (C-6; HS-6). Refers to individuals who were assigned the male gender at birth and currently identify as female, and it includes those who are at different stages of their transition or gender affirmation process. See also *F2M or FTM (Female-to-Male)*.

MAC (C-7; HS-3). *Master Addictions Certification* provided by *NBCC.*

Machismo (C-7; HS-7). A Spanish word used to denote a strong sense of male pride or emphasis placed on masculine characteristics. Sometimes associated with male chauvinism. Contrast with *Marianismo.*

Macro Level (C-7; HS-7). The focus on the community or the public at large versus the *micro level*, which focuses on the individual or student.

Macroaggression (C-7; HS-7). Overtly aggressive behavior towards individuals in marginalized populations. This typically includes outward acts of bigotry and oppression. See also *Stereotypes*, *Prejudice*, and *Discrimination.*

Madanes, Cloé (1940 -) (C-6; HS-4). An author, teacher, and presenter of family therapy techniques and one of the originators of *strategic family therapy.*

Magical Thinking (C-5; HS-4). Ways of thinking that attribute causal relationships between human thoughts or behaviors to making other behaviors or experiences happen in the absence of evidence to this effect. For example, thinking one's thoughts can control others' behaviors or that if one behaves a certain way, say wearing a special hat or shirt, this will effect behavior in oneself or others, like winning a football game. In some cases, this is related to superstition, ritual, prayer, or other practices.

Magnification/Minimization (C-6; HS-4). Magnifying the negative or minimizing the positive. See also *Cognitive Distortion.*

Mahler, Margaret (1897 - 1985) (C-5; HS-3). A Hungarian physician, *psychoanalyst*, and a key *object relations therapy* theorist focusing on *child development.*

Mahoney, Michael (1946 - 2006) (C-5; HS-3). An American *psychologist* and educator known for his contributions to *constructivist therapy.*

Mainstreaming (C-7; HS-5). The practice of placing students with *intellectual disabilities* or *learning disorders* into general (or mainstream) classrooms as opposed to isolating them in special classrooms.

Maintenance Stage (C-8; HS-3). Stage 4 of *Donald Super's lifespan developmental approach to career counseling*, occurring between ages 44 and 64 years, where the individual confirms *career* choice and hopes to avoid stagnation. See also *Growth*,

Exploration, Establishment, and Deceleration/Disengagement Stages

Major Depression (C-8; HS-7). A mood disorder characterized by feelings of sadness, diminished interest in pleasure, a significant increase or decrease in appetite, diminished ability to concentrate, feelings of worthlessness, and/or suicidal thoughts. See also *Depression.*

Malcolm X (1925 - 1965) (C-4; HS-4). See *Al Hajj Malik El-Shabazz.*

Malingering (C-4; HS-4). The purposeful fabrication of mental or physical health symptoms with the intention of gaining a secondary reward (i.e. attention, pity, time off work). Also known as manipulation.

Malpractice (C-8; HS-8). Improper treatment by a medical or mental health professional that leads to harm or injury to a client. Can be the result of purposeful harmful behaviors or *negligence.* See also *Malpractice Insurance.*

Malpractice Insurance (C-9; HS-6). Insurance that can be obtained by a medical or mental health professional to protect oneself in case one is sued. See also *Liability Insurance.*

Managed Health Care (C-9; HS-6). Organizations whose intent it is to contain health care costs, usually by limiting the doctors to whom patients can go and by overseeing treatment by approving *diagnoses* and limiting services to what they believe are needed. Includes *HMOs*, *PPOs*, and *EAPs.*

Mandala (C-5; HS-3). Within Hinduism and Buddhism, complex, concentric creative images made to represent divinity or connection to the divine, unity, or harmony. *Jung* noted that individuals who were approaching a *holistic* integration of the *unconscious* and *conscious* parts would create unique images similar to these religious symbols found in many *cultures.*

Mandated Reporter (C-10; HS-10). Any individual who comes in regular or professional contact with individuals from a class of protected persons and is required to report *abuse* or harm to the authorities, like police or *child protective services* agencies. In many U.S. states, this includes the following professionals: teachers, counselors, human service professionals, physicians, or other school or agency workers (including administrative and janitorial staff) who may come into contact with children, older persons, pregnant women, or other protected classes of people. Some states now require all citizens to be mandated reporters for certain types of abuse. The laws governing mandated reporters, who and how they qualify, and which classes of people are protected vary from state (or jurisdiction) to state (or jurisdiction).

Mania (C-6; HS-5). Periods of euphoric excitement, over activity, and delusional thinking. Often found in *bipolar and related disorders.*

Manifest Meanings (C-6; HS-3). The obvious or surface meanings of a dream.

Mann-Whitney U Test (C-6; HS-2). Also known as *U test*, a *nonparametric statistical test* of the *null hypothesis* of two samples within the same population of a study. The null hypothesis is tested against an alternative hypothesis in this test.

***Manpower Development and Training Act* (C-5; HS-5).** One of a number of legislative acts during the 1960s that provided opportunities for minorities and the poor and helped to reshape attitudes toward social problems; resulted in increased job opportunities for human service professionals and counselors.

Mapping (C-7; HS-4). Examining the communication sequences in couples and families in order to understand how individuals relate to one another.

Marathon Groups (C-7; HS-5). Groups that last for an extended period of time.

Marginalized Groups (C-8; HS-8). See *Minority Groups.*

Marianismo (C-4; HS-4). A Spanish word used to denote a strong sense of traditional femininity, placing emphasis on forbearance, self-sacrifice, and nurturance. Contrast with *Machismo.*

Marijuana (C-8; HS-8). See *Cannabis.*

Marriage, Couples, and Family Counseling (C-8; HS-7). A specialty area that focuses on the marriage dyad or the family system in which individuals with an advanced degree sometimes work. Marriage, couples, and family counseling programs are accredited by the *Council for Accreditation of Counseling and Related Educational Programs* or the *Commission on Accreditation for Marriage and Family Therapy Education.* See also *Marriage, Couples, and Family Counselors.*

Marriage, Couples, and Family Counselors (C-8; HS-7). An individual who has obtained at least his or her master's degree in counseling or a related field and has focused upon marriage and *family counseling.* See also *Marriage, Couples, and Family Counseling.*

Maslow, Abraham (1908 - 1970) (C-7; HS-3). An influential American *psychologist* and one of the founders of the field of *existential-humanistic approaches* to counseling and education. See also *Maslow's Hierarchy of Needs.*

Maslow's Hierarchy of Needs (C-8; HS-8). In *Abraham Maslow's* hierarchical theory, the postulation that lower order needs must be fulfilled before higher-order needs. The order of needs fulfillment, in ascending order, is (1) physiological, (2) safety, (3) *love and belonging*, (4) *self-esteem*, and (5) *self-actualization.*

MAST (C-7; HS-4). See *Michigan Alcoholism Screening Test.*

Master Addictions Counselor (MAC) (C-7; HS-3). Specialty *certification* for *addiction counselors* that is offered by the *National Board for Certified Counselors.*

Master's in Psychology and Counseling Accreditation Council (MPCAC) (C-6; HS-2). A new *accreditation* body for master's level training programs in *psychology* and *counseling.* This accreditation body competes with the *Council for the Accreditation of Counseling and Related Educational Programs*, but currently only has accredited a handful of programs.

Master's in Social Work (MSW) (C-9; HS-9). Graduate degree for *social workers.*

Master's-Level Standards (CACREP) (C-9; HS-9). Standards set by the *Council for Accreditation of Counseling and Related Educational Programs* for earning a master's degree in counseling that includes four primary areas: *learning environment*, *professional counseling identity*, *professional practice*, and *evaluation of the program.*

Mastery Learning (C-7; HS-5). See *Criterion-Referenced Assessment.*

May, Rollo (1909 - 1994) (C-7; HS-5). An influential *existential* theorist, writer, and *psychologist* who contributed to the diversity of the counseling field during the 1950s and 1960s.

McAuliffe's Definition of Culturally Competent Helping (C-4; HS-4). The perspective that *culturally competent helping* involves a helper's consistent willingness to learn about the cultural dimensions of clients' lives and to integrate cultural considerations into the helping process. Developed by Garrett McAuliffe.

***McKinney-Vento Homeless Assistance Act* (C-6; HS-6).** Enacted in 1987 for the purpose of providing mental health services, *substance abuse* treatment, outreach services, emergency food and shelter, housing, health care, education, job training, and child care for the homeless and the poor.

McPheeters, Harold (1923 -) (C-2; HS-10). A *psychiatrist* who received a grant for the funding of some of the first mental health and *human services* programs at community colleges. He is often said to be the founder of the human services field.

Mead, Margaret (1901 - 1978) (C-7; HS-7). An influential American anthropologist who made *ethnographic research* popular through her studies of aboriginal youth in Samoa.

Mean (C-9; HS-9). A statistical property referring to the average of all scores in a set of numbers or values. A type of *measure of central tendency*. See also *Median* and *Mode*.

Meaninglessness (C-8 HS-5). In *existential therapy*, the idea that life has no inherent meaning, life is absurd, and the recognition that all meaning given to existence is created by the person.

Meaning-Making System (C-5; HS-3). The manner in which one comes to understand the world. See also *Subject/Object Theory*.

***Measurement and Evaluation in Counseling and Development* (C-6; HS-3).** Journal of the *Association for Assessment and Research in Counseling* (*AARC*).

Measures of Central Tendency (C-8; HS-6). Statistical procedures that provide information about the middle range of scores as described by the *mean*, *median*, and *mode*.

Measures of Variability (C-8; HS-5). Statistical procedures that provide information on the extent to which scores vary as described by the *range*, *interquartile range*, and *standard deviation*.

Median (C-9; HS-9). A *measure of central tendency* that is the middle score, or the score at which 50% of scores fall above and 50% fall below. In a *skewed curve* or skewed distribution, the median is generally the most accurate measure of central tendency since it is not affected by unusually high or low scores. See also *Mean* and *Mode*.

Medicaid (C-6; HS-7). One of the social insurance programs often called *medical assistance* run by the U.S. federal government to provide health coverage for low-income individuals and families.

Medical Assistance (C-6; HS-7). The generic named used to refer to various social insurance programs, like *Medicaid*, providing medical and mental health coverage to low-income individuals or individuals who are living with disabilities.

Medical Model (C-8; HS-8). The view, often held by adherents of the *deterministic* view of human nature and in contrast with the *wellness approach*, asserting that mental illness is most likely caused by genetic/biological factors and therefore can be *diagnosed* and treated as a physical illness.

Medicare (C-6; HS-7). One of the social insurance programs run by the U.S. federal government that provides health coverage for adults aged 65 or older, who have contributed to the Medicare system during their working life, or other select groups of individuals.

Medication Management (C-6; HS-6). Refers to the on-going use of prescribed medications (i.e., drugs) for the treatment of individuals with medical, psychological, or psychiatric conditions. Ideally, such treatment is overseen by a prescribing *psychiatrist* or other physician with specialty in treating the conditions in question.

Medication-Induced Movement Disorders and Other Adverse Effects of Medications (C-7; HS-5). A group of *mental disorders* that manifest as a result of adverse and severe side effects to medications, although a causal link cannot always be shown. Some of these disorders include neuroleptic-induced Parkinsonism, neuroleptic malignant syndrome, medication-induced dystonia, medication-induced acute akathisia, tardive dyskinesia, tardive akathisia, medication-induced postural tremor, other medication-induced movement disorder, antidepressant discontinuation syndrome, and other disorders as a result of adverse effects of medication.

Meditation (C-7; HS-7). Various types of relaxation, self-regulation, internal energy transference, contemplation, and other *mindfulness* techniques individuals use to change *consciousness* or for related purposes (e.g., relaxation, anxiety-reduction, pain management, mental focusing). Meditation is used within many medical and mental health therapeutic contexts and has roots as a practice in a wide variety of religions. See also *Mindfulness.*

Mehrabian, Albert (1939 -) (C-4; HS-4). A psychological researcher who in the early 1970s demonstrated that words accounted for 7% of what was being communicated, while voice intonation accounted for 38%, and body language for about 55%.

Meichenbaum, Donald (1940 -) (C-7; HS-3). A cognitive therapist who believes that it is not only the behavior of the individual that becomes reinforced, but the ways in which the individual thinks.

Melting Pot Myth (C-6; HS-6). The misnomer that various values and customs of different *cultures* become integrated and subsumed into the larger culture. See also *Cultural Mosaic.*

Member Checks (C-7; HS-3). A method of ensuring *trustworthiness* in *qualitative research*, that involves going back to individuals who participated in the research and reviewing their participant data to check for accuracy.

Membership Benefits (C-4; HS-4). Membership in *professional associations* provides a number of unique opportunities and benefits, including subscriptions to professional journals, professional development opportunities, *networking* opportunities, *consultation* on ethical issues and ethical dilemmas, legislative updates and policy setting alerts, links to listservs and interest networks, computer-assisted *job* search services, professional liability insurance, scholarships, and more.

Men (C-4; HS-4). See *Diverse Populations Human Service Professionals Work With.*

Men's Issues Therapy (C-5; HS-5). A *gender aware* counseling approach that focuses on specific tasks to be achieved in the helping relationship when the client is a man.

Mental Disorder (C-10; HS-10). A condition that influences one's thoughts, feelings, or behaviors that causes suffering or inhibits one's ability to function. A list and descriptions of mental disorders can be found in the *Diagnostic and Statistical Manual-5.*

Mental Filter (C-7; HS-5). Focusing only on negative aspects of oneself, of another, or of a situation. See also *Cognitive Distortion* and *Faulty Logic.*

Mental Functions (Thinking, Feeling, Sensing, Intuiting) (C-7; HS-4). In *analytical psychology* (*Jungian therapy*), the *thinking function*, *feeling function*, *sensing function*, and *intuiting function*, along with our *attitudes* (*extrovert* or *introvert*), that make up the *psychological type* of the person. *Judging* and *perceiving* mental functions were later added by *Myers and Briggs.*

Mental Health America (MHA) (C-4; HS-5). A leading community-based nonprofit association that is focused on addressing the needs of those with mental illness and promoting the mental health of Americans. Formerly called the *National Mental Health Association* (*NMHA*).

Mental Health Counseling (C-9; HS-7). Counseling or *psychotherapy* that focuses on mental health concerns, including possible *mental disorders.* Usually conducted by *mental health counselors*, although others with related degrees can also practice mental health counseling.

Mental Health Counselor (C-9; HS-7). A subspecialty in the counseling profession focusing on *mental health counseling.* The mental health counselor has at least a master's degree in counseling. See also *Counselor.*

Mental Health Professionals (C-10; HS-10). A blanket term referring to a number of professionals who work in a variety of capacities to support the recovery, well-being, and improved functioning of their clients, including but not limited to: *psychiatrists*, *psychologists*, *social workers*, *counselors*, *human services professionals*, and *nurse practitioners.* Oftentimes, mental health professionals work together on *interdisciplinary teams*; however, each profession has a unique and distinct professional identity with an area of expertise.

***Mental Health Study Act* (C-7; HS-6).** Passed in 1955, a broadly based effort to study the *diagnosis* and treatment of mental illness.

Mental Health Support (C-5; HS-7). The process of offering general support and advice to clients concerning their mental health. Not as intensive as *mental health counseling*, this type of work is usually performed by human service professionals.

***Mental Measurements Yearbook* (C-8; HS-3).** See *Buros Mental Measurement Yearbook*

Mental Research Institute (MRI) (C-6; HS-3). This institute was formed out of the work of a number of theorists at *Palo Alto.* The institute was led by *Bateson*, *Jackson*,

Haley, Satir, Madanes, Watzlawick, and Weakland, who focused on communication and family process and influenced a number of *couples and family counseling* approaches. See also *Palo Alto Mental Research Institute.*

Mental Retardation (C-8; HS-8). An outdated, and now viewed as a derogatory, term used for *intellectual disability.*

Mental Status Exam (C-8; HS-7). An *informal assessment* of a client in four areas, including: (1) how the client presents himself or herself (appearance and behavior); (2) the client's emotional state (*affect*); (3) the client's ability to think clearly (thought components); and (4) the client's memory state and orientation to the world (cognition).

Mental Status Report (C-6; HS-5). A one or two paragraph written report by the helper about the findings from a *mental status exam.*

Mescaline (C-5; HS-5). The primary psychoactive substance found in the cactus *Peyote.* It can produce psychedelic, transcendent, and altered *consciousness* effects when ingested. It is used recreationally, ritualistically, and medically. It is a *controlled substance* in the United States. See also *Peyote.*

Mesmer, Franz (1734 - 1815) (C-7; HS-5). A German physician and predecessor of *Freud* who influenced him to practice *hypnosis.* The name from which the word *mesmerize* was derived.

Mesmerize (C-4; HS-4). To gain control or power over individuals or their actions via *hypnosis* or related techniques. Mesmerism lead to the development of hypnosis as a mental health technique. See also *Mesmer, Franz.*

Meta-Analysis (C-8; HS-5). A type of research that involves reviewing, summarizing, or analyzing a collection of previously published research on a related topic, such as a meta-analysis of research on practitioner's experiences with suicide prevention.

Meta-Cognition (C-6; HS-4). Knowledge, beliefs, and awareness of one's own thought processes. Meta-cognitions are often associated with intelligence and contribute to our ability to be successful learners.

Metaphors and Analogies (C-5; HS-3). Using *symbols,* allegories, and a logical analysis to make a comparison between a client's current situation and an external event to establish *empathy* by responding in a manner in which the client feels heard and understood at a deep level. For example, for a client who is feeling disconnected and lost from others in life, the helper may explain how the client is adrift at sea far from shore in a boat with no paddle. Considered an *advanced empathic response.*

Metatheory Stage of Integrative Counseling (C-4; HS-3). The fourth stage of developing an *integrative approach to counseling,* in which the counselor develops a full appreciation of many theories and ties together commonalities among them into a single integrative approach. See also *Eclecticism.*

Methadone (C-8; HS-8). A synthetic *opioid* drug used most often in the *recovery* treatment of and *detoxification* from more dangerous opioid *addiction,* such as *heroin.* Methadone is a *controlled substance* that itself can be abused and used addictively; individuals using the drug in their recovery are said to be on *Methadone maintenance.*

Methadone Maintenance (C-7; HS-7). When an individual is prescribed *Methadone* as part of a program for *detoxification* and/or *recovery* from *opioid* drug abuse. See also *Methadone.*

Methodology (C-8; HS-6). In research, the methodology, or procedures, section which includes a description of how the study was conducted and is based on the type of research that was conducted.

MCGA (C-8; HS-3). See *Military and Government Counseling Association.* A division of the *American Counseling Association.*

***Michigan Alcoholism Screening Test* (*MAST*) (C-6; HS-4).** A popular *test* used for the assessment of *alcohol abuse* and use.

Micro Level (C-7; HS-7). Focusing on the individual or student versus the *macro level*, which focuses on the system or community at large.

Micro Skills (C-5; HS-4). In the training of human service professionals, refers to the various individual skills that effective practitioners must master with their clients, such as *empathy*, *genuineness*, *reflection of feeling*, and many related micro skills.

Microaggressions (C-9; HS-9). Subtle, brief, and often *unconscious* behaviors aimed at demeaning a person based on his or her *culture*, *ethnicity*, *gender*, *sexual orientation*, or *other minority status*. Related to the concepts of *discrimination*, *prejudice*, and *stereotypes.*

Microcounseling Skills Training (C-7; HS-5). Based on many of the skills deemed critical by *Carl Rogers* and other *humanistic* counselors and *psychologists*, these packaged ways of training counselors focus on the learning of basic counseling skills, such as *attending behaviors*, *listening*, and *empathic understanding*. These approaches showed that the learning of such skills could occur in a relatively short amount of time and that the practice of such skills has a positive impact on counseling outcomes. See also *Common Factors.*

Middle School Counselor (C-7; HS-7). One of three levels of *school counseling*. U.S. states sometimes credential K-12 or sometimes credential at specific grade levels.

Milan Group (C-5; HS-2). Inspired by *Gregory Bateson* and *Jay Haley*, this group developed an approach to *couples and family counseling* that stressed *cognitive* and *constructivist therapy* and believed that language was critical to meaning making.

Milgram, Stanley (1933 - 1984) (C-8; HS-7). An American social *psychologist* who conducted controversial, deceptive research on obedience that was one factor which eventually led to restraints being placed on the ways research could be conducted. In his study, subjects believed they were shocking individuals when they did not adequately complete a task. In fact, the individuals who were "shocked" were actors. The purpose of the study was to test the extent to which participants would follow instructions from an authority figure to exert harm on another person. See also *Institutional Review Board.*

Milieu Therapy (C-4; HS-4). A form of *counseling* where individuals join a therapeutic community of multiple individuals (typically 30 people) focusing on responsibility for self and for others, based on set rules and consequences. More advanced, or senior clients, take on more responsibility and model behaviors for others in these communities.

Military and Government (C-3; HS-3). Setting where *clinical mental health counselors*, and related professionals, may be employed such as with the Army or Veteran's Administration.

Military and Government Counseling Association (MCGA) (C-8; HS-3). A division of the *American Counseling Association* that mostly focuses on military counselors and other counselors and educators in government.

Mill, James (1773 - 1836) (C-5; HS-4). A British historian, philosopher, and economist who believed the mind is a *blank slate* upon which ideas are generated. See also *Tabula Rasa.*

Miller, Jean Baker (1927 - 2006) (C-7; HS-4). An American *psychiatrist*, *psychoanalyst*, and author known for developing *relational-cultural theory*, considered a type of *gender aware therapy* focused on women. See also *Feminist Therapy.*

Miller, W. R (1947 -) (C-6; HS-3). An educator in the field of *psychology* and one of the founders of *motivational interviewing.*

***Millon Clinical Multiaxial Inventory* (C-7; HS-5).** An *objective personality test* that is a comprehensive psychological *assessment* of personality, *psychopathology*, and *psychiatric disorders.*

Mimesis (C-4; HS-2). In *Structural Family Therapy*, a *joining* technique counselors use with their clients to gain trust via gently and respectively mimicking their behaviors and patterns of communication in sessions.

Mindfulness (C-8; HS-8). A wide variety of techniques used to focus an individual's *self-awareness* or *consciousness* in the present moment, including all thoughts, feelings, and bodily experiences. Mindfulness is sometimes seen as a type of *meditation* or focusing practice and is used in many counseling approaches, such as in *Dialectical Behavior Therapy*, to help clients become aware of their issues.

Mind-Reading (C-6; HS-3). Making assumptions about what other people are thinking while discounting other possibilities. A type of *Cognitive Distortion.*

Miner, J. B. (C-4; HS-1). Developed one of first group interest inventories in 1922 to assist large groups of high school students in selecting an *occupation.*

Mini Mental Status Exam (C-7; HS-3). A commonly used standardized questionnaire to measure mental status in clients. See also *Mental Status Exam.*

***Minnesota Multiphasic Personality Inventory-II (MMPI-II)* (C-8; HS-7).** A commonly used *objective personality test* that measures *psychopathology* and personality traits in people. The *test* includes ten content scales, a lie scale, and a defensiveness scale, amongst other things.

Minnesota Point of View (C-7; HS-2). Developed by *E. G. Williamson* during the 1930s and based on *trait-and-factor theory*, this approach is seen as the *first comprehensive theory of counseling* (as distinguished from *Freud's* theory of *psychoanalysis*).

Minority Groups (C-8; HS-8). A group of people being singled out because of their cultural or physical characteristics and who are being systematically oppressed by those individuals who are in a position of power. See also *Oppression.*

Minuchin, Salvador (1921 -) (C-7; HS-4). An influential Argentinean-American family *therapist* who developed *structural family therapy* and highlighted the importance of understanding *situational crises* and developmental milestones when working with families. See also *Joining* and *Structural Family Therapy.*

Miracle Question (C-8; HS-7). Within *solution-focused brief therapy*, a type of *preferred goals question* focused on quickly identifying where the client wants to be in the future and helping the client accomplish his or her desired goals. Often put in a framework which asks, "If you were to wake up in the morning and find your world to be what you want it to be, what would that look like," or "what would be different?" See also *Solution-Focused Questions.*

Mirror Neurons (C-8; HS-6). Neurons within the brain that fire when one observes a behavior in another that mimics a behavior the observer has had. Mirror neurons appear to be related to the ability to express *empathy*, in that neurons in the observer will "mirror" (or fire) when the person being observed expresses feelings or shows behaviors that the observer has experienced. It appears that individuals can increase the number of mirror neurons being fired with practice.

***Mirror of Men's Lives* (C-5; HS-1).** A book written by *Sanchez de Arevalo*, in 1468, which included one of the first *job* classification systems.

Mirroring (C-6; HS-6). A therapeutic technique in which the helper attempts to replicate the client's physical presentation in session by maintaining a similar *affect*, *posture*, and other body language as the client. Used as a method of *joining* with the client.

Mistaken Beliefs (C-9; HS-6). Beliefs a person holds about *self* or the world that are not based on accurate information.

Mitwelt (C-7; HS-6). In *existential* terms, our social dimension, and it has to do with the ways in which we relate to one another and the common experiences that we all have and can understand. The challenge of mitwelt is to come to a balance between *isolation* from our social world and immersion within our social world. A term popularized by the philosopher *Ludwig Binswanger.* See also *Eigenwelt*, *Uberwelt*, and *Umwelt.*

Mixed Methods Approach (C-9; HS-7). Combining *quantitative* and *qualitative* methods of research in one's *research design.*

***MMPI-II* (C-8; HS-7).** See *Minnesota Multiphasic Personality Inventory-II.*

Mob Instinct (C-4; HS-3). The phenomenon that individuals, when around a group of others, naturally take on a *herd instinct* in the sense that they act together in unison concerning a belief and disregard their individual perspectives. Sometimes seen as a genetically based tendency and associated with *psychodynamic approaches.*

Mobile Therapy (C-5; HS-5). Various models of helping where the helper goes to the client within the community (e.g., client's home or sees the client at a school setting) to offer services.

Mobilizer (C-1; HS-5). A human service professional who organizes client and community support to provide needed services. One of the original 13 roles or functions of human service professionals as defined by the *Southern Regional Education*

Board.

Mode (C-9; HS-9). A statistical property referring to the most frequent *test* score of the group. A type of *measure of central tendency*. See also *Median* and *Mean*.

Modeling (C-9; HS-8). The subtle or deliberate ways that the helper, or others, can demonstrate new behaviors for the client in an effort for the client to practice, learn, and adopt those behaviors. Also called *social learning*, *imitation*, or *behavioral rehearsal*. See also *Inadvertent* and *Intentional Modeling*.

Modernism (C-7; HS-5). The idea that science can find the answer to most problems and can discover inherent structures relevant to the understanding of mental health problems (e.g., *id*, *ego*, *superego*, *schemas*). Contrast with *Post-Modernism*.

Monoamine Oxidase Inhibitors (C-5; HS-4). An older classification of *antidepressant* medications that are used to treat *depression* and *anxiety* disorders.

Mood (C-8; HS-7). The psychological state that a person is in, which can be habitual or short term. Moods are often described as less specific than *emotions* and are likely to be influenced by a multitude of variables as opposed to one trigger that creates emotions. One aspect of a *Mental Status Exam*.

Mood-Stabilizing Drugs (C-7; HS-6). A group of *psychotropic medications* that are used to treat *bipolar and related disorders*.

Moral Anxiety (C-8; HS-5). In *psychoanalysis*, *anxiety* that comes from fear of violating (or of getting caught violating) one's standards, morals, or values, such as the *anxiety* experienced by a religious teen getting caught looking at pornography by his parents.

Moral Development (C-8; HS-7). The manner in which a person develops a moral conscience. *Kohlberg* and *Gilligan* both developed moral models, although Gilligan suggested that women's *moral development* is different than men's.

Moral Dilemmas (C-5; HS-5). Problems of a moral nature that have no clear-cut answers. Given to children by *Lawrence Kohlberg* that gave direction for his *moral development* theory. See also the *Heinz Dilemma*.

Moral or Neurotic Guilt (C-7; HS-5). In *existential therapy*, feelings of guilt or remorse someone feels from engaging in behavior that is damaging to others or to oneself.

Moral Reasoning (C-6; HS-6). The manner in which individuals come to understand meaning relative to how they should behave in the world. Related to one's sense of right and wrong.

Morality (C-7; HS-7). Appropriate individual conduct as defined by one's family, *culture*, society, and religious writings. In counseling, related to some types of *ethical decision-making*. See also *Moral Models of Ethical Decision Making*.

Moreno, Jacob L. (1889 - 1974) (C-6; HS-4). An Austrian-American *psychiatrist* influential in the field of *group counseling* and the creator of *psychodrama*.

Morphine (C-7; HS-7). An *opiate* that is found organically in a number of plants and is used to treat pain. It can be taken orally, injected through the muscle, smoked, or administered intravenously and is a highly addictive *controlled substance* that some people abuse recreationally.

Motivational Interviewing (C-7; HS-4). An approach to helping rooted in the assumption that motivation is a key to change, is multidimensional, is dynamic and fluctuating, is influenced by social interactions, can be modified, and is influenced by the helper's style. The main task of helpers is to be collaborative, evocative, and honoring of their clients. They do this using four basic principles: expressing *empathy*, developing discrepancies, rolling with *resistance*, and supporting self-efficacy.

Mourning (C-7; HS-7). Another term for the grief and loss process and emotional or behavioral experiences from this process. See also *Grief, Stages of.*

MSW (C-9; HS-9). See *Master's in Social Work.*

Multicultural and Social Justice Counseling Competencies (C-9; HS-9). Areas of proficiency that were created to assist helpers when working with diverse clients that are sectioned into four domains: (1) counselor [helper] *self-awareness*, (2) client worldview, (3) counseling relationship, and (4) counseling and *advocacy interventions.* Critical to these competencies are the *attitudes and beliefs*, *knowledge*, *skills*, *and actions* of the counselor. Helpers should be aware of these competencies and how to work with clients using them. Previously called the *Multicultural Counseling Competencies.*

Multicultural Counseling (C-9; HS-9). The ways in which a helper works effectively with a client who is different from the helper's *culture*, *gender*, *sexual orientation*, *religion*, *ethnicity*, or other distinguishing aspects. In such cases, the helper should develop maximum competencies to work with the client and should have developed *cultural competence.*

Multicultural Counseling Competencies (C-9; HS-9). See *Multicultural and Social Justice Counseling Competencies.*

Multicultural/Multiracial Student Services (C-5; HS-5). An office, in higher education, where *student affairs and college counselors*, and other related human service professionals, sometimes find employment working with culturally and racially diverse students. See also *Biracial/Multiracial Identity Development.*

Multigenerational Family Therapy (C-7; HS-5). Approaches to family *therapy* that use the ideas of *Murray Bowen*, *Ivan Boszormenyi-Nagy*, and other related *family therapy* theorists.

Multimodal Therapy (C-6; HS-3). A *cognitive-behavioral approach* to counseling, developed by *Arnold Lazarus*, that assesses a wide range of client domains, including behavior, *affect*, sensation, imagery, cognition, interpersonal factors, and drug/biological considerations, generally referred to as the *BASIC ID.*

Multiple Aptitude Test (C-7; HS-4). A type of *aptitude test* that measures a broad range of abilities which are associated with *occupational* choice.

Multiple-Perspective-Taking (C-7; HS-5). Understanding a number of different points of view. Related to *cognitive complexity*. See also *Multiple Realities.*

Multiple Realities (C-6; HS-3). The ability to identify multiple origins, or perspectives on the world, that led to the present understanding of reality. Particularly important in *narrative therapy.*

Multiple Regression (C-6; HS-2). A commonly used type of statistical analysis within *multivariate correlational studies.* It is used to determine the extent to which a combination of *predictor variables* predicts scores on one or more *criterion variables.*

Multiplicity (C-6; HS-4). The stage, after *dualism* and before *relativism*, in *Perry's* theory of intellectual development. Represents movement out of dogmatic thinking and into *multiple perspective taking.*

Multistoried (C-6; HS-3). The concept, in *narrative therapy*, that all of our lives have multiple *narratives* and that we tend to stress some, called our *dominant narratives*, more than others.

Multivariate Analysis of Variance (MANOVA) (C-7; HS-4). In *quantitative research*, a statistical analysis used when two or more *dependent variables* are being examined in reference to one or more *independent variables.*

Multivariate Correlational Studies (C-7; HS-4). In *quantitative research*, the examination of the relationship among more than two *variables.*

Murray, Henry (1893 - 1988) (C-7; HS-3). An American *psychologist* who developed the *Thematic Apperception Test (TAT)*, which asks a subject to view a number of standard pictures, one at a time, and create a story that has a beginning, middle, and end which is later interpreted by the test administrator.

Mustabatory Irrational Beliefs (C-8; HS-5). See *Grandiose Irrational Beliefs* and *Rational Emotive Behavior Therapy.*

Musturbation (C-6; HS-4). When an individual engages in *grandiose irrational beliefs* or related *absolutistic musts and shoulds* type thinking in life. See also *Rational Emotive Behavior Therapy.*

Mutuality (C-6; HS-4). In *Kegan's subject/object theory*, movement from narcissism to a sense that we have shared interests and can satisfy each other's needs.

***Myers-Briggs Type Indicator* (*MBTI*) (C-7; HS-5).** An *objective personality* test used to measure common personality qualities based on *Jung's mental functions* and *attitudes* as well as two additional mental functions developed by *Katherine Cook Briggs* and her daughter *Isabel Briggs Myers.* This test is used to assess for normal personality styles and is often used to help people understand how they are different from one another and how their personality styles may fit certain types of *jobs.* Individuals are found to be one of 16 personality types that are a combination of *extroverted* (E) *or introverted* (I), *sensing* (S) or *intuiting* (N), *thinking* (T) or *feeling* (F), and *judging* (J) or perceiving (P) (e.g., ENFP).

Myers, Isabel Briggs (1897 - 1980) and *Katherine* Cook Briggs (1875 - 1968) (C-6; HS-4). This mother and daughter team developed the *Myers-Briggs Type Indicator.*

Mystery, Respectful Curiosity, Awe (C-7; HS-5). The manner in which *a narrative therapist* brings himself or herself into the *counseling relationship*, which shows respect for the client and focuses on a positive curiosity about the client and his or her life.

Myth of the Independent Mind (C-3; HS-1). In *relational and subjectivity therapy*, the concept that we are brought up believing we are independent, but in actuality, our sense of *self* is developed through *mutuality.*

NAADAC (C-4; HS-4). See *National Association of Alcoholism and Drug Abuse Counselors.*

NACMHC (C-7; HS-4). See *National Academy for Certified Mental Health Counselors.*

NAMI (C-7; HS-7). See *National Alliance for Mental Illness.*

Narcan (C-8; HS-8). See *Naxolene.*

Narcolepsy (C-6; HS-4). A *sleep disorder* leading to sleepiness in the daytime and cataplexy (sudden muscle weakness while fully conscious). *Stimulants* have been found somewhat successful in the treatment of this disorder.

Narcotics (C-7; HS-7). A class of *controlled substances* that contains *opioid* drugs, such as *morphine*, *heroin*, *codeine*, *Percocet*, *oxycodone*, and other related *opiates*, although other drugs, such as *cannabis* and *cocaine* are often included in this general category. Some narcotics are prescribed for pain relief and other medical uses and these drugs are frequently abused recreationally and can be highly addictive.

Narcotics Anonymous (C-7; HS-7). A type of *support group* for individuals who are living with *addictions* to *narcotic* substances and related addiction behaviors.

Narrative Family Therapy (C-7; HS-4). A type of *family therapy* based on a belief that it is critical to understand the stories that families tell to help them *deconstruct* how they come to understand their family, with the goal being able to recreate how the family understands itself. Based on *post-modernism*, the approach examines how language is used to develop individuals' understandings of reality and how it also can oppress individuals. It also examines how individuals and families can come to understand and recreate their *dominant stories* in life. See also *Narrative Therapy.*

Narrative Reasoning (C-4; HS-2). The understanding of an individual's unique life story. Used in *narrative family therapy* and *narrative therapy.*

Narrative Therapy (C-8; HS-5). Developed by *Michael White* and *David Epston*, a *post-modern* approach that suggests reality is a social construction and that each person's reality is maintained through his or her *narrative* or language discourse. Values held by those in power are often disseminated through language and become the norms against which individuals compare themselves. Therefore, problems individuals have, including *mental disorders*, are seen as a function of how people compare themselves to what they have been told are the norms of society. Thus, individuals sometimes end up believing their lives are filled with problems that are demonstrated by the *problem-saturated stories* or narratives they generate. By being humble, asking respectful questions, listening to exceptions to the problem-saturated stories, and listening to subtle positive stories, narrative therapists help clients create new, *preferred stories.* See also *Post-Modernism* and *Social Constructionism.*

Narratives (C-7; HS-6). In *narrative therapy*, the stories defining who and what clients are in life.

Nasal Reflect Neurosis (C-4; H-2). Developed by *Wilhem Fliess*, this theory suggested that there were similarities between nasal and genital tissue and that surgery, or other treatment of the nose, could lessen certain psychological symptoms. This theory influenced *Freud*, although he later distanced himself from it.

NASP (C-6; HS-5). See *National Association of School Psychologists.*

NASPA (C-6; HS-2). National Association of Student Personnel Administrators. Now the *Student Affairs Administrators in Higher Education* but keeping the *NASPA* acronym.

NASW (C-9; HS-9). See *National Association of Social Workers.*

National Academy for Certified Mental Health Counselors (NACMHC) (C-7; HS-3). During the 1970s, this national academy offered one of the first *certifications* for counselors. Today, this *certification* is subsumed by the *National Board for Certified Counselors* and is called a *Certified Clinical Mental Health Counselor (CCMHC).*

National Alliance on Mental Illness (NAMI) (C-7; HS-7). A large education and *advocacy* organization for mentally ill individuals in the United States.

National Assessment of Educational Progress (NAEP) (C-4; HS-1). Sometimes called "the nation's report card," these *assessment* instruments allow each U.S. state to compare progress in achievement within its own state and to other states around the country.

National Association for Advancement of Colored People (NAACP) (C-7; HS-7). A civil rights organization formed in 1909 to fight *prejudice*, *Jim Crow laws*, and to advance the *status* of people of color in America.

National Association for Poetry Therapy (NAPT) (C-4; HS-3). A U.S. national *professional association* that has established guidelines and support for the practice of *poetry therapy* and related written word uses in counseling. See also *Creative and Expressive Therapists.*

National Association of Alcoholism and Drug Abuse Counselors (NAADAC) (C-6; HS-6). An independent U.S. association for *substance abuse* counselors representing over 85,000 bachelor's and master's level *addiction counselors.*

National Association of School Psychologists (NASP) (C-6; HS-5). An independent *professional association* for *school psychologists* in the U.S.

National Association of Social Workers (NASW) (C-9; HS-9). The U.S. national *professional association* representing bachelor's and master's level *social workers.*

National Association of Women Deans, Administrators, and Counselors (NAWDAC) (C-4; HS-2). A U.S. *professional association* for female college deans, administrators, and counselors.

National Board for Certified Counselors (NBCC) (C-9; HS-3). A U.S. organization that sponsors *certification* of counselors as *National Certified Counselor (NCCs)* and in three specialty areas: *National Certified School Counselor*, *Certified Clinical Mental Health Counselor*, and *Master Addiction Counselor.*

National Board for Professional Teaching Standards (C-4; HS-3). Developed a *certification* process for *school counselors* in the U.S.

National Career Development Association (NCDA) (C-7; HS-3). A division of the *American Counseling Association* that focuses on vocational and *career assessment* and counseling.

National Certified Counselor (NCC) (C-10; HS-3). *Certification* as a counselor that requires a master's degree and additional training and *supervision* offered by the *National Board for Certified Counselors (NBCC)*. Requires passing the *National Counselor Exam (NCE)*.

National Certified School Counselor (NCSC) (C-7; HS-7). A subspecialty *certification* for *school counselors* that is offered by the *National Board for Certified Counselors (NBCC)*.

National Certified School Psychologist (NCSP) (C-6; HS-5). A U.S. *certification* that one can gain after having successfully graduated from a state-approved *school psychology* program.

National Clinical Mental Health Counselor (NCMHC) (C-7; HS-3). A subspecialty *certification* for mental health counseling offered by the *National Board for Certified Counselors (NBCC)*.

National Clinical Mental Health Counselor Exam (NCMHCE) (C-6; HS-3). The examination that one must pass to become a *National Clinical Mental Health Counselor.*

National Coalition of Creative Arts Therapies (C-4; HS-3). A U.S. *professional association* for counseling and human service professionals specializing in creative art therapies, such as art, music, dance/movement, or *drama therapy*. See also *Creative and Expressive Therapists.*

National Committee for Mental Hygiene (C-6; HS-6). In 1909, *Clifford Beers* helped to establish the *National Committee for Mental Hygiene*, which lobbied the U.S. Congress to pass laws that would improve deplorable conditions in mental institutions.

National Counselor Exam (NCE) (C-7; HS-3). Examination that one must pass to become a *National Certified Counselor (NCC)*. Becoming an NCC demonstrates experience and knowledge in the field, and some U.S. states use the exam as part of the process of becoming a *licensed professional counselor.*

National Credentialing Academy (NCA) (C-5; HS-2). The U.S organization that offers *credentialing* as a *certified family therapist*, sponsored by the *International Association of Family Counselors.*

***National Defense Education Act* (*NDEA*) (C-7; HS-3).** Passed in 1958 as a direct response to the Soviet Union's launching of *Sputnik*, this U.S. act provided funding for the expansion of counseling programs in schools in order to identify gifted students. Was critical to the spread of *school counselors.*

National Employment Counseling Association (NECA) (C-8; HS-3). A division of the *American Counseling Association* focused on issues related to employment and *career counseling.*

National Institute of Mental Health (NIMH) (C-7; HS-7). Created by the U.S. Congress in the late 1940s, this agency was the federal government's first real effort at confronting mental health issues and in sponsoring systematic research and training in the mental health field.

***National Mental Health Act* (C-6; HS-6).** An act passed in 1946 that granted U.S. states funding for research, training, *prevention*, *diagnosis*, and treatment related to *mental disorders.*

National Mental Health Association (NMHA) (C-4; HS-5). See *Mental Health America* (*MHA*).

National Office for School Counselor Advocacy (C-5; HS-2). Affiliated with the College Board, this office has resources to help *school counselors* with their college and *career* readiness mission.

National Organization for Human Service Education (C-2; HS-8). See *National Organization for Human services.*

National Organization for Human Services (NOHS) (C-2; HS-10). Founded in 1975 as the *National Organization for Human Service Education*, this *professional association*: (1) provides a link between human service educators, practitioners, and organizations, (2) supports the *credentialing* of human service professionals, (3) provides educative materials, ethical guidelines, and workshops for human service professionals, (4) supports creative approaches toward meeting clients' needs, (5) and promotes the professional identity of human service professionals. The association has six regions, a journal called the *Journal of Human Services* (formerly, *Human Service Education*), a newsletter called *The Link*, a national conference, and much more.

National Rehabilitation Counseling Association (NRCA) (C-6; HS-5). A *professional association* for *rehabilitation counselors* in the U.S.

National Standards for School Counseling Programs (C-5; HS-2). Standards of *accreditation* published by the *American School Counselor Association;* contains the standards and competencies (knowledge, attitudes, and skills) that students are expected to gain in the academic, *career*, and personal/social domains. These standards were revised in 2004 as the *ASCA National Standards for School Counseling Programs* and again in 2014 as the *ASCA Mindsets and Behaviors for Student Success: K-12 College- and Career-Readiness Standards for Every Student.*

National Training Laboratory (NTL) (C-7; HS-5). Founded in the 1940s by *Kurt Lewin* and other prominent theorists, this U.S. institution examines group dynamics and trains individuals to understand the special interactions that occur in *groups.*

National Vocational Guidance Association (NVGA) (C-8; HS-2). Founded in 1913 as a U.S. *professional association* for *vocational guidance counselors*, it is considered to be the forerunner of the *American Counseling Association* (*ACA*).

Nationally Certified School Psychologists (NCSP) (C-4; HS-3). A U.S. national *credential* for *school psychologists.*

Native Americans (C-6; HS-6). In the U.S., Native Americans consist of two major groups: American Indians and Alaskan Natives (mostly Aleut and Inuit). See also *Indigenous People.*

Natural Consequences (C-7; HS-5). Behavioral consequences that would normally or naturally occur if behaviors are left to run their typical course, such as allowing a child who doesn't want to wear his or her coat to not wear the coat when it is cold out. After experiencing the cold, the child is likely to wear a coat in the future.

Originally developed for *individual psychology*. See also *Logical Consequences.*

Natural Responses (C-5; HS-5). Reflecting a client's affect and content while using a natural tone and fluid response.

Naturalistic Observation (C-7; HS-4). A research approach where one observes individuals (and phenomena) in their natural state or environment without interfering.

Naturalistic-Phenomenological Philosophy (C-7; HS-4). The basis of *qualitative research*, this approach assumes there are many ways in which reality can be interpreted and experienced by individuals. See also *Phenomenology.*

Nature-Versus-Nurture (C-7; HS-7). The ongoing discussion of whether genes or environment play a more crucial role in human/animal development. Most individuals believe there is a dynamic interaction between genes and the environment.

NAWDAC (C-4; HS-2). See *National Association of Women Deans, Administrators, and Counselors.*

Naxolene (C-8; HS-8). Often sold under the brand name *Narcan*, this medication blocks the effects of *opioids* (e.g., *heroin*, *cocaine*) and can be lifesaving if given to a person who is overdosing. Most U.S states have adopted its use by paramedics and, when injected into the muscle, it can work in as little as 5 minutes, or 2 minutes if injected intravenously.

NBCC (C-9; HS-3). See *National Board for Certified Counselors.*

NBPTS (C-6; HS-2). See *National Board for Professional Teaching Standards.*

NCA (C-5; HS-2). See *National Credentialing Academy.*

NCC (C-10; HS-3). See *National Certified Counselor.*

NCDA (C-8; HS-3). See *National Career Development Association.*

NCE (C-7; HS-3). See *National Counselor Exam.*

NCSC (C-7; HS-7). See *National Certified School Counselor.*

NCSP (C-6; HS-5). See *National Certified School Psychologist.*

***NDEA* (C-7; HS-3).** See *National Defense Education Act.*

NECA (C-8; HS-3). See *National Employment Counseling Association.*

Necessary and Sufficient Conditions (C-6; HS-6). The six conditions in *person-centered counseling* that are necessary if counseling is to be successful, and are sufficient enough that no other *intervention* is needed. They include: (1) two people are in psychological contact; (2) one, the helper, is *congruent* within the helping relationship; (3) the second, the client, is *incongruent*; (4) the helper shows *unconditional positive regard*; (5) the helper shows *empathy*; (6) and, to some degree the client recognizes the unconditional positive regard and the empathy.

Need Fulfillment (C-6; HS-5). In *Gestalt therapy*, the process of ensuring all *needs*, past and present, are in some manner addressed so that one might avoid *unfinished business.*

Need Identification (C-6; HS-5). In *Gestalt therapy*, the process of identifying current and past unfulfilled *needs* to ensure need satisfaction.

Need Satisfaction Cycle (C-6; HS-2). A cycle, in *Gestalt therapy*, that suggests that *needs* become noticed and addressed in the following sequence: sensation, awareness, contact, satisfaction, and withdrawal (or "zero point).

Need to be Regarded (C-6; HS-5). See *Positive Regard, Need for.*

Needs (C-6; HS-5). In *reality therapy*, it is believed that individuals are born with five needs of varying strengths, including *survival* (*self-preservation*), *love and belonging*, *power* (*inner control*), *freedom* (*independence*), and *fun* (*enjoyment*).

Needs Assessment (C-7; HS-7). The formal *assessment* process of exploring and addressing needs, gaps, or problem areas that exist between present conditions and desired outcomes, which is often used in *program evaluation* to improve an existing structure, such as a business, program, or organization.

Need-Strength Profile (C-7; HS-4). In *reality therapy*, the unique, genetically-based profile of the strength of our five needs, that includes *survival* (or *self-preservation*), *love and belonging*, *power* (or *inner control*), *freedom* (or *independence*), and fun (or *enjoyment*).

Negative Automatic Thoughts (C-8; HS-6). Ongoing, *preconscious* thoughts that impact how we act and feel in problematic ways and are related to our *intermediate thoughts* and our *core beliefs* (e.g., I don't think I can write this paper adequately). See also *Cognitive Therapy.*

Negative Correlation (C-8; HS-5). A type of *correlation* that occurs when increases in the value of one *variable* is associated with decreases in the value of another variable (or vice versa). See also *Correlation.*

Negative Feedback Loop (C-6; HS-4). In *cybernetics* and from systems view of *family therapy*, interactional processes (or feedback) that occur within systems that have the effect of minimizing irregularities and contributing to the stability of the system (which could be healthy or unhealthy, depending on the nature of the system). For example, when a spouse becomes angry, the other spouse has a way of diffusing the first spouse's anger, thus returning the system to a calm state and its more usual way of functioning. Contrast with *Positive Feedback Loop.*

Negative Punishment (C-7; HS-6). In *behavior therapy*, the removal of a *stimulus* that leads to a decrease in a specific (or targeted) behavior. For example, a teacher takes away recess due to a child's acting out in class. See also *Punishment.*

Negative Reinforcement (C-8; HS-7). In *behavior therapy*, any *stimulus* that, when removed following a response, increases the likelihood of that response. For example, if an older sibling is not doing homework due to the screaming of her baby sister in the room, removing the baby from her sibling's presence yields an increase in homework behavior.

Negatively Skewed Curve (C-8; HS-5). A set of *test* scores or data distribution where the majority of scores fall at the upper, or positive, end of the curve. It is said to be a negatively skewed curve or distribution because the tail of the distribution points toward the "negative" or low-end of curve (the tail points to the left).

Neglect (C-7; HS-8). A type of abuse in which parents or caregivers of children, disabled adults, the elderly, or others in need fail to provide food, clothing, shelter, medical care, or supervision to the extent that the individual's health, safety, and well-being are at-risk of harm or death.

Negligence (C-7; HS-7). The unintentional breach of a duty that one person owes another. In the helping relationship, it is when a client sustains emotional or physical harm as a result of a helper not taking proper care or acting in a reasonable manner in the helping relationship. Negligence can result in *malpractice* suits against helpers.

Neo-Freudian Approaches (C-8; HS-5). Although still emphasizing early child-rearing, the *conscious*, and the *unconscious*, these approaches tend to focus more on *psychosocial forces* and relationships in the building of *self*, and play down the influence of *instincts*. They also tend to be less deterministic than the classic *psychodynamic approaches* and sometimes more interactive between the *analyst* and client. Some include *Erik Erikson's psychosocial theory*, *object relations theories*, and *relational-intersubjectivity approaches*.

Networking (C-7; HS-7). The process of becoming involved in numerous professionally related activities, and the professionals associated with them, in an effort to become more knowledgeable about a field and to learn from or collaborate with others. It can lead to opportunities for new jobs or schools and scholarship opportunities with others who share similar interests.

Neurocognitive Disorders (C-8; HS-6). A group of *mental disorders* that are *diagnosed* when one's decline in cognitive functioning is significantly different from the past and is usually the result of a medical condition (e.g., Parkinson's, *Alzheimer's disease*), the use of a substance/medication, *traumatic brain injury*, or other related conditions. Examples of *neurocognitive disorders* (*NCD*) include delirium, and several types of major and mild *NCDs* such as frontotemporal *NCD*, *NCD* due to Parkinson's disease, *NCD* due to *HIV* infection, *NCD* due to *Alzheimer's disease*, substance- or medication-induced *NCD*, and vascular *NCD*, among others.

Neurodevelopmental Disorders (C-8; HS-7). A group of *mental disorders* that refer to *diagnoses* that typically manifest during early development, although diagnoses are sometimes not assigned until adulthood. Examples of neurodevelopmental disorders include *intellectual disabilities*, communication disorders, *autism spectrum disorders* (incorporating the former categories of autistic disorder, *Asperger's disorder*, childhood disintegrative disorder, and pervasive developmental disorder), *ADHD*, specific *learning disorders*, motor disorders, and other neurodevelopmental disorders.

Neurofeedback (C-8; HS-7). See *Neurological and Psychophysiological Therapies*.

Neuroleptics (C-6; HS-5). *Antipsychotic drugs* that are generally used in the treatment of *schizophrenia*. There are three broad classes of these drugs that include the conventional antipsychotics, the atypical antipsychotics, and the new, second-generation antipsychotics.

Neuro-Linguistic Programming (NLP) (C-4; HS-1). Developed by Richard Bandler and John Grinder, a highly controversial approach to counseling, personal communication, and self-help that aims to reprogram limiting beliefs, thoughts, or values into positive ones. It incorporates ideas from *Virginia Satir*, *hypnotherapy*, *Milton Erickson*, *Gregory Bateson* and other sources.

Neurological and Psychophysiological Therapies (C-7; HS-5). Called by some the final frontier of counseling, a wide range of approaches that are based on the *neuroplasticity* of the brain, involve *neuroprocessing*, *neurofeedback*, and assume that there is an intimate relationship between psychological and neurological change. See also *Neuropsychology*.

Neuroplasticity (C-7; HS-4). The ability of the brain to change neural pathways and develop new neural pathways at all stages of life. See also *Neuropsychology*.

Neuroprocessing (C-7; HS-4). The ability to take in and understand information and how such information impacts the neural pathways. See also *Neuropsychology*.

Neuropsychological Assessment (C-6; HS-2). A specialized *assessment* that evaluates the central nervous system for functioning. It is frequently applied after a traumatic brain injury, illnesses that may have caused brain damage, or with older persons that may be experiencing changes in brain functioning. See also *Neuropsychology*.

Neuropsychology (C-7; HS-7). A domain of *psychology* that examines brain–behavior relationships. See also *Neurological and Psychophysiological Therapies*.

Neurosis (C-9; HS-9). A common term used to describe any of a series of symptoms that generally do not meet the diagnostic categories in *Diagnostic and Statistical Manual-5* but cause some type of distress and limited impairment in functioning.

Neurotic Anxiety (C-7; HS-5). According to *Freud*, *anxiety* stemming from the *unconscious* fear that one's *id* may take control of one's behaviors, and thus, cause harm to *self* or others in some way.

Neurotransmitters (C-7; HS-6). Structures in the brain that perform as chemical communicators of electrical signals across the brain's synapses, from one cell to another cell. Chemical deficits in neurotransmitters lead to a wide range of psychological disorders and can be treated by face-to-face counseling and medication.

Neutral Stimulus (C-7; HS-7). In *behavior therapy*, a *stimulus* that, normally, produces no specific response.

Nietzsche, Friedrick (1844 - 1900) (C-6; HS-3). A German philosopher, scholar, and writer whose ideas contributed to *existential therapy*, development of nihilism, and to the concept of the superior man who could rise above others, among other contributions to philosophy and *culture*.

NIMH (C-7; HS-7). See *National Institute of Mental Health*.

***No Child Left Behind (NCLB) Act* (C-7; HS-5).** A U.S law passed in the year 2002 that was intended to help all students meet minimum educational competencies and, to a large degree, led to *high stakes testing* to ensure that all school systems were making adequately yearly progress toward this goal. This act impacted *school counselors'* roles in that it placed pressure on them to ensure that part of their job was focused on facilitating academic excellence (e.g., running study skills groups, academic success groups).

No Gossiping (C-6; HS-5). In *Gestalt therapy*, a technique in couples, family, or *group counseling* where individuals talk directly to another person rather than talking about that person.

NOHS (C-2; HS-10). See *National Organization for Human services.*

Nominal Scale (C-7; HS-4). A *scale of measurement* in which each category is discrete and the only calculation possible is to count the frequencies of the separate categories. For example, examining the numbers of White, Black, Asian, and "other" racial categories can be accomplished through nominal scaling.

Nonbenzodiazepines (C-6; HS-4). A classification of medications that act in very similar ways to *benzodiazepines*, this class of drug has a different chemical structure than the *benzodiazepines*. These are *controlled substances*, that are considered hypnotic drugs. Two examples are Buspar and Geprione.

Nondirective Approach (C-8; HS-7). Beginning with *Rogers' person-centered therapy*, various approaches to helping where the helper does not provide direction or guidance in sessions but permits clients to express themselves and establish their own focus and pace for the helping relationship.

Non-Dogmatic (C-9; HS-9). Closely related to being *nonjudgmental*, refers to individuals who are open to understanding the views of others, open to feedback, and even open to changing their perception of the world after hearing other points of view. Such individuals are relatively free from *biases* and can accept people in their differences, regardless of dissimilar cultural heritage, values, or beliefs.

Non-Dominant Groups (C-9; HS-9). A term used instead of the word *minority* due to negative conations sometimes associated with that word. See also *Minority Groups* and *Marginalized Groups.*

Non-Experimental Research (C-8; HS-6). A type of *quantitative research* that does not involve manipulation of *variables* by the researcher; rather, this approach tends to look at relationships between variables or to describe the attitudes, beliefs, and behaviors of a group being surveyed. Non-experimental research includes *correlation research* (bivariate and multivariate), *survey research*, and *ex post facto* (*causal-comparative*) research.

Non-Genuineness (C-8; HS-6). Also referred to as *incongruence* in *person-centered therapy*, non-genuineness occurs when a person's feelings, thoughts, and behaviors are not in sync, usually because *conditions of worth* have been placed on the person by people he or she highly regards. Thus, the person acts how others want him or her to act, and not how the person actually is. The person's *actualizing tendency* has been thwarted in an effort to be regarded by significant others.

Non-Judgmental (C-10; HS-10). Showing clients, or others, that you respect and accept them as they express their thoughts and *emotions*. Accepting a person without strings attached. See also *Acceptance* and *Unconditional Positive Regard.*

Non-Maleficence (C-8; HS-6). One of *Kitchener*'s moral ethical principles that involves how a helper should first and foremost avoid doing harm to clients and to others. See also Hippocratic Oath.

Non-Normative (SFBT) (C-6; HS-4). Within *solution-focused brief therapy* (*SFBT*), the recognition that there is no normal way of being—no one reality to aspire to. Thus, SFBT helpers do not hold their clients to an external standard of behavior.

Non-Parametric Statistical Tests (C-6; HS-3). A series of statistical analyses not requiring the data to meet the parameters of a *normal distribution*.

Non-Pathologizing of the Client (C-8; HS-7). The process by which a helper meets with a client and treats him or her respectfully as a *holistic* person. Clients are perceived as "living with" mental health issues as opposed to "having" them or "being" mentally ill.

Non-Profit Organizations (C-7; HS-7). See *Not-For-Profit Organizations*.

Non-Standardized Assessment Procedures (C-5; HS-3). *Assessment* instruments that are not necessarily given under the same conditions and in the same manner at each administration. These instruments tend be informal and have lower *validity* and *reliability* than *standardized assessment procedures*, although sometimes they can be more practical.

Nonverbal Behaviors (C-10; HS-10). Communication that is not verbal or spoken, such as one's *body positioning*, *tone of voice*, *eye contact*, *personal space*, and *touch*.

Nonverbal Intelligence Tests (C-8; HS-5). *Intelligence tests* that rely on little or no verbal expression.

Norm Group (C-8; HS-7). A peer group to which one compares oneself. Often used in *testing* and other *assessments*.

Norm Group Comparisons (C-8; HS-6). In *testing* and *assessment*, comparing one's scores to one's peer group to understand the relative placement of the scores.

Norm(s) (C-7; HS-7). See *Social Norms*.

Normal/Bell-Shaped Curve (C-8; HS-6). When test scores or other data result in a "bell shaped" distribution as a result of the laws of probability. The properties of such a distribution enable *norm group comparisons* of *test* score results or of data.

Normal Curve Equivalents (NCE) Scores (C-6; HS-2). A type of *derived score* with a *mean* of 50 and a *standard deviation* of 21.06. Often used with educational *testing*.

Norming (C-7; HS-6). *Tuckman's* second *stage of group development*, where the *group* begins developing cohesion and normalizing with each other towards finding common ground.

Norm-Referenced Test (C-8; HS-4). *Assessment* instruments in which examinees' scores can be compared to those of their peer or *norm group*.

North American Drama Therapy Association (NADTA) (C-2; HS-2). A U.S. national *professional association* establishing guidelines and support for the practice of *drama therapy*.

Not Knowing Posture (SFBT) (C-6; HS-5). Within *solution-focused brief therapy*, a perspective helpers adopt that lets clients know they are the experts on their lives and that therapeutic interpretations are tentative, cautious, humble, respectful, and curious attempts to understand. See also *Being Tentative*.

Not-For-Profit Organizations (C-7; HS-7). Organizations that have a shared mission to improve society, and whose objective is to achieve this mission without requiring profit from cost of services or sales of a product. These organizations typically rely on public or private donations and grants for funding. Common settings in which human services professionals and counselors work. Also known as *Non-profit Organizations.*

NRCA (C-6; HS-5). See *National Rehabilitation Counseling Association.*

NTL (C-7; HS-5). See *National Training Laboratory.*

Nuclear Family Emotional System (C-5; HS-4). A term that describes the extent to which a family is *enmeshed.* The more enmeshed, the more the family cannot distinguish *emotions* and develop a sense of *self* from one another. Used in *Bowenian family therapy* and *multigenerational family therapy.*

Nude Encounter Groups (C-4; HS-2). A type of *encounter group* conducted by participants in the nude, run mostly during the 1960s, that eventually raised some ethical concerns and led to *Guidelines for Psychologists Conducting Growth Groups* by the *American Psychological Association.*

Null Hypothesis (C-8; HS-6). In *quantitative research*, a *hypothesis* that researchers hope to show is false; that is, the researcher wants to disprove the hypothesis and show that the treatment has caused differences between groups, thus demonstrating treatment effects. See also *Alternative Hypothesis.*

Numerical Scale (C-6; HS-2). A type of *rating scale* in which a statement or question is followed by a choice of numbers arranged from high to low along a number line.

NVGA (C-8; HS-2). See *National Vocational Guidance Association.*

O*NET (aka O*NET Online) (C-7; HS-6). Developed by the United States Department of Labor, this online resource offers comprehensive information on close to 1,000 *occupations*, including information on *job* tasks, tools and technology, knowledge, skills, abilities, work activities, detailed work activities, work context, job zone, education, *credentials*, interests, *work* styles, work values, related occupations, wages and employment, job openings, and additional information. Can be cross-referenced with the *Occupational Outlook Handbook.*

***O*NET Interest Profiler* (C-7; HS-5).** An *interest inventory*, associated with *O*NET*, that is based on the *Holland code* and results can be cross-referenced with *O*NET* and the *Occupational Outlook Handbook.*

One-Group Pretest-Posttest Design (C-7; HS-3). A single group is examined before treatment and after treatment and changes are assumed to be the result of the treatment. There is no control group or comparison group. A type of *pre-experimental design.*

One-Shot Case Study Design (C-7; HS-3). One single group is examined at one point in time after a treatment is assumed to have affected change. There is no control group or comparison group.

Object Permanency (C-8; HS-7). A developmental milestone in which an infant develops the capacity to recognize that objects continue to exist when they are beyond the child's sensory awareness (seen, touched, tasted, smelled, or heard). First studied by *Jean Piaget.*

Object Relations Theory (C-6; HS-3). In contrast to the instincts of *sex* and aggression driving human behavior, object relations theory stresses the importance of relationships in motivating people. Some well-known theorists of this theory include *Melanie Klein*, *Margaret Mahler*, and *Harry Stack Sullivan.*

Object Relations Therapy (C-6; HS-3). Approaches to professional helping that follow *object relations theory.* See also *Object Relations Theory.*

Objective Factors (C-5; HS-3). In *Social Cognitive Career Theory*, it is believed that people are impacted by both objective factors (e.g., real factors, such as economic hardship) and *perceived environmental factors* (e.g., how our cognitive filters impact our understanding of the world).

Objective Personality Testing (C-8; HS-4). Multiple-choice or true/false type question formats that assess various aspects of personality. Often used to increase client insight, to identify *psychopathology*, and to assist in *treatment planning.* It is a type of *personality test.*

Objective Test (C-7; HS-4). Various types of *tests* in which right or wrong answers exist and the test can be scored objectively, such as standardized *achievement tests* given in schools, *aptitude tests* like the *SAT/PSAT*, and certain personality tests that use multiple choice and true/false answers.

Oblique Rotation (C-7; HS-3). See *Factor Rotation.*

Observable Variables (C-8; HS-6). *Variables* that can be directly detected and measured. See also *Latent Variables.*

Observation (C-8; HS-7). Observing behaviors of an individual to develop a deeper understanding of one or more specific behaviors (e.g., observing a student's acting-out behavior in class, assessing a client's ability to perform hand-eye coordination tasks to determine potential vocational placements). As a research tool, it includes *time sampling*, *event sampling*, and *time and event sampling.* It is also a type of *informal assessment.*

Observational Learning (C-9; HS-8). See *Modeling.*

Observational Method (C-8; HS-6). Refers to research methods employing observational strategies of individuals, events, or processes. See also *Observation.*

Observer Effect (C-7; HS-5). See *Hawthorne Effect.*

Obsessive-Compulsive and Related Disorders (C-8; HS-6). A group of *mental disorders* that involve obsessive thoughts and compulsive behaviors that are uncontrollable and the client feels compelled to perform. *Diagnoses* in this category include obsessive-compulsive disorder, body dysmorphic disorder, hoarding disorder, trichotillomania (or hair-pulling disorder), and excoriation (or skin-picking) disorder.

Occam's Razor (C-5; HS-4). Derived from the Latin meaning of "law of parsimony," or the principle that when solving a problem with multiple courses of action, the simplest and most logical solution is likely the correct one. Considered to have been developed by William of Occam (or Ockham), a 13th to 14th century English monk. *Steve de Shazer*, one of the developers of *solution-focused brief therapy*, was said to use this philosophy.

Occupation/Occupational (C-7; HS-7). Of or relating to *jobs* of a similar nature that can be found within several *work* environments and connote the kinds of work a person is pursuing.

***Occupational Outlook Handbook* (*OOH*) (C-7; HS-6).** A website developed by the U.S. Bureau of Labor Statistics that offers information on hundreds of common *jobs* in 25 broad *occupational* groups. Information about the jobs includes a summary of the job, what one does on the job, the *work* environment, what one needs to do to get that job, pay, job outlook state, and area data for the job, similar occupations, and a section with additional information about the job. There is also a cross-walk between the *Occupational Outlook Handbook* and *O*NET Online*.

Occupational Therapist (C-6; HS-5). A professional specializing in *occupational therapy*. See also *Rehabilitation Counseling*.

Occupational Therapy (C-7; HS-6). A form of professional *therapy* that focuses on helping people to regain, maintain, or develop work/*occupational* skills due to physical, psychological, and cognitive disabilities. See also *Rehabilitation Counseling*.

Odd-Even Reliability (C-8; HS-3). A method of determining *reliability* that involves dividing the items on a measure in some rational manner that assumes that scores on the first half of the *test* should be equivalent to scores on the second half. The two halves are then correlated to show the accuracy of the test. Also called *Split-Half Reliability*.

Oedipus Complex (C-8; HS-3). The concept, from *psychoanalysis*, that during the *phallic stage*, the boy's realization that some people don't have a penis (e.g., his mother) and the resulting *unconscious* fearful fantasy, called *castration anxiety*, that his father will castrate him in an effort to rid him of his sexual desires for his mother (and make him like his mother). Resolution occurs through the boy's *repression* of his feelings for his mother, as he realizes he is no match for his father. At this point, he has no choice but to identify with his father, and displace the sexual feelings he has toward his mother to girls and later to women. This identification leads to internalization of male *sex* role behaviors as the son joins the "club" of men.

Offender Counseling (C-7; HS-7). A wide variety of counseling formats or programs that focus on people within the criminal justice or correctional system (e.g., *substance abuse* and *mental health counseling* for inmates in prison, *batterers intervention programs* in the community). See also *Correctional Facilities*.

Offering Alternatives (C-7; HS-7). The process by which a helper suggests to the client that there may be a variety of ways to address a problem and provides varying possible options from which the client can choose. Contrast with *Advice Giving* and *Information Giving*.

Office Atmosphere/Environment (C-9; HS-9). An important aspect of building the relationship with clients is the client's level of comfort in the helper's office, which should be inviting, warm, comfortable, and pleasant while also being private and welcoming to all persons and *cultures*. See also *Environment*.

Office of Assessment and Evaluation (C-6; HS-4). One area in higher education dealing with campus and student *assessment* and evaluations that individuals with a master's or higher in *student affairs and college counseling* sometimes work.

Office of Intercultural Student Services (C-7; HS-6). One area in higher education that individuals with a master's or higher in *student affairs and college counseling* sometimes work that focuses on cultural issues on campus and/or foreign students. This office is an important referral source for students struggling with cross-cultural issues.

Office of Residence Life and Housing Services (C-7; HS-4). One area in higher education focusing on issues connected to student housing and residential student living that individuals with a master's or higher in *student affairs and college counseling* sometimes work.

Office of Student Activities Services (C-7; HS-4). An area in higher education focusing on campus activities for students that individuals with a master's or higher in *student affairs and college counseling* sometimes work.

Office of the Registrar (C-7; HS-4). An area in higher education handling college and course registration and academic records that individuals with a master's or higher in *student affairs and college counseling* sometimes work.

One-Group Pretest-Posttest Design (C-6; HS-2). A *research design* in which one single group is examined in a study at two different points of time, first before the treatment and second, after the treatment. Any noted changes are assumed to be the result of the treatment. However, because no control group or comparison groups are used, this assumption is considered weak. A type of *Pre-Experimental Design.*

One-Shot Case Study Design (C-6; HS-2). A *research design* in which one group is given a treatment and studied after the treatment should have caused change. This group is then examined relative to what would have been expected based on that treatment. However, no control group or comparison groups are used; therefore, evidence for its effectiveness is limited. A type of *Pre-Experimental Design.*

Online Counseling (C-7; HS-7). See *Counseling Online.*

Onset (C-7; HS-7). The beginning or start of a *mental disorder.* Often, the *Diagnostic and Statistical Manual of Mental Disorders* will provide information regarding the onset of various *pathologies.*

***OOH* (C-7; HS-6).** See *Occupational Outlook Handbook.*

Open Groups (C-7; HS-7). *Groups* which readily allow new members to enter.

Open Questions (C-8; HS-8). *Questions* that enable the client to have a wide range of responses and that encourage more than a yes/no or a *forced choice* response (e.g., "What do you think about that?"; "How does that make you feel?").

Operant Conditioning (C-9; HS-7). The shaping of behavior that is brought about through the use of *positive reinforcement*, *negative reinforcement*, *positive punishment*, or *negative punishment.* See also *Behavior Therapy.*

Operational Definition (C-8; HS-6). Within research, a word or term that explains that word or term in measureable ways so that it can be understood and researched. Frequently, this may include words, terms, and concepts that are taken for granted, yet are highly conceptual and not normally measured, such as *empathy*, *racism*, *spirituality*, happiness, etc. See also *Operationalize.*

Operationalize (C-8; HS-6). To take an abstract construct (for example, *empathy*) and develop a means to define, measure, and quantify it. See also *Operational Definition.*

Opiate or Opioids (C-8; HS-8). A classification of *controlled substances*, derived from the opium poppy, used often in medicine for pain relief and for severe cough or diarrhea. Also used illegally to produce a numbing effect and for its "high." Common opiates include *morphine*, *heroin*, *oxycodone*, *Percocet*, *hydrocodone*, and *fentanyl.* Opioids are also referred to as analgesics or *narcotics.*

Oppression (C-9; HS-9). The process by which one group unjustly uses its power to control, rule, suppress, deny rights to, or otherwise inflict harm to individuals or groups of people, called *minorities* or *marginalized groups*, who have less power than the oppressors. See also *Minority Groups*, *Non-dominant Groups*, and *Marginalized Groups.*

Oral Histories (C-8; HS-6). In *qualitative research*, an *interview* (or life story) with an individual who has participated in an event or observed an event in question.

Oral Stage (C-9; HS-4). *Sigmund Freud's* first *psychosexual stage of development*, occurring between birth and age 1 year, in which a child's emotional gratification is derived from intake of food, by sucking, and later by biting. See also *Anal Stage*, *Genital Stage*, *Latency Stage*, and *Phallic Stage.*

Ordinal Scale (C-7; HS-4). A scale of measurement in which the magnitude or rank order is implied; however, the distance between measurements is unknown.

Organ Inferiority (C-7; HS-3). In *individual psychology*, the *feelings of inferiority* that individuals have due to deficits that are sometimes expected (e.g., a 1-year-old falling down) and sometimes unique (e.g., a person born without a limb). How one deals with these feelings is a function of parental messages and can result in *compensatory behaviors* that assuage the feelings of inferiority. Some compensatory behaviors can be positive, but often they result in individuals not following their natural paths in life as they try to avoid feelings of inferiority.

Organismic Valuing Process (C-8; HS-6). In *person-centered counseling*, the process of evaluating one's environment and drifting toward those individuals who positively value one's natural tendencies, or ways of being, and drifting away from people who negatively value him or her.

Organizational Climate (C-8; HS-7). A measure of the atmosphere or *culture* within an agency or organization. Including *overt norms*, *covert norms*, and *hierarchies* within organizations.

Organizational Systems (C-8; HS-7). Organizational systems, such as agencies, follow the basic tenets of *general systems theory.* Thus, issues related to *boundaries*, *rules*, *hierarchy*, and *homeostasis* all play a role in the system dynamics. Counselors and human service professionals need to know how to work effectively within such systems.

Organizations That Partner or Support ACA (C-8; HS-2). Affiliates and organizations that partner with the *American Counseling Association* and contribute to the betterment of the counseling profession in unique ways. Some of these include *National Board of Certified Counselors*, *Council for the Accreditation of Counseling and Related*

Educational Programs, Council on Rehabilitation Education, Chi Sigma Iota, and *American Counseling Association Foundation.*

Orthogonal Rotation (C-7; HS-3). See *Factor Rotation.*

Orthopsychiatry (C-6; HS-5). A sub-field of *psychiatry* that specializes in psychological and behavioral disorders related to childhood and adolescent development.

Other Conditions That May Be a Focus of Clinical Assessment (C-7 HS-5). Reminiscent of Axis IV of the previous edition of the *Diagnostic and Statistical Manual (DSM)*, this last part of Section II of the *Diagnostic and Statistical Manual-5* ends with a description of concerns that could be clinically significant, such as abuse/*neglect*, relational problems, psychosocial, personal, and environmental concerns, educational/occupational problems, housing problems, economic problems, and problems related to the legal system. These conditions, which are not considered mental disorders, are generally listed as *V codes*, which correspond to the 9th edition of the *International Classification of Diseases*, or *Z codes*, which correspond to the 10th edition of the *International Classification of Diseases*. See also *International Classification of Diseases.*

Other Mental Disorders (C-7; HS-4). This diagnostic category includes *mental disorders* that do not fall within specifically listed groups and do not have unifying characteristics. Examples include other specified mental disorders due to another medical condition, unspecified mental disorders due to another medical condition, *other specified mental disorders*, and *unspecified mental disorders.*

Other Specified Disorders (C-7; HS-3). Relative to *Diagnostic and Statistical Manual-5*, used when a provider believes an individual's impairment to functioning or distress is clinically significant; however, the symptoms do not meet the full criteria. Example "Other Specified Depressive Disorder, depressive episode with insufficient symptoms."

Otis-Lennon School Ability Test (C-4; HS-1). A type of *cognitive ability test* to examine one's potential in school. A type of *aptitude test.*

Outcome Evaluation (C-7; HS-6). See *Summative Evaluation.*

Outcome Research (C-7; HS-5). Research conducted to find the most effective outcome(s), or result(s), for a particular treatment, approach, or program in mental health and related social science studies. This research is often done to compare results between one or more treatment approaches.

Outcome Variable (C-10; HS-7). See *Dependent Variable.*

Outing (C-6; HS-6). The process in which an individual discloses another's *sexual orientation*, *gender identity*, *intersex* status, or other privately held identities without permission or consent.

Outpatient Facilities (C-10; HS-10). Settings where *clinical mental health counselors* and other helping professionals provide help to clients outside of a hospital setting (or *inpatient facilities*), which include a wide range of helping organizations and programs (e.g., *private practice settings*, *community-based mental health centers*).

Outreach Worker (C-6; HS-8). A human service professional who may go out into the community to work with clients. This term also refers to professionals who act as *advocates* or liaisons within various community groups and organizations, in some cases with specific populations or to address specific topics, such as doing outreach to high risk users of drugs, etc. One of the original 13 roles and functions of human service professionals as defined by the *Southern Regional Education Board.*

Outsider Witness Groups (C-8; HS-2). See *Definitional Ceremonies.*

Overcorrection (C-6; HS-5). In *behavior therapy*, this technique involves having a person engage in corrective behaviors that take effort and are contingent on, and the result of, exhibiting inappropriate behaviors, such as having a child who was told to clean his or her room weekly, and does not do it, and then has to clean his or her room daily.

Overeaters Anonymous (C-8; HS-8). An organization and *12 step group* dedicated to helping people overcome compulsive eating issues, such as overeating and food *addiction.* They also help individuals with other *eating disorders* such as *anorexia nervosa*, *bulimia nervosa*, and *binge eating disorder.*

Overgeneralization (C-6; HS-4). Making large generalizations from a small event. See also *Cognitive Distortion.* See also *Catastrophizing.*

Overindulged/Frustrated (C-7; HS-4). Relative to *psychoanalysis*, when a child is *overindulged* or *frustrated* during a *psychosexual stage*, his or her *libido* becomes *fixated* resulting in unfinished psychological issues and behaviors in adulthood.

Overt Rehearsal (C-5; HS-2). A counseling technique, similar to *role-playing*, in which clients must openly state or enact their intentions with others.

Overt Rules (C-8; HS-6). Clearly defined rules made by families that affect how members of the family interact with one another. Contrast with *Covert Rules.*

Oxycodone (C-7; HS-7). An *opiate* that is used to treat pain and often recreationally abused. It is generally taken orally, and is a highly addictive *controlled substance.*

Palo Alto, CA (C-4; HS-1). Location where a number of well-known theorists and family *therapists* worked to develop helping approaches related to *general systems theory*, *cybernetics*, and communication skills. See also *Mental Research Institute* (MRI).

Panic Attack (C-10; HS-10). See *Anxiety Attack.*

Pansexual (C-6; HS-6). A *sexual orientation* in which the individual is emotionally, physically, and/or sexually attracted to persons of any *sex* or *gender* (but not to all individuals equally or indiscriminately). See also *Bisexual.*

Paradigm Shift (C-6; HS-4). The concept that knowledge builds on itself, that new discoveries are based on past knowledge, and that periodically, new knowledge creates a shift in the basic foundation of our *schemas.*

Paradoxical Directive (C-7; HS-3). A directive given by a helper whereby the helper expects the client to not adhere to the directive, usually because of client *resistance.* However, either adherence or non-adherence will be beneficial. Used in *strategic therapies.* For example, a person who cannot sleep due to obsessive worries at night is told to clean his or her house when the worries begin. This results in either a very clean house, or going back to sleep, both of which are beneficial.

Paradoxical Effect (C-7; HS-6). The discovery, during the 1950s, that *amphetamines*, which generally make individuals hyperactive, were found to have the opposite effect in many children diagnosed with *attention deficit disorder with hyperactivity*. Instead, they seemed to calm them down and help them focus.

Paradoxical Intention (C-6; HS-2). In *existential therapy*, when clients are encouraged by the helper to do more of a symptom that is causing problems. Paradoxically, prescribing more may result in the symptom recurring less or stopping altogether, perhaps because people see they have control over the symptom. Some helpers call this *prescribing the symptom*.

Parallel Analysis (C-6; HS-2). A method for determining the appropriate number of *factors* to extract when doing a *factor analysis* that involves generating a random data set, computing *eigenvalues* from the random data set, comparing the eigenvalues from the random data to the sample data, and extracting the number of factors from the sample data with larger eigenvalues than the random data.

Parallel Form Reliability (C-8; HS-3). See *Alternate Form Reliability*.

Parallel Process (C-7; HS-5). A phenomenon that occurs when something that happens between a client and a helper repeats itself between the helper and *supervisor*. This offers the *supervisor* the ability to show how to treat the client by responding to the *supervisee* in a manner that is helpful and which the helper can emulate with his or her client.

Parametric Statistics (C-8; HS-4). A group of statistical analyses used to analyze a representative *sample* of data and make inferences to the larger population, with the assumption that the sample population matches the larger population.

Paraphilic Disorders (C-9; HS-5). A group of *mental disorders* diagnosed when the client is sexually aroused to circumstances that deviate from traditional sexual stimuli *and* when such behaviors result in harm or significant emotional distress. The disorders include exhibitionistic disorder, voyeuristic disorder, frotteurisitc disorder, sexual sadism and sexual masochism disorders, fetishistic disorder, transvestic disorder, pedophilic disorder, and other specified and unspecified paraphilic disorders.

Paraphrasing (C-10; HS-10). A helping skill that involves the helper reflecting back the general feelings and content of what the client said by using similar words and phrases of the client.

Parapraxis (Parapraxes) (C-9; HS-5). See *Freudian Slip*.

Paraprofessional (C-10; HS-10). Individuals in a variety of different fields, such as human services or education, who assist professionals but do not have professional *credentials* themselves. For example, human service assistants who help other human service professionals, teaching assistants who help teachers in a classroom, or nurses' aides who provide support service to licensed nurses. Often, these people have obtained training or education related to the professional field they are working in but not at the same level as those who are credentialed.

Parasuicide (C-5; HS-5). Behaviors that are generally defined as suicidal but do not result in death. Sometimes seen as a failed or half-hearted attempt at suicide in an effort to gain attention. See also *Suicidal Ideation* and *Suicidality, Assessment for Lethality*.

Parsons, Frank (1854 - 1908) (C-10; HS-2). An American educator, social *advocate*, and author who is the founder of *vocational guidance* and an important figure in the subsequent development of the counseling profession. Parsons has been referred to as the *founder of the counseling field* and the *founder of vocational guidance*.

Participant Observation (C-7; HS-5). Research in which information is gathered by a researcher who joins a group and interacts with (or observes) its members.

Pastoral Counseling (C-7; HS-5). A variety of counseling approaches that incorporate *spirituality* or *religion* and/or are related to pastoral and other faith-based counseling approaches. Sometimes, this form of counseling is provided by a minister (i.e., pastor) or other spiritual/religious leader, but may be incorporated into *psychotherapy* or provided at settings (e.g., agencies, hospitals) or private practices focusing on this kind of counseling. See also *Pastoral Counselor*.

Pastoral Counselor (C-7; HS-5). A counselor who specializes in spiritual and/or *pastoral counseling* issues (or related faith-based counseling approaches), who may or may not have a master's degree in counseling. In some cases, pastoral counselors are ministers (i.e., pastors), imams, chaplains, or other ministerial leaders or lay-leaders, but this is not required. Although, it is not a specialty area of *Counseling and Related Educational Programs*, pastoral counselor education programs can qualify for *accreditation*. See also *Pastoral Counseling*.

Pastoral, Religious, and Spiritual Counseling Agencies (C-7; HS-5). Settings where *clinical mental health counselors* may be employed and where a focus of counseling is on areas related to *pastoral counseling* and spiritual counseling approaches, such as religious counseling centers (e.g., Christian counseling agencies), churches, mosques, or *private practice settings* focusing on this type of counseling. See also *Pastoral Counseling* and *Pastoral Counselor*.

Path Analysis (C-7; HS-3). A type of *multivariate correlational research* that is based on *structural equation modeling* in which the causal connections or pathways between *variables* are estimated.

Pathologizing (C-7; HS-7). The process by which a helper sees a client and treats that person as if he or she has a problem or disease, or only sees the person as a *diagnosis*.

Pathology (C-7; HS-7). The study of the origin, *diagnosis*, and development of disease in medicine, psychology, and other biological fields.

Patient(s) (C-9; HS-3). An older term used to describe the person(s) on the receiving end of the *therapy* or treatment. This term is primarily used by medical professionals and human service professionals with medical training, such as *psychiatrists*. Contrast with *Client*.

Pause Time (C-5; HS-5). The amount of silence between statements made during an *interview*. This may be adjusted to meet the expectations of people from different *cultures*.

Pavlov, Ivan (1849 - 1936) (C-9; HS-9). A Russian physiologist and behavioral researcher who was the originator of *classical conditioning*. Through his research, he showed that a hungry dog that salivated when shown food would learn to salivate to a tone if that tone was repeatedly paired or associated with the food. See also *Behavior Therapy*.

PCP or Phencyclidine Hydrochloride (C-7; HS-7). A central nervous system depressant and *controlled substance* that has unpredictable side effects, such as agitation, *hallucinations*, and disorientations. An illicit drug that is often sold on the streets.

Peak Experiences (C-6; HS-6). Developed by *Maslow*, a euphoric or exhilarating sensation that comes from achieving *self-actualization*.

Pedersen, Paul (1936 -) (C-6; HS-4). An American *psychologist* and author of some of the seminal works on *cross-cultural counseling*.

Peer Counseling (C-7; HS-7). The process by which counseling-related activities (e.g., listening, offering compassion, emotional support) are provided by peers rather than by professional counselors. Peer counseling may include training and can be offered in many settings, such as teens as peer mentors in schools or individuals with mental illness who are actively recovering who act as peer support helpers to clients with similar mental health concerns at a mental health center. Often, peer counseling is overseen by professional staff.

Peer Review (C-8; HS-7). The process that occurs when a manuscript is sent out to reviewers by an editor of a journal. The manuscript is sent out blind, with no identifying information about the authors so that the reviewers can read the manuscript in an unbiased manner and assist in making a decision about whether or not the manuscript should be published in a journal.

Penis Envy (C-8; HS-5). According to *Freud*, envy females experience due to the realization they do not have a penis. It is connected to feelings of envy for the power represented in the male penis and to being male in society. Largely disavowed in recent years, as highlighted in the Woody Allen joke: "I worked with Freud in Vienna. We broke over the concept of penis envy. Freud felt that it should be limited to women."

People-Rating (C-6; HS-4). A *cognitive distortion*, in *rational emotive behavior therapy*, in which an individual makes assumptions about a person (e.g., rates a person good or bad) and fails to see the complexities of people.

Perceived Environmental Factors (C-3; HS-1). In *social cognitive career theory*, it is believed that people are impacted by both *objective factors* (real factors--e.g., economic hardship) and perceptions of factors (perceived environmental factors).

Perceiving Mental Function (C-7; HS-6). In the *Myers-Briggs Type Indicator*, based on *Jung's mental functions*, the perceiving mental function is part of the fourth dimension of one's psychological type which includes both the *judging* and the *perceiving* mental functions. Individuals with a *perceiving* type prefer a flexible, loose, or spontaneous approach to the world.

Percentages (C-9; HS-9). A proportion of the whole. A type of *descriptive statistic* often used in *survey research*.

Percentile Rank (C-7; HS-5). See *Percentiles*.

Percentiles (C-7; HS-5). A method of comparing raw scores to a *norm group* by calculating the *percentage* of people falling below an obtained score, with ranges from 1 to 99, and 50 being the mean.

Perception of Problems (C-7; HS-3). The belief by *narrative therapists* that the perception of problems, and the language used in describing problems, are directly related to the development of problems.

Percocet (C-7; HS-7). An *opiate* and *controlled substance* that is a combination of *oxycodone* and Tylenol that is used to treat pain. It is generally taken orally, and is highly addictive.

Performance-Based Assessment (C-7; HS-3). The evaluation of an individual using a variety of *informal assessment* procedures that are often based on real world responsibilities (e.g., seeing how quickly and properly a potential firefighter can run into a building and carry out a dummy that is the weight of a person). This kind of *assessment* tends to not focus on cognitive skills and these procedures are sometimes seen as an alternative to *standardized testing* (e.g., a portfolio). Type of *informal assessment.*

Performing (C-7; HS-6). *Tuckman's* fourth *stage of group development.*

Periods (C-4; HS-3). In *Levinson's Seasons of a Man's Life* and *Seasons of a Woman's Life* developmental theory, the time, during an *era*, when a person makes crucial choices in his or her life (the stable period) and when a person is at the end of an era and is ready to move onto another era (the *transitional periods*).

Perls, Fritz (1893 - 1970) (C-10; HS-4). A German *psychiatrist*, *psychotherapist*, and *existential-humanistic* theorist who developed *Gestalt therapy.* One of the many theorists that fueled the diversity of counseling theories during the 1950s and 1960s.

Permeable Boundaries (C-7; HS-6). *Boundaries* in a system that allow information to come in and be digested or analyzed, and then that information is allowed to adjust the system in a healthy manner. See also *Rigid Boundaries* and *Semipermeable Boundaries.*

Perry, William G. (1913 - 1998) (C-6; HS-4). An American educational *psychologist*, professor, and adult developmental theorist who emphasized the learning process and *cognitive development* of college students. See also *Dualism*, *Multiplicity*, *Relativism*, and *Commitment in Relativism*, and *Perry's Scheme of Intellectual and Ethical Development.*

Perry's Scheme of Intellectual and Ethical Development (C-6; HS-4). A model and theory of traditional aged college student development of knowledge and morality created by *William Perry* that includes the stages *dualism*, *multiplicity*, *relativism*, and *commitment in relativism.* Each stage is further divided into nine different positions organized under the various stages (e.g., basic dualism, full dualism). In this theory, students generally move from black and white, concrete thinking to more flexible and complex thinking while increasingly understanding the grays in life. See also *Perry, William G.*

Persona (C-7; HS-6). In *analytical psychology*, an *archetype* that represents the face that one shows to the world.

Personal Growth Group (C-8; HS-7). A kind of *self-help group* or *counseling group* that offers support and opportunities for introspection to *group* members while encouraging expression of feelings and exploration of individual growth.

Personal Space (C-7; HS-7). The amount of physical space between a helper and client which sends an immediate message to the client about the helping relationship and can positively or negatively affect the relationship.

Personal Unconscious (C-7; HS-4). In *analytical psychology*, where all one's unique repressed material is stored in the *unconscious* mind.

Personality Assessment (C-8; HS-4). *Tests* that assess the *affective* realm. Personality assessment includes *objective personality tests*, which measure aspects of personality through some kind of *forced choice* method (e.g., true/false or multiple choice questions), *projective testing*, which assesses personality by having individuals respond to unstructured *stimuli* and then making interpretations about their responses (e.g., "inkblots"), and *interest inventories*, which assess an individual's likes and dislikes related to the world of *work*.

Personality Disorders (C-7; HS-4). The 10 personality disorders in the *Diagnostic and Statistical Manual-5* all involve a pattern of experiences and behaviors that are persistent, inflexible, and deviate from one's cultural expectations for healthy individual personality development. Usually, this pattern emerges in adolescence or early adulthood and causes severe distress in one's interpersonal relationships. The personality disorders are grouped into the three following clusters which are based on similar behaviors: (1) Cluster A: paranoid, schizoid, and schizotypal. These individuals seem bizarre or unusual in their behaviors and interpersonal relations, (2) Cluster B: antisocial, borderline, histrionic, and narcissistic. These individuals seem overly emotional, are melodramatic, or unpredictable in their behaviors and interpersonal relations, and (3) Cluster C: avoidant, dependent, and obsessive-compulsive (not to be confused with obsessive-compulsive disorder). These individuals tend to appear anxious, worried, or fretful in their behaviors.

Personality Tests (C-8; HS-4). See *Personality Assessment.*

Personality Theory of Occupational Choice (C-8; HS-3). See *Holland's Personality Theory of Occupational Choice.*

Personalization (C-6; HS-4). A type of *cognitive distortion* where a person assumes that he or she is the cause of another person's negative behavior.

Person-Centered Consultation (C-6; HS-4). *Consultation* that applies *person-centered counseling* principles.

Person-Centered Counseling (C-10; HS-8). Developed by *Carl Rogers* and part of the *existential-humanistic approach* to *counseling*, this approach suggests we all have an *actualizing tendency* that directs us to reach our full potential. This tendency, however, can be thwarted by an individual's desire to be regarded by significant others, who, will sometimes place *conditions of worth* on the individual. Such conditions result in an *incongruent* self. Person-centered helpers suggest that the way to facilitate change is by the helper exhibiting *empathy*, *unconditional positive regard*, and *congruence* (*genuineness*). An *anti-deterministic approach*. See also *Existential-Humanistic Approaches* and *Necessary and Sufficient Conditions.*

Person-Centered Group Counseling (C-8; HS-7). The practice of *group counseling* using the basic tenets of *person-centered counseling.*

Person-Environment Fit (C-7; HS-5). The level of compatibility (or fit) an individual and his or her characteristics have within the environment, or how well one's environment is compatible with one's individual characteristics. Particularly important in *career counseling*. See also *Holland Code.*

Peyote (C-6; HS-6). A small cactus known for its *psychoactive drug* properties, primarily via *mescaline*, that can produce psychedelic, transcendent, and altered *consciousness* effects when ingested. It is used recreationally, ritualistically, and medically. It is a *controlled substance* in the United States. See also *Mescaline.*

Phallic Stage (C-9; HS-4). *Sigmund Freud's* third *psychosexual stage of development*, occurring between ages three and five years, when the child becomes aware of his/her and the opposite sex's genitals and receives pleasure from self-stimulation. See also *Anal Stage*, *Genital Stage*, *Latency Stage*, and *Oral Stage.*

Phenomenological Designs/Research (C-6; HS-3). A *qualitative research design* in which researchers seek to describe the lived experience of a phenomenon and the contextual factors that influence that experience. See also *Phenomenology.*

Phenomenological Psychology (C-7; HS-4). Emphasizes the nature of existence and the study of reality. See also *Existential Psychology* and *Phenomenology.*

Phenomenology (C-7; HS-3). The study of subjective experience and individual *consciousness.* See also *Phenomenological Designs/Research.*

Philadelphia Child Guidance Clinic (C-6; HS-3). Now called the Philadelphia Child and Family Therapy Training Center, this was the counseling and training center of *Salvador Minuchin* and his *Structural Family Therapy* approach to counseling. It continues to exist under the new name.

Philosophical Conditioning (C-5; HS-2). In *rational emotive behavior therapy*, the belief that every individual develops a particular way of understanding the world due to dedication to his or her own unique philosophy (e.g., *values*, beliefs, ideas) which is usually created early in life. Each person's philosophy becomes habitual and supports either rational or *irrational beliefs*, being reinforced and sustained by the person, and can lead to healthy ways of living or emotional distress and dysfunction concomitant with the rational or irrational beliefs.

Philosophical Pragmatism (C-5; HS-2). *William James* suggested this philosophy, which states that reality is continually constructed as a function of its utility or practical purpose.

Phobia (C-9; HS-8). Persistent, intense and/or irrational fears of things, situations, or events (and the responses to these fears) such as phobias of heights, spiders, public speaking, or the number 13. Oftentimes, the intense fear associated with a phobia is so debilitating for clients that it interferes with their ability to go about their daily routines.

Phony Layer (C-7; HS-3). Also called the *role-playing* layer, in *Gestalt therapy* a part of the *structure of neurosis* where individuals put forth a fake personality to others.

Physical Self (C-6; HS-4). One of the five factors of the *indivisible self model.* It includes the part of ourselves that is reflected through our biological and physical aspects of *self* and is related to ensuring that we have adequate physical activity in our lives (e.g., exercise) and that we eat well, have a good diet, and avoid being overweight or underweight (e.g., nutrition).

Piaget, Jean (1896 - 1980) (C-10; HS-9). A Swiss *psychologist* and child theorist who approached intelligence from a developmental perspective by observing how children's cognitions were shaped as they grew. See also *Piaget's Theory of Cognitive Development.*

Piaget's Theory of Cognitive Development (C-10; HS-9). *Piaget* examined how *cognitive development* unravels in childhood and identified a number of stages that he called *sensorimotor*, *preoperational*, *concrete-operational*, and *formal-operational.* He also believed that cognitive development is adaptive, and he conceived the concepts of *assimilation* and *accommodation.*

Pinel, Philippe (1745 - 1826) (C-6; HS-6). A French physician and founder of the field of *psychiatry* who approached insanity and mental illness from a scientific perspective and advocated for humane treatment of the mentally ill.

***PL94-142* (C-8; HS-6).** See *Education for All Handicapped Children Act.*

Placebo Effect (C-8; HS-7). A phenomenon that occurs when one receives a fake treatment or *intervention* and still makes an improvement due to his or her expectation that the treatment will be helpful.

Plasticity (C-7; HS-6). The idea that the individual has the ability to stretch and change cognitively, physically, interpersonally, intrapsychically, morally, and spiritually.

Plato (born circa 428 BCE to 348 BCE) (C-7; HS-6). An early Greek philosopher who considered problems of the human condition to have physical, moral, and spiritual origins.

Play Therapy (C-8; HS-8). A broad range of counseling techniques that utilize play as the primary therapeutic *intervention.* Play therapy is primarily used with children but can have applications for other client populations. Many different theoretical approaches can be used in play therapy and it can be on a continuum from *nondirective* to *directive* in varying degrees.

Pleasure Principle (C-8; HS-5). In *psychoanalysis*, the idea that the *id* is always seeking pleasure. The id is said to be driven by the pleasure principle.

Plotinus (born circa 204 AD to 207 AD) (C-5; HS-4). A Greek-speaking philosopher who believed in duality or the concept that the soul is separate from the body.

Poetry Therapy (C-6; HS-5). A *creative and expressive therapy* that utilizes poetry and other *bibliotherapy* techniques as counseling *interventions.*

Pointing Out Conflicting Feelings or Thoughts (C-5; HS-4). The process by which a helper makes a client aware of discrepancies between his or her thoughts, feelings, or behaviors. A type of *advanced empathic response.*

Polarities (C-6; HS-3). In *Gestalt therapy*, related to the concept of *figure-ground*, *Perls* believed that dimensions of *self* can be viewed as an infinite number of opposing pairs or polarities (e.g., good self and bad self). One such polarity Perls popularized is the *topdog/underdog.*

Political Correctness (C-7; HS-7). Avoiding the use of terms, actions, and other forms of expression that are considered to offend, exclude, or marginalize groups of individuals who are socially, physically, or emotionally disadvantaged or *discriminated* against.

Polysubstance Abuse (C-7; HS-7). When an individual experiences *substance abuse* through use of multiple substances as a means of *intoxication* and/or developing dependency, thus not specifically having a substance of choice. Many polysubstance users mix *alcohol* with other drugs or medications and many users seek to increase the effects of intoxication via their polysubstance usage.

Poor Laws (C-6; HS-8). Established by the English government in 1601, this was one of the first attempts at legislating aid for the poor. In many ways, the American system of *social welfare* was modeled after the Poor Laws.

Portability (C-8; HS-3). Sometimes called *reciprocity*, the extent to which one can easily "move" their *credential* from one U.S. state to another. This is often difficult, as states set the requirements for many credentials, such as *licensure*, and requirements could vary dramatically from state to state. For instance, *licensed professional counselors* often have difficulty moving their license from state to state and the *American Counseling Association* and other associations are currently assisting states in developing licensure portability for them.

Portfolio Assessment (C-7; HS-6). A type of performance-based *assessment* in which a number of items are collected and eventually shown to such individuals as potential employers or potential colleges as an indication of the applicant's ability. Sometimes used in lieu of *standardized testing* and can be considered a type of *performance-based assessment.*

Positive Addiction (C-7; HS-6). Coined by *William Glasser* in a book of the same name, the idea of engaging in healthy behaviors (e.g., exercise) that can lead to self-improvement.

Positive Correlation (C-9; HS-6). A type of correlation between two or more *variables* in which increases in the level of one variable are associated with increases in the level of the other variable(s).

Positive Feedback Loop (C-6; HS-4). In *cybernetics* and systems views of *family therapy*, when changes within one part of a system lead to changes within another part of the system, which in turn leads to changes in the first part of the system, thereby creating an unstable environment (which could lead to growth, conflict, or other changes to the system). For example, the continued escalation of an argument between spouses (positive feedback loop) can eventually lead to the decision to separate or go to counseling. Contrast with *Negative Feedback Loop*.

Positive Helping (C-7; HS-6). An approach to helping that is optimistic, future-oriented, strength-based, and focused on a large number of human contexts. See also *Positive Psychology*.

Positive Psychology/Counseling (C-7; HS-6). This optimistic, *wellness*-oriented approach suggests that individuals can learn how to increase their positive cognitions and *emotions* and change their behaviors to match this new positive focus.

Positive Punishment (C-7; HS-6). In *behavior therapy*, the addition of a *stimulus* that leads to a decrease in behavior. For example, yelling "no" at a child after they run into the street stops the child from running into the street again. See also *Punishment*.

Positive Regard (C-8; HS-8). Having a positive, open, and inviting attitude toward another. A trait humanists consider necessary for creating a nurturing environment. See also *Acceptance*, *Nonjudgmental*, and *Unconditional Positive Regard*.

Positive Regard, Need for (C-7; HS-7). In *person-centered counseling*, one's need to be *positively regarded* by important others in one's life or to feel loved, supported, and appreciated by significant others. This is a particularly strong need in childhood development. It is directly related to *conditions of worth* that are sometimes placed on an individual and how such conditions supersede one's *actualizing tendency*. See also *Positive Regard*.

Positive Reinforcement (C-8; HS-8). In *behavior therapy*, any *stimulus* that, when presented following a response, increases the likelihood of that response. For example, when a child says "please," they are given a reward for their good manners.

Positively Skewed Curve (C-7; HS-3). A set of scores in which the majority falls at the lower or negative end. It is said to be a positively skewed curve or distribution because there are fewer, "positive," or high-end scores, toward the right. In other words, the curve is stretched, or skewed, to the right.

Possibility Therapy (C-4; HS-2). Similar to *solution-focused brief therapy*, generally a brief therapeutic approach, created by Bill O'Hanlon, that stresses respect and collaboration and utilizes the client's ideas, *emotions*, and responses to develop solutions in counseling but incorporates other clinical ideas from *Carl Rogers* and *Milton Erickson* to validate clients and interpret their statements and ideas.

Postconventional Level (C-7; HS-5). *Lawrence Kohlberg's* third level of *moral development* (age 14 years and older), when a person makes a moral decision based on acceptance of a social contract that is related to democratically recognized universal truths (Stage 5), or based on individual *conscience* as a result of self-examined ethical principles (Stage 6). See also *Conventional Level* and *Preconventional Level*.

Post Hoc Analysis (C-5; HS-2). A variety of follow-up analyses to an *analysis of variance*, that are used when statistically significant findings emerge for *independent variables* that have three or more levels. For example, if statistical significance was found when examining the effects of three treatments groups (e.g., *cognitive therapy*, *solution-focused brief therapy*, and no treatment) on *depression* in clients, which groups were significant is not immediately known. A follow-up post hoc analysis would identify which groups are significantly different (e.g., the *cognitive therapy* group showed lower depression rates compared to the control and solution-focused groups).

Post-Interview Stage (C-7; HS-7). The sixth, or final *stage of the helping relationship* marked by completion of paperwork, billing, follow-up, and so forth. See also *Stages of the Helping Relationship*.

Post-Modern Approaches (C-8; HS-3). Conceptual orientations that include *narrative therapy*, *solution-focused brief therapy*, *relational-cultural theory*, *gender aware therapy*, and other approaches to the helping relationship based on the philosophies of *post-modernism* and *social constructionism*. Post-modern approaches question many assumptions about what is truth and emphasizes that language usage propagates beliefs that people end up viewing as truth. These approaches question many of the assumptions of other therapies, such as the belief in certain *diagnoses*, that intrinsic problems exist, or that certain words define who we are (e.g., *id*, *ego*, *superego*, *conscious mind*, *actualizing tendency*, *quality world*, *core beliefs*). Instead, they believe clients develop problems due to the rules and language developed by those who are in powerful positions (e.g., the family members, aristocracy, the wealthy, politicians). The purpose of these approaches is to help clients see how they have become a prisoner to the language and rules used in society and to help them use new language, define new rules, and find new solutions to their problems. Counselors, in dialogue with clients, can find exceptions to client problems and help move them toward new solutions to their problems. See also *Post-Modernism*, *Structuralism* and *Post-Structuralism.*

Post-Modernism (C-8; HS-4). The questioning of modernism, or many of the truths we have come to know and believe. Post-modernists tend to believe that we should question reality and that much of what one believes is a function of dominant language found in one's social milieu, especially language promulgated by those in positions of power. A philosophy adhered to by *narrative therapists*, *solution-focused brief therapists*, *relational-cultural theorists*, and others. See also *Post-Modern Approaches.*

Post-Modernist (C-7; HS-3). A person who embraces *post-modernism* and thus questions many of the basic assumptions taken for granted as a result of so-called *empiricism* and the *scientific method* and suggests there is no one way to understand the world, no foundational set of rules to make sense of who we are, and no one way of understanding a person. These individuals question "truth" and question many of the basic tenets of popular therapies that suggest certain structures cause mental health problems. See also *Post-Modernism*, *Structuralism* and *Post-Structuralism.*

Post-Psychoanalytic Models (C-8; HS-4). Counseling models that have moved significantly away from stressing the role *instincts* play in the formation of the *ego* and toward the importance of relationships in ego formation. Some of the more popular approaches include *Erikson's psychosocial theory*, *relational psychoanalysis*, *self-psychology*, and *relational-intersubjectivity approaches.*

Post-Secondary Counseling (C-7; HS-3). Another term for *student affairs and college counseling.*

Post-Structuralism (C-6; HS-3). A subset of *post-modernism*, the questioning of many of the structures we have been taught to believe in. In counseling and helping, such structures include things like: *id*, *ego*, *superego*, *schemas*, *self-actualizing tendency*, *core beliefs*, *internality*, and *mental disorder.* See also *Post-Modernism and Structuralism.*

Post-Traumatic Stress Syndrome (PTSD) (C-10; HS-10). A client's response to *trauma* that involves re-living aspects of the traumatic event and experiencing distress that is significant enough to interfere with his or her ability to function. See also *Trauma and Stressor-Related Disorders.*

Posture (C-7; HS-7). How we present ourselves physically to our clients, i.e., how we sit, stand, or otherwise position our body.

Power Differential (C-6; HS-6). Differing degrees of control, authority, or influence over others that can be real or perceived and are a function of such things as *race*, *class*, *gender*, *occupation*, *socioeconomic status*, or a host of other factors.

Power Dynamics (C-6; HS-6). The result of the force that some individuals, institutions, or society place on other individuals and the resulting undue demands that cause stressful behaviors that many people call *abnormal.*

Power Need (in Reality Therapy) (C-5; HS-3). One of five needs that make up one's *need-strength profile* of *reality therapy*. Also called *inner control need.*

Power Test (C-7; HS-3). See *Statistical Power.*

PPO (C-7; HS-3). See *Preferred Provider Organization.*

Practicality (C-8; HS-4). The practical considerations associated with selecting a *test* or measurement instrument, including time of administration, cost, format, readability, and ease of administration, scoring, and interpretation of results. One of the cornerstones of *test worthiness.*

Practitioner-Scientist (C-5; HS-4). The idea that all mental health professionals use research in some manner to drive the way they practice helping.

Preconscious (C-6; HS-4). In *psychoanalysis*, thoughts or *emotions* that are *unconscious* or unaware to the client but have not been fully *repressed* and thus are able to be accessed, explored, and brought into the clients' *self-awareness* (or made *conscious*).

Preconventional Level (C-8; HS-8). *Lawrence Kohlberg's* first level of *moral development* (ages 2–9), when a person makes a moral decision based on perceived power others hold and the desire to avoid *punishment* (Stage 1), or the egocentric desire to satisfy one's own need to gain personal rewards (Stage 2). See also *Conventional Level* and *Postconventional Level.*

Predictive Correlational Research (C-8; HS-4). A type of *quantitative research* used to investigate *correlations* between *variable(s)* or to predict scores on a variable based on scores obtained from another *variable(s)*.

Predictive Validity (C-9; HS-3). Evidence that test scores are able to predict a future criterion or standard. For instance, the *American College Test* and the *Scholastic Aptitude Test* should be able, to some degree, to predict first-year college grades otherwise they do not have predictive *validity*. A type of *criterion-related validity.*

Predictor Variable (C-8; HS-4). A *variable* which is predictive of something in the future. Used in *correlational research* and *multiple regression* analyses.

Pre-Experimental Design (C-8; HS-3). As in *true experimental* and *quasi-experimental designs*, the purpose of pre-experimental designs is to show a cause-and-effect relationship between the *intervention* and specific outcomes. However, unlike the other experimental designs, pre-experimental designs do not have built in controls for threats to *internal validity*; therefore, it is very difficult to determine if the treatment is responsible for any differences in participants. See also *One-Shot Case Study Design*, *One-Group Pretest-Posttest Design*, and *Static-Group Comparison.*

Preferred Futures (C-8; HS-5). The goals and the imagined future that are focused upon in *solution-focused brief therapy.*

Preferred Gender Pronouns (PGP) (C-7; HS-7). A set of pronouns that a client prefers (e.g., him, he, she, her, his, her, they) based on their *gender identity*. It is appropriate, and preferred, for counselors and human service professionals to ask for a person's preferred gender pronoun when meeting for the first time.

Preferred Goals Questions (C-8; HS-5). *Questions* asked by helpers to assist clients to focus on the future and their chosen goals for change. Most associated with *solution-focused brief therapy*. See also *Miracle Question*.

Preferred Provider Organization (PPO) (C-6; HS-4). Sometimes called a participating providing organization, a type of *managed health care* organization that has contracted with medical providers and hospitals to provide services, at a lower cost, within their network of providers. Going to a non-PPO provider generally incurs larger costs to the consumer.

Preferred Stories (C-8; HS-3). In *narrative therapy*, the new and healthier stories that are developed in therapy which can become the client's *dominant narratives* as they take precedence over *problem-saturated* or unhelpful stories.

Pregenital Stage (C-4; HS-1). In *Freud's psychosexual stages of development*, the stage of infantile development where the genitals have not yet become the dominant force in development.

Pregroup Stage (C-8; HS-8). The *stage of group development* in which the *group* leader screens potential group members before forming the group.

Prejudice (C-10; HS-10). As pertains to *stereotyping*, *racism*, and *discrimination*, any negative opinions and attitudes held about all members of a particular group, such as towards certain ethnic or cultural groups.

Premack's Principle (C-6; HS-4). Also known as the *relativity theory of reinforcement* or *grandma's law*, this principle states that more desirable behaviors, which are more probable, can be utilized as reinforcements for less desirable behaviors, which are less probable. For example, a person decides to take himself or herself to see an anticipated movie if he or she completes the house chores the person is dreading.

Preoperational Stage (C-10; HS-8). *Jean Piaget's* second stage of *cognitive development* (ages 2–7 years), when a child develops language ability and can maintain mental images. Here, children can engage in symbolic play (e.g., making believe a box is a house), but tend to respond intuitively rather than think logically. They also cannot take on different points of view. See also *Concrete-Operational Stage*, *Formal-Operational Stage*, and *Sensorimotor Stage*.

Preparing for Listening (C-9; HS-9). Refers to a variety of strategies that helpers can use to increase the chances that they will listen to their clients effectively, including calming oneself down, not talking or not interrupting, showing interest, not jumping to conclusions, actively listening, concentrating on feelings, concentrating on content, maintaining eye contact, having an open body *posture*, being sensitive to personal space, and not asking questions.

Prescribing the Symptom (C-6; HS-2). See *Paradoxical Intention*.

Presenting Concerns (C-10; HS-10). The various primary reason(s) (i.e., problems) that clients seek services from human service professionals and other helpers.

Presenting Problem(s) (C-10; HS-10). See *Presenting Concerns.*

Presuppositional Questions (in Assessment) (C-7; HS-4). *Questions* that imply something is true, or assuming what one wants to prove, by the manner in which you ask a question. For instance, asking the question: "Can you tell me how your husband has mishandled you?" is a leading question. Since all husbands have likely done something that is perceived negatively by their spouses during their relationship, this "begs the question" that the client is likely to come up with some event when the husband responded poorly to or mistreated the spouse. See also *Leading Questions.*

Presuppositional Questions/Language (in Post-Modern Helping) (C-7; HS-3). *Questions* that imply something will change between the time the question is asked and the next meeting of the client. Often used in *post-modern approaches.* For instance, between the making of an appointment and coming in for the first appointment, a helper might ask, "Has anything changed since you made your appointment?"

Preventive Education (C-7; HS-7). Offering *psychoeducation*, oftentimes in a *group* setting, in an effort to ward off, or prevent, future problems.

Primal Therapy (C-5; HS-2). A type of *therapy*, somewhat popular during the 1960s and rarely used today, in which a client is encouraged to have a *catharsis* by bringing back *repressed* memories, especially memories from early childhood and even memories of being born.

Primary Attachment Figure (C-5; HS-5). The predominant parent, guardian or caregiver to whom an infant securely bonds with emotionally and psychologically. In order to have a healthy attachment style, one requires at least one sensitive and reactive attachment figure who meets the child's needs and to whom the child can perceive as safe, warm, and loving.

Primary Feelings of Inferiority (C-5; HS-2). In *individual psychology*, universal *feelings of inferiority*, such as when infants and young children struggle to overcome their natural physical, cognitive, and psychological hurdles of life (e.g., a toddler attempts to walk).

Primary Function (Jungian) (C-5; HS-2). In *analytical psychology*, concerning the *mental functions* of *thinking* vs. *feeling* or *intuiting* vs. *sensing*, the one function people tend to favor.

Primary Obligation: Client, Agency, or Society (C-8; HS-8). Ethical codes generally assert that the human service professional's *primary obligation* is ensuring the client's right to *confidentiality*, right to be respected, and right for self-determination; however, there are instances in which professionals also recognize, and sometimes favor, the right of other individuals and of society to be protected from harm.

Primary Prevention (C-7; HS-7). Concentrating on the prevention of emotional problems prior to them occurring through such things as *psychoeducation* and by promoting a *wellness approach* to helping. Contrast with *Secondary Prevention* and *Tertiary Prevention.*

Primary Process (C-8; HS-3). In *psychoanalysis*, the raw, irrational impulses from which the *id* operates.

Primary Reinforcer (C-7; HS-7). In *operant conditioning*, reinforcers with biological origins such as food, pain, or pleasure. See also *Secondary Reinforcer.*

Primary Sources (C-8; HS-5). Using original records (e.g. someone's actual *diaries*), as opposed to *secondary sources* (e.g., a book about or discussing the diaries), in collecting data for research. Particularly important in *historical research.*

Primary Survival Triad (C-6; HS-5). The triad between parents and each child which is responsible for the child's *self-esteem.*

Primordial Images (Jungian) (C-7; HS-4). In *analytical psychology*, images, or *archetypes*, residing in the *psyche* inherited by all people and which provide the psyche with its tendency to perceive the world in certain ways that people identify as "human."

Principal Axis Factoring (PAF) (C-5; HS-1). A method of *factor extraction* used when conducting a *factor analysis* to reveal the *latent variables* of a model. A PAF captures a more representative latent factor structure because *error variance* is not included in the analysis. See also *Principal Component Analysis.*

Principal Component Analysis (PCA) (C-5; HS-1). A method of *factor extraction* used when conducting a *factor analysis* to reveal the *latent variables* of a model. A PCA includes *error variance* in the model which captures a larger percentage of variance in the total model; however, the inclusion of error variance is a threat to the factorial *validity* of the emergent factor structure. There is an ongoing debate among statisticians about whether PCA is a type of factor analysis or only a method of item-reduction. See also *Principal Axis Factoring.*

Principle Ethics Model (C-6; HS-5). A type of moral model of ethical decision-making that suggests *ethical decision-making* should revolve around certain principles. See also *Kitchener, Virtue Ethics Models,* and *Ethical Decision-Making, Moral Models.*

Principled Activist (C-6; HS-3). The fourth *stage of racism* where the professional can understand and accept that all people hold varying values and beliefs. In this stage, the helper is ready to embrace *social justice* actions. Developmental theory formulated by *D'Andrea and Daniels.* See also *Affective/Impulsive*, *Dualistic Rational*, and *Liberal Stages of Racism.*

Principled Conscience Orientation (C-7; HS-5). Stage 6 of *Kohlberg's postconventional morality level*, where moral decisions are based on a sense of universal truths, personal *conscience*, and principles of *justice* that are seen as being valid beyond current laws and social contracts.

Private Logic (C-7; HS-3). In *individual psychology*, the internal thoughts that people have that drive them toward our *subjective final goal.* Based on how a person responded to early *feelings of inferiority.*

Private Practice Settings (C-10; HS-9). Settings where *clinical mental health counselors* and other *licensed clinicians* may be employed, which are privately owned businesses where the counselor is self-employed or teams with other counselors in a profit sharing or related structure (e.g., franchise) to see clients. Some private practices take insurance or are *fee for service*, or a combination of the two.

Privilege (C-9; HS-9). Exclusive rights, powers, or recognitions given to members of particular groups simply because they are members of that group, as opposed to merit-based rights. For example, *White privilege* has been common in America, extending special unspoken rights to White people over people of color.

Privileged Communication (C-10; HS-6). The legal right of a professional to not reveal information about a client and the information that is protected under this legal right. This legal right is determined by U.S. states, and relative to human service professionals, this generally only includes *licensed* mental health professionals. See also *Confidentiality*.

Probability Level (C-9; HS-5). See *Alpha Level*.

Problem-Free Language/Talk (C-8; HS-5). In *post-modern approaches*, such as *narrative therapy* and *solution-focused brief therapies*, language that does not focus on the problem, but instead focuses on solutions and alternatives to the problem.

Problem Identification Stage (C-7; HS-7). The second stage of the helping relationship where the client feels comfortable to discuss his or her problems due to trust that was built during the first stage. See also *Stages of the Helping Relationship*.

Problem-Saturated Stories/Narratives (C-8; HS-4). In *narrative therapy*, those stories presented by clients that are filled with the problems and problem talk. *Narrative therapists* strive to help clients view their lives in *multistoried* ways so that they can find solutions to their problems.

Problem-Solving Models of Ethical Decision-Making (C-8; HS-8). *Ethical decision-making models* that provide a step-by-step approach to making ethical decisions. One such model includes eight steps: (1) identifying the problem; (2) identifying the potential issues involved; (3) reviewing the relevant ethical guidelines; (4) knowing relevant laws and regulations; (5) obtaining consultation; (6) considering possible and probable courses of action; (7) listing the consequences of various decisions; (8) and deciding on what appears to be the best course of action.

Problem-Solving Therapy (C-7; HS-3). Developed by *Jay Haley*, this type of *strategic therapy* focuses on solving problems without necessarily focusing on the problem. The goal is to do whatever is necessary, and legal and ethical, to induce change.

Process Addiction(s) (C-7; HS-7). Seen as functioning similarly to *substance abuse*, addictive behaviors to activities (or processes) such as *sex*, video gaming, gambling, shopping, and eating. See also *Addiction*.

Process Evaluation (C-7; HS-6). See *Formative Evaluation*.

Process Notes (C-8; HS-8). Written notes that are usually brief (often one to three paragraphs long) to help the counselor remember salient points of a session. Clients typically do not have a right to see these as per the *Health Insurance Portability and Accountability Act* regulations. Contrast with *Progress Notes*.

Process-Oriented Consultation Model (C-7; HS-4). An approach to *consultation* in which the *consultant* either does not have the answer or withholds expertise, with the belief that the most effective resolution would be for the system members to find their own solution.

Process Self-Disclosure (C-7; HS-5). Similar to the concept of *immediacy*, involves the helper sharing with the client his or her moment-to-moment experience of *self* in relation to the client. See also *Self-Disclosure.*

Pro-Counselor (C-5; HS-2). See *Triad Model.*

Professional Associations (C-10; HS-10). In the mental health and human services fields, a variety of organizations that support the philosophical beliefs of a particular discipline and offer a wide range of professional activities and benefits, like the *ACA* or *NOHS*.

Professional Counseling Identity (C-6; HS-2). The second primary area that the *Council for the Accreditation of Counseling and Related Educational Programs* reviews, this focuses on the *foundation of the program* and the *counseling curriculum* as they relate to counselors-in-training developing their identity as professional counselors. More generically, it is the total process of developing one's identity as a counselor. See also *Master's-Level Standards.*

Professional Disclosure Statement (C-10; HS-10). An informational document about the helper and helping relationship that reflects important values upheld in ethical codes and provides information about the helping process. It is usually given to clients when first meeting them. Such a statement often includes: (1) how the helping process will unravel, (2) the theoretical approach of the helper, (3) potential risks and limitation of the helping relationship, (4) the helper's *credentials*, (5) the limits of *confidentiality*, (6) the right of the client for self-determination, (6) respect for the client relative to his or her unique cultural identity, (7) fee for services. (8) and other pertinent information or related things.

Professional Practice (C-5; HS-2). The third primary area that the *Council for the Accreditation of Counseling and Related Educational Programs* requires for program *accreditation* that focuses on the students' development of counseling theory and skills while under *supervision*. See also *Master's-Level Standards.*

***Professional School Counseling* (C-5; HS-2).** Journal of the *American School Counselor Association* (*ASCA*).

Professional Standards for the Training of Group Workers (C-6; HS-2). Standards developed by the *Association for Specialists in Group Work* that guide the training of *group counselors.*

Professional Will (C-7; HS-4). A transfer plan to another helper in case a helper becomes incapacitated while working with clients, such as due to illness or death.

Prognosis (C-7; HS-7). The clinical term for the length, breadth, and expected course of a client's condition/illness and his or her response to or outcome of treatment, positive or negative.

Program Accreditation (C-8; HS-8). Relative to human service professionals, a broad range of standards that programs must meet to show competence in the training of human service professionals or counselors for *accreditation.* See also the *Council for Standards in Human Service Education* (*CSHSE*) and the *Council for Accreditation of Counseling and Related Educational Programs* (*CACREP*).

Program Evaluation (C-7; HS-7). The process of systematically assessing a program to determine if it has achieved its goals and objectives and has worth and value. This can involve a variety of *informal* and formal *assessment* and evaluation tools to measure the effectiveness and efficiency of programs. Some components include *process evaluation*, *formative evaluation*, and *outcome evaluation*, sometimes called *summative evaluation*.

Progress Notes (C-8; HS-8). Clinical notes written by human service professionals that include such things as type of *treatment plan*, *diagnosis*, *medications*, *prognosis*, and *frequency of treatment*. Clients have rights to see these. Contrast with *Process Notes*.

Progress Toward Client Goals (C-6; HS-6). A part of the *case management* process, this involves ensuring that client goals are being monitored and assessed.

Progressive Muscle Relaxation (C-7; HS-5). Similar to the concept of *reciprocal inhibition*, a *relaxation exercise* in which clients are taught how to progressively relax by focusing on each major muscle group in the body and then tightening and feeling the muscle relax until the whole body is relaxed. Originally developed by *Edmund Jacobson*. See also *Meditation*.

Project Pigeon (C-5; HS-3). A project developed by *B.F. Skinner* during World War II that taught pigeons to steer gliders with explosives into targets, even under heavy enemy fire and other adverse conditions. Although highly effective, it was abandoned due to the development of radar.

Projection (C-8; HS-7). See *Defense Mechanisms*.

Projective Personality Tests (C-8; HS-5). *Tests* that present a *stimulus* to which individuals can respond. Personality factors are interpreted based on the individual's responses. Often used to identify *psychopathology* and to assist in *treatment planning*. Examples are the *Rorschach Inkblot Test* and *sentence completion test*. A type of *personality test*.

Protection of a Title (C-7; HS-4). The protection of professional *credentials* that attest to a person's attainment of a certain level of *competence*, but does not speak to one's *scope of practice*.

Protective Factors (C-6; HS-6). Influences in clients' lives that guard against the likelihood of the client committing suicide or homicide. Some include pregnancy, stable employment, medication compliance, children living at home, being connected with a *therapist*, easy access to clinical *interventions*, having children under the age of 18, strong family or community supports, positive coping and problem-solving skills, and having strong religious or spiritual beliefs.

Provider (C-7; HS-7). A generic term for any professional, individual, or organization offering helping services to clients. For example, one's primary medical provider refers to the doctor one usually goes to for common ailments (e.g., a family physician).

Providing Information (C-6; HS-6). The communication of factual knowledge. A commonly used *counseling skill*.

Provisional Diagnosis (C-5; HS-4). Tentative *diagnoses* that are made when a *clinician* has a strong inclination that a client will meet the criteria for a *diagnosis*, but does not yet have enough information to make the diagnosis officially.

Prozac (C-7; HS-6). A type of *psychotropic medication* and *controlled substance* used in the treatment of *depression* and some *anxiety disorders*.

Prudent (C-6; HS-5). In a *moral model of ethical decision-making*, one way a counselor's character may be important. In other words, the counselor being prudent, or careful and tentative, in his or her decision making.

Psy.D (C-8; HS-6). Doctorate of *psychology* degree; an alternative, clinically-focused degree path to a doctorate in psychology instead of the Ph.D. See also *Psychologist.*

Psyche (C-4; HS-2). All of that which makes up one's *conscious* and *unconscious* mind. In *psychoanalysis*, it includes the *id*, *ego*, and *superego*. In *Jungian therapy*, it includes the *conscious*, the *personal unconscious*, and the *collective unconscious*. In other approaches, it may include other aspects of the individual.

Psychiatric Disorders (C-10; HS-10). See *Mental Disorder.*

Psychiatric-Mental Health Nurse Credentialing (C-5; HS-3). A professional *credential* for *psychiatric-mental health nurses*. See also *Psychiatric-Mental Health Nurse.*

Psychiatric-Mental Health Nurse or Psychiatric Nurse-Practitioner (C-7; HS-6). Also referred to as a *psychiatric nurse* or nurse-practitioner who has received specialized training as a mental health professional. The advanced psychiatric-mental health nurse is called an *Advanced Practice Registered Nurse* (*APRN*).

Psychiatric Nurse (C-7; HS-6). See *Psychiatric-Mental Health Nurse or Psychiatric Nurse-Practitioner.*

Psychiatric Social Worker (C-7; HS-7). A *social worker* with specialized mental health training who works in psychiatric settings, such as *inpatient hospitalization* units.

Psychiatrist (C-10; HS-10). A medical physician who generally has completed a residency in *psychiatry* with extensive training in some kind of mental health setting. Traditionally, most psychiatrists also did *psychotherapy* but in recent years many oversee *medication management* and work with patients with biological-related disorders. See also *Psychiatry.*

Psychiatry (C-7; HS-7). The medical specialty concerned with *psychiatric disorders* and their treatment, often through *medication management* and *psychotherapy*. See also *Psychiatrist.*

Psychiatry Credentialing (C-7; HS-6). The *credentialing* process for *psychiatrists* that involves becoming a *licensed physician* and usually a *board-certified psychiatrist.*

Psychic Energy (C-8; HS-5). In *psychoanalysis*, the belief that our mental energy is composed of *instincts* made up of our *life instinct* (*Eros*) and our *death instinct* (*Thanatos*).

Psychoactive Drugs (C-8; HS-8). Drugs and medications that alter brain functioning and create changes in *consciousness*, moods, and/or perceptions in individuals. They have medical, ritualistic, and recreational usage. This category of substances includes *cocaine*, *LSD*, *peyote*, *morphine*, and others. Most are *controlled substances.*

Psychoanalysis (C-8; HS-5). Also known as "talk therapy," the therapy approach based on *Freud*'s ideas, such as the belief that *instincts* (e.g., hunger, thirst, survival, aggression, *sex*) are strong motivators of behavior and satisfying them is mostly an *unconscious* process. *Defense mechanisms* (e.g., *rationalization*, *repression*) are developed to manage instincts. Early child-rearing practices, as applied through the *oral*, *anal*, and *phallic psychosexual stages of development* in the first six years of life, are responsible for how defenses are developed and result in normal or *abnormal* personality development. Effects of early childhood practices are observed in adolescence and adulthood in what are called the *latency* and *genital psychosexual stages*.

Psychoanalyst (C-8; HS-7). A person trained in *psychoanalysis*, usually at one of a number of post-graduate training centers around the country and world. Today, these may or may not be licensed individuals, as few U.S. states provide *licensure* for psychoanalysis.

Psychoanalytic Group Therapy (C-6; HS-4). *Group therapy* using *psychoanalytic* procedures.

Psychoanalytic Movement (C-5; HS-2). The first comprehensive *psychotherapeutic* system. Developed by *Sigmund Freud*, *psychoanalysis* was influenced by the new emphasis on the scientific method.

Psychobiology (C-6; HS-5). The study of the mind/body interactions that influence the development and functioning of the personality.

Psychodrama (C-7; HS-4). An approach that focuses on individuals acting out their experiences in front of an audience or via *group* participation. This form of *therapy* emphasizes *role-playing*, *here-and-now* interactions, expressions of feelings, and feedback from the audience (the group), and is considered by some the forerunner of *group counseling*. Developed by *Jacob L. Moreno*.

Psychodynamic Approaches (C-8; HS-6). A conceptual orientation that includes *psychoanalysis*, *analytical psychology* (*Jungian therapy*), *individual therapy* (*Adlerian therapy*), and other approaches to the helping relationship based on psychodynamic theories. To some degree, all suggest the *unconscious* and *conscious* impact the functioning of the person in deeply personal and dynamic ways, look at early child-rearing practices as important in the development of personality, and believe that the past and the dynamic interaction of the past with conscious and unconscious factors are important in the therapeutic process.

Psychodynamic Approaches to Career Counseling (C-7; HS-4). A *career development theory*, which bases its approach on *psychodynamic* principles. One such approach was developed by *Anne Roe*, who based *career* choice on the type of early parenting received and classified individuals in one of eight orientations toward the world of *work*. Roe hypothesized that parents can be classified as either warm or cold, and that these two styles result in one of three types of emotional climates, emotional concentration on the child, acceptance of the child, or avoidance of the child.

Psychodynamic Consultation (C-5; HS-3). Approaches to *consultation* that apply *psychodynamic approaches* including *psychoanalysis* counseling principles.

Psychodynamic Family Therapy (C-5; HS-3). An approach to *family counseling* based on *psychodynamic* theory and practiced by *Robin Skynner* and others.

Psychoeducation (C-7; HS-7). An approach to helping that incorporates educational information and/or classroom teaching in combination with other techniques to prevent problems.

Psychoeducational Groups (C-8; HS-8). Types of *groups* that are focused on preventing future problems by providing individuals with educational information in combination with traditional group techniques to process any issues that may come up while or after presenting the educational information. Formerly called *guidance groups*. See also *Psychoeducation.*

Psychological and Educational Tests (C-8; HS-6). Any of a variety of *personality tests*, *achievement tests*, and *aptitude tests* for educational and psychological *assessment* purposes.

Psychological Type (C-6; HS-5). In *analytical psychology*, the attitudes of *extroversion* and *introversion* and the *mental functions* of *thinking* and *feeling* and of *sensing* and *intuiting*. *Carl Jung* suggested we are all born more extroverted or introverted, and we become a thinking or feeling person and a sensing or intuiting person. The combination which we are (e.g., extroverted, intuiting, and thinking) is our *psychological type*. *Katherine Cook Briggs* and *Isabel Briggs Myers* added two more mental functions, *judging* and *perceiving*. See also *Myers-Briggs Type Indicator.*

Psychologist (C-8; HS-7). Generally, a person who holds a doctoral degree (Ph.D. or *Psy.D*) in counseling psychology or clinical psychology, and has completed an internship at a mental health facility and has passed specific U.S. state requirements to obtain *licensure* as a psychologist. See also *Psychology.*

Psychology (C-6; HS-5). The broad field of academic, medical, and other scientific studies of the mind (or *psyche*) and behavior. This professional field is vast and includes areas devoted to clinical, counseling, animal, developmental, educational, school, paranormal, and many other dedicated areas focusing on the mind and behavior of animals, individuals, groups, and organizations, etc., and innumerable interconnected concepts such as cognition, perception, development, and relationships.

Psychology Board Certifications (C-5; HS-4). Established by the *American Board of Professional Psychology* (*ABPP*), one of 14 *board certifications* for *psychologists*, including clinical child and adolescent psychology, clinical health psychology, clinical neuropsychology, clinical psychology, cognitive and behavioral psychology, counseling psychology, couples and family psychology, forensic psychology, group psychology, organizational and business consulting psychology, police and public safety psychology, psychoanalysis, rehabilitation psychology, and school psychology.

Psychology Credentialing (C-7; HS-5). Credentials in *psychology* that most commonly include *licensed psychologist*, *psychology board certifications*, and credentialed *school psychologist* (*licensed* or *certified* as a function of the U.S. state nomenclature used).

Psychometrics (C-7; HS-5). An area of research that focuses on the development, validation, and implementation of *psychological and educational tests.*

Psychopathology (C-7; HS-7). The study of unusual or abnormal *mental disorders* and their origin, progression, and treatment. Additionally, this term refers to the development of mental disorders and their symptoms in individuals.

Psychopharmacology (C-8; HS-7). The scientific *study* and practice of using medications to treat an array of disorders. Sometimes called *Psychotropic Medications.*

Psychosexual Stages of Development (C-8; HS-5). As posited by *Sigmund Freud*, the five stages of individual development: *oral stage*, *anal stage*, *phallic stage*, *latency stage*, and *genital stage*. See also *Psychoanalysis*.

Psychosis (C-7; HS-4). A *mental disorder* in which one's emotional life and thinking is severely impaired as indicated by the person being out of touch with reality. Often, psychosis is also associated with unusual behavior. Psychosis may or may not include *hallucinations or delusions*.

Psychosocial and Environmental Stressors (C-6; HS-5). Sources of client distress that are common concerns (e.g., job loss, marital problems, homelessness, relationship issues) and are assessed through the use of *V Codes* or *Z Codes* in the *Diagnostic and Statistical Manual-5*.

Psychosocial Development (C-7; HS-7). The development of personality based on the impact of social factors, including *culture*, society, family, significant others, etc. This approach tends to be based on an *anti-deterministic* view of human nature and opposed to *Freud's deterministic view of human nature*. See also *Erikson's Psychosocial Theory* and *Psychosocial Development, Stages of*.

Psychosocial Development, Stages of (C-8; HS-7). As developed by *Erik Erikson*, eight stages of lifespan development that affect the formation of the personality of a human being. The stages are: *trust vs. mistrust*, *autonomy vs. shame and doubt*, *initiative vs. guilt*, *industry vs. inferiority*, *identify vs. role confusion*, *intimacy vs. isolation*, *generativity vs. stagnation*, and *ego integrity vs. despair*. Erikson suggested that as individuals pass through the eight stages, they are faced with a *task*, sometimes called a *crisis*. Portrayed as a pair of opposing forces, Erikson described the first opposing task in each stage as *syntonic*, or positive emotional quality, and the second task as *dystonic*, or negative emotional quality. He suggested that individuals needed to experience both syntonic and dystonic qualities.

Psychosocial Forces (C-6; HS-6). The notion that social forces affect the development of our *psyche* (e.g., parenting, peer relationships, work relationships).

Psychosomatic (Illnesses) (C-7; HS-6). Referring to body-based symptoms or illnesses whereby there is no known biological cause, but rather the cause of the body-based symptom or illness appears rooted in a person's *anxiety disorder* or related *mental disorders*. For example, in some individuals or *cultures*, *depression* or other *anxiety* symptoms occur as stomach pains or pain in other areas of the body, rather than being seen as mental experiences.

Psychotherapist (C-7; HS-7). Although generally not licensed by U.S. states, on a practical level this is a person who has an advanced degree in *psychiatry*, *psychology*, *social work*, or counseling and who works in a mental health setting or in *private practice*, providing individual, marital, or *group therapy*. Because many states do not legislate the term *psychotherapist*, anyone can call himself or herself a psychotherapist; however, he or she cannot do *psychotherapy* because those skills are usually legislated as limited to licensed therapists.

Psychotherapy (C-7; HS-7). Generally seen as the practice of doing long-term therapy with a client in the *there and then* and focusing on life stories, deep-seated issues, personality reconstruction, the *unconscious*, and deep client revelations, which can be painful for the client. See also *Counseling* and *Therapy*.

Psychotherapy Groups (C-7; HS-7). Also called *group therapy*, these groups typically focus upon deep-seated, long-term issues, remediation of severe *pathology*, and personality reconstruction.

Psychotic Disorders (C-8; HS-7). See *Schizophrenia Spectrum and Other Psychotic Disorders*.

Psychotropic Medications (C-7; HS-6). Medications that affect psychological functioning and include five groups: *antipsychotics*, *mood-stabilizing drugs*, *antidepressants*, *antianxiety agents*, and *stimulants*. See also *Psychopharmacology*.

PsycINFO (C-7; HS-5). An indexing *electronic database* that includes millions of *peer-reviewed* sources that are related to the research and practice of *psychology* and other mental health disciplines. See also *Gale*, *EBSCO*, and *ERIC*.

Public Arena (C-5; HS-5). One of the three areas that is covered in the *advocacy competencies* related to *advocacy* within the public sphere (or wider community) beyond clinical settings.

Public Assistance (C-6; HS-7). The generic term for government assistance to individuals, often called *social welfare*, such as *Temporary Assistance for Needy Families* (*TANF*) and *Medicaid*.

Public Information (C-6; HS-5). Informing the public about issues that have far reaching effects. An aspect of the *advocacy competencies*. See also *Public Arena*.

Publication Manual of the American Psychological Association (C-7; HS-7). The official *APA* style manual that sets rules for how to write, cite, organize, and reference within publications. This is the most commonly used style guide for writing within social science fields.

Publisher-Type Scores (C-7; HS-2). Created by *test* developers who generate their own unique *standard scores* that employ a *mean* and *standard deviation* of the publisher's choice.

Punishment (C-7; HS-7). Applying an aversive *stimulus* or removing a positive stimulus following a behavior in an effort to decrease a specific behavior. This method of changing behavior can sometimes lead to undesirable side effects (e.g., counter-aggression). With *positive punishment*, when the stimulus is presented, the behavior will decrease. With *negative punishment*, when the stimulus is removed, the behavior will decrease.

Punishment-Obedience Orientation (C-7; HS-7). *Kohlberg's* stage 1 of the *preconventional level*, where moral decisions are made to avoid *punishment* or gain rewards from individuals in authority

Purposeful Sample (C-7; HS-5). The deliberate selection of individuals from a specific group due to the focus of one's research.

***P*-Value (C-10; HS-6).** See *Alpha Level*.

Pygmalion Effect (C-8; HS-5). See *Rosenthal Effect*.

QCSW (C-6; HS-5). See *Qualified Clinical Social Worker*.

Q-Sort Technique (C-6; HS-3). An assessment technique in which subjects' viewpoints can be analyzed by having them sort a number of items (e.g., feeling words) into categories and then having them rank order the categories. Analysis between pre and post a treatment (e.g., therapy) can often be computed. *Carl Rogers* used this technique to analyze changes in perceptions of the *self* of clients, noting that clients discrepancy between their *idealized self* and their *real self*, lessened over time.

Qualified Clinical Social Worker (QCSW) (C-6; HS-5). See *Licensed Clinical Social Worker.*

Qualitative Research (C-10; HS-5). Rather than using the *scientific method*, as in *quantitative research*, qualitative research relies on the researcher to observe, describe, and interpret phenomena carefully within a natural setting or social context and to employ aspects of researcher *subjectivity* (or viewpoint) as components of study. This type of research assumes everything is subjective and that objective reality is elusive or non-existent. For these reasons, qualitative research allows one to examine phenomena that quantitative research cannot explore, like our understanding of abstract concepts such as *empathy* and the spiritual nature of our lives. It includes *grounded theory*, *phenomenological*, *ethnographic*, and *consensual qualitative research.*

Quality World (C-8; HS-5). In *reality therapy*, the pictures in our minds of what we want to have in order to have our needs met for our unique *need-strength profile.*

Quantitative Research (C-10; HS-5). An approach to research with the underlying assumption that there is an *objective reality* that can be verified. The researcher begins with a *hypothesis*, or a conjecture, about the nature of human phenomena and uses the *scientific method*, or a systematic process of observation, measurement, and experiment, to test the *hypotheses*, find possible answers to the *research question* being asked, or both. The two main types of quantitative research are *experimental* and *nonexperimental research.* Experimental research includes *true experiment*, *quasi experiment*, *single-subject*, and *pre-experimental designs.* Nonexperimental research includes *ex post facto*, *correlational*, and *survey research.*

Quasi-Experimental Research (C-8; HS-4). Instead of *random assignment*, as is found in *true-experimental research*, quasi-experimental research examines already existing intact groups, giving one or more groups the treatment, while not giving the other groups the treatment. *Causal relationships* can be obtained from the analysis.

Queer (C-9; HS-9). Traditionally seen as a derogatory word to describe *gays* and *lesbians*, in recent years this word has been embraced by the *lesbian*, *gay*, *bisexual*, *transgender*, *queer*, *questioning*, *intersex*, and *ally* community as a means of regaining power and not buying into existing ways of seeing the world. It has also taken on a nebulous meaning of anyone who does not identify as a *heterosexual.*

Questioning (C-9; HS-9). A type of *sexual orientation* in which one is wondering about, or not sure of, his or her sexual attractions or *sexual identity.*

Questions (C-10; HS-10). A commonly used helping skill that includes a wide variety of questions, some of which should be used cautiously as they can cause defensiveness (e.g., *why questions*). Some of the more frequently used questions include *open* and *closed questions*, *tentative questions*, *solution-focused questions* (*preferred goals*, *evaluative*, *coping*, *exception-seeking*, *solution-focused*), and why questions. See also *Interview.*

Quincunx (C-4; HS-2). Developed by *Galton*, and sometimes called *Galton's Board*, this device demonstrates the natural occurring nature of the *normal curve*. It highlights the notion that many items in life (e.g., traits, test scores) result in a *bell-shaped curve* or *normal distribution.* Balls are dropped on a board that has a series of rows of pins equidistant from one another. On the top of the board is one pin, below that is the next row with two pins, below that is three pins and so forth until you have about 8 rows. As the balls are dropped, by probability, they have an equal chance of going left or going right. Ultimately, due to the laws of probability, the dropping of the balls results in a bell-shaped curve or *normal distribution*.

Race (C-10; HS-10). Traditionally, a way of dividing people based on what was considered shared, common genetic, phenotypical, and biological characteristics; however, in reality, it has been found that race is a socially constructed concept with little or no basis in biology. In today's world, it has been shown that many individuals who assume they are a race, genetically are a mix of many "races," and that there is more genetic variation within any single "race" than between other "races." Additionally, the heritability of most characteristics goes beyond race, demonstrating this concept as a social construction.

Racial Identity Development (C-9; HS-9). Encompasses various models that look at the development of racial identity in individuals. Most models are stage-based and reflect a general continuum from awareness of one's identity, to the embracing of one's identity, to the acceptance and appreciation of other identities. See also *Racial Identity Development for People of Color*, *Helms White Identity Model*, and *Stages of Racism.*

Racial Identity Development for People of Color (RIDPOC) (C-7; HS-4). A 5-stage *developmental model* of racial identity that states that people of color may pass through unique stages that reflect their cultural selves. The stages include conformity, dissonance and beginning appreciation, resistance and *immersion*, *introspection* and *internalization*, and universal inclusion.

Racism (C-10; HS-10). The belief that one *race* is superior to another.

Racist Attitudes (C-10; HS-10). Having preconceived notions about the characteristics of an individual or a group that are based on generalizations about *race* or the characteristics of the individual or group.

Radical Behaviorist (C-7; HS-6). *Behaviorists* that believe the *unconscious* and other "mentalistic concepts" like the *id*, proposed by *Freud* and other theorists, should not be considered in understanding behavior as all *conditioning* occurs at the level of behaviors, and is not an internal process. See also *B.F. Skinner* and *Black Box.*

Radical New Approaches (C-6; HS-2). New approaches to counseling that have significantly impacted the manner in which counseling is delivered. Some of these approaches include *neuroprocessing*, *neurofeedback*, *hypnotherapy*, *eye movement integration therapy*, *cerebral electric stimulation*, *neurological and psychophysiological therapies*, *eye movement desensitization response*, *complementary*, *alternative*, *and integrative therapies*, and others.

Random Assignment (C-9; HS-6). A method for assigning participants to conditions in a research study in which subjects are randomly assigned to different treatment groups, or to an *experimental group* and *control group*. Random assignment helps to ensure that the groups are similar to one another in most aspects and lessens the likelihood of error in statistical measurement when finding results. It is usually used in *experimental research.*

Random Sample (C-9; HS-6). A sampling technique that involves collecting data from a *sample* of participants who were randomly selected from a larger population. For a sample to be truly random, everyone in the population must have an equal chance of being selected.

Range (C-10; HS-6). A *measure of variability* that examines the spread of *test* scores from highest to lowest for the group. Range is the lowest score subtracted from the highest score, or the lowest score subtracted from the highest score plus 1 (to account for all scores).

Rank Order Scales (C-7; HS-6). A type of *rating scale* that asks individuals to place their responses from highest to lowest preference on an *ordinal scale.*

Rank, Otto (1884 - 1939) (C-4; HS-2). An influential Austrian *psychoanalyst* and theorist who was a colleague and friend of *Sigmund Freud.* His work post-Freud was influential in *existential-humanistic* counseling approaches and *objection relations theory*, and many other professional areas. He was particularly known as one of the first *therapists* to highlight the importance of *here-and-now* emotional expression in therapy and for the importance he placed on attachment and birth trauma.

Rapid Eye Movement (C-6; HS-2). Used in the practice of *Eye Movement Desensitization Response Therapy*, individuals' rapid eye movements following a practitioner's hands or an object. See also *Eye Movement Desensitization Response Therapy (EMDR).*

Rapport and Trust Building Stage (C-8; HS-8). The first stage of the helping relationship where basic skills and a focus on the *working alliance* allow the client to feel safe in the helping relationship. See also *Stages of the Helping Relationship.*

Rating Scales (C-7; HS-5). Scales developed to assess any of a number of attributes of the examinee. These can be rated by the examinee or someone who knows the examinee well. Some commonly used rating scales include *numerical scales*, *Likert-type scales* (*graphic scales*), *semantic differential scales*, and *rank-order scales.* A type of *informal assessment.*

Ratio Scale (C-8; HS-5). A scale of measurement that has a meaningful zero point and equal intervals, and thus, can be manipulated by all mathematical principles and easily used in statistical computations.

Ratio Scale of Reinforcement (C-6; HS-4). In *behavior therapy*, *schedules of reinforcement* that involve reinforcing a client after a certain number (or ratio) of behaviors are exhibited. They can be *fixed* or *variable ratio schedules of reinforcement.*

Rational Emotive Behavior Therapy (REBT) (C-10; HS-5). Developed by *Albert Ellis*, *rational emotive behavior therapy* suggests individuals are born with the potential for *rational thinking* or *self-defeating thoughts and irrational thinking*, and it is the belief about an event that is responsible for one's reaction to the event. Thus, an *activating event* (A) precedes the *beliefs* (B) about the event, and it is the beliefs that result in the *consequences* (C), or the feelings and behaviors that follow. *Irrational beliefs* (iB) result in negative feelings and behaviors and *rational beliefs* (rB) result in appropriate and reasonable feelings and behaviors. Ellis offers three *core irrational beliefs* that many people buy into. Helpers assist clients in *disputing* (D) irrational beliefs by changing their thoughts and by having the client practice new behaviors.

Rational-Emotional Role-Play (C-6; HS-2). A *rational emotive behavior therapy* technique that permits clients to *role-play*, or act out, as they have a debate between the rational and emotional parts of themselves. Often, the counselor will begin by acting out the client's rational part and having the client act out the emotional, or dysfunctional, part and then the counselor and client will switch roles to get the client to act out being rational.

Rational Functions (Jungian) (C-6; HS-2). According to *Jung*, the *mental functions* of *thinking* and *feeling*, called rational due to people getting information via collected evidence, rather than being based on perceptions as are the *sensing* and *intuiting mental functions*. See also *Irrational Functions (Jungian)*.

Rational Thinking (C-7; HS-5). Used in *rational emotive behavior therapy*, whereas *irrational thinking* creates dysfunctional behaviors and negative feelings, rational thinking creates functional behaviors and reasonable or good feelings. It is believed, in this approach, that the *belief*, not the *activating event*, causes the *consequences* (feelings and actions). Contrast with *irrational thinking*.

Rationalization (C-6; HS-3). See *Defense Mechanisms.*

Raw Score (C-9; HS-4). An untreated score before manipulation or processing to make it a *standard score*, as must be done for all *norm-referenced tests*. Raw scores tell us little, if anything, about how a person has done on a *test*.

Reaction Formation (C-6; HS-3). See *Defense Mechanisms.*

Readiness Tests (C-6; HS-3). *Tests* that measure one's readiness for moving ahead in school. Often used to assess readiness to enter kindergarten or first grade. Generally, they are a type of *achievement test.*

Readiness, Not Resistance (SFBT) (C-7; HS-5). In *solution-focused brief therapy* counselors do not refer to client *resistance*, but instead view clients as being at different levels of readiness for change, which include *customers* (ready to work), *complainants* (able to identify problems, but unsure of solutions), and *visitors* (those just shopping around) in descending order of readiness for change.

Real Self (C-6; HS-5). One's genuine, true *self*. Used in *person-centered counseling.* Contrast with *Ideal Self* and *Idealized Self.*

Reality Principle (C-8; HS-5). In *psychoanalysis*, manner in which the *ego* is seen as dealing with the world.

Reality Therapy (C-8; HS-4). Developed by *William Glasser* and based on *choice theory*, reality therapy suggests we are born with five needs: *survival* (*self-preservation*), *love and belonging*, *power* (*inner control*), *freedom* (*independence*), and *fun* (*enjoyment*). These needs are said to drive one's behavior and are sometimes satisfied in dysfunctional ways. The role of the counselor is to understand the pictures in the client's *quality world* that drive the client toward the satisfaction of these needs and to assist the client in developing new pictures and new behaviors that can help the client find more functional ways of acting. See also *Choice Theory* and *Needs.*

Realness (C-9, HS-8). The characteristic, or trait, where helpers are open and genuine with participants and clients about their thoughts, feelings, and intentions. Sometimes called *congruence*, *genuineness*, or *authenticity*.

Re-Author (C-7; HS-4). The concept, in *narrative therapy*, that we can *deconstruct* our current meaning-making system, or way of understanding the world, and construct a new one.

Recapitulation of Early Family Patterns (C-5; HS-4). Term used to describe how early family patterns of behaviors are repeated with other individuals or groups.

Reciprocal Inhibition (C-7; HS-5). In *behavior therapy*, and connected to *relaxation exercises*, a *classical conditioning* concept where clients are taught how to progressively relax by focusing on each major muscle group in the body, tightening and then feeling the muscle relax until the whole body is relaxed. Also known as *progressive muscle relaxation*.

Reciprocity (C-8; HS-3). See *Portability*.

Recognized ASCA Model Program (RAMP) (C-5; HS-1). The recognition that a school has developed and implemented the *ASCA National Model*.

Records and Personal Documents (C-6; HS-4). Assessing behaviors, values, and beliefs of an individual by examining such items as *autobiographies*, *journals and diaries*, *genograms*, or school records. It is a type of *informal assessment*.

Recovery (C-8; HS-8). The process of seeking to maintain *sobriety* or to actively abstain from *substance abuse* or *process addictions*. One is said to be in *recovery*, or in active recovery, if one is working towards a life free from substance abuse or addiction.

Reductionistism (C-7; HS-5). The idea, proposed by some theorists, that the individual can be understood by examining the person at simpler, more fundamental levels. Includes *Freud*, who examined the individual components of the *id*, *ego*, and *superego*, and the *learning theorists*, who believed that development of personality can be reduced to behavioral contingencies, such as *positive reinforcement* and *negative reinforcement*.

Reed, Anna (1871 - 1946) (C-8; HS-3). A prison reformer and *advocate* who established *guidance* services in the Seattle school system in the late 1800s. By 1910, 35 other cities had plans for the establishment of *vocational guidance* in their schools.

Reeducation and Reorientation (C-8; HS-3). Fourth phase of *individual psychology*.

Referral (C-8; HS-8). The process and reason a helper has his or her client see another helper or professional. It involves discussing the referral with the client, obtaining permission for the referral, monitoring the client's progress with the referral, and ensuring *confidentiality*. One aspect of the *case management* process.

Reflecting Deeper Feelings (C-7; HS-5). The process by which a helper reflects the client's underlying feelings of which the client might not be aware. A type of *advanced empathic response*.

Reflection (C-10; HS-10). In most helping approaches, a key technique whereby the helper listens deeply to the client (including observations of body *posture*, *tone of voice*, emotional display, etc.) and repeats, mirrors, or paraphrases back the words and feelings of the client, sometimes extending to deeper emotional levels than the client may be aware of. See also *Reflection of Content* and *Reflection of Feeling.*

Reflection of Content (C-9; HS-9). The process by which a helper repeats back to the client specific cognitive statements (or implied statements) that the client made using the same or slightly different words. Contrast with *Reflection of Feeling.*

Reflection of Feeling (C-9; HS-9). The process by which a helper repeats back to the client specific feelings (or implied feelings) that the client made using either the same feeling word or a feeling word related to the one the client used. Contrast with *Reflection of Content.*

Reflective Teams (C-7; HS-3). In *narrative therapy*, when *therapists* not directly involved with the client, or individuals familiar with the client's situation, observe the client with his or her therapist and later share their thoughts about what was observed and experienced with the client and therapist. This is sometimes a technique used in *supervision* and counselor training.

Reflexivity (Narrative Therapy) (C-7; HS-3). In *narrative therapy*, a process where the client is invited to comment on the helping process so that the helper, or counselor, can learn from the client the impact the helping process is having on the client, and thus make changes if needed.

Reflexivity (Qualitative Research) (C-7; HS-4). In *qualitative research*, the researcher's subjective experience of, and impact on, the research process. Reflexivity is frequently used in studies through tools like *journals and diaries* or examined through processes like *bracketing.*

Refocusing (C-5; HS-2). See *De-Reflection.*

Reframing (C-8; HS-4). The technique used in some therapies that suggests certain problem symptoms can be viewed differently (and usually more positively) than the individual, or family members, has/have typically viewed the symptoms (e.g., a very quiet child could be seen as thoughtful).

Registered Art Therapist (ATR) (C-6; HS-6). A type of *certification* for *art therapists.*

Registered Nurse-Psychiatric Mental Health Nurse (C-6; HS-6). A *psychiatric nurse* who is a registered nurse and works with individuals with psychiatric disorders. See also *Psychiatric-Mental Health Nurse or Psychiatric Nurse-Practitioner.*

Registration (C-7; HS-7). The least rigorous type of *credentialing.* See also *Certification* and *Licensure.*

Regression (C-7; HS-3). See *Defense Mechanisms.*

Regression to the Mean (C- 7; HS-4). A statistical phenomenon that occurs when a measure or data point that is extreme the first time it is measured, has a tendency to be less extreme (or closer to the *mean*) on subsequent measures. A threat to *internal validity*

Rehabilitation Act of 1973 **(C-6; HS-6).** A law that ensured access to *vocational* rehabilitation for adults, based on three conditions: a severe physical or mental *disability*, a disability that interferes with obtaining or maintaining a job, and employment that is feasible.

Rehabilitation Agencies (C-7; HS-6). Setting where *clinical mental health counselors*, *rehabilitation counselors*, and sometimes human service professionals may be employed to assist individuals needing mental, physical, or social rehabilitation and/or *vocational* rehabilitation. Also, an important *referral* agency for clients who need such services. See also *Rehabilitation Counseling* and *Clinical Rehabilitation Counseling*.

Rehabilitation Counseling (C-7; HS-4). A 48-credit counseling specialty area, accredited by the *Council on Rehabilitation Education* (*CORE*), that involves helping clients manage the physical, emotional, and social effects of *disabilities*. The July 2017 merger of CORE and the *Council for the Accreditation of Counseling and Related Educational Programs* (*CACREP*) means that all CORE accredited rehabilitation programs are now CACREP accredited rehabilitation programs, from this point forward. See also *Clinical Rehabilitation Counseling*.

Rehabilitation Counseling Bulletin **(C-6; HS-4).** Journal of the *American Rehabilitation Counseling Association* (*ARCA*).

Rehabilitation Counselor (C-8; HS-7). A person who has obtained a master's degree or higher in *rehabilitation counseling* from a *Council on Rehabilitation Education* or *Council for the Accreditation of Counseling and Related Educational Programs* accredited counseling program. See also *Clinical Rehabilitation Counseling*.

Rehearsal (C-6; HS-5). Used in *Gestalt therapy* and other counseling approaches, when the client tries out new ideas or behaviors in session through *role-play* or other techniques.

Reich, Wilhelm (1897 - 1957) (C-5; HS-2). An Austrian *psychoanalyst* whose ideas had great influence on *Gestalt therapy*, *body-oriented therapies*, and other counseling approaches, and is known for his development of *vegetotherapy*, among other ideas.

Reinforcement (C-9; HS-9). In *Behavior therapy* and related helping approaches, the presentation of a *stimulus* to change a client's behavior. *Positive reinforcement* is the presentation of a stimulus that yields an increase in behavior, whereas *negative reinforcement* is the removal of a stimulus that yields an increase in behavior.

Reinforcement Contingencies (C-8; HS-8). Based on *operant conditioning*, the process in which a *stimulus*, that follows a client's actions or behaviors, increases the likelihood that the behavior will be repeated.

Relapse (C-9; HS-8). The process during *recovery* when the person has a recurrence of his or her addictive behaviors (e.g., gambling, using drugs) or, in some cases, fully returns to the *addiction*. It is a common and expected aspect of recovery that should be addressed within on-going efforts of *sobriety*. Often referred to as "falling off the wagon."

Relapse Prevention (C-9; HS-8). Various treatment methods to assist someone coping with *addictions* from having a *relapse* that include counseling, *psychoeducation*, use of *support groups*, and other methods to prevent and cope with relapse and promote *sobriety*.

Relational and Intersubjective Therapies (C-5; HS-1). A variety of counseling approaches that suggest individuals have internalized images of significant, early relationships in their lives (e.g., with parents) and that remnants of these images impact how people relate to themselves and others and how they make decisions in life.

Relational and Subjectivity Therapy (C-5; HS-1). A newer form of *psychodynamic therapy*, this approach highlights the myth of the independent mind, suggesting that it is through interactions that the *self* is formed. Those who practice this perspective develop a deep, intimate, self-disclosing relationship with their clients and give attention to *transference* and to carefully timed *self-disclosures* of the therapist's *countertransference* as well.

Relational-Cultural Theory (C-8; HS-5). Developed by *Jean Baker Miller* and others, this theory is connected to *feminism* and *multicultural and social justice approaches* to counseling. It encourages individuals to develop mutually-growth-fostering relationships in which all persons are validated and feel a sense of worth, among other principles.

Relationship Building (C-7; HS-7). The idea that it is critical to find some mechanism that allows one to build effective relationships with clients, and that the therapeutic relationship can be formed in many different ways, depending on the personality of the helper. Closely related to what some have called the *working alliance.*

Relativism (C-7; HS-5). The second stage in *William Perry's* theory of adult *cognitive development*, where a person begins to think abstractly, to allow for differing opinions, and to understand there are many ways to view the world. See also *Dualism* and *Commitment to Relativism.*

Relativity Theory of Reinforcement (C-6; HS-4). See *Premack's Principle.*

Relaxation and Systematic Desensitization (C-7; HS-6). A treatment approach where clients learn basic *relaxation exercises* and apply them to the alleviation of specific phobias (e.g., fear of elevators). It is a type of *Exposure Therapy*. See also *Systematic Desensitization* and *Subjective Units of Discomfort Scale.*

Relaxation Exercises (C-7; HS-6). A wide-range of techniques or activities, such as *progressive muscle relaxation* or *meditation*, to teach clients how to de-*stress*, reduce *anxiety*, focus, and decrease fear. Used in many counseling and helping approaches, including *behavior therapy*.

Release of Test Data (C-6; HS-5). An ethical issue that asserts that *test* data should be released to others only if the client has signed a release form. The release of such data is generally granted only to individuals who can adequately interpret the test data, and professionals should assure that those who receive such data do not misuse the information. See also *Confidentiality.*

Reliability (C-9; HS-5). The consistency of *test* scores. Some of the more common types of reliability are *internal consistency*, *split-half reliability*, *parallel forms reliability*, and *test–retest reliability*. One of the four qualities that make up *test worthiness.*

Relics (C-6; HS-3). Any of a variety of objects of historical significance that can provide evidence about a *culture* or past event. Often used in *qualitative research*. See also *Artifacts.*

Religion (C-6; HS-6). An organized or unified set of practices (or dogma) and beliefs that have moral underpinnings and define a group's way of understanding the nature of the world or view of God or other higher powers. Acceptance of differing religious and spiritual perspectives is critical in *cultural competence.* Contrast with *Spirituality.*

Re-Membering (C-7; HS-3). In *narrative therapy*, the process of helping clients reconstruct their identities by accepting and expanding on specific positive memories and de-focusing *problem-saturated stories* and memories.

Reparative Therapy (C-8; HS-8). See *Conversion Therapy* and *Sexual Orientation Change Efforts.*

Repressed Memory (C-8; HS-7). When painful memories are forgotten and placed into the *unconscious* in an effort to block out the distressing feelings. See also *Defense Mechanisms.*

Repression (C-6; HS-5). See *Defense Mechanisms.*

Research Design (C-8; HS-6). The research methodological approach one takes to study and evaluate a particular question, after developing a *hypothesis* or *research question* and doing a *review of the literature.* See also *Quantitative Research* and *Qualitative Research.*

Research Problem (C-9; HS-5). See *Statement of the Problem.*

Research Question (C-8; HS-6). Based on prior research and theory, a question that is developed to examine a particular problem. See also *Hypothesis.*

Researcher Bias (C-9; HS-8). See *Bias.*

Residential Treatment Centers (C-8; HS-8). An *inpatient treatment* setting where individuals can live for a specified amount of time and focus on their particular problem, *addiction*, or *mental disorder* with the goal to return to "normal" living. It is a setting where *clinical mental health counselors* and human service professionals may be employed.

Resistance (C-8; HS-8). The assumption that the client is acting in a defensive manner because he or she is fearful of revealing something painful. Particularly noted in *psychoanalysis*, although it is also a common word used to describe a wide range of client non-compliance.

Respectful (C-6; HS-6). In a *moral model of ethical decision-making* that focuses on *virtue ethics*, one way a helper's character may be important. Using this model, the helper attempts to be courteous, humble, and polite in the ethical decision-making process.

Respectful Curiosity (C-8; HS-7). The manner in which *narrative therapists*, and other *post-modern* helpers, view their clients with an open, curious form of respect and non-judgment.

RESPECTFUL Model (C-7; HS-6). An acronym that speaks to the ingredients needed by the culturally competent mental health professional. Includes understanding religion, economic class, *sexual identity*, psychological development, *ethnicity*, chronological disposition, trauma, family history, unique physical traits, and language. Developed by *D'Andrea, Michael and Daniels.*

Respondent Conditioning (C-8; HS-8). See *Classical Conditioning.*

Response to Intervention (RTI) (C-5; HS-1). A data-driven and multiple-level approach to helping students struggling with academics.

Re-Story (C-7; HS-4). In *narrative therapy*, clients are encouraged to re-author, or re-write, their *problem-saturated stories* focusing instead on healthier *narratives* in sessions.

Restructuring (C-6; HS-3). In *structural family therapy*, the rearranging of boundaries and hierarchies in order to help the family communicate more effectively and feel better about *self* and others.

Results (C-7; HS-5). The section in a research paper or manuscript where the data is described.

Retell (C-7; HS-4). In *narrative therapy*, the repeating of new stories by the client in an effort to embrace and accept them fully.

Reticence (C-5; HS-4). A positive way of describing *resistance*. See also *Resistance*.

Retroflection (C-5; HS-2). In *Gestalt therapy*, similar to *repression* and inhibition, refers to the holding back of an impulse intended toward others and substituting it with another one toward *self*.

Revenge Seeking (C-5; HS-4). From *individual psychology*, one manner in which a child deals with *feelings of inferiority*.

Review of the Literature (C-8; HS-7). One of the first sections of a scholarly paper or manuscript which involves a thorough examination of major research done in a particular area and generally references information found in *peer-reviewed* journal articles and in books.

Rhythmic Stimulation (C-6; HS-2). Used in the practice of *EMDR*, when the *rapid eye movement* is done in a rhythmic way. See *Eye Movement Desensitization Response Therapy (EMDR)*.

RIASEC (C-9; HS-4). The acronym of the *Holland code* which is used in describing one's personality type that can be matched to specific *jobs*. Includes six codes: realistic, investigative, artistic, social, enterprising, and conventional. Successful matching of a person's Holland code with the code of a job has been shown to be related to job satisfaction.

Richer/Thicker Descriptions (C-8; HS-5). In *phenomenological research* and other types of *qualitative research*, and in *narrative therapy*, when the researcher or helper looks for descriptions of the participants, or clients, to become deeper, more complex, and detailed.

Richmond, Mary (1861 - 1928) (C-5; HS-6). An influential American *social worker* who developed one of the first *social work* training programs.

RIDPOC (C-7; HS-4). See *Racial Identity Development for People of Color*.

Rigid Boundaries (C-7; HS-6). As pertains to *general systems theory*, a framework that does not allow information to flow easily into and out of the system, thus impeding the change process. See also *Diffuse Boundaries* and *Semipermeable Boundaries*.

Risk Factors (C-7; HS-7). Influences in a client's life that increase the likelihood of the client committing suicide or homicide. Some of the more common risk factors include prior attempts, a history of abuse, family history, giving things away, *alcohol* and/or *substance abuse*, feelings of hopelessness, severe *depression*, extreme agitation, *anxiety*, loss of purpose, having access to a lethal means, relationship breakup, problems with anger, severe eating or sleeping problems, and related symptoms. See also *Suicidality, Assessment for Lethality* and *Homicidality, Assessment for Lethality*.

Ritalin (C-8, HS-8). A *stimulant* and *controlled substance* often used in the treatment of *attention deficit hyperactivity disorder* (*ADHD*), this medication tends to have a *paradoxical effect* with individuals who are living with ADHD in that it calms them down and helps them to focus.

Rochester Guidance Center (C-5; HS-3). Located in upstate New York, one of the first clinics where *Carl Rogers* worked. Here, he worked from a *psychodynamic* perspective but soon adapted his own approach and became one of the most well-known *existential-humanistic* theorists.

Roe, Anne (1904 - 1991) (C-5; HS-2). An American *clinical psychologist* whose research contributed to *occupational psychology* and *career counseling*. See *Psychodynamic Approaches to Career Counseling*.

Rogers, Carl (1902 - 1987) (C-10; HS-10). An American *psychologist* frequently listed as one of the most influential people in the fields of counseling and *psychology*. He was one of the founders of the *humanistic approach* to counseling and education as well as the person who developed *person-centered counseling*. He was a proponent of the importance of *empathy*, *congruence* (*genuineness*), and *unconditional positive regard* (*acceptance*) in the helping relationship. See also *Common Factors*.

Role-Playing (C-9; HS-9). A way of rehearsing new behaviors through acting out different parts, ideas, or behaviors with clients.

Rollnick, Stephen (1952 -) (C-6; HS-2). A *clinical psychologist* and one of the founders of *motivational interviewing*.

Rorschach, Herman (1884 - 1922) (C-7; HS-4). A Swiss *psychiatrist* and student of *Carl Jung*, he created the *Rorschach Inkblot Test* by splattering ink onto sheets of paper and folding them in half. He believed the interpretation of an individual's reactions to the resulting splatter forms could tell much about the individual's *unconscious* life.

***Rorschach Inkblot Test* (C-7; HS-5).** A *projective test* developed by *Herman Rorschach* in which inkblots splattered onto sheets of paper are shown to a client and the client's *unconscious* interpretations of the resulting splatter forms are used as a basis for *personality assessment* and to gather information about the client's worldview.

Rosenthal Effect (C-7; HS-7). Also known as the *Pygmalion effect*, when having high expectations results in a better performance on tasks. For example, when teachers expect more out of their students, even those perceived as under-performing, the students have a tendency to perform better and achieve more.

Rule-Out (C-5; HS-4). A type of *provisional diagnosis* that is given when the client meets many of the symptoms, but not enough of them to make a *diagnosis* at this time. In this case, diagnosis should thus be considered further.

Rules (C-7; HS-6). In *systems theory*, the ways in which a system is defined as a result of *boundaries*, *information flow*, and *homeostasis*. These can be *overt* or *covert rules*.

Rush, Benjamin (1746 - 1813) (C-6; HS-6). An American founding father, physician, politician, social reformer, and educator. He is known for his progressive and *humanistic* treatment of the mentally ill in the first "modern" mental institutions.

SAD (C-7; HS-5). See *Seasonal Affective Disorder.*

SAMHSA (C-6; HS-6). See *Substance Abuse and Mental Health Services Administration*

SAMIC-3 (C-6; HS-2). An acronym, developed by *Robert Wubbolding*, to address effective client planning in *reality therapy*. It stands for simple, attainable, measurable, immediate, controlled, consistent, and committed.

Sample (C-8; HS-7). A process used in *quantitative research* and *qualitative research* where a subset of a larger population is accessed for research. See also *Random Sample.*

Sampling Distribution (C-6; HS-3). Based on a specific *sample*, the probability that a given statistic accurately represents the larger population.

Sartre, Jean-Paul (1905 - 1980) (C-6; HS-4). An influential French e*xistential* philosopher and author.

***SAT* and/or *PSAT* (C-7; HS-3).** U.S. college admissions exams. The PSAT, or preliminary SAT, is given to high school sophomores as a preparatory exam for the SAT and to determine recipients of the National Merit Scholarship Program. The SAT is one of the most commonly used college entrance exams. Currently, the reading and writing section and the math section of the SAT has *means* that approximate 500 and *standard deviations* that approximate 100 for a national *sample* of high school students, regardless of whether they go to college. Also known as the *Scholastic Aptitude Test* and the Pre-Scholastic Aptitude Test.

Satir, Virginia (1916 - 1988) (C-7; HS-5). An American *social worker* and *family counselor* who was instrumental in popularizing a *systemic perspective* to counseling. She believed that a *primary survival triad* exists that includes parents and the child, with each child's sense of well-being and *self-esteem* the result of this triad. She stressed the importance of communication in families. Individuals with low self-esteem yield one of four unhealthy universal communication patterns: (1) the placater, who appeases people so that others won't get angry at him or her; (2) the blamer, who accuses others in an effort to diffuse hurt; (3) the computer, who acts cool, calm, and collected in an attempt to deal with the world as if nothing could hurt him or her; (4) and the distracter, who goes off on tangents in an effort to treat threats as if they do not exist. Her approach has been called the *human validation process model* and *communication theory*.

Saturation (C-7; HS-3). The point in *qualitative research* where no new themes emerge from the data being examined, and thus, the data collection phase can stop.

Scaffolding (C-6; HS-4). A process of slowly building up low-risk changes, tasks, or alterations of *problem-saturated stories* to higher-risk changes so clients can gradually achieve and or accept the changes. Used in several counseling approaches, including *narrative therapy*.

Scaled Scores (C-7; HS-3). See *Standard Score.*

Scales of Measurement (C-7; HS-3). Ways of defining the types of scores collected from a research study so that the correct statistics can be applied. The four types of measurement scales are *nominal*, *ordinal*, *interval*, and *ratio*.

Scaling (C-7; HS-6). An evaluative *question* where clients are asked to subjectively rate themselves on an imaginary scale between 0 and 10 to assess their experiences, *emotions*, or behaviors. For example, a client is asked to rate his or her *depression* symptoms from 0 to 10, with 0 being no depression to 10 being suicidal. Almost anything can be evaluated via scaling.

Scapegoat (C-8; HS-8). An individual, within a system, who is *unconsciously* given the blame for problems in the system. The scapegoat is often the individual who is showing some type of symptoms, but is not the source of the problem, such as a child who is acting out in a home where *interpersonal violence* exists. The source of the problem, in this case, may be the violence. See also *Triangulate*.

Scapegoating (C-8; HS-8). The process of an individual being singled out by a system (or family) as the source of all problems and taking the blame and/or consequences, even though this person, "the *scapegoat*," is not the source of the problem, such as a child acting out in a home where *interpersonal violence* exists be scapegoated. See also *Triangulate*.

Scatterplot (C-7; HS-4). A graph of two sets of *test* scores used to visually display the relationship or correlation (one score is on the *x*-axis and the second is on the *y*-axis, resulting in one "dot"). If the dots are closer to a straight line, the correlation is moving toward a positive or negative 1. If the dots are spread out or completely random, the correlation is closer to zero. For example, imagine placing *SAT* scores on the *x*-axis and grade point average during the first year of college on the *y*-axis and plotting that graph. How would the graph look, if instead, you were plotting height and weight of all men in the United States?

Schedules of Reinforcement (C-7; HS-5). In *behavior therapy*, when a reinforcer is delivered on a *fixed ratio*, *fixed interval*, *variable ratio*, or *variable interval* amount of time (or schedule of reinforcement). A fixed ratio schedule is when a behavior is reinforced based on number of fixed times (e.g., every two times behavior is exhibited). A fixed interval schedule is when a behavior is reinforced after a fixed amount of time (e.g., every two minutes). A variable ratio schedule is when a behavior is reinforced after an indeterminate number of times, but averages out to a certain number of times (e.g., averages out to every third time a behavior is exhibited). A variable interval schedule is when a behavior is reinforced after an indeterminate amount of time, but averages out to a specific time period (e.g., 1 minute and 6 minutes; and 5 minutes and 2 minutes—averages every 3.5 minutes).

Schema (C-7; HS-4). The blueprint of our cognitive framework or how we come to understand the world. Sometimes used interchangeably with the concept of *core beliefs*.

Schema of Apperception (C-6; HS-2). In *individual psychology*, the cognitive rules, or *schemas*, individuals have developed when *assimilating* their experiences. It is the way people have come to understand and make sense of experiences in their lives.

Schemata (C-7; HS-4). Organized, mental ways of perceiving and responding to complex situations or *stimuli*.

Schizophrenia (C-8; HS-7). A *psychotic disorder* characterized by misrepresentation of and retreat from reality, *delusions*, *hallucinations*, and withdrawn, bizarre, or regressive behavior. It is popularly and erroneously called split personality. See also *Schizophrenia Spectrum and Other Psychotic Disorders*.

Schizophrenia Spectrum and Other Psychotic Disorders (C-8; HS-7). The disorders in the *Diagnostic and Statistical Manual-5* that all have one feature in common: psychotic symptoms (i.e., *psychosis*), that is, *delusions*, *hallucinations*, grossly disorganized or *abnormal* motor behavior, and/or negative symptoms. The disorders include schizotypal personality disorder, delusional disorder, brief *psychotic disorder*, schizophreniform disorder, *schizophrenia*, schizoaffective disorder, substance/medication-induced psychotic disorders, psychotic disorders due to another medical condition, and catatonic disorders.

***Scholastic Aptitude Test* (*SAT*) (C-7; HS-3).** *See SAT and/or PSAT.*

School/Community (C-5; HS-2). One of the three areas for *advocacy* included in the *advocacy competencies* focusing on school and community settings.

School Counseling (C-10; HS-10). Previously called *guidance* counseling, a specialty area in counseling and one of the areas accredited by the *Council for the Accreditation of Counseling and Related Educational Programs*. Professional *school counselors* help students in primary and secondary educational settings with emotional, behavioral, social, *career*, educational, and other areas of student and personal development utilizing counseling skills. See also *ASCA National Model* and *American School Counselors Association* (*ASCA*).

School Counselor (C-10; HS-10). An individual with a master's degree or higher in counseling and a sub-specialty in *school counseling*. See also *Counselor* and *American School Counselors Association* (*ASCA*).

School Counselor Competencies (C-6; HS-2). Created by the *American School Counselors Association* (*ASCA*) to describe *school counselors'* knowledge, abilities, skills, and attitudes in implementing a *Comprehensive School Counseling Program* (*CSCP*) and meeting students' academic, *career*, and personal/social needs. See also *ASCA National Model*.

School Counselor Performance Appraisal (C-5; HS-1). Included in the *ASCA National Model*, a tool that can be used by supervising administrators to evaluate *school counselors' job* performance.

School Psychologist (C-10; HS-10). An individual who holds a master's degree or higher in school psychology and has expertise in conducting *testing* and *assessment* and in assisting in the development and implementation of behavior plans for children in school settings.

School Social Worker (C-10; HS-10). A *social worker* who officially works within a school setting, offering services to students and families.

***School-to-Work Opportunities Act* (C-4; HS-3).** Passed in 1994 by Congress, this act provides incentives to help schools and community colleges develop programs that integrate academic learning with on-the-job experiences.

Scientific Method (C-8; HS-7). An approach to research used in *quantitative research*, the systematic process of observation, measurement, and experiment, to test the *hypotheses*, find possible answers to the *research question* being asked, or both.

Scope of Practice (C-9; HS-7). Designates the areas and activities a *credentialed*, usually *licensed*, professional can work in and where he or she can do this work.

Scree Plot (C-6; HS-2). A graphical representation of *eigenvalues* which is used to visually display the appropriate number of factors to extract when doing a *factor analysis*. See also *Kaiser Criterion* and *Parallel Analysis*.

Sculpting (C-6; HS-3). A technique in counseling where individuals are posed, or placed, in a visual depiction of situations as the client is experiencing them. Most often, this technique is used in *family therapy*, but it has other applications. First developed by *Virginia Satir*. See also *Family Sculpting*.

***SDS* (C-5; HS-3).** See *Self-Directed Search*.

Seasonal Affective Disorder (SAD) (C-7; HS-5). A condition where individuals experience *depression* symptoms due to the on-set of winter or other low sunlight settings.

Secondary Feelings of Inferiority (C-5; HS-2). In *individual psychology*, *feelings of inferiority* that lead to discomfort, strife, or maladaptive behaviors to compensate for the feelings which occur as the result of psychological struggles from poor parenting, child abuse or *neglect*, and social injustice (e.g., *racism*). Contrast with *Primary Feelings of Inferiority*.

Secondary Prevention (C-9; HS-9). A type of *prevention* that focuses on the control of non-severe mental health problems. Contrast with *Primary Prevention* and *Tertiary Prevention*.

Secondary Process (C-8 HS-3). In *psychoanalysis*, related to *ego* functioning, regulation of the *reality principle* which functions between the *preconscious* and *conscious*. See also *Primary Process*.

Secondary Reinforcer (C-7; HS-7). Based on *operant conditioning*, a type of reinforcement contingency that reinforces an action or behavior after it has been associated with a *primary reinforcer* (e.g., biological reinforcer such as food). See also *Token Economy*.

Secondary Sources (C-7; HS-7). Documents or verbal information obtained from sources that did not actually experience the event and used by researchers in collecting data for historical studies. Generally, secondary sources should not be used if *primary sources* are available.

Secondary Traumatic Stress (C-6; HS-6). When a helper, or others, mimics a client's trauma-related symptoms, or takes on undue *stress*, due to their exposure to the individual's trauma. See also *Compassion Fatigue*.

***Section 504 of the Rehabilitation Act* (C-7; HS-5).** This act applies to all U.S. federally funded programs receiving financial assistance and was established to prevent *discrimination* based on *disability*. Relative to schools, it protects those children with disabilities who are not protected by the *Individuals with Disabilities Education Act* by establishing a mechanism to assist such children in their learning.

Secure Base (C-5; HS-5). See Primary Attachment Figure.

Sedatives (C-6; HS-6). Drugs that are generally tranquillizing and can be used to induce sleep. Often, these controlled substances are *anxiolytics* or *benzodiazepines.*

Seguin, Edouard (1812 - 1880) (C-4; HS-3). A French-American physician who worked with individuals with *intellectual disabilities* and developed the form board to increase his patients' motor control and sensory discrimination. This was the forerunner to *intelligence testing* based on one's nonverbal performance, and he suggested that sensory motor ability was related to intelligence.

Selective Serotonin Reuptake Inhibitor (SSRI) (C-7; HS-6). A class of *antidepressant* drugs that became popular in the latter part of the 20th century and used to treat *depression*, *obsessive-compulsive and related disorders*, some types of other *anxiety disorders*, and more.

Self (C-7; HS-6). The core of the person that regulates and oversees all other parts of the person. The term is used in a number of theories, although defined somewhat differently from theory to theory. In *analytical psychology*, an *archetype* that represents the unity of *consciousness* and *unconsciousness* and is symbolic of "the God within us." It is related to *individuation* and aims for integration of the "whole" self as people age.

Self-Actualization (C-7; HS-7). Being fully in touch with oneself, including being *congruent*, *genuine*, *non-dogmatic*, *introspective*, and being whole. It means having harmony with *self*, others, and nature and knowing and understanding one's feelings. Relative to *Maslow's hierarchy of needs*, it is the highest of all needs and something many people strive for but never obtain.

Self-Actualized Person (C-7; HS-7). *Abraham Maslow's* term for a person who has achieved *self-actualization.*

Self-Awareness (C-8; HS-8). The extent to which an individual has personal insights into the *conscious* understanding of his or her thoughts, feelings, motivations, personality traits, and desires.

Self-Concept (C-8; HS-8). A person's understanding and perception of "oneself," or of one's self-identity (e.g., *self*). It includes such aspects as *sexual identity*, personality orientation, perceptions of ability, etc.

Self-Defeating and Irrational Thinking (C-8; HS-5). In *rational emotive behavior therapy*, beliefs and thoughts that individuals have about themselves and the world around them that prevent them from living rational, healthy lives. See also *Core Irrational Beliefs* and *Irrational Beliefs.*

Self-Defeating Emotions (C-7; HS-4). In *rational emotive behavior therapy*, dysfunctional or unreasonable *emotions* resulting from *irrational beliefs.*

Self-Determination (C-7; HS-7). The process of looking within to make choices about oneself as opposed to allowing others to direct one's life.

***Self-Directed Search* (*SDS*) (C-7; HS-3).** A type of *interest inventory* that uses the *Holland Code*, can be taken quickly, and scored and interpreted quickly by a helper. It is particularly useful for individuals who do not have in-depth knowledge of the world of *work* and want to get a sense of where they might fit.

Self-Disclosure (C-7; HS-7). A helping skill by which the helper reveals a part of his or her personal life in an effort to communicate to the client an understanding about the client's experience or to act as a model which the client can emulate. Self-disclosure should only be conducted to advance the client's understanding of *self* and/or to help the client learn new behaviors, and not for the helper's benefit. Sometimes, self-disclosure can be used as an *advanced empathic response*. See also *Content Self-Disclosure* and *Process Self-Disclosure*.

Self-Efficacy Theory (C-7; HS-6). A theory that states the types of choices we make are based on our current beliefs about whether we can perform certain behaviors. It can be applied to *career counseling* and personal counseling and was popularized by *Albert Bandura*, among others.

Self-Esteem (C-9; HS-9). The extent to which a person values and feels good about himself or herself.

Self-Fulfilling Prophecy (C-5; HS-5). A phenomenon that occurs when a person makes a prediction about the outcome or result of an event based on his or her positive or negative expectations. The prediction influences one's behaviors and increases the chances that the expected result will occur. This, in turn, is then seen as proof of the prediction's accuracy. However, in reality, the outcome or result occurred because of the person's behavior and not because of his or her prediction. For example, predicting that one will fail a *test* and therefore choosing not to study brings about the expected result of failing, making it look like the prediction was accurate, when in reality this happened due to the lack of studying.

Self-Help Groups (C-7; HS-7). Also called *support groups*, meetings of individuals, generally run by nonprofessionals, whose purpose is to educate and affirm *group* members. An example is *Alcoholics Anonymous*.

Self-Injurious Behavior (C-8; HS-8). The deliberate, repetitive, impulsive, non-lethal harming of oneself, such as through cutting or burning oneself. Also referred to as self-mutilation, self-harm, and self-abuse.

Self-Management Techniques (C-7; HS-6). Used in *cognitive-behavioral approaches* and *behavior therapy*, techniques where clients learn how to apply any of a number of behavioral counseling techniques on their own and monitor their own progress.

Self-Preservation Need (in Reality Therapy) (C-5; HS-3). See *Survival Need*.

Self-Psychology (C-5; HS-2). An adaptation to traditional *psychoanalysis*, approaches that involve focusing on a client's inner subjective experience. Developed by *Heinz Kohut*.

Self-Regulation (C-5; HS-3). In *Gestalt therapy*, the process of regulating the *self* through a process of *need identification* and *need fulfillment*.

Self-Report (C-8; HS-6). Types of *assessments*, *tests*, *questionnaires*, or surveys that rely on the individual to complete them, as opposed to them being given to the individual by an interviewer or clinician.

Self-Study Report (C-4; HS-4). A written report by a training program, seeking *accreditation* or re-accreditation, which specifies how the program meets each of the sections of an accreditation body's standards (e.g., *Council for the Accreditation of*

Counseling and Related Educational Programs). This report is sent to the main office of the accreditation body at which point it is reviewed and a decision is made as to whether an accreditation review team should be sent to the college or university to review the program.

Self-Support (Gestalt) (C-5; HS-3). The process by which individuals learn to rely on their *self* to locate ways of meeting their needs in life.

Self-Talk (C-7; HS-6). The internal dialogues that individuals have with themselves. This internal dialogue can be either positive or negative and has influence over decision-making, *emotions*, and behaviors. This is highlighted in different forms of *cognitive therapy*.

Seligman, Martin (1942 -) (C-6; HS-5). An American *psychologist* and author who originally became known for his work on *learned helplessness* and, more recently, has written on learned optimism and *positive psychology*.

Selye, Hans (1907 - 1982) (C-6; HS-5). An Austrian-Hungarian scientist who stated that *stress* is a healthy response to a changing situation, but can become unhealthy if not properly dealt with by the individual.

Semantic Differential Scales (C-6; HS-2). A type of *rating scale* in which a person is asked to identify which of two opposing words, in a series of choices, most represents his or her best choice (e.g., love and hate; *introvert* and *extrovert*).

Semipermeable Boundaries (C-7; HS-6). As pertains to *general systems theory*, when certain systems (e.g., family, community) have *boundaries* that allow information to enter the system and be processed, incorporated, or flow out of the system. Generally, semipermeable boundaries are seen as a type of healthy boundary flow as opposed to systems that have *loose boundaries* or *rigid boundaries*.

Semi-Structured Interview (C-7; HS-6). When conducting an *interview* with a client or participant, it is the process of using prescribed items and also allowing leeway for the examiner to explore other relevant information the client mentions, such as an important area in his or her life. See also *Structured Interview* and *Unstructured Interview*.

Senility (C-8; HS-8). See *Dementia* and *Alzheimer's Disease*.

Sensing Mental Function (C-7; HS-6). In *analytical psychology* (*Jungian therapy*), one of the four *mental functions* that makes up one's *psychological type*. Individuals who primarily use this mental function use their senses (e.g., touching, hearing, smelling, taste, seeing) to understand the world. See also *Intuiting Mental Function*, *Feeling Mental Function*, and *Thinking Mental Function*.

Sensitivity Groups (C-7; HS-5). Also called *encounter groups*, training groups, or *T-groups*, *group therapy* settings where the goal is personal awareness and growth via interaction with other *group* members and the agenda and topics are set by the group members as the group evolves.

Sensorimotor Stage (C-10; HS-8). *Jean Piaget's* first stage of cognitive development (from birth to 2 years), when the child responds only to physical and sensory experiences. See also *Concrete-Operational Stage*, *Formal-Operational Stage*, and *Preoperational Stage*.

Sensory Distortion (C-4; HS-2). The misinterpretation of reality related to the senses of touching, hearing, smelling, taste, and seeing. In *Erikson's psychosocial theory of development*, too much trust leads to sensory distortions.

***Sentence Completion Test* (C-8; HS-4).** A *projective test* where stems (beginning of sentences) are offered to clients and the client is asked to complete them (e.g., my mother is….).

Separation of Self (C-6; HS-2). In *object relations theory*, individuals move from an *enmeshed* state (*symbiosis*) with parents to individuality, or separation of *self.*

Service Learning (C-6; HS-7). Encompasses a wide variety of educational programs that place students within the community to engage in project-based or other applied learning experiences, focusing on service (or giving back) to community members.

SES (C-8; HS-8). See *Socioeconomic Status.*

Settlement Houses (C-7; HS-7). Houses where social activists would go to live within a poor community to help those in need. See also *Settlement Movement*, *Jane Addams*, and *Hull House.*

Settlement Movement (C-7; HS-8). Arising in the United States in the 1800s, the attempt by social activists, while living with the poor, to change communities through community action and political activities. See also *Settlement Houses*, *Jane Addams*, and *Hull House.*

Severity (C-8; HS-5). A manner of discriminating, in the *Diagnostic and Statistical Manual of Mental Disorders*, the extent of a *diagnosis* (e.g., mild, moderate, or severe).

Sex (Act of) (C-9; HS-6). The act of engaging in sexual intercourse or related sexual activities.

Sex (Assigned at Birth) (C-10; HS-7). See *Assigned Sex.*

Sex Reassignment Surgery (C-9; HS-9). Medical surgery, combined with administration of hormones, to change a *transgender* individual's *sex* characteristics to those of the opposite sex from which he or she was assigned at birth (i.e., his or her *biological sex*). Also called *gender reassignment surgery*, *gender affirmation surgery*, *and* other related terms.

Sex Therapy (C-9; HS-7). Counseling approaches that specialize in issues of human sexuality, sexual function, or sexual education and any attending physical or psychological issues connected to sexual health.

Sexism (C-10; HS-10). *Discrimination*, denigration, or stigmatizing of others due to their *biological sex* or *gender identity.*

Sexual Dysfunctions (C-8; HS-7). Disorders that are related to problems which disrupt sexual functioning or one's ability to experience sexual pleasure. They occur across *sexes* and include delayed ejaculation, erectile disorder, female orgasmic disorder, and premature (or early) ejaculation disorder, among others.

Sexual Identity (C-9; HS-9). One's personal identification of sexual or romantic attraction, such as *heterosexual*, *lesbian*, *gay*, *bisexual*, *asexual*, or other sexual identities.

Sexual Minorities (C-8; HS-8). An outdated term for *lesbian*, *gay*, *bisexual*, *transgender*, *queer, questioning, intersex,* and *ally, gender non-conforming,* and other non-*heterosexual* or non-*cisgender* individuals. Many people take offense to this term, denying that there is anything minor about them.

Sexual Orientation (C-10; HS-10). The *gender* or *sex* (or multiple sexes or genders) toward which a person consistently has sexual or romantic attraction, feelings, longings, and attachments.

Sexual Orientation Change Efforts (SOCE) (C-10; HS-10). Efforts to change a person from *homosexuality* to *heterosexuality*. This approach is in disrepute and the *professional associations* warn against referring to *therapists* who practice these approaches. See also *Conversion Therapy* and *Reparative Therapy.*

Sexual Preference (C-10; HS-10). The belief that *sexual orientation* is a choice or preference. This term is outdated and false, although some people still adhere and agree with it today.

Sexual Prejudice (C-9; HS-9). Negative attitudes or beliefs generally targeted toward *homosexual, bisexual,* or *heterosexual* individuals (or other *sexual orientations*).

Sexual Relationships with Clients (C-10; HS-10). The strict ban, in ethical codes, on *sex* or dating with clients or the family members or friends of clients. In counseling, the ban on having a sexual relationship with a client, which is highlighted in *the American Counseling Association's* ethical code, is a minimum of 5 years . Other restrictions, in addition to the 5 years, are also placed upon counselors. Having a sexual relationship with a client is among the most damaging of all ethical violations and virtually all helping professions have issued prohibitions against it. See also *Dual and Multiple Relationships.*

Shadow (C-8; HS-4). In *analytical psychology*, an *archetype* that represents the part of *self* which one is afraid to show or acknowledge (e.g., a mean person may be afraid to show his or her soft side, a kind person may be afraid to show his or her anger).

Shamans (C-4; HS-4). Individuals who have special *status* because of their healing and sometimes mystical powers in tribal (i.e., *indigenous people*) or other cultural and religious settings and who frequently engage in induced trance states as forms of communication with spirits, gods, or other higher powers. Shamans may also include tribal priests or curanderos, depending on term usage and *culture.*

Shame-Attacking Exercises (C-6; HS-3). In *rational emotional behavior therapy*, the practicing of behaviors in public which one would normally be afraid to do in an effort to become comfortable with trying out new behaviors.

Shaping (C-7; HS-6). In *operant conditioning*, the ways in which behaviors are emphasized for selective reinforcement until they become fully formed in the manner in which one wants them to be. For example, parents can actively modify or shape certain behaviors in infants through reinforcement. Behaviors can be shaped purposefully or inadvertently. Shaping is also called *successive approximations.*

Shapiro, Francine (1948 -) (C-7; HS-3). An American *psychologist* known for creating *eye movement desensitization response therapy* (EMDR).

Shared Journey (C-7; HS-5). *In existential therapy*, the idea that *therapy* is a joint journey where the helper and client develop a strong *I-thou relationship.*

Shelter (C-7; HS-8). A place within a community which offers temporary safety or refuge to victims of *interpersonal violence (IPV)* or to others needing temporary safety or housing (e.g., homeless individuals) until permanent (and safe) accommodations can be secured. Shelters for victims of IPV are generally hidden from the general public and many shelters are *non-profit organizations* or related helping agencies (e.g., YWCA).

Shock Therapy (C-8; HS-7). See *Electroconvulsive Therapy (ECT).*

Should and Must Statements (C-8; HS-5). Believing if one does not act in a specific manner, it is horrible. They are particularly highlighted in *rational emotive behavior therapy.* See also *Cognitive Distortion.*

Showing Curiosity, Respect, and Acceptance (C-8; HS-5). Ways of being with clients that are humble and assist in the building of the helping relationship and often used by *narrative, solution-focused brief therapy,* and other *post-modern helpers.* See also *Showing Mystery.*

Showing Mystery (SFBT) (C-7; HS-5). In *solution-focused brief therapy,* an attitude towards clients which helpers embrace to explore the counseling relationship from a place of awe and respect, rather than a place of expert knowledge and authority. This helps to de-mystify and strengthen the discourse of the *therapeutic alliance.* See also *Showing Curiosity, Respect, and Acceptance.*

***SIGI-Plus* (C-6; HS-2).** See *System of Interactive Guidance Information- Plus.*

Significance Level (C-9; HS-7). See *Alpha Level.*

Silence and Pause Time (C-7; HS-7). Helping skills in which a helper is intentionally quiet during a session to allow the client opportunity to reflect on what he or she has been saying, while also allowing the helper to process the session and formulate his or her next response. The amount of silence and pause time has been shown to be different based on the clients' *culture.*

Simon, Theodore (1872 - 1961) (C-7; HS-2). A French *psychologist* known for his work with *Alfred Binet* on the creation of the *Binet-Simon scale,* one of the first instruments to assess intelligence.

Simple Correlational Studies (C-7; HS-4). A type of *correlational research* that explores the relationship between two variables. See also *Predictive Correlational Research.*

Single Aptitude Tests (C-7; HS-4). See *Special Aptitude Tests.*

Single-Subject Experimental Design (C-6; HS-3). Where participants serve as their own controls by providing at least three baseline measures of the *dependent variable* before treatment. This is followed by the treatment and then, usually, followed by a second baseline. Sometimes, treatment and baselines can continue for multiple times. See also *ABA Design.*

Situational Assessments (C-7; HS-4). A type of *environmental assessment* used to examine how an individual is likely to respond in a contrived but natural situation. An example of this type of procedure is when a potential doctoral student counsels a *role-playing* client. It is a type of *informal assessment.*

Situational Crisis (C-7; HS-7). An unexpected event, with which a person or family must address.

Situational Stress (C-7; HS-7). Unexpected *stress* that affects an individual and/or a family (e.g., job loss, natural disaster). Contrast with *Developmental Stress.*

Sixteen Personality Factor Questionnaire (16PF) (C-7; HS-3). A common *personality test*, based on *self-report*, used by human service professionals for exploration of healthy personality and *diagnosis* of psychiatric disorders and their treatment.

Skewed Curve (C-8; HS-5). A set of *test* scores that do not fall along the *normal curve* and tend to have more scores at the lower (*positively skewed*) or higher (*negatively skewed*) end of the curve.

Skewness (C-8; HS-4). A descriptive statistical measure of the extent to which a data distribution is similar or dissimilar to a *normal distribution*. Skewness is a measure of the symmetry of the distribution.

Skill Standards (C-2; HS-9). Twelve competencies, and skills associated with them, identified in a national project as being important to the work of the human service professional. The competencies are participant empowerment; communication; *assessment*; community and service networking; facilitation of services; community and living skills and support; education, training, and self-development; *advocacy*; *vocational*, education, and *career* support; crisis *intervention*; organizational participation; and *documentation*.

Skinner, B. F. (1904 - 1990) (C-10; HS-9). A well-known American *behaviorist*, *psychologist*, and scientist who believed that one's personality is developed through *reinforcement contingencies*. He was the developer of *operant conditioning theory*.

Skinner Box (C-8; HS-6). A box-like laboratory device developed by *B.F. Skinner* for use in animal behavioral studies in *operant conditioning*. It is frequently and falsely confused for his *baby-tender*.

Skynner, Robin (1922 - 2000) (C-6; HS-2). A British child *psychiatrist* and *family therapist* known for his work in *psychodynamic family therapy*.

Sleep-Wake Disorders (C-6; HS-3). A category, in the *Diagnostic and Statistical Manual-5*, which includes *mental disorders* where one's sleep patterns are severely impacted, and they often co-occur with other disorders (e.g., *depression*, *anxiety*). Some examples include insomnia disorder, hypersomnolence disorder, restless legs syndrome, narcolepsy, and nightmare disorder. A number of sleep-wake disorders involve variations in breathing, such as sleep-related hypoventilation, obstructive sleep apnea hypopnea, or central sleep apnea.

SNAP (C-6; HS-8). See *Supplemental Nutritional Assistance Program.*

S.O.A.P. Format (C-5; HS-5). A method of writing *progress notes* for clients. The acronym stands for subjective, objective, assessment, and plan.

Sober (C-10; HS-10). The state of not being intoxicated. See also *Intoxication.*

Sobriety (C-10; HS-10). An individual who is in active *recovery* from *substance abuse* or *process addiction(s)* or in the process of *recovery*. See also *Sober* and *Recovery.*

Social Casework (C-5; HS-7). An early focus of *social workers* to help people solve problems that came out of the work of those in *charity organization societies* and the *settlement movement*. See also *Case Management.*

Social Class (C-10; HS-10). The grouping of people according to such things as wealth, ancestry, position, prestige, and the ranking and subsequent perception of an individual's worth to society based on these groupings. See also *Socioeconomic Status.*

Social Cognitive Career Theory (C-6; HS-5). Rooted in *social cognitive theory*, an approach to *career counseling* that focuses on three main ideas of self-efficacy, outcome expectations, and goals. It embraces the belief that people are impacted by both *objective factors* (e.g., real factors such as economic hardship) and *perceived environmental factors* (e.g., factors that are a function of one's perception), such as *discrimination* that does not exist). See also *Social Cognitive Theory.*

Social Cognitive Theory (C-7; HS-5). Developed by *Albert Bandura*, this theory, used in various fields (e.g., *psychology*, education) states that individuals gain much of the knowledge about the world through psychosocial interactions with others, through personal experiences, and through viewing of media (e.g., movies, the Internet, TV). The theory suggests that individuals will tend to repeat or *model* behaviors if they have high *self-efficacy* toward the behavior, whether they get reinforced for the response they get after the behavior is performed, and whether the environment is conducive to the behavior.

Social Concern (C-6; HS-3). In *individual psychology*, the concept of *social interest* or *community feeling*. One has social interest if one is not impeded by *compensatory behaviors* and if one's *style of life* is not based on *faulty logic* and *secondary feelings of inferiority*. See also *Social Interest*, *Gemeinschaftsgefühl*, and *Community Feeling.*

Social Constructivism (or Constructionism) (C-8; HS-5). This philosophy has to do with how values are transmitted through language by the social milieu (e.g., family, *culture*, society) and suggests that the person is constantly changing with the ebb and flow of the influences of significant others, culture, and society. *Social constructivists* generally agree that those in positions of power control the type of language that is used in cultures and society and thus individuals who are not in power (e.g., *non-dominant groups* such as minorities and women) are at a disadvantage and may be oppressed by the power structure that prevails. Part of the basis of the *post-modern approaches* to counseling.

Social Constructivist Consultation (C-7; HS-2). Consultation that applies *social constructivism* counseling principles. See also *Social Constructivism.*

Social Constructivist Model of Ethical Decision-Making (C-7; HS-4). A perspective to *ethical decision-making* that sees knowledge (e.g., knowledge in ethics codes) as intersubjective, changeable, and open to interpretation. This approach suggests that reality is socially constructed, constituted through language, and organized and maintained through *narrative* (stories), and that there are no essential truths. Thus, this type of ethical decision-making sees the value in language and conversation occurring between all involved parties in an ethical dilemma, including the client. See also *Social Constructivism.*

Social Constructivist Perspective (C-8; HS-4). A perspective that suggests realities are socially constructed, constituted through language, and organized and maintained through *narrative* (stories), and that there are no essential truths. An important philosophy embraced by the *post-modern approaches*. See also *Social Constructivism.*

Social Constructivists (or Constructionist) (C-8; HS-5). Professionals who follow *social constructivism* in their work, such as a social constructivist educator.

Social Contract Orientation (C-7; HS-6). Stage 5 of *Kohlberg's post-conventional* morality level which requires formal operational thinking where people believe in the process of democratically devised social contracts (e.g., laws) that can be analyzed, interpreted, and changed, and which ultimately take precedence over individual needs.

Social Exchange Theory (C-4; HS-3). A theory that suggests relationships are created out of an analysis of the cost and benefits awarded to each person as he or she interacts with others and compares the benefits of these transactions. It suggests that the worth of an exchange is based on the rewards received minus the costs involved.

Social Exclusion (C-8; HS-8). See *Time Out.*

Social Interest (C-6; HS-3). Also called *gemeinschaftsgefühl*, and discussed in *individual psychology* (*Adlerian therapy*), the concept that those individuals who are living out their lives fully have a natural desire to give back to society and have deep *empathy* for others.

Social Justice (C-9; HS-9). Work that impacts the broader system (e.g., agencies, cities, country, government) to affect positive change for clients and overcome barriers to change such as *discrimination*, poverty, or other social ills. See also *Multicultural and Social Justice Counseling competencies.*

Social Justice Advocacy (C-9; HS-9). Counseling and helping-related activities that involve *advocacy* for clients by empowering them, by helping them find resources, by advocating for them locally, and by advocating for systemic change nationally and internationally. See also *Social Justice* and *Multicultural and Social Justice Counseling Competencies.*

Social Justice Advocate (C-9; HS-9). One who practices *social justice advocacy.*

Social Justice Orientation (C-9; HS-9). Having a mindset about and living out the behaviors inherent in *social justice advocacy.* See also *Social Justice* and *Multicultural and Social Justice Counseling Competencies.*

Social Justice Work (C-9; HS-9). See *Social Justice Advocacy.*

Social Learning (C-9; HS-8). The process by which one learns from watching the behavior of others and then acting out those behaviors. See also *Modeling.*

Social Norms (C-7; HS-7). Informal, often *unconscious*, understandings, rules, attitudes, or beliefs regarding the expected behaviors of a group or society. Often, simply called *norms.*

Social/Political Advocacy (C-7; HS-7). An aspect of the *advocacy competencies*, this has to do with sensitivity to the concerns of *non-dominant groups* and that professionals have a responsibility to take action (i.e., *advocacy*) if a group is being *discriminated* against.

Social Security (C-7; HS-8). An American government *social welfare* system where workers pay into the system a percentage of their annual earnings (or payroll tax) in exchange for guaranteed payments upon retirement, *disability*, or to survivors, under certain circumstances. The more one earns, and thus contributes a higher tax, the more income one receives, although the upper limit is capped.

Social Self (C-6; HS-4). One of the five factors of the *indivisible self model.* The social self is related to how we are connected to others through our friendships, intimate relationships, and through family. It is composed of the ability to connect with others in supportive, emotional, and sometimes sexual ways and is also the part of us that can share deeply with others and be mutually respectful and appreciative. It is related to friendship and love.

Social Welfare Policy (C-7; HS-8). Programs and policies provided by the government for the social good or *social welfare* (or government assistance) of its citizens. It includes *social security*, *temporary assistance for needy families*, *Medicare*, *Medicaid*, and other programs.

Social Work (C-8; HS-10). The daily activities of helping performed by *social workers* and the broad name forglasser the social science field of helping from a *social justice* and empowerment philosophy. See also *Social Worker.*

Social Worker (C-8; HS-8). A mental health professional who engages in work for the benefit, or *welfare*, of individuals, social groups, or communities rooted in a *social justice* and empowerment philosophy. These individuals can have a bachelor's, master's, or doctoral degree in *social work*. They can be found working in a wide-variety of settings and often work with human service professionals and counselors in agencies. See also *Master's Degree in Social Work (MSW).*

Society for Individual Psychology (C-3; HS-1). First called the Society for Free Psychoanalysis, this was an organization founded by *Alfred Adler* in 1911 as a breakaway from *Freud*'s Viennese Analytic Society over disagreements between Adler and Freud.

Society for Psychoanalytic Endeavors (C-3; HS-1). *Carl Jung* founded this organization, following his break with *Freud's* ideas, to support his own ideas of *psychoanalysis.*

Society for Psychotherapy (C-3; HS-1). An early organization dedicated to *psychotherapy* in Europe. Prior to World War II, the German chapter banned Jews from membership and in response *Jung* assumed the presidency of the *International General Medical Society for Psychotherapy* to permit Jews membership in a larger, umbrella organization.

Socioeconomic Status (SES) (C-10; HS-10). The *status* one (or one's family) has in society based on a combination of social and economic symbols one possesses, which are normally defined by things like amount of income and education one has and the types of work one does as well as the quality of one's housing and other material possessions (e.g., swimming pool, expensive cars, high fashion clothing). Although, individuals are born to the SES of their family, in most societies it is changeable as the person elevates his or her status in terms of wealth, education, and other cultural markers of success. In some *cultures*, SES ascribed at birth is seen as fixed, such as the Indian caste system (although, this is changing somewhat today). It includes statuses such as lower, middle, and upper class. Also called *Social Class.*

Sociometric Instruments (C-6; HS-3). A type of *classification inventory* where the relative position of an individual within a group is mapped, such as when one asks preschool children which students in class they like best and then arrows are drawn between students' names based on preferences voiced.

Socratic Questioning (C-8; HS-6). A type of focused and deliberate *question* asking that attempts to get people to examine ideas in complex and new ways and to uncover new assumptions about life.

Solution-Focused Brief Therapy (SFBT) (C-10; HS-9). A pragmatic, optimistic, *anti-deterministic*, and future-oriented approach to counseling that believes in the ability of the client to change. SFBT rejects the notion that individuals have an inherent tendency toward mental health problems or illnesses and focuses almost exclusively on solutions and on client strengths, not on client deficits or problems. It assumes that focusing on "problems" could be detrimental and that it is important to focus on the future. This approach can be viewed through a series of six stages that include pre-session change, forming a collaborative relationship, describing the problem, establishing preferred outcomes, problem-to-solution focus, reaching preferred outcomes, and ending therapy. See also *Solution-Focused Questions*, *Steve de Shazer*, and *Insoo Kim Berg*.

Solution-Focused Family Therapy (C-8; HS-6). Based on *solution-focused brief therapy*, this brief type of therapy suggests that language and perceptions of problems are related to the development of problems. Therefore, they have clients examine alternative ways of viewing themselves, and they focus solely on helping clients find solutions to their problems based on their existing strengths. Since each member can do this on his or her own, solution-focused family therapists do not need to see the couples or whole family together in *therapy*. See also *Solution-Focused Brief Therapy*.

Solution-Focused Questions (C-8; HS-6). *Questions* aimed at helping clients focus on solutions instead of problems in *solution-focused brief therapy*, a number of different types of *questions* are employed, including: *evaluative questions*, which help clients distinguish behaviors that have led to preferred goals from those that have not; *coping questions*, which help clients focus on past behaviors that have been successful in dealing with problems; *exception-seeking questions*, which help clients examine when they haven't had the problem in their lives to explore how they previously lived a problem-free life; *preferred goals questions*, which are used to assist clients to focus on the future; and *solution-oriented questions*, which are future-oriented and offer clients the opportunity to develop new, positive ways of reaching their preferred goals. See also *Miracle Question*.

Solution-Oriented Questions (C-8; HS-6). Questions which broadly ask clients how their lives would be different if the problem did not exist in the future and which provide opportunities for new, positive ways of reaching preferred goals. One type of *solution-focused question*. See also *Miracle Question*.

Solution Talk (C-8; HS-6). In *solution-focused brief therapy*, a shift in talk from the client's *problem-saturated* discussions to discussions focused on solutions. Respectfully permitting some problem focus, helpers should quickly shift to solution talk in sessions.

Somatic Symptom and Related Disorders (C-7; HS-4). Somatic symptom disorders were previously referred to as "somatoform disorders" and are characterized by the experiencing of a physical symptom without evidence of a physical cause, thus suggesting a psychological cause. Somatic symptom disorders include somatic symptom disorder, illness anxiety disorder (formerly hypochondriasis), conversion (or functional neurological symptom) disorder, psychological factors affecting other medical conditions, and factitious disorder.

Soup Kitchen (C-8; HS-9). A general term for various organizations or programs set up to provide free meals to homeless individuals in the community.

Southern Regional Education Board (SREB) (C-1; HS-9). Relative to human service professionals, this board provided grant money during the 1960s to develop some of the first human services programs. It also assisted in the development of 13 roles and functions necessary for a qualified human service professional. They included *outreach worker*, *broker*, *advocate*, evaluator, *teacher/educator*, *behavior changer*, *mobilizer*, *consultant*, *community planner*, *caregiver*, *data manager*, *administrator*, and *assistant to specialist.*

Sparkling Outcomes (C-8; HS-5). In *narrative therapy*, a reference to *unique outcomes*, or *exceptions to the problem*, relative to the dominant, *problem-saturated narrative* or stories of a client's life. Seeking exceptions to these problems, clients learn to find times they successfully coped with or avoided their problems and then work to increase these positive outcomes in life.

Spearman, Charles Edward (1863 - 1945) (C-6; HS-3). An English *psychologist* who believed in a two-factor approach to intelligence that included a *general (g) factor* that mediates general intelligence and a *specific (s) factor* that mediates certain focused abilities (e.g., math, music, art), both of which he considered important in understanding cognitive ability. See also *Spearman-Brown Formula.*

Spearman-Brown Formula (C-5; HS-2). A mathematical formula that can be used with *split-half* or *odd-even reliability* estimates to increase their accuracy, which is impaired because of the shortening (splitting in half) of the test. See also *Spearman, Charles Edward.*

Special Aptitude Test (C-7; HS-4). A type of *aptitude test* that measures a specific ability (e.g., mechanical ability) and is often used for *job* placement and acceptance into specialty schools.

Specialty Area Domains in Counseling (C-9; HS-3). Specialty areas in counseling that are accredited by *CACREP.* They include *clinical mental health counseling*, *school counseling*, *student affairs and college counseling*, *career counseling*, *addiction counseling*, *clinical rehabilitation counseling*, and *marriage, couples, and family counseling.*

Specialty Credentials in Social Work (C-3; HS-4). Specialty areas in which *social workers* can earn additional *certifications.* They include clinical work, *gerontology*, *hospice* and palliative work, youth and family, military, leadership, health care, *addictions*, *case management*, and education.

Specific (*s*) Factors of Intelligence (C-7; HS-3). The belief that some aspects of intelligence are mediated by very specialized aspects of human functioning (e.g., math, music, art) and largely not influenced by the *general (g) factor.* Popularized by *Charles Edward Spearman.*

Specific State Certifications (C-8; HS-8). U.S. states often offer a variety of specialty *certifications* in which the state decides the level of education and experience needed to obtain said *certification* (e.g., state-certified *substance abuse counselors*).

Specified and Unspecified Disorders (C-6; HS-4). A *diagnosis* that can be used when a provider believes an individual's impairment of functioning or distress is clinically significant; however, it does not meet the specific diagnostic criteria in that category. The "other specified" code should be used when the *clinician* wants to communicate specifically why the criteria does not fit. The "unspecified disorder" code should be used when the clinician does not wish, or is unable to, communicate specifics. For example, if someone appeared to have significant *panic attacks* but only had three of the four required criteria, the diagnosis could be "Other Specified Panic Disorder—due to insufficient symptoms." Otherwise, the clinician would report "Unspecified Panic Disorder."

Specifiers (C-7; HS-4). A way of distinguishing a *diagnosis* in the *Diagnostic and Statistical Manual-5* based on certain circumstances. These are not mutually exclusive, so a person can have a diagnosis with more than one specifier. For instance, for a recent bipolar episode, a client might have any of the following specifiers: includes mixed features, anxious distress, melancholic features, atypical features, psychotic features, and catatonic features.

Speed Test (C-5; HS-1). *Tests* developed to see how quickly a test taker can complete particular tasks, or test items, within a specified period of time. Particularly important in memory tests or tests of motor coordination, etc.

Spielrein, Sabina (1885 - 1942) (C-5; HS-2). A Russian *psychiatrist*, and one of the first female *psychoanalysts*, who was famously known as a patient and student of *Jung*, with whom she had a sexual relationship.

Spirituality (C-8; HS-7). Seen as residing within a person, and not defined by a group (e.g., a *religion*), spirituality defines the person's understanding of *self*, self in relationship to others, and self in relationship to things larger or beyond the self (e.g., God, nature, the universe). It is related to one's existential views on life concerning meaning, purpose, and connection to self and others. Spirituality does not require a belief in a god or a higher power. See also *Religion.*

Spitting in the Client's Soup (C-8; HS-5). In *individual psychology* (*Adlerian therapy*), pointing out a behavior to a client that she or he is exhibiting and why it is dysfunctional, thus bringing it to *consciousness* and decreasing the likelihood it will occur again.

Split (Gestalt) (C-6; HS-2). In *Gestalt therapy*, when one polarity is more dominant than the other. This is called a split in one's personality. See also *Polarities.*

Split-Half Reliability (C-8; HS-3). See *Odd-Even Reliability.*

Splitting (C-7; HS-4). The tendency for people to separate others into concrete, and oftentimes opposing, categories of "good or bad," especially done if one had received poor parenting early in life.

Spontaneous Recovery (C-7; HS-6). After treatment for behavior change, the recurrence of former, unwanted behaviors.

Sport Psychology (C-5; HS-4). The study of how participation in sport and exercise effects psychological and physical aspects of individuals, as well as, how psychological factors affect sport performance.

SREB (C-1; HS-9). See *Southern Regional Education Board.*

Stages of Change (C-6; HS-2). See *Transtheoretical Model of Behavior Change.*

Stages of Group Development (C-7; HS-6). The typical stages that a *group* progresses through in the group process, including the *pregroup stage*, *initial stage*, *transition stage*, *work stage*, and *closure stage*. These somewhat parallel the classic stages of *Tuckman*, i.e., *forming*, *storming*, *norming*, *performing*, and *adjourning*.

Stages of Racism (C-7; HS-4). A developmental theory by *D'Andrea and Daniels* that suggests helpers will pass through stages of *racism* that include *affect/impulsive*, *dualistic rational*, *liberal*, and *principled activist stages*.

Stages of the Helping Relationship (C-7; HS-3). A series of predictable stages that clients pass through in the helping relationship. The stages include *rapport and trust building*, *problem identification*, *deepening understanding and goal-setting*, *work*, *closure*, and *post-interview*.

Standard Deviation (SD) (C-8; HS-3). A measure of *variability* that describes how scores vary around the *mean*. In all *normal curve equivalents*, the percentage of scores between the mean and +1SD, and the mean and -1SD is the same (about 34%); as is the percentage of scores between +1SD and +2SD, and -1SD and -2SD (about 14%); as is the percentage of scores between +2SD and +3SD and -2SD and -3SD (about 2%), and so forth. Hence, by knowing the standard deviation and the mean, much can be understood about a particular set of test scores. The standard deviation is the square root of the variance.

Standard Error of Estimate (C-7; HS-1). The band of scores (range of scores) a person is predicted to obtain based on his or her score from a previous known *test*. The equation allows use of the score on instrument "X "to predict a range of scores on instrument "Y." For instance, to a certain degree, scores on the *SAT* exam should predict first year college grade point average.

Standard Error of Measurement (C-7; HS-2). The range of scores where a person's score is expected to fall if he or she took the instrument over and over again—in other words, where a "true" score might lie. It is calculated by taking the square root of 1 minus the *reliability* and multiplying that number by the *standard deviation* of the desired score. For example, if a person took an intelligence *test* and scored a 103, his or her "true" score might actually be somewhere between a 99 and a 107.

Standard Error of the Mean (C-6; HS-1). A measure of the *standard deviation*, or the *variability*, between multiple sample *means* from a larger population.

Standard of Caring (C-8; HS-6). The concept, by *Carol Gilligan*, that women's *moral development* is different than men's and that women have a greater sense of caring about others and awareness of the impact of their decisions on others, when making moral decisions.

Standard Scores (C-8; HS-2). Scores derived by converting an individual's raw score to a new score that has a new *mean* and new *standard deviation*. Standard scores are generally used to make test results easier for the examinee to interpret. Includes such scores as *percentiles*, *z-scores*, *T-score*, *deviation IQs*, *stanines*, *sten scores*, *normal curve equivalents* (*NCE*), college or graduate school entrance exam scores (e.g., *SAT*, *GRE*, and *ACT*), *publisher-type scores*, or by using *developmental norms* such as *age comparisons* and *grade equivalent scoring*. Also called *converted scores*, *derived scores*, and *scaled scores*.

Standardized Assessment Procedures (C-9; HS-6). An *assessment* instrument that is administered in the same way every time it is given. The assessment results may be compared with those of a *norm group*. An example is the *Scholastic Aptitude Test* (*SAT*). It is also called *standardized testing*.

Standardized Testing (C-9; HS-6). See *Standardized Assessment Procedures*.

Standards for Counseling Supervisors (C-6; HS-2). Developed by the *Association of Counselor Educators and Supervisors* (*ACES*) and adopted by *ACA*, these sets of standards have been developed for the best practices of counseling *supervision*.

Standards for Educational and Psychological Testing (C-4; HS-1). Developed by the American Educational Research Association, the *American Psychological Association*, and the National Council on Measurement in Education, these are premier standards for guidance on *assessment* and *testing*, published and updated since 1966 to its current 2014 edition.

Standards for Multicultural Assessment (C-5; HS-1). Developed by the *Association for Assessment and Research in Counseling* (*AARC*), it provides 68 multicultural *assessment* standards in the areas of *advocacy*, selection of assessment procedures, and administration and scoring, interpretation and application of results, and training in the use of assessments.

Standards for the Preparation of Counselors and Other Personnel Service Specialists (C-3; HS-1). Requirements that set the minimal standards for training programs in counselor education and related fields. Unofficially used as early as 1973, it was not until 1979 that the *American Personnel and Guidance Association* (*APGA*), now the *American Counseling Association* (*ACA*), officially adopted them, and in 1981 APGA created the *Council for the Accreditation of Counseling and Related Educational Programs*, which sets and approves such standards.

Standards in Assessment (C-7; HS-2). Any of a number of standards developed to help guide practitioners on the proper use of *tests* and inform test users of their rights.

Stanford Achievement Test (C-6; HS-2). A type of *survey battery achievement test*. See also *Thorndike, Edward*.

Stanford-Binet Intelligence Scale **(C-8; HS-3).** An *intelligence test*, which has its origins in the first *intelligence test*, the *Binet-Simon Scale*. See also *Binet, Alfred*.

Stanine (C-8; HS-3). Derived from the term "standard nines," a *standard score* frequently used in schools. Often used with *achievement tests*, stanines have a *mean* of 5 and a *standard deviation* of 2, and range from 1 to 9.

State-Approved School Counseling Program (C-8; HS-4). U.S. programs, approved by *State Boards of Education*, for the training of *school counselors*.

State Boards of Education (C-8; HS-4). U.S. professional bodies in education, in each state, that set the standards for the *credentialing* of teachers, *school counselors*, and other school personnel.

Statement of the Problem (C-9; HS-5). In research, the problem or question that is being explored and it may also be called the *research problem* or *research question*. Based on one's *literature review*.

Static-Group Comparison (C-6; HS-2). A type of *pre-experimental design* in which one group that is given a treatment is compared to another group that has not had the treatment and differences are observed. This is considered a weak design as no control group is employed and the non-treatment group could have many initial differences from the treatment group.

Statistical Power (C-8; HS-4). Research and statistical procedures that are conducted a priori, or before *quantitative research* is conducted, to determine that researchers have parameters in place that will allow them to find *statistical significance* if statistical significance is present. Common considerations for statistical power include, *sample* size, confidence interval, *alpha level*, and *effect size*.

Statistical Significance (C-9; HS-6). The concept that researchers use to show that non-random differences have occurred between the *control group* and the *experimental group*. Statistical significance is determined by an *alpha level*.

Statistics (C-5; HS-4). The process of gathering, analyzing, presenting, and applying statistical (i.e., numerical) data to solve problems, improve conditions, and gain insight.

Status (C-6; HS-6). The social standing or rank of an individual or groups of individuals (e.g., doctors, artists, professionals, or other categories) within a *culture*, society, organization, or group. Often based on one's *privilege* or marginalization in society, which in turn is often based on *socioeconomic status*. See also *Socioeconomic Status*.

Steinem, Gloria (1934 -) (C-4; HS-4). An influential American *feminist* author, activist, and journalist whose criticism of *Freud's* concept of *penis envy* in her essay "What if Freud were Phyllis?" helped to challenge his ideas. Also known for writing a book on *self-esteem*.

Sten Scores (C-8; HS-3). Derived from the name "standard 10," a *standard score* that is commonly used on personality inventories and questionnaires. Stens have a *mean* of 5.5 and a *standard deviation* of 2.

Stereotypes (C-10; HS-10). Rigidly held beliefs about a group of people based on the false assumption that most or all members of the group have certain behaviors or beliefs that tend to be unique to that group. Generally viewed as a negative concept, some stereotypes are positive yet still can lead to *discrimination*, *microaggressions*, or other mistreatment of groups. For example, all Asians are good at math is an example of a positive stereotype that is not accurate and can lead to assumption-based behaviors that can cause mistreatment of individuals.

Stereotyping (C-10; HS-10). When one actively *stereotypes*. See also *Discrimination*.

Stimulants (C-9; HS-9). A class of drugs that are *controlled substances* used to increase psychological or physical functioning and generally result in increased alertness and locomotion. Examples of legal stimulants are *Adderall*, *amphetamines*, and *Ritalin*. Examples of illegal stimulants are *cocaine* and *crystal meth*.

Stimulus Control (C-6; HS-5). Where a *stimulus* is altered or removed and a new, healthier behavior is reinforced (e.g., a binge eater places a lock on the refrigerator to prevent eating).

Stimulus/Stimuli (C-7; HS-6). Something(s) that causes a physiological, psychological, or behavioral response.

Storming (C-8; HS-6). *Tuckman's* second *stage of group development*, which involves *group* members challenging and clashing, or storming, with each other in sessions. If navigated well, successful passage through this stage leads to greater group cohesion and a more effective *working alliance*, but if navigated poorly, group members remain at odds with each other and may actively work against each other.

Strategic Family Therapy (C-7; HS-4). An approach to *family counseling*, developed by *Jay Haley* and *Cloe Madanes*, that focuses on strategies for change that will help couples and families feel better. Focused on doing whatever is necessary to help the clients, strategies are not necessarily obviously related to the problem, although they do alleviate the problem. See also *Strategic Therapy*.

Strategic Therapy (C-7; HS-4). A type of therapy developed by *Jay Haley* that focuses on strategies for change and is less concerned with the past and more focused on doing whatever is necessary to help the individual feel better. Strategies are not necessarily obviously related to the problem, although they do alleviate the problem

Strengths-Based Model (C-7; HS-6). An approach to helping that puts primary emphasis on *client strengths* and seeks to increase positive exceptions (i.e., *exceptions to the problem*) that the client has had in his or her life. This model asks what clients are doing well and how can they increase what they are doing well. It is a type of *positive counseling*. Contrast with *Deficit Model*.

Stress (C-8; HS-8). The normal physiological and psychological responses to changing situations. In moderation, it is a healthy response; however, too much stress can cause psychological and physical problems, thus stress can be seen as negative or positive.

Stress Inoculation Therapy (C-5; HS-3). An approach to counseling where clients are taught how to handle difficult or stressful situations successfully or with a reduced level of negative responses prior to the situations occurring. See also *Stress*.

Striving for Perfection (C-7; HS-4). A term used in *individual psychology* that stresses how a person's *subjective final goal* drives a person towards certain behaviors which the individual believes he or she has to accomplish perfectly.

Striving for Superiority (C-7; HS-4). A term used in *individual psychology*, when individuals respond to *feelings of inferiority* by compensating for those feelings and developing maladaptive ways of behaving in the world. *Adler* later changed this term to *striving for perfection*, then to *fictional final goal*, and finally to *subjective final goal*.

Striving for Wholeness (C-7; HS-4). See *Striving for Perfection*.

Strong, Edward K., Jr. (1884 - 1963) (C-5; HS-2). An American *psychology* professor who led a team of researchers in the 1920s to develop the *Strong Vocational Interest Blank*. The test is now known as the *Strong Interest Inventory* and is still one of the most popular interest inventories ever created.

Strong Interest Inventory **(C-8; HS-4).** A popular and empirically-tested *interest inventory* that examines one's likes and dislikes as well as one's personality orientation as related to the world of *work*. Amongst other things, the test yields *Holland Code* results and is used in *career counseling*. See also *Strong, Edward K., Jr.*

Strong Vocational Interest Blank **(C-6; HS-2).** One of the first major *interest inventories*, developed in 1927. This *test*, in its revised form, is now called the *Strong Interest Inventory* and is still one of the most widely used instruments of its kind. It revolutionized *vocational counseling*. See also *Strong, Edward K., Jr.*

Structural Equation Modeling (C-4; HS-1). A series of mathematical and statistical analyses used in *confirmatory factor analysis* and *path analysis*.

Structural Family Therapy (C-7; HS-4). An approach to *family counseling*, developed by *Salvador Minuchin*, that focuses on the structure, hierarchy, and problems of function of the family.

Structuralism (C-6; HS-3). In counseling and *psychology*, this philosophical concept suggests the existence of inherent structures that influence individual personality development. Contrast with *Post-Structuralism*.

Structured Interview (C-7; HS-6). An *interview* that focuses on specific *questions*/items in order to cover a broad base of information in a specific, predetermined method. Contrast with *Unstructured Interview* and *Semi-Structured Interview*.

Structures of Neurosis (C-5; HS-2). In *Gestalt therapy*, a model that suggests that individuals have layers of *self* that go from the *cliché layer* ("small talk"), to the role-playing or *phony layer* ("presenting a front"), to the *impasse layer* (realizing one's roles one is playing), to the *implosive layer* (being frozen or in limbo after realizing one's roles), and lastly to the *explosive/authentic layer* (realness, orgasm, sadness, anger, joy, experiencing).

Structures of Personality (C-9; HS-5). *Freud's* concepts of *id*, *ego*, and *superego*. See also *Psychoanalysis*.

Struggles of Living (C-5; HS-4). One area that is focused upon in *existential therapy*, referring to the everyday struggles individuals face getting through life.

Student Affairs Administrators in Higher Education (C-3; HS-1). Formerly, the *National Association of Student Personnel Administrators*, but keeping the *NASPA* acronym, the primary *professional association* for *student affairs* professionals.

Student Affairs and College Counseling (C-4; HS-2). A specialty area accredited by the *Council for the Accreditation of Counseling and Related Educational Programs* that focuses on college *student affairs and college counseling*. This area examines the development and mental health of students within the college setting. See also *Student Affairs Specialists, Roles and Functions* and *College Counseling*.

Student Affairs and College Counselors (C-6; HS-3). A professional who has obtained his or her master's degree or higher in *student affairs and college counseling*. See also *Student Affairs Specialists, Roles and Functions* and *College Counseling*.

Student Affairs Specialists, Roles and Functions (C-4; HS-1). The areas of specialty for *student affairs* professionals include the following: (1) advising and helping; *assessment*, *evaluation*, and research; (2) equity, *diversity*, and inclusion; (3) ethical professional practice; (4) history, philosophy, and values; (5) human and organizational resources; (6) law policy and governance; (7) leadership; (8) personal foundations; (9) and student learning and development.

Student Affairs Specialists, Where You Find Them (C-4; HS-1). The settings you will find student affairs professionals on a college campus include: *admissions office*, *academic support services*, *career development services*, *commuter services*, *counseling centers*, *distance learning site directors*, *financial aid office*, *health services*, *human resources*, *intercultural student services*, *office of assessment and evaluation*, *office of educational accessibility*, *office of the registrar*, *residence life and housing services*, *student activities services*, and *women's/men's centers*.

Student Personnel Point of View (C-4; HS-1). The resurgence of *student affairs* practice that started during the 1940s.

Student Services (C-5; HS-3). This college campus *student affairs* office focuses on areas of student advising, recruitment, academic success, *career development*, and related areas. It is one area you will find professionals with a master's degree or higher in *student affairs and college counseling* working.

Style of Life (C-7; HS-4). All behaviors, feelings, values, and so forth that define the person and show how he or she is moving forward in life. This term is used in *individual psychology*.

Subceive (Subception) (C-5; HS-4). *Carl Rogers's* term for the professional's ability to perceive feelings and deeper meanings beyond what the individual expresses.

Subcultures (C-8; HS-8). Groups of people whose behaviors and values may differ from those of the larger *culture*, such as punk rockers, anarchists, or hippies, among others.

Subject/Object Theory (C-6; HS-2). The basis for *Robert Kegan's constructivist model* of development. The conjecture that individuals pass through specific developmental stages in constructing their unique ways of making meaning of the world. See also *Incorporative Stage*, *Imperial Stage*, *Impulsive Stage*, *Interpersonal Stage*, *Institutional Stage*, and *Interindividual Stage*.

Subjective Final Goal (C-7; HS-3). The goal that drives the person and may be the product of *feelings of inferiority* and compensatory behaviors that result from such feelings. Based on *individual psychology* ideas. See also *Striving for Superiority*, *Striving for Perfection*, and *Fictional Final Goal*.

Subjective Units of Distress Scale (SUDS) (C-9; HS-7). Also known as Subjective Units of Discomfort Scale or Subjective Units of Disturbance Scale, in *behavior therapy*, this is a scale from 0 to 100 asking clients to indicate their level of total relaxation (at 0) to highest levels of *anxiety* (at 100) when being introduced to anxiety-producing experiences. It is used to determine whether the helper, engaged in *exposure therapy* *techniques*, should advance the client to the next level.

Subjectivity (C-8: HS-6). In *qualitative research*, methods of ensuring the researcher's voice and presence (i.e., their humanness) in the study, such as through use of *diaries/journals*. It is part of *trustworthiness* strategies.

Sublimation (C-7; HS-5). See *Defense Mechanisms.*

Substance Abuse (C-10; HS-10). The harmful or *addictive* use of *alcohol*, drugs, medications, and other *controlled substances.* See also *Substance-Related and Addictive Disorders* and *Substance Use Disorder.* Contrast with *Substance Dependence.*

Substance Abuse and Mental Health Services Administration (SAMHSA) (C-6; HS-6). A branch of the U.S. Department of Health and Human Services, this government agency is focused on the research and treatment of *substance abuse* and mental illness.

Substance Abuse Disorder (C-9; HS-8). See *Substance Abuse*, *Substance-Related and Addictive Disorders* and *Substance Use Disorder.*

Substance Abuse Settings (C-9; HS-9). Settings where *clinical mental health counselors* and *substance abuse counselors* and other helpers may be employed, in which the primary focus of treatment is on *substance abuse recovery* or prevention. Such settings include *outpatient facilities*, *inpatient facilities*, *rehabilitation agencies* (aka rehabs), and related treatment settings.

***Substance Abuse Subtle Screening Inventory (SASSI)* (C-7; HS-6).** An empirically-tested *assessment* screening tool used to determine presence and severity of an individual's *alcohol use disorder* and/or *substance abuse disorder.* See also *Substance Abuse.*

Substance Dependence (C-8; HS-7). Involves the physical and psychological reliance (or dependence) of the body on *alcohol*, drugs, medications, and other *controlled substances*, in which *withdrawal* and other behavioral symptoms (e.g. *delirium tremens*) are experienced when usage of the substances is stopped. In severe cases, substance dependence can result in significant impairment up to death due to changes to the body's neurology and organ damage (e.g., cirrhosis of the liver). Contrast with *Substance Abuse.*

Substance-Related and Addictive Disorders (C-8; HS-7). A classification of *mental disorders* that includes disruptions in functioning as the result of a craving or strong urge due to *substance abuse* and *process addictions.* Often caused by prescribed and illicit drugs or the exposure to toxins, with these disorders the brain's reward system pathways are activated when the substance is taken (or in the case of gambling disorder, when the behavior is being performed). Some common substances include *alcohol*, caffeine, nicotine, *cannabis*, *opioids*, *inhalants*, *amphetamine*, *phencyclidine (PCP)*, *sedatives*, *hypnotics* or *anxiolytics*. *Substance use disorders* are further designated with the following terms: *intoxication*, *withdrawal*, induced, or unspecified.

Substance Use Disorder (C-8; HS-5). The current *Diagnostic and Statistical Manual-5* diagnostic term encompassing *substance-related and addictive disorders.* See also *Substance Abuse* and *Substance Dependence.*

Subsystems (C-8; HS-6). In *family counseling*, usually groups of individuals that make up part of a system (e.g., parental subsystem, child subsystem).

Subtractive (C-5; HS-4). On the *Carkhuff scale* of empathic responses, any score below a 3.0 made by human service professionals is considered non-empathic, or subtractive to the counseling session. See also *Carkhuff scale* and *Empathy*.

Success Identity (C-6; HS-5). In *reality therapy*, the process by which individuals develop a sense of responsibility and self-worth for their achievement as opposed to having a failure identity.

Successive Approximations (C-7; HS-6). See *Shaping*.

SUDS (C-9; HS-7). See *Subjective Units of Distress Scale*.

Sue and Torino's Definition of Culturally Competent Helping (C-4; HS-2). The perspective that *culturally competent helping* uses both universal and *culture*-specific helping skills, highlights individual, group, and universal dimensions of clients, and understands individualism and collectivism when assessing clients in the development of treatment goals.

Sue, Derald Wing (C-6; HS-4). An influential American professor of counseling *psychology* and one of the seminal authors of publications in the area of *cross-cultural counseling* and *diversity* issues.

Suggesting Alternatives (C-8; HS-8). A means of gently confronting a client by offering new ways, or alternatives, of viewing the world. See also *Confrontation*.

Suicidal Ideation (C-10; HS-10). Refers to thoughts of suicide by an individual and is seen as a key step towards completing the act of suicide, although some people experience suicidal thoughts (or ideation) without attempting or completing suicide. See also *Suicidality, Assessment for Lethality*.

Suicidality, Assessment for Lethality (C-9; HS-9). The process for evaluating if clients are posing an imminent danger to themselves, including but not limited to the degree to which the client has developed a plan, has the means to carry out the plan, is prepared to implement the plan, has rehearsed the plan, and has acted on the plan. See also *Suicidal Ideation*, *Risk Factors* and *Protective Factors*.

Sullivan, Harry Stack (1892 - 1949) (C-5; HS-2). An influential American *psychiatrist* and *psychoanalyst* who was a key *object relations therapy* theorist.

Summative Evaluation (C-8; HS-7). In *program evaluation*, the assessment of a program after the program is completed. Contrast with *Formative Evaluation*.

Super, Donald (1910 - 1994) (C-8; HS-3). An American *vocational* counselor and educator who formulated an early developmental model of *career development* that is still in use today. It includes the following stages: *growth*, *exploration*, *establishment*, *maintenance*, *deceleration/disengagement*. See also *Super's Developmental Self-Concept Theory*.

Superego (C-9; HS-8). According to *Freud's* theory, the partly *conscious* portion of the *psyche* that internalizes parental and societal rules and serves as the rewarder or punisher by dictating moral attitudes, *conscience*, and a sense of guilt. See also *Ego* and *Id*.

Super's Developmental Self-Concept Theory (C-8; HS-3). A five-stage *career development* theory that is founded on the belief that we make career choices based on our view of *self* through the lifespan. It includes the following stages: *growth* (birth through 14), *exploration* (14-25), *establishment* (25-45), *maintenance* (45-60), and *deceleration/disengagement* (over 60). See also *Super, Donald.*

Supervisee (C-10; HS-10). The individual whose work is being overseen by another more experienced person in a supervisory relationship. Contrast with *Supervisor.* See also *Supervision, Approved Clinical Supervisor* and *Clinical Supervision.*

Supervision (C-10; HS-10). The process of having one's work overseen by a *supervisor* who assesses and evaluates the *supervisee's* performance to: (1) help the *supervisee* become a better human service professional or counselor and, (2) facilitate client growth. See also *Approved Clinical Supervisor* and *Clinical Supervision.*

Supervisor (C-10; HS-10). Individuals who have gained expertise to oversee the clinical work of *mental health professionals* through the application of appropriate *supervision* models. Contrast with *Supervisee.* See also *Approved Clinical Supervisor* and *Clinical Supervision.*

Supplemental Nutritional Assistance Program (SNAP) (C-6; HS-8). Formally called Food Stamps, a form of U.S. federal *public assistance* given to individuals from low-income households to support the purchase of food.

Supplemental Security Income (SSI) (C-7; HS-7). A U.S. government *social welfare* program offering assistance to individuals who are aged, blind, or disabled and who have low income.

Support (C-8; HS-8). A general term that acknowledges that one role of the helper is to let clients feel as if there is someone in their lives who they can rely on for aid, assistance, and to promote their general well-being.

Support Groups (C-7; HS-7). Also called a *self-help group*, meetings of individuals, generally run by non-professionals, whose purpose is to educate and affirm *group* members. An example is *Alcoholics Anonymous.*

Suppression (C-7; HS-5). See *Defense Mechanisms.*

Suprasystems (C-6; HS-6). Systems that are larger than the one being examined. With families, the community is an example of a *suprasystem.*

Survey Battery Tests (C-7; HS-3). Multiple choice and true/false *tests* usually given in school settings, which measure broad content areas. Often used to assess progress in school, they are types of *achievement tests.*

Survey Research (C-8; HS-5). A research methodology in which specific information is gathered from a target population using some form of a questionnaire (or survey). It can be done in person, via email, on the Internet, etc.

Survival Need (in Reality Therapy) (C-5; HS-3). The most basic, and typically first need developed by people as identified by *reality therapy.* It has to do with acquiring the basic needs of shelter, food, safety, and continuing one's existence. *William Glasser* suggested that all other needs eventually grow out of this need. It is one of five needs that make up one's *need-strength profile* and is also called *self-preservation.*

Symbiosis (C-6; HS-4). In *object relations theory*, individuals move from an *enmeshed* state (symbiosis) with parents to individuality, or separation of *self.*

Symbols (C-7; HS-4). In *analytical psychology* (*Jungian therapy*), symbols represent deeper meaning about *self* and are often related to universal concepts (e.g., a person's obsession about shark teeth may represent that person's need to be powerful).

Symptom Checklist (C-6; HS-6). A variety of screening tools, often in questionnaire form, that lists various symptoms of medical or mental health illnesses. It is used to assist in *diagnosis* and *treatment planning* for clients and may be used as part of an *intake interview*.

Synanon (C-5; HS-4). A type of *substance abuse recovery* therapy where extreme confrontation was used. Its efficacy was questionable and it is no longer used.

Synchronicity (C-7; HS-4). In *analytical psychology*, the idea *Jung* developed to describe the process by which a psychic event happens seemingly at the same time as a physical event. These two events develop a meaningful relationship to each other, although there is no causal link between the two. For example, synchronicity occurs if one gets news of a significant other's death at the same time the black dress one recently ordered is delivered to one's home. These two events appear to be linked, but the one did not cause the other.

Synchronous (C-7; HS-7). Something that occurs moment-to-moment or "live," particularly in reference to communication and technology as it relates to distance learning and related usage. For instance, live counseling via a video camera or on the phone is considered synchronous. Contrast with *Asynchronous*.

Synthetic Drugs (C-7; HS-7). Drugs or medications with an altered (i.e., man-made) chemical structure designed to have similar effects of substances created from natural ingredients. Usually, these are created to circumvent restrictions against illegal substances, such as synthetic *cannabis* (often called Spice) and frequently have severe and dangerous side effects. Also known as designer drugs.

Syntonic (C-5; HS-4). *Erikson* suggested that as individuals pass through the eight stages of psychosocial development, they are faced with a task, sometimes called a crisis. Portrayed as a pair of opposing forces, Erikson described the first opposing task in each stage as *syntonic*, or having a positive emotional quality, and the second task as *dystonic*, or having a negative emotional quality. He suggested that individuals needed to experience both syntonic and dystonic qualities in their development.

***System of Interactive Guidance and Information-Plus* (*SIGI-Plus*) (C-6; HS-2).** A comprehensive computer-based *career awareness* program.

System Rules (C-8; HS-7). The kinds of procedures, both *overt* and *covert*, that lend direction to the way in which a system operates.

Systematic Desensitization (C-7; HS-6). A *behavioral technique* developed by *Joseph Wolpe* that is used primarily to treat *phobias* and panic disorders. This treatment involves a helper working with a client to first create a hierarchy of *stimuli* that causes the client *anxiety* (e.g., a client with a fear of elevators may start by imagining an elevator, then imagining walking into an elevator). The helper then teaches the client *progressive muscle relaxation*. Next, the helper takes the client through the hierarchy while the client practices progressive muscle relaxation to alleviate the anxiety. A type of *exposure therapy*.

Systematic Training for Effective Parenting (STEP) (C-4; HS-2). A training program developed by *Don Dinkmeyer*, based on principles of *individual psychology*, to address effective parenting.

Systemic Changes (C-7; HS-6). Changes made by individuals that impact the lives of other individuals and larger systems.

Systemic Perspective (C-6; HS-6). Used in *family counseling*, *group therapy*, and *consultation*, this involves taking into account all of the systems that may impact on the client(s) and developing treatments that take those systems into consideration. See also *Systems Advocacy.*

Systems Advocacy (C-7; HS-7). Having an understanding of system wide barriers that negatively impact clients and developing a plan for eliminating such barriers through *social justice* action and political power. An aspect of the *advocacy competencies.* See also *Systems Perspective.*

Systems Theory (C-7; HS-5). See *General Systems Theory.*

Szasz, Thomas (1920 - 2012) (C-6; HS-5). An American *psychiatrist*, *psychoanalyst*, and educator, who believed that *abnormal* behavior is a function of power dynamics in relationships; he was a strong *advocate* against the use of *diagnosis.*

Tabula Rasa (C-6; HS-5). Latin phrase meaning "smoothed or erased tablet" or *blank slate.* Refers to the mind in its blank or empty state before receiving outside impressions.

Tactile Response (C-3; HS-1). A helping skill in which the helper relates direct observations of the helper's own body sensations in an effort to communicate understanding to the client. These sensations are a response to what the client has said and are reflective of the client's feelings as the helper allows himself or herself to be a vessel for the client's feelings. For instance, a helper might say "My stomach turned when you told that story. I imagine that's how you must have felt." Tactile responses are *advanced empathic responses.* See also *Self-Disclosure.*

Talking Cure (C-7; HS-7). A term used to describe the verbal interaction undertaken in *psychotherapy.* It was originally phrased by Bertha Pappenheim, a patient of *Josef Breuer*, who was also a colleague of *Sigmund Freud.* Freud adopted the term to describe the fundamental work of *psychoanalysis.*

TANF (C-7; HS-8). See *Temporary Assistance for Needy Families.*

Tarasoff Case (C-9; HS-5). The landmark Supreme Court case that set a precedent for the responsibility that mental health professionals have, called the *duty to protect* or *duty to warn.* This case states that one must act to prevent a client from harming self or others by reporting *foreseeable danger/harm* to authorities and potentially informing the person at risk, even if that means breaking *confidentiality.* Specifically, the legal case was Tarasoff vs. Regents of the University of California which occurred in 1976, involving Prosenjit Poddar who murdered Tatiana Tarasoff after telling a *psychologist* he had intentions of killing her.

Tardive Dyskinesia (C-6; HS-4). Side effects of some *antipsychotic drugs* that can include involuntary movements of the tongue, lips, and facial muscles.

Task/Crisis (C-5; HS-3). Within each of *Erikson's* eight stages, people face a task/crisis where they have to find a balance between *syntonic* and *dystonic* emotional qualities. Tasks revolve around the following, respective of each of the 8 stages: hope, will, purpose, competence, fidelity, love, caring, and wisdom.

Task Groups (C-8; HS-6). A type of *group work* that emphasizes *conscious* behaviors and focuses on how *group* dynamics affect the successful completion of a product or task. Often, these are short-term groups ending after the completion of the targeted task.

Tau Upsilon Alpha (TUA) (C-1; HS-8). The honor society for the *National Organization for Human Services.*

Tavistock Institute of Human Relations (C-6; HS-4). Founded in 1946 in England, this organization studied *group* and organizational behavior from a *psychodynamic* perspective. Many famous persons in the field, such as *Carl Jung* and *Melanie Klein*, were affiliated with the institute during their careers.

TBI (C-7; HS-7). See *Traumatic Brain Injury.*

Teacher/Educator (C-3; HS-6). One who tutors, mentors, and models new behaviors for clients. One of the original 13 roles or functions of human service professionals as defined by the *Southern Regional Education Board.*

Technology (C-7; HS-7). Relative to the mental health field, the increasing numbers of online training programs as well as the recognition of the myriad ways helping and *supervision* have been greatly impacted by computers and that helping can now be delivered in unconventional ways, such as via the Internet.

Teleology (C-6; HS-2). In *individual psychology*, the term that suggests that all individuals are goal directed.

Telling and Retelling (C-7; HS-3). In *narrative therapy*, the process of telling and retelling healthy, non-problem-saturated new stories to oneself, the therapist, and to others in an effort to reinforce one's newly developed identity. See also *Problem-Saturated Stories/Narratives.*

Temperament (C-7; HS-3). A natural predisposition to certain psychological and emotional traits. Temperaments, such as introversion or extroversion, are often regarded as innate rather than learned.

Temporary Assistance for Needy Families (TANF) (C-6; HS-8). Formerly called *Aid to Families with Dependent Children*, a U.S. government *social welfare* program designed to assist needy families in developing self-sufficiency. Funded by block grants provided by the federal government to state governments.

Tentative Questions (C-8; HS-8). *Questions* that are asked cautiously and curiously. Sometimes, akin to an *empathic response*, they tend to be more facilitative when trying to build a relationship with a client (e.g., "So, it seems like you might be feeling upset about your relationship?").

Terman, Lewis (1877 - 1956) (C-8; HS-3). An American *psychologist* and professor at Stanford University who analyzed the *Binet-Simon* scale and made a number of revisions to create the *Stanford-Binet intelligence test* that is still used today. Terman was the first to incorporate in his *test* the ratio of chronological age and mental age and times it by 100, calling it the *intelligence quotient* or *IQ* (e.g., mental age of 8 divided by chronical age of 6, times 100 = an IQ of 125).

Termination (C-8; HS-8). The process of ending the helping relationship either due to successful completion of treatment or due to other reasons, such as the client's need for a different form of treatment, the retiring of a helper, the leaving of the helper, the illness of a helper, etc. Appropriate termination processes are often spelled out in *ethical codes.*

Tertiary Prevention (C-7; HS-7). In mental health, the control and reduction of the impact of a *mental disorder*, or problem that has occurred, in an effort to ensure that the individual remains stable or gets better. Tertiary prevention could involve ongoing counseling, referral to *support groups* and other resources, medication, and more. Contrast with *Primary Prevention* and *Secondary Prevention.*

Test (C-8; HS-6). A subset of *assessment*, which involves providing an instrument that assesses an individual's cognitive and/or *affective* realms and the obtaining of scores based on the instrument in an effort to collect data about the individual. Tests can be used individually or be used as part of a total assessment process.

Test Administration (C-8; HS-6). The process of giving a *test.* Tests should be administered appropriately as defined by the way they were established and standardized. Alterations to this process should be noted and interpretations of test data adjusted if conditions were not ideal. See also *Standardized Assessment Procedures.*

Test-Retest Reliability (C-8; HS-3). A form of *reliability* that involves giving the *test* twice, to the same group of people, and then correlating the scores of the first test with those of the second test to determine the reliability or consistency of test scores. Doing so measures *error* in the test, not changes in people.

Test Scoring and Interpretation (C-8; HS-3). The process of examining *tests* and making judgments about test data. Professionals should reflect on how issues of *test worthiness* (i.e., *reliability*, *validity*, *cross-cultural fairness*, and *practicality*) impact test scoring and interpretation.

Test Security (C-8; HS-5). Professionals have the responsibility to make reasonable efforts to assure the integrity of *test* content and the security of the test itself. Professionals should not duplicate tests or change test material without the permission of the publisher.

Test Worthiness (C-9; HS-3). The worthiness of *tests* is determined by an objective analysis of each test in four critical areas: (1) *validity*—whether or not it measures what it is supposed to measure; (2) *reliability*—whether or not the score an individual receives on a test is an accurate measure of his or her true score; (3) *cross-cultural fairness*—whether or not the score the individual obtains is a true reflection of the individual and not a reflection of cultural bias inherent in the test, (4) and, *practicality*—whether or not it makes sense to use a test in a particular situation (e.g., based on cost, length, ease of administration, etc.).

Tests in Print (TIP) (C-8; HS-3). A comprehensive sourcebook of most *tests* published. The online version is mostly used today.

T-Groups (C-7; HS-5). See *Sensitivity Groups.*

Thanatos (C-8; HS-3). See *Death Instinct* and *Libido.*

The Counseling Psychologist **(C-6; HS-4).** A premier professional journal focusing on counseling *psychology* and related areas of mental health research and practice.

The Family Journal: Counseling & Therapy for Couples & Families **(C-6; HS-3).** Journal of the *International Association of Marriage and Family Counselors (IAMFC).*

The Principles for Diversity-Competent Group Workers (C-7; HS-4). Developed by the *Association for Specialists in Group Work*, a division of the *American Counseling Association* that helps guide the work of counselors when doing *group work.*

Thematic Apperception Test (TAT) **(C-7; HS-3).** One of the first *projective tests* developed by *Henry Murray.* The TAT is based on Murray's needs-press theory which suggests those needs of a person that are pressed upon in the environment will become evident when a person is shown an ambiguous picture and is asked to tell a story that has a beginning, middle, and end. Examiners review individuals' responses and particularly focus on who in the story the examinee is identifying with, the content of the story, and the type of beginning and ending the story has.

Theoretical Blueprint (C-6; HS-1). A visual depiction, typically in the form of a table, that is used when developing a measurement instrument for mapping out the content and the domains of a theoretical construct to ensure *content validity* by accounting for the full breadth of material that is related to the construct that is being measured.

Theoretical Integration Stage (C-6; HS-3). The third stage of developing an *integrative approach to counseling* in which the *clinician* has thoroughly learned one theory and is comfortable integrating one or more other theories into his or her approach.

Theory (C-9; HS-6). Relative to professional helping, the comprehensive system or philosophy related to the helping process that enables the helper to understand his or her clients, apply techniques, predict change, and evaluate results. Theories are *heuristic*, which means they are testable. Some of the major schools that encompass a number of helping theories include *psychodynamic*, *cognitive-behavioral*, *existential-humanistic*, *post-modern*, and *systemic perspective.*

Theory of Vocational Choice (C-8; HS-3). See *Holland's Personality Theory of Occupational Choice.*

Therapeutic Alliance (C-9; HS-9). See *Working Alliance.*

Therapeutikos (C-6; HS-4). The Greek word meaning "caring for another." With the word *psyche* ("spirit or soul") it is part of the formation of the word *psychotherapy.*

Therapist (C-8; HS-8). Normally, a term that broadly refers to those professionals focusing on *clinical counseling.* It can refer to *licensed professional counselors*, *licensed psychologists*, *licensed clinical social workers*, *psychoanalysts*, *psychiatrists*, or any other number of human service professionals engaged in some form of "talk therapy." The term has also gained generic usage and can refer to other professions such as physical therapists or respiratory therapists. In these cases, it is generically referring to "helping" people in these contexts.

Therapy (C-9; HS-9). Broadly, the process of *clinical counseling* or "talk therapy," referring to the talking-based treatment of mental health and related issues with clients. The term is also used generically to refer to a wide range of helping behaviors. See also *Counseling* and *Psychotherapy*.

Therapy Group (C-9; HS-8). A meeting of individuals whose purpose is to effect behavior change and increase *self-awareness*, similar to a *counseling group* but with more personal disclosure and personality reconstruction expected from members. See also *Group Work*.

There and Then (C-6; HS-4). In *Gestalt therapy* and other helping approaches, a reference to clients' tendencies to talk about experiences that happened to them in the past or when they talk about other people rather than focusing on their own experiences in the present. Contrast with *Here-and-Now*.

Thick Descriptions (C-8; HS-5). In *qualitative research* and in *narrative therapy*, the inclusion of rich, in-depth accounts of experiences by individuals. When *interviewed*, these individuals can share their personal experiences in deep detail, can identify multiple origins that led them to where they are today, understand multiple perspectives to situations, and describe their experiences in expansive detail. The interviewing process can sometimes help a person move from *thin descriptions* to thick descriptions.

Thin Descriptions (C-8; HS-5). In *qualitative research* and in *narrative therapy*, underexplored and weakly detailed accounts of experiences by individuals. They may stem from individuals with a tendency to think in simple, *dualistic*, and black and white ways who typically adhere to a single perspective of reality. The interviewing process can sometimes help a person move from thin descriptions to *thick descriptions*.

Thinking Mental Function (C-7; HS-6). In *analytical psychology* (*Jungian therapy*), one of the four *mental functions* that make up one's *psychological type*. Individuals, who primarily use their thinking mental function, evaluate or judge information as they employ logic and reasoning in examining data and causal relationships. See also *Feeling Mental Function*, *Sensing Mental Function*, and *Thinking Mental Function*.

Third Force Psychology (C-7; HS-6). A reference to the *humanistic approach* of *psychology* and *counseling*, with *psychoanalysis* and *behavior therapy* referred to as the first two forces.

Third Gender (or Third Sex) (C-8; HS-6). A *gender identity* where a person does not categorize or define one's self as either masculine or feminine (or male or female) but instead the person identifies as a third (or fourth or fifth) *gender* beyond male or female. Some North American *indigenous people* use the related term Two Spirit to describe the third gender. In reality, there have always been multiple genders in many *cultures* throughout history, but Western culture has traditionally only recognized two-male/female or masculine/feminine, depending on usage.

Third-Party Reimbursement (C-7; HS-6). Generally, used to describe the payment, by insurance companies (the third party), for medical and mental health services.

Third Wave of Viennese Psychology (C-7; HS-6). A reference to *existential therapy*, initially developed by *Victor Frankl* in the form of *logotherapy*, as it followed the first waves, also developed in Vienna, of *Freud's psychoanalysis* and *Adler's individual psychology*.

Thorazine (C-5; HS-4). A *psychotropic medication* that is an *antipsychotic drug* and *controlled substance*; it is one of the earliest of such drugs developed and can have seriously damaging neurological side effects from long-term use.

Thorndike, Edward (1874 - 1949) (C-5; HS-2). An American *psychologist* who believed that *tests* could be given in a format that was more reliable than previous methods. His work culminated with the development of the *Stanford Achievement Test* in 1923.

Thought Disorder (C-7; HS-5). Refers to cognitive impairment disorders where disorganized thinking or speech are primary features.

Thought-Stopping (C-7; HS-5). One of a number of techniques to prevent a person from using *cognitive distortions*, the person is taught to stop the problematic thought through a variety of techniques from yelling (or mentally yelling) "stop" or flicking a rubber band on the wrist for *punishment* when the negative thought occurs.

Thurstone, Louis (1887 - 1955) (C-5; HS-1). An American scientist and *psychometric* specialist who *hypothesized* a multifactor approach to intelligence that included seven primary factors: verbal meaning, number ability, word fluency, perception speed, spatial ability, reasoning, and memory.

Tillich, Paul (1886 - 1965) (C-5; HS-2). A German-American *existential philosopher* and Christian theologian whose ideas were influential on the development of *existential therapy*.

Time-Limited, Brief-Counseling Groups (C-6; HS-4). *Counseling groups*, which are of a limited duration of time, such as a 6-week period, and which use brief-counseling techniques, such as those in *solution-focused brief therapy*.

Time Management (C-7; HS-7). The planning of activities involved in the *case management* process. Effective time management is important in avoiding *burnout*, ensuring that all clients are seen within a reasonable period of time, and assisting professionals in remembering meetings, appointment times, and other obligations.

Time Out (C-8; HS-8). In *behavior therapy* and in educational and parenting strategies based on *behavior modification*, a period of time in which a person (usually a child) is isolated from others and/or from his or her environment following the commission of unacceptable behaviors. One minute per age has been traditional, generally, up to a maximum of 5 minutes for time out length. It is also called *social exclusion*.

Time Sample (C-5; HS-3). In *testing* and *assessment*, especially with *observation*, using a *sample* of time to observe a behavior; there is an assumption that the sample is accurate. For example, a *supervisor* might examine 3, 5-minute segments of a person's *clinical interview* with a client to obtain a sample of the trainee's ability.

***Title VII* (C-6; HS-5).** Title VII of the 1964 *Civil Rights Act* prohibits *discrimination* against women and *minority groups* in all aspects of employment.

***Title IX* (C-8; HS-7).** Title IX of the Education Amendments of 1972 prohibits *discrimination* based on sex for any education programs or activities (e.g., sports) receiving federal funds.

Token Economies (C-9; HS-7). A behavioral technique that is based on *operant conditioning*, where a token, which is a *secondary reinforcer*, is given to an individual when an identified appropriate behavior is exhibited. After a certain number of tokens have been collected, and/or a specified amount of time has passed, the individual can exchange the tokens for a reward, sometimes called a *backup reinforcer*. Originally devised for individuals with *intellectual disabilities*, it is now used with a wide variety of client populations.

Tomm, Karl (C-3; HS-1). A Canadian *family therapist*, *psychiatrist*, and educator who was influential in the development of *narrative therapy* through his mentorship of *Michael White*. He is director of the Family Therapy Program at the University of Calgary.

Tone of Voice (C-7; HS-7). One's means of communicating nonverbally and adding emphasis or meaning to communication through variations in the inflection, pitch, rate, and force of speech. See also *Nonverbal Behavior*.

Tonics of the Counseling Relationship (C-6; HS-4). In *Wubbolding's WDEP* approach to *reality therapy*, the positive qualities the helper shows to build a relationship.

Top Dog/Underdog (C-7; HS-4). One of the *polarities* that *Perls* popularized and which seems to characterize a polarity which many people demonstrate. Some people act like the top dog, or the part of *self* that is bossy and the "master," while others act like the underdog, or the part of self that is passive, slave like, and inept.

Total Behavior (C-7; HS-3). In *reality therapy*, one's total actions, thinking process, feelings, and physiological responses. A person can only choose his or her actions and thoughts, which are jointly called *doing*. One's feelings and physiology results from those choices.

Total Educational Context (C-5; HS-1). Suggested by *John Brewer* who believed that *guidance counselors* (now *school counselors*) should be involved in a variety of functions in the schools, including adjustment counseling, assistance with curriculum planning, classroom management, and, of course, *occupational guidance*.

Total Quality Management (TQM) (C-5; HS-2). Developed by Edward Demming, a management approach to customer satisfaction that applied *humanistic* and systems principles to business and industry settings. It was influential toward helping *William Glasser* create *choice theory* and expand *reality therapy*. In particular, it helped him develop his concept of the *quality world*.

Touch (C-7; HS-7). A *nonverbal behavior* that involves physical contact between a helper and a client. Traditionally, helpers have been taught to rarely touch the client. However, some appropriate or therapeutic touch may be natural and enriching to the helping relationship. Research suggests that cross-cultural differences exist in the ways that clients perceive and respond to touch and other nonverbal helper behaviors.

Toxic Behaviors (C-7; HS-7). Behaviors and attitudes that are debilitative to another person's well-being and are sometimes responsible for fostering low *self-esteem*.

Toxins of the Counseling Relationship (C-6; HS-4). In *Wubbolding's WDEP* approach to *reality therapy*, the negative qualities the client shows to building a relationship.

Trail Making Test (C-3; HS-1). A *neuropsychological assessment* tool used to measure task switching and visual attention in individuals.

Trait and Factor Theory (C-8; HS-3). The *first comprehensive theory of counseling* also known as the *Minnesota point of view*, which was developed by *E. G. Williamson*. This theory initially grew out of the ideas of *Frank Parsons*. Although originally *vocationally* oriented, the approach was modified and became a generic approach to counseling and *psychotherapy* and involved five steps: analysis, synthesis, *diagnosis*, counseling, and *follow-up*. See also *Trait-and-Factor Approach*.

Trait-and-Factor Approach (C-9; HS-2). As developed by *Frank Parsons*, a systematic approach to *vocational guidance* that involves knowing oneself, knowing *job* characteristics, and making a match between the two through "true reasoning." Today, this approach has been expanded and includes a number of other steps and concepts. See also *Trait and Factor Theory*.

Traits (C-5; HS-3). Relative to the *Diagnostic and Statistical Manual-5*, when a person does not meet the necessary criteria for a *diagnosis*, but has many of the features (e.g., borderline traits, narcissistic traits).

Transactional Analysis (C-4; HS-2). A popular approach to *therapy* during the 1960s and 1970s that examined parent, adult, and child *ego states* within each person and how a person's ego states communicate with ego states in other people.

Transactional Rules (C-5; HS-4). Rules that are maintained by families that help to keep consistency with their *boundaries*, communication sequences, and help to establish *homeostasis*.

Transferable Skills (C-5; HS-5). Skills from one *job* or activity that are similar enough to allow transferability from that job or activity to another job or activity.

Transference (C-10; HS-7). The client's redirection of both negative and positive feelings and desires, especially those *unconsciously* retained from childhood, toward a helper. Transference is a primary aspect of *psychodynamic approaches* to therapy. Contrast with *Countertransference*. See also *False Connection*.

Transference Relationship (C-9; HS-5). A phenomenon that can occur in the helping relationship when the client transfers his or her early ways of relating (usually relating to parents) to the *therapist*. In *psychoanalysis*, this *transference* relationship can be interpreted at the appropriate time in *therapy*. This occurs when the client is capable of understanding that he or she *unconsciously* treats others as a result of these earlier relationships.

Transforming School Counseling (C-6; HS-1). Initiatives sponsored by the *Education Trust* and by *ASCA* to change the manner in which *school counselors* worked and *school counseling* programs were formed. It led to the *ASCA National Model* and other *comprehensive school counseling programs* (*CSCP*).

Transgender (C-10; HS-10). A term for individuals who do not identify with the *sex* of their birth or conform to the *gender binary* of masculine vs. feminine. These persons may or may not live in *congruence* with the *gender identity* to which they internally believe they match. This term originally existed as a specific concept, often referring to *transsexual* people, but has become an umbrella term for many individuals who do not conform to their birth sex or *gender* assigned at their birth, including *cross dresser*, *transsexual*, *intersex*, and other people self-identifying under this umbrella term.

Transition (C-8; HS-8). The process a client may go through to explore, discover, and affirm his or her *gender identity*. This may, but does not always, include taking hormones, having surgeries, or going through *therapy*.

Transition Stage (C-8; HS-8). The third *stage of group development* in which goals and rules are understood by *group* members, some *anxiety* and *resistance* still exists, and an effort is made to assist members in focusing on themselves and moving toward the working stage.

Transitional Periods (C-6; HS-4). The periods between *eras* that foster a smooth transition from one era to the next in *Levinson's Seasons of a Man's Life and Seasons of a Women's Life* theories.

Transparency (C-9; HS-8). The characteristic or *trait* where researchers and practitioners are open and sincere with participants and clients about their thoughts, feelings, and intentions. It is sometimes called *congruence*, *genuineness*, *realness*, or *authenticity*.

Transparent Self (C-5; HS-3). Developed by *psychologist* Sidney Jourard, when an individual does not hide his or her hidden parts of the *self*. Related to the concept of *transparency*, Jourard believed that concealing of the self leads to ill health and maladaptive behaviors and encouraged people to be open to others. See also *Johari Window*.

Transphobia (C-8; HS-8). The fear of, *prejudice* to, or *discrimination* against people of the *transgender* community or those who identify as *gender non-conforming*. Transphobia describes individuals who harbor a range of negative attitudes, thoughts, and intents toward transgender people. See also *Transgender*.

Transsexual (C-8; HS-8). A person who does not identify with the *sex* of one's birth and attempts to realign one's sex with one's *gender identity*. See also *Transgender*.

Transtheoretical Model of Behavior Change (or Stages of Change) (C-6; HS-2). A model of behavioral change developed by James Prochaska and Carlo Di Clemente that includes the stages of: (1) pre-contemplation (not ready for change); (2) contemplation (thinking about change); (3) preparation (getting ready for change); (4) action (doing the change); (5) maintenance (maintaining the change for at least six months); (6) and termination (not being tempted by the behavior and certain one will maintain the new change).

Transvestite (C-8; HS-8). See *Crossdresser*.

Tranxene (C-6; HS-6). A *benzodiazepine psychotropic medication* that is an *antianxiety agent* and a *controlled substance*.

Trauma and Stressor-Related Disorders (C-8; HS-5). A new category for *Diagnostic and Statistical Manual-5*, trauma and stressor-related disorders emphasize the pervasive impact that life events can have on an individual's emotional and physical well-being. *Diagnoses* include reactive attachment disorder, disinhibited social engagement disorder, posttraumatic stress disorder, acute stress disorder, and adjustment disorders.

***Trauma Symptom Checklist-40* (*TSC-40*) (C-5; HS-4).** A *self-report assessment* tool for the *diagnosis* and treatment of *post-traumatic stress syndrome* and other symptoms from traumatic experiences (e.g., sexual or physical abuse).

Traumatic Brain Injury (C-7; HS-7). Any type of brain injury that leads to serious problems in psychological, physical, social, or intellectual functioning. It can be caused by any of a number of incidents such as an injury from war, an accident, an overdose, a stroke, or other injuries.

Treatment Planning (C-8; HS-8). Accurately assessing client needs in order to develop *diagnoses*, *prognoses*, client goals, and a written plan to address the treatment of presenting problems. *Assessment* in treatment planning can include: (1) conducting a *clinical interview*; (2) administering *tests*; (3) using *informal assessment instruments*; (4) and coming up with a diagnosis. See also *Case Management*.

Triad Model (C-7; HS-5). A team-based training model that provides a safe environment for the helper so that he or she can learn to better understand culturally different clients. The team members are the *client*, the *counselor*, the *anti-counselor* (who highlights the differences in values and expectations between the counselor and client), and a *pro-counselor* (who highlights the similarities).

Triadic Relationship (C-7; HS-6). In *consultation*, the relationship between the *supervisor*, the *supervisee*, and a third party (or parties), who is impacted by the supervisor/supervisee relationship, such as the client.

Triadic Supervision (C-7; HS-6). A type of *supervision* in which one *supervisor* meets with two *supervisees* in the same session.

Triangulate (C-8; HS-7). When parents' issues are projected onto children and the children get blamed or *labeled* for a problem that really originated with the parents' inability to talk with one another or get along. See also *Scapegoating*.

Triangulation (C-9; HS-5). In research, using multiple methods of gathering data to ensure accuracy of the results. It is often used in *qualitative research* methods.

Triarchic Theory (C-6; HS-4). A theory of intelligence developed by Sternberg that has three components or sub-theories, including componential (analytical), experiential (creative), and practical (contextual) aspects.

Tricyclics (C-6; HS-4). One of the older classes of *antidepressants*.

Tripartite Model of Personal Identity (C-6; HS-4). Suggests that human service professionals understand their clients in three spheres: (1) the *Individual Level*, which represents the client's uniqueness, (2) the *Group Level*, which is related to aspects of the person that can vary based on the cultural and ethnic groups to which the client belongs, and (3) and the *Universal Level*, which is related to common experiences people share, such as (a) biological and physical similarities, (b) common life experiences (birth, death, love, sadness, etc.), (c) self-awareness, and (d) the ability to use symbols such as language.

True Experimental Research (C-9; HS-6). A type of *experimental research* in which the researcher randomly assigns subjects to particular groups and then manipulates the *independent variable(s)* to measure its effect on the *dependent variable(s)*.

True Reasoning (C-7; HS-2). *Frank Parsons* suggestion that *vocational guidance* involved a three-step process that included knowing oneself, knowing *job* characteristics, and making a match between the two (thoughtful analysis).

Trust vs. Mistrust (Ages Birth–1 year) (C-9; HS-7). *Erikson's* first stage of *psychosocial development* where the infant develops a sense of trust or mistrust based on the type of caretaking received. Healthy infant caretaking leads to trust, whereas dysfunctional infant caretaking leads to distrust.

Trusting, Collaborative, Equal Relationship (C-8; HS-7). The type of relationship the helper works to build with clients when conducting *solution-focused brief therapy* and some other, usually *post-modern*, forms of therapy.

Trustworthiness (C-8; HS-4). In *qualitative research*, strategies to ensure the quality or worth of the research, similar to *validity* in *quantitative research*. It entails many strategies, such as using *audit trails*, *bracketing*, and *thick descriptions*.

T-Score (C-9; HS-3). A type of *standard score* that can be easily converted from a *z-score*. *T-scores* have a *mean* of 50 and a *standard deviation* of 10 and are generally used with *personality tests*.

T-Test (C-7; HS-3). A statistical measure that is used in *quantitative research* to examine differences between two group *means*. A "dependent-samples t-test," sometimes called a "matched-pairs t-test," is used for comparing the mean scores between the same participants in a *one-group pretest-posttest design*. An "independent-samples t-test," sometimes called a "paired-samples t-test," is used for comparing the means between two different independent samples.

Tuckman, Bruce Wayne (1938 - 2016) (C-7; HS-3). An influential researcher on *group* dynamics who theorized that groups typically progress through the following stages: *forming*, *storming*, *norming*, *performing*, and *adjourning*.

Tunnel Vision (C-5; HS-4). Only seeing the downside, negative aspects, or specific viewpoints of a situation, as in looking down a tunnel or with blinders on where one cannot accurately see the whole picture. See also *Cognitive Distortions*.

Twelve Competency Areas (C-1; HS-10). Based on the *Skill Standards*, areas that are typically performed by human service professionals; these are a set of skills or *job* functions related to each competency, and activity statements or tasks that the human service professional would undertake to fulfill the job functions.

Twelve Steps (12 Steps) (C-9; HS-9). The 12 guiding principles, originally developed by *Alcoholics Anonymous*, that have been used for many related *support groups* often connected with *substance abuse* and *process addictions* or obsessive-compulsive disorders. Examples of the *12 steps* include admitting one is powerless over the *addiction*, making amends to those one wronged, and relying on a higher power for strength in *recovery*.

Twelve Step Group (12 Step Group) (C-9; HS-9). Any *support group* that follows the guiding principles found in the *12 steps* of *Alcoholics Anonymous* or related *self-help groups.*

(Twenty-Twenty) 20/20 Vision (C-10; HS-5). A vision for the future of the counseling field that is being sponsored by the *American Counseling Association*. The 20/20 vision represents the coming together of 31 counseling associations to develop a common definition and vision of counseling. See also *Counseling.*

Two Spirit (C-8; HS-6). See *Third Gender (or Third Sex).*

Type A Personality (C-6; HS-6). This describes individuals who are highly motivated, organized, competitive, driven, focused, or aggressive.

Type B Personality (C-6; HS-6). This describes individuals who are laid-back, relaxed, and more leisurely in their goals and behaviors.

Type I Error (C-8; HS-4). Also referred to as *alpha error*, this occurs when the *null hypothesis* is true and is rejected by the researchers. In other words, the researchers conclude that there are statistically significant differences between groups when, in reality, there are not differences between groups.

Type II Error (C-8; HS-4). Also referred to as *beta error*, this occurs when the *alternative hypothesis* is true and is rejected by researchers. In other words, the researchers conclude that there are not statistically significant differences between groups when, in reality, differences between groups exist.

U Test (C-6; HS-2). See *Mann-Whitney U Test.*

Uberwelt (C-7; HS-5). In *existential* terms, the manner in which we relate to our spiritual *self*, or to the unknown. See also *Eigenwelt*, *Mitwelt*, and *Umwelt.*

Umwelt (C-7; HS-5). In *existential* terms, it is being grounded in our biology and has to do with how we experience the world around us based on our biological foundations. See also *Eigenwelt*, *Mitwelt*, and *Uberwelt.*

Unconditional Positive Regard (C-10; HS-10). Accepting a person without conditions or without strings attached. One of *Carl Rogers'* core conditions of helping along with *empathy* and *congruence.*

Unconditioned Response (C-8; HS-83). A reaction to a *stimulus* that happens automatically or naturally.

Unconditioned Stimulus (C-8; HS-8). A *stimulus* that, when paired with a *conditioned stimulus*, will develop the same responses as the conditioned stimulus.

Unconscious (C-10; HS-9). Proposed by early *psychodynamic* theorists, the idea that there is a hidden part of all individuals that motivates and impacts behavior in complex ways. The goal of many counseling approaches today is to make parts of the *unconscious*, *conscious.* Contrast with *Conscious.*

Unconscious Factors (C-6; HS-6). A concept stating that much of our behavior is caused by factors beyond our everyday awareness. See also *Unconscious.*

Undifferentiated Ego Mass (C-7; HS-3). A term used by *Murray Bowen* to explain the lack of *individuation* in family members.

Unfinished Business (C-7; HS-6). Unresolved problems and experiences brought from an earlier life stage that affect interpersonal relationships. A concept most associated with *Gestalt therapy* but popularized and also used by helpers from other theoretical approaches.

Unhelpful Stories (C-6; HS-3). In *narrative therapy*, stories clients tell that feed into oppressive *narratives* and work against the client's attempts to be healthy.

Unique Outcomes (C-7; HS-3). In *narrative therapy*, a reference to *sparkling outcomes*, or exceptions, to the dominant, *problem-saturated narrative* of a client's life. Seeking *exceptions to the problems*, the client learns to find times he or she successfully coped with or avoided the problems and works to increase these positive outcomes in life.

Universal Identity (C-7; HS-6). Relative to a cross-cultural understanding of the person, along with *individual identity* and *group identity*, one of three identities that make up the person. This identity represents common or universal themes which all people share.

Universal Level (C-6; HS-4). In the *tripartite model of personal identity*, things related to common experiences, such as (a) biological and physical similarities, (b) common life experiences (birth, death, love, sadness, etc.), (c) *self-awareness*, and (d) the ability to use symbols such as language.

Universal Rules (C-7; HS-5). In *couples and family counseling* approaches, rules that are shared across many *cultures* and often related to hierarchical structure (e.g., the Golden Rule, prohibitions against stealing, the importance of children obeying parents).

Universal Skills (C-4; HS-4). Generic counseling skills and techniques that are believed to be effective at working with diverse groups of clients.

Unreliable Assessment and Research Instruments (C-7; HS-5). Clinical and research *assessments* that fail to produce consistent results which suggests that the assessment instrument has poor consistency and does not demonstrate *test worthiness*. More often a concern for the *reliability* of assessment and research instruments when used with diverse clients.

Unspecified Mental Disorders (C-7; HS-3). Relative to the *Diagnostic and Statistical Manual-5*, used when a provider believes an individual's impairment to functioning or distress is clinically significant; however, the provider does not specify the reason why the full criteria are not met. For example, a *clinician* identifies *delusions*, *hallucinations*, and *depression*, but does not specify a *diagnosis*, but instead, the clinician states "*Other Specified Disorder*."

Unstructured Interview (C-7; HS-6). An *interview* in which the examiner does not have a pre-established list of items or *questions* to which the participant can respond; instead, participant responses to examiner inquiries establish the direction for follow-up questioning. Contrast with *Structured Interview*.

Use of Power (C-6; HS-3). From *individual psychology*, one manner in which children deal with *feelings of inferiority* through how they use power in their life.

Use-of-Time Assessment (C-4; HS-1). An *assessment* from the management element of the *ASCA National Model* that assesses how much time *school counselors* are spending on different activities.

Using "Now" Language (C-6; HS-4). In *Gestalt therapy* and other counseling approaches, an emphasis by the counselor on using language that focuses on how the client is experiencing things "now" and that helps to keep the client in the present as opposed to the *there and then* aspects of life or talking about problems. See also *Here-and-Now.*

Using Irony or Satire (C-4; HS-3). Using mockery, caricature, humor, etc. to point out the faulty logic and negative behavior of a client. It is one method of *confrontation* used with clients and should be done carefully (and some suggest not used at all).

V Codes (C-7; HS-5). A diagnostic classification system for *environmental and psychosocial stressors* in individuals used in the *Diagnostic and Statistical Manual of Mental Disorders* and associated with the *International Classification of Diseases.* See also *Other Conditions That May Be a Focus of Clinical Assessment.*

Vaillant, George (1934 -) (C-5; HS-3). An American professor and *psychiatrist* who formulated a theory of adult development that was unique in that it spoke to how adults overcome major psychiatric illnesses.

Validity (in Assessment) (C-10; HS-4). The degree to which all of the accumulated evidence (e.g., types of validity) supports the legitimacy of a *test.* Validity can be measured in a number of ways and attempts to answer the question, "How well does a test measure what it's supposed to measure?" Some of the various types of validity include *content validity*, *criterion-related validity*, and *construct validity.*

Validity (in Quantitative Research) (C-7; HS-5). The ability to control *extraneous variables* when conducting research or the degree to which the research is accurate or measures what it claims to measure. Two types of validity that impact research are *internal validity* and *external validity.*

Valium (C-6; HS-6). A *benzodiazepine psychotropic medication* that is an *antianxiety agent* and *controlled substance.*

Values in the Helping Relationship (C-8; HS-8). The ethical responsibility of helpers to ensure that their values or biases are not imposed upon their clients. In the most recent version of the *American Counseling Association's* ethics code, one cannot refer out a client simply due to values differences between the counselor and the client. See also *Referral.*

Variable (C-8; HS-6). Any characteristic or quality that can be measured. See also *Observed Variable* and *Latent Variable.*

Variable Interval Schedule of Reinforcement (C-7; HS-5). A *schedule of reinforcement* that is based on an indeterminate or unpredictable amount of time, but averages out to a specific amount of time (e.g., every four minutes). In this case, variable means inconsistent and interval refers to the amount of time.

Variable Ratio Schedule of Reinforcement (C-7; HS-5). A *schedule of reinforcement* that occurs when a behavior is reinforced after an indefinite or unpredictable number of responses, but averages out to a certain number of times (e.g., on average, gets reinforced every three times). Slot machines are a good example of a variable ratio schedule. In this case, variable means inconsistent and ratio refers to the number of responses.

Variance (C-7; HS-3). A statistical measure of the extent to which values in a data set are spread out around the *mean*. The variance is the *standard deviation* squared.

Varimax Rotation (C-7; HS-3). See *Factor Rotation.*

Vegetotherapy (C-4; HS-1). Developed by *Wilhelm Reich*, a *psychodynamic*-based *therapy* which involves massaging and using other body techniques with clients to elicit physical release of *emotions* held within the body. See also *Body-Oriented Therapies.*

Ventura School of Girls (C-6; HS-2). A girls' *correctional facility* that *William Glasser* consulted with and where he implemented early applications of his *reality therapy* approach.

Veracity (C-8; HS-7). In *Kitchener*'s moral model of *ethical decision-making*, being truthful in the ethical decision-making process.

Vernon, Philip (1905 - 1987) (C-4; HS-2). A British *psychologist* who believed that subcomponents of intelligence could be added in a hierarchical manner to get a score for a cumulative or *general (g) factor. Intelligence testing* continues to use this concept.

Vicarious Learning (C-4; HS-4). Learning that occurs through indirect means or *observation*, as in learning about the dangers of explosives from hearing a friend describe how he injured himself playing with fireworks. An important concept in *modeling* and *behavior therapy*, it was originally defined by *Albert Bandura.*

Vicarious Traumatization (C-3; HS-3). See *Compassion Fatigue.*

Vienna Psychoanalytic Society (C-5; HS-1). The oldest *psychoanalytic movement* society in the world, many prominent *psychoanalysts* were president of this society, including *Adler* (its first president) *Freud*, *Reich*, *Jung*, and others.

View of Human Nature (C-9; HS-7). The manner in which an individual makes sense of the world. In counseling theory, the way that an individual applies his or her meaning of the world to the counseling relationship.

Virtue Ethics Model (C-7; HS-5). Any of a number of models that suggests *ethical decision-making* should be based on the helper's character. For instance, some suggest that helpers should be *prudent* or tentative in their ethical decision-making, maintain *integrity*, be *respectful*, and be *benevolent*. See also *Ethical Decision-Making, Moral Models of.*

Virtue/Strength (C-6; HS-4). Every one of the eight stages of *Erikson's psychosocial theory* of development has a virtue/strength associated with it that individuals have to tackle. In order of his eight stages, they include hope and drive, willpower and self-control, purpose and direction, competence and method, fidelity and devotion, love and affiliation, care and production, and wisdom and renunciation.

Visitor (C-8; HS-6). In *solution-focused brief therapy*, clients that come to counseling as tourists, to see what it is about but are not ready to identify issues, goals, or develop solutions to their problems. Contrast with *Customers* and *Complainants.* See also *Readiness, Not Resistance*.

Vocation/Vocational (C-8; HS-5). Of or relating to one's *work*, *job*, *career*, or *occupation.*

Vocational Bureau (C-9; HS-1). Established by *Frank Parsons* during the turn of the twentieth century, this bureau assisted individuals in choosing an *occupation*, preparing themselves for it, finding an opening in it, and building a *career* of efficiency and success.

Vocational Education Act **(C-5; HS-1).** In 1946, the U.S. government passed this act which provided federal funds to support *guidance*, counseling, and counselor training and leadership at the local and state levels.

Vocational Guidance (C-6; HS-3). The original counselors, near the beginning of the twentieth century, practiced vocational guidance or *career counseling*. For some counselors, this is still part of their role. See also *Vocation/Vocational.*

Vocational Guidance Counselors (C-6; HS-3). In the history of counseling, vocational guidance counselors were the first counselors who assisted individuals with *career* and *vocational* issues. They later became mental health, school, couples and family counselors.

Vocational Guidance Movement (C-7; HS-2). In the early 1900s, there became a major focus on *vocational* and *occupational counseling* that set the stage for the establishment of the counseling profession. Much of this movement was a response to societal changes after the industrial revolution and World War I.

Vocational Rehabilitation Centers (C-7; HS-5). During the 1950s, these centers became increasingly popular as they addressed the physical and psychological needs of individuals, especially those who had been seriously injured during World War II. Today, vocational rehabilitation centers continue to be important settings for *occupational* and psychological counseling.

Voice Intonation and Tone (C-10; HS-10). A *nonverbal behavior* related to the pitch, tone, and volume in a helper's voice. See also *Tone of Voice.*

Voting Rights Act **(C-5; HS-4).** Federal legislation in the United States that forbids racial *discrimination* in voting. One of a number of legislative acts during the 1960s that provided opportunities for *minority groups* and the poor and helped to reshape attitudes toward social problems. It resulted in increased *job* opportunities for counselors and human service professionals.

Wagner O'Day Act **(C-6; HS-2).** In 1932, this federal act established the U. S. Employment Service.

Walking Into Agency (C-8; HS-8). See *Agency Atmosphere*.

Wants (C-7; HS-4). In *reality therapy*, the desires of the client as opposed to the needs.

Ward v. Wilbanks **(C-8; HS-5).** A precedent setting legal case that states that counselors must counsel all clients regardless of client characteristics or differing values with their clients. In *Julea Ward's* situation, she was a graduate student of Eastern Michigan University who, based on her conservative religious values, refused to counsel a client who was *gay*. After refusing to comply with a remediation plan to address her response to the client, and after a formal hearing, she was dismissed from her program. She eventually sued the university, but lost. However, upon appeal the case was settled out of court. The *Julea Ward* case was the driving force behind the statement in the current *ACA Code of Ethics* that directly reinforced the notion that one should not refer a client due to differences between personal counselor values and client characteristics or values, but *referrals* should be made based on *scope of practice* and client needs. See also *Julea Ward* and *Referral.*

Watson, John B. (1878 - 1958) (C-7; HS-5). An American *psychologist* and one of the first to apply the concepts of *classical conditioning* to the clinical setting. See also *Little Albert.*

Watzlawick, Paul (1921 - 2007) (C-6; HS-2). An influential Austrian-American *psychologist* and *family therapist* who worked at the *Brief Family Therapy Center* inside the *Mental Research Institute* (*MRI*) at *Palo Alto.*

Ways of Relating (C-6; HS-3). In *Boszormenyi-Nagy*'s *multigenerational approach*, this speaks to how ways of relating are passed down through the generations.

WDEP System (C-8; HS-5). A system developed by *Robert Wubbolding* that is applied to clients when using a *reality therapy* approach. W = client wants, D = what the client is doing in his or her life's direction, E = evaluating if what the client is doing is working, and P = creating a plan of action for change. See also *SAMIC-3.*

Weakland, John (1919 - 1995) (C-6; HS-2). An influential American *family therapist* who worked at the *Brief Family Therapy Center* inside the *Mental Research Institute* (*MRI*) at *Palo Alto.*

Weaver, Eli (1862 - 1922) (C-7; HS-2). A New York City school principal who wrote a booklet called *Choosing a Career* and is considered an early *advocate* of *vocational guidance.*

***Wechsler Adult Intelligence Scale* (*WAIS*) (C-8; HS-7).** See *Wechsler Intelligence Scales.*

***Wechsler Intelligence Scale for Children* (*WISC*) (C-8; HS-7).** See *Wechsler Intelligence Scales.*

***Wechsler Intelligence Scales* (C-8; HS-7).** A series of *psychometric tests* that have been developed to measure intelligence (i.e., *IQ*) and thinking abilities in people. There are several variations of them for children and for adults, including the *Wechsler Preschool and Primary Scale of Intelligence* (*WPPSI*), the *Wechsler Intelligence Scale for Children* (*WISC*), and the *Wechsler Adult Intelligence Scale* (*WAIS*).

***Wechsler Memory Scale* (C-6; HS-4).** A *psychometric test* developed to measure memory in people.

***Wechsler Preschool and Primary Scale of Intelligence* (*WPPSI*) (C-8; HS-8).** See *Wechsler Intelligence Scales.*

WEIRD People (C-5; HS-2). The acronym for "western, educated, industrialized, rich, and democratic" that represents characteristics of individuals and societies who comprise the largest group of clients and research participants in social sciences research. However, WEIRD people represent only a small proportion of the global population. It is therefore essential that mental health professionals practice *culturally competent helping* and consider *cross-cultural fairness* in the research and assessment process.

Welfare of Client (C-9; HS-9). In the helping professions, the ethical duty to promote those things that benefit or help the client and avoid harm to the client.

Well-Being Therapy (C-7; HS-6). See *Positive Psychology.*

Wellness (C-8; HS-8). Attending to all aspects of the individual's life that lead to health and happiness. Ensuring that one is addressing his or her own health in a number of domains, such as one's *creative self*, *coping self*, *social self*, *essential self*, and *physical self.* Some ways to address one's wellness is through exercise, being in one's own *therapy*, *meditation*, prayer, journaling, etc. One of the *common factors.* See also *Indivisible Self Model.*

Wellness Approach (C-8; HS-8). The view, supported by adherents of the *anti-deterministic view of human nature* and contrasted with the *medical model*, which espouses the ability of the individual to change through attention to his or her *wellness*, personal choices, *holism* aspects of *self*, and other things in the client's control. See also *Wellness*, *Indivisible Self Model*, and *Positive Psychology.*

Whitaker, Carl (1912 - 1995) (C-6; HS-3). An influential American physician and *family therapist* known for contributing to the *Experiential Approach to Family Therapy.*

White Identity Development (C-7; HS-6). Proposes specific stages of White *racial identity development* that individuals are likely to pass through as they become increasingly cross-culturally aware. One well known model was developed by *Helms.*

White Privilege (C-7; HS-7). See *Privilege.*

White, Cheryl (1955 -) (C-1; HS-4). The widow of *narrative therapy* developer *Michael White*, her interests in *feminism* and *social justice* were influential in the development of *narrative therapy.* She is currently director of the Dulwich Centre in Australia.

White, Michael (1948 - 2008) (C-7; HS-3). An Australian *social worker* who founded the *post-modern social constructivist* theory of *psychotherapy* known as *narrative therapy.*

Wholeness (Jungian) (C-5; HS-2). In *analytical psychology*, *Jung's* emphasis on finding completeness and involves an expanded *consciousness*, through integrating the *conscious* with the *personal unconscious* and the *collective unconscious.*

Why Question (C-10; HS-10). A type of *question*, which starts with "why," and attempts to get to the underlying issue(s) of a client's problems. Why questions, however, are generally not recommended because they tend to make clients feel defensive or judged.

***Wide Range Achievement Test 4* (*WRAT-4*) (C-7; HS-3).** Currently in its fourth variation, an *achievement test* designed to measure a child or adult's reading, sentence comprehension, spelling, and math skills. It assesses for learning problems.

Wilcoxon Ranked-Sum Test (C-6; HS-3). The *nonparametric* equivalent to an independent-sample *t-test.* This procedure is used to test for statistical significance between two independent samples.

Will to Meaning (C-7; HS-4). In *existential therapy*, *Frankl's* term for a person's active search to find meaning in life.

Williamson, E. G. (1900 - 1979) (C-8; HS-2). An American *psychologist* credited with developing the *first comprehensive theory of counseling*, also known as the *Minnesota point of view* or *trait and factor theory*. Williamson's approach initially grew out of the ideas of *Frank Parsons*.

Willing-Denial (C-7; HS-4). In *existential therapy*, the many ways people deny the possibilities and choices that exist in life, often through deadening themselves to the world around them, living in a fantasy world, or other methods of *denial*.

Winnicott, Donald (1896 - 1971) (C-5; HS-2). A British pediatrician and *psychoanalyst* who was a key *object relations therapy* theorist.

Winslade, John (1953 -) (C-2; HS-1). A U.S.-based, New Zealand counselor and professor of counselor education who was an early and well-known proponent of *narrative therapy*.

Withdrawal (Alcohol and Other Substances) or Withdrawal Symptoms (C-10; HS-10). The various physical, psychological, and emotional symptoms that can result from stopping or reducing intake of certain drugs, *alcohol*, or other substances (including many prescription medications).

Withdrawal (C-4; HS-3). In *Erikson's psychosocial theory* of development, too much mistrust leads to disconnection and distance from others (i.e., withdrawal).

Witnesses (C-7; HS-4). In *narrative therapy*, individuals are brought in to observe (or witness) the client discuss his or her newfound ways of understanding the world. These witnesses are not there to validate the person, but to hear the client and possibly ask questions to help the client focus his or her understanding of this newfound way of being.

Wittgentstein, Ludwig (1889 - 1951) (C-5; HS-2). An Austrian-British philosopher whose work was influential on *post-modernism* and thus the development of *solution-focused brief therapy*.

Wolf, Toni (1888 - 1953) (C-4; HS-2). An early client of *Carl Jung* who eventually became a *Jungian therapist*, had a long term relationship with Jung, and helped him develop some of his ideas.

Wolfe, Janet (1941 -) (C-4; HS-1). *Albert Ellis's* companion for much of his life who eventually became a *clinical psychologist* and executive director of the *Albert Ellis Institute*.

Wolpe, Joseph (1915 - 1997) (C-7; HS-5). A South African *psychiatrist*, and one of the first to apply the concepts of *classical conditioning* to the clinical setting. One of the many theorists that fueled the diversity of counseling therapies during the 1950s and 1960s. He developed *reciprocal inhibition* and *systematic desensitization techniques*.

Women (C-8; HS-8). See *Diverse Populations Human Service Professionals Work With*.

Women, Infants, and Children (WIC) (C-5; HS-7). A form of *public assistance* that is a U.S. federally funded financial support program offered to low-income mothers with children between the ages of birth and five years old.

Women's/Men's Centers (C-7; HS-3). Centers on college campuses that focus on men's or women's issues and one area in higher education that individuals with a master's or higher in *student affairs and college counseling* sometimes work.

***Woodcock Johnson Test of Cognitive Abilities* (C-6; HS-2).** A *test* to determine a broad range of possible intellectual abilities and *learning disabilities.*

***Woodworth's Personal Data Sheet* (C-4; HS-1).** An instrument developed to screen World War I recruits for their susceptibility to mental health problems. It is considered the precursor of modern-day *personality testing.*

***Word Association Test* (C-8; HS-4).** A *projective test* of mental function and personality where the participant explores associations of related words grouped together. Such tests were originally developed by *Carl Jung.*

Work (C-8; HS-5). Effort expended in pursuit of a *job*, *occupation*, or *avocation* to produce or accomplish something.

Work Incentive Program (C-5; HS-7). One of a number of legislative acts during the 1960s that provided opportunities for *minority groups* and the poor to find *work* and helped to reshape attitudes toward social problems. These resulted in increased *job* opportunities for mental health professionals.

Work Stage (in Group Counseling) (C-8; HS-8). The fourth stage of *group work*, where trust has already been built, goals are defined, and the clients begin to accomplish their goals (i.e., work on their issues). See also *Stages of the Helping Relationship.*

Work Stage (in Individual Counseling) (C-8; HS-8). The fourth stage of the helping relationship, where trust has already been built, goals defined, and the client begins to accomplish his or her goals (i.e., work on his or her issues). See also *Stages of the Helping Relationship.*

Working Alliance (aka Therapeutic Alliance) (C-9; HS-9). Along with the *ability to deliver one's theoretical approach*, one of the two *common factors* to effective helping relationships between client and counselor, and one of the most critical factors toward positive client outcomes in the helping relationship. It can include *empathy*, *acceptance*, *genuineness*, *embracing a wellness perspective*, *cultural competence*, and the *it factor.* See also *Common Factors.*

World Is Largely Unpredictable (C-5; HS-3). A basic tenet of chaos theory, used in *chaos theory consultation*; put simply, it assumes that the world functions randomly and unpredictably rather than according to a predictable plan or pattern.

Worldview (C-6; HS-6). The ways in which one sees the world or the lens through which one views things (i.e. one's perspective on life). See also *View of Human Nature.*

Wounded Healer (C-9; HS-9). A concept, originally highlighted by *Carl Jung*, that helpers are compelled into the helping professions because they are wounded themselves, thus seeking out a *career* that aligns with their own wounded selves.

Wubbolding, Robert (1944 -) (C-7; HS-4). An American *psychologist*, educator, trainer, and presenter of *reality therapy* known for being the first director of training for the William Glasser Institute and for his own academic writing on reality therapy, including the *WDEP system.*

Wundt, Wilhelm (1832 - 1920) (C-8; HS-5). A German physician, educator, and philosopher who developed one of the first psychological laboratories. He also set out to create "a new domain of science" that he called physiological psychology, which later became known as *psychology*.

Xanax (C-6; HS-6). A *benzodiazepine psychotropic medication* that is an *antianxiety agent* and *controlled substance*.

Yalom, Irvin (1931 -) (C-7; HS-6). An American *psychiatrist*, educator, and author who is well-known for his contributions to *existential therapy* and to *group therapy*. In addition to his nonfiction works on therapy, he has also written several fiction books on related topics, some of which have been turned into movies.

YAVIS (C-6; HS-5). The acronym for "young, attractive, verbal, intelligent, and successful," it stands for the positive bias for these types of clients found in many mental health professions, meaning many professionals prefer this type of client and have a negative bias toward other clients.

Yerkes, Robert (1876 - 1956) (C-5; HS-2). An American *psychologist* and primatologist who was president of the *American Psychological Association* during World War I. He chaired a special committee designed to screen new military recruits which developed the *Army Alpha* test.

Yes/No Closed Question (C-7; HS-7). A type of *closed question* where the client is being asked to answer the question with a "yes" or with a "no" response. These types of questions are very limiting and should be used sparingly in counseling sessions or interviews. Contrast with *Open Questions*.

You/But Statements (C-6; HS-6). One method of *confrontation* with clients where the helper points out contradictions between what the client says and what he or she is doing or emotionally displaying. For example, "you said you were angry…but you are crying."

Youth Services Agencies (C-7; HS-7). Settings where *clinical mental health counselors* and human service professionals may be employed where the focus is on adolescents, such as *child protective services*, the YMCA, adoption agencies, or juvenile correctional centers.

Z Codes (C-7; HS-5). A diagnostic classification system for environmental and psychosocial stressors in individuals used in the *Diagnostic and Statistical Manual-5* and associated with the 10th edition of the *International Classification of Diseases*. See also *Other Conditions That May Be a Focus of Clinical Assessment*.

Zero Point (C-6; HS-2). See *Need Satisfaction Cycle*.

Zoloft (C-7; HS-6). A *psychotropic medication* that is an *antidepressant* and *controlled substance*.

***z*-score (C-9; HS-2).** The most fundamental *standard score*, which is created by converting an individual's raw score to a new score that has a *mean* of 0 and a *standard deviation* of 1.

INDEX OF COUNSELING WORDS AND TERMS

The following words and terms are in order, based on their rankings. A ranking of 10 means that in the opinion of the authors, the item has a very good chance of finding its way on a credentialing exam. A ranking of 1 means it is unlikely to be found on an exam. If you are studying for such an exam, we encourage you to focus on the higher numbers (perhaps 7 through 10), and if you have time, then review the numbers below those. Good luck!

RANKINGS OF "10"

RANKINGS OF "9"

RANKINGS OF "8"

RANKINGS OF "7"

RANKINGS OF "6"

RANKINGS OF "5"

RANKINGS OF "4"

Vernon, Philip
Vicarious Learning
Withdrawal
Wolf, Toni
Wolfe, Janet
Woodworth's Personal Data Sheet

RANKINGS OF "3"

AACN
ABAP
Accreditation Council for Genetic Counseling
American Association of Colleges of Nursing (AACN)
American Psychiatric Nurses Association (APNA)
AMTA
APNA
Art Therapy Credentials Board
Assistant to Specialist
Association for Play Therapy (APT)
Augustine
Baby-Tender (aka Skinner Air Box)
Bogust v. Iverson
Boston Civic Service House (CSH)
Broker
Bronfenbrenner, Urie
Buckley Amendment
Class Interval
Commuter Services
Conant, James Bryant
Control Theory
Cooper's Cube Model
CSCORE
Data Manager
Delusive Perceptions
Democratically Held Discussion Groups
Demonstrating the 3 C's
Developing an Understanding of Self and Others (DUSO)
Developmental Norms
Dinkmeyer, Don
Duhka
Entropy
Esquirol, Jean
Evaluation of the Program
Expert Review
Foundational Rules
Fry, William
Generalist
Griggs v. Duke Power Company
Guntrip, Harry
Hayes, Steven
Health Services
HS--BCP
Human Resources (Field of)
Human Services—Board Certified Practitioner (HS-BCP)
Iatrogenic Disorder
Impulsivity (as per Erikson)
Institute for Sex Research
Janet, Pierre
Journal of Human Services
Learning Environment
Licensure Committee
Military and Government
Myth of the Independent Mind
Perceived Environmental Factors
Society for Individual Psychology
Society for Psychoanalytic Endeavors
Society for Psychotherapy
Specialty Credentials in Social Work
Standards for the Preparation of Counselors and Other Personnel Service Specialists
Student Affairs Administrators in Higher Education
Tactile Response
Teacher/Educator
Tomm, Karl
Trail Making Test
Vicarious Traumatization

RANKINGS OF "2"

American Public Human Services Association (APHSA)
APHSA
Ellis, Debbie Joffe
Encounters with Self
International General Medical Society for Psychotherapy
Letting Down of Boundaries
McPheeters, Harold
National Organization for Human Service Education
National Organization for Human Services (NOHS)
NOHS
North American Drama Therapy Association (NADTA)
Skill Standards
Winslade, John

RANKINGS OF "1"

Council for Standards in Human Service Education (CSHSE)
CSHSE
Ethical Standards of Human Service Professionals
Human Service Professionals, Roles and Functions
Link, The
Mobilizer
Southern Regional Education Board (SREB)
SREB
Tau Upsilon Alpha (TUA)
Twelve Competency Areas
White, Cheryl

INDEX OF HUMAN SERVICES

WORDS AND TERMS

The following words and terms are in order, based on their rankings. A ranking of 10 means that in the opinion of the authors, the item has a very good chance of finding its way on a credentialing exam. A ranking of 1 means it is unlikely to be found on a credentialing exam. If you are studying for such an exam, we encourage you to focus on the higher numbers (perhaps 7 through 10), and if you have time, then review the numbers below those. Good luck!

RANKINGS OF "10"

RANKINGS OF "9"

RANKINGS OF "8"

Superego
Supplemental Nutritional Assistance Program (SNAP)
Support
TANF
Tau Upsilon Alpha (TUA)
Temporary Assistance for Needy Families (TANF)
Tentative Questions
Termination
Therapist
Therapy Group
Time Out
Transition
Transition Stage
Transparency
Transphobia
Transsexual
Transvestite
Treatment Planning
Unconditioned Stimulus
Values in the Helping Relationship
Walking Into Agency
*Wechsler Preschool and Primary Scale of Intelligen*ce (*WPPSI*)
Wellness
Wellness Approach
Women
Work Stage (in Group Counseling)
Work Stage (in Individual Counseling

RANKINGS OF "7"

Antipsychotic Drugs
Asperger's Disorder
Assigned Sex
Autism Spectrum Disorder
Autonomy vs. Shame and Doubt (ages 1-3 years)
Backup Reinforcer
Body Positioning
Codeine
Coming Out
Co-Morbidity
Cross-Cultural Symptomatology, Misunderstanding
Data Manager
Debriefing
Deepening Understanding and Goal Setting Stage
Defense Mechanisms
Deinstitutionalization
Delirium Tremens (DTs)
Democratically Held Discussion Groups
Dependent Variable
Designer Drugs
Determinism
Developmental Crisis
Developmental Models
Developmental Models of Cultural/Racial Identity
Developmental Norms
Developmental Stress
Diaries/Journals
Directive Approach
Directive Theories
Disaster Counseling
Discussion, Implications, and Conclusions
Dix, Dorothea
ECT
Ego Identity (Adolescents)
Electroconvulsive Therapy (ECT)
Enable
Enabler
Encounter Group
End-of-Life Care
Enmeshment
Enuresis
Environmental Assessment
Environmental Contexts
Epistemology
Erikson's Psychosocial Theory of Development
Ethical Codes, Limitations of
Ethical Hot Spots
Existential Crisis
Existential-Humanistic Approaches
Experimental Group
Experimental Psychologists
Extinguished
Family-Based Helping/Counseling
Family Guidance
Fee for Service
Feeding and Eating Disorders
Feeling Word Checklist
Feminist Counseling/Therapy
Fentanyl
Fifth Force
Fight or Flight Response
Fixated
Forced Choice Closed Question
Forming
Friendly Visitors
Full Potential (Rogers)
Gatekeeping
Gender Binary
Gender Expression
Gender Identity
Gender Neutral
Gender Non-Conforming (GNC)
Generalizability
Generalization
Generativity vs. Stagnation (Middle/Late Adulthood)
Genetic Counseling
Genogram
Gerontological Settings
Gilligan, Carol
Gilligan's Theory of Women's Moral Development
Glasser, William
Great Society
Grief, Stages of
Group Cohesion
Group Counseling
Group Dynamics
Group Process
Group Therapy
Guidance

RANKINGS OF "6"

RANKINGS OF "5"

RANKINGS OF "4"

RANKINGS OF "3"

RANKINGS OF "2"

Academic Support Services
Causal-Comparative Research
Constructivist Career Counseling
Constructivist Career Development Theory
D'Andrea, Michael and Daniels, Judy
Davis, Jesse
de Shazer, Steve
Decentration from Self
Definitional Ceremonies
Deflection
Delusive Perceptions
De-Reflection
Derived Score
Diathesis-Stress Model
Differential Analysis
Digital Communication
DISCOVER
Discriminant Analysis (DA)
Disqualifying or Discounting the Positive
Distance Learning Sites (and Directors of)
Dreikurs, Rudolf
Duhka
Dummy Coding
Eigenvalue
Einfühlung
Endogenous Variable
Enneagram
Entropy
Epistemological Reflection
Eras
Ethics Code of the American Counseling Association
Explanatory Correlation
Exploratory Factor Analysis
Exploratory Research
Explosive/Authentic Layer
Ex-Post Facto Research
Face Validity
Factor Loading
Fairbarn, W. R. D.
Faith Development, Fowler's Theory of
False Connection
Financial Aid Office
First Comprehensive Theory of Counseling
Fisch, Dick
Fliess, Wilhem
Fluid Intelligence
Founder of the Counseling Field
Founder of Vocational Guidance
Galton, Sir Francis
Galton's Board
General, Typical, Variant
Gestalt Consultation
G.I. Bill
Gnosticism
Going Around
Goodness-of-Fit
Gould, Roger
Heidegger, Martin
Hermeneutical Psychology
Heterosexual-Homosexual Rating Scale
High-Level Distancing Tasks
Histogram
Holistic Process
Iatrogenic Disorder
Impasse Layer
Impersonal Unconscious
Implosive Layer
Impulsivity (as per Erikson)
Inadequacy
Indebtedness
Insight and Interpretation
Institute for Sex Research
Integrative Models of Supervision
Internal Consistency Reliability
International Board for the Certification of Group Psychotherapists (IBCGP)
International Registry of Counselor Education Programs (IRCEP)
Interquartile Range
Inverted Pyramid Method (IPM)
Iowa Test of Basic Skills
IRCEP
Journal for Individual Psychology
Journal for Social Action in Counseling and Psychology
Journal for Specialists in Group Work
Journal of College Counseling
Journal of Creativity in Mental Health
Journal of Employment Counseling
Journal of Humanistic Counseling
Journal of LGBT Issues in Counseling
Kernberg, Otto
Kraepelin, Emil
Layers of Neurosis
Liberal Stage
Low-Level Distancing Tasks
Loyalties
Mann-Whitney U Test
Master's in Psychology and Counseling
Accreditation Council (MPCAC)
Milan Group
Mimesis
Minnesota Point of View
Multiple Regression
Narrative Reasoning
Nasal Reflect Neurosis
NASPA
National Association of Women Deans,
Administrators, and Counselors (NAWDAC)
National Credentialing Academy (NCA)
National Office for School Counselor Advocacy
National Standards for School Counseling Programs
National Vocational Guidance Association (NVGA)
NAWDAC
NBPTS
NCA

RANKINGS OF "1"

Index of Human Services Words

Appendix A

Websites of the American Counseling Association and Its Divisions

National Association
ACA: American Counseling Association
Website: www.counseling.org/

Divisions of the American Counseling Association
AADA: Association for Adult Development and Aging
Website: www.aadaweb.org/

AARC: Assessment for Assessment and Research in Counseling
Website: aarc-counseling.org/

ACAC: Association for Child and Adolescent Counseling
Website: acachild.org/

ACC: Association for Creativity in Counseling
Website: www.creativecounselor.org/

ACCA: American College Counseling Association
Website: www.collegecounseling.org/

ACES: Association for Counselor Education and Supervision
Website: www.acesonline.net/

AHC: Association for Humanistic Counseling
Website: afhc.camp9.org/

ALGBTIC: Association for Lesbian, Gay, Bisexual, and Transgender Issues in Counseling
Website: www.algbtic.org/

AMCD: Association for Multicultural Counseling and Development
Website: www.multiculturalcounseling.org/

AMHCA: American Mental Health Counselors Association
Website: www.amhca.org/

ARCA: American Rehabilitation Counseling Association
Website: www.arcaweb.org/

ASCA: American School Counselor Association
Website: https://www.schoolcounselor.org/

ASERVIC: Association for Spiritual, Ethical, and Religious Values in Counseling
Website: https://www.aservic.org/

ASGW: Association for Specialists in Group Work
Website: www.asgw.org/

CSJ: Counselors for Social Justice
Website: https://counseling-csj.org/

IAAOC: International Association of Addictions and Offender Counselors
Website: www.iaaoc.org/

IAMFC: International Association of Marriage and Family Counselors
Website: www.iamfconline.org/

MGCA: Military and Government Counseling Association
Website: acegonline.org/

NCDA: National Career Development Association
Website: www.ncda.org/aws/NCDA/pt/sp/home_page

NECA: National Employment Counseling Association
Website: www.employmentcounseling.org/

Appendix B

Websites of the National Organization of Human Services and Its Regions

National Association
National Organization for Human Services (NOHS)
Website: www.nationalhumanservices.org/

Regional Associations
MACHS: Mid-Atlantic Consortium for Human Services
Website: www.nationalhumanservices.org/machs
Contact: machs@nationalhumanservices.org

MWOHS: Mid-West Organization of Human Services
Website: www.nationalhumanservices.org/mwohs-who
Contact: mwohs@nationalhumanservices.org

NEOHS: New England Organization for Human Services
Website: www.nationalhumanservices.org/neohs
Contact: neohs@nationalhumanservices.org

NWHS: Northwest Human Services Association
Website: http://www.northwesthumanservices.org/
Contact: nwest@nationalhumanservices.org

SOHS: Southern Organization for Human Services
Website: www.nationalhumanservices.org/sohs
Contact: sohs@nationalhumanservices.org

Western NOHS: Western Region of Human Service Professionals
Website: www.nationalhumanservices.org/west-2013-regional-conference
Contact: west@nationalhumanservices.org

Appendix C

Websites of Select Professional Associations in the Mental Health Professions

AAPC: American Association of Pastoral Counselors
Website: www.aapc.org

AATA: American Art Therapy Association
Web site: www.arttherapy.org/aata-educational-programs.html

AAMFT: American Association for Marriage and Family Therapy
Website: www.aamft.org

APA: American Psychiatric Association
Website: https://www.psychiatry.org/

APHSA: American Public Human Services Association
Website: www.aphsa.org/

APsaA: American Psychoanalytic Association
Website:

APA: American Psychological Association
Website: www.apa.org/

APNA: American Psychiatric Nurses Association
Website: www.apna.org

NASP: National Association of School Psychologists
Website: https://www.nasponline.org/

NASW: National Association of Social Workers
Website: www.socialworkers.org/

Appendix D

Ethics Codes, Competencies, and Credentialing Bodies of Select Professional Associations

Ethics Codes

AAMFT: American Association for Marriage and Family Therapy
Ethics Code: www.aamft.org/iMIS15/AAMFT/Content/Legal_Ethics/Code_of_Ethics.aspx

ACA: American Counseling Association
Ethics Code: www.counseling.org/knowledge-center/ethics

ACES: Association for Counselor Education and Supervision
Ethics Code: www.acesonline.net/resources/ethical-guidelines-supervisors

AMHCA: American Mental Health Counselors Association
Ethics Code: www.amhca.org/?page=codeofethics

APA: American Psychiatric Association
Ethics Code: https://www.psychiatry.org/psychiatrists/practice/ethics

APA: American Psychological Association
Ethics Code: www.apa.org/ethics/code/

ASCA: American School Counselor Association
Ethics Code: https://www.schoolcounselor.org/school-counselors-members/legal-ethical

CSJ: Counselors for Social Justice
Ethics Code: www.psysr.org/jsacp/Ibrahim-v3n2_1-21.pdf

IAMFC: International Association of Marriage and Family Counselors
Ethics Code: www.iamfconline.org/public/department3.cfm

NASW: National Association of Social Workers
Ethics Code: https://www.socialworkers.org/pubs/code/default.asp

NBCC: National Board for Certified Counselors
Ethics Code: http://www.nbcc.org/InteractiveCodeOfEthics/

NCDA: National Career Development Association
Ethics Code: ncda.org/aws/NCDA/pt/sp/guidelines

NOHS: National Organization for Human Services
Ethics Code: www.nationalhumanservices.org/ethical-standards-for-hs-professionals

Competencies

ALGBTIC: Association for Lesbian, Gay, Bisexual, and Transgender Issues in Counseling
Competencies for counseling LGBQQIA individuals and transgender clients
Website: www.algbtic.org/competencies.html

ASERVIC: Association for Spiritual, Ethical, and Religious Values in Counseling
Spiritual competencies
Website: www.aservic.org/resources/spiritual-competencies/

ASGW: Association for Specialists in Group Work
Best practice guidelines in group work
Website: www.asgw.org/s/ASGW_Best_Practices.pdf

AMCD: Association for Multicultural Counseling and Development
Multicultural and social justice counseling competencies
Obtain from: Ratts, R., Singh, A. A., Nassar-McMillan, Butler, S. K., McCullough, J. R. (2016). Multicultural and social justice counseling competencies. *Journal of Multicultural Counseling and Development*, 44, 28–48.

Credentialing in Human Services and Counseling

CCE: Center for Credentialing in Education
Credential: HS—BCP: Human Services Board Certified Practitioner
Website: hwww.cce-global.org/

CRCC: Commission on Rehabilitation Counselor Certification
Credential: CRC: Certified Rehabilitation Counselor
Website: www.crccertification.com

NBCC: National Board for Certified Counselors
Credential: NCC: National Certified Counselor
Credential: CCMHC: Certified Clinical Mental Health Counselor
Credential: MAC: Master Addictions Counselor
Credential: NCSC: National Certified School Counselor
Website: www.nbcc.org

Appendix E

Graduate Programs in Counseling, Human Services, and Related Professions

The following lists a number of master's and doctoral programs for a variety of mental health related professions.

Graduate Programs in Counseling:
Council for Accreditation of Counseling and Related Educational Programs
1001 North Fairfax Street, Suite 510
Alexandria, VA 22314
Phone: 703.535.5990
Website: www.cacrep.org
Related association: American Counseling Association

Book: Counselor Preparation: Programs, Faculty, Trends (13th ed.) (2012).
Authors: *Schweiger, Henderson, McCaskill,, Clawson, & Collins*
Routledge Publishing Company
7625 Empire Drive
Florence, Kentucky 41042-2919
Phone: 800.634.7064
Web site: www.routledge.com/
Email: orders@taylorandfrancis.com

Graduate Programs in Human Services
GradSchools.com: Human Services Graduate Programs
GradSchools.com
3803 W Chester Pike, Suite 125
Newtown Square, PA 19073
Phone: 866.472.3266
Website: https://www.gradschools.com/programs/human-services

Council for Standards in Human Service Education
3337 Duke Street
Alexandria, VA 22314
Phone: 571-257-3959
Website: www.cshse.org
Email: info@cshse.org

Doctoral Programs in Counseling and Clinical Psychology:
American Psychological Association (APA)
750 First Street NE
Washington, DC 20002
Graduate and Postdoctoral Education
Phone: 800.374.2721 TDD/TTY: 202.336.6123
Website: www.apa.org/education/grad/index.aspx
Related association: American Psychological Association (www.apa.org)

Graduate Programs in Rehabilitation Counseling:
Council on Rehabilitation Education
1699 Woodfield Rd., Suite 300
Schauburg, IL 60173
Phone: 847.944.1345
Email: sdenys@cpcredentialing.com
Web site: www.core-rehab.org
Rehabilitation Counselors and Educators Association (rehabcea.org/)

Graduate Programs in Marriage And Family Therapy:
Commission on Accreditation for Marriage and Family Therapy Education
112 South Alfred Street,
Alexandria, VA 22314-3061
Phone: 703.253.-0473
Website: www.aamft.org

Clinical Pastoral Programs:
Association for Clinical Pastoral Education, Inc.
1 West Court Square #325 Decatur, GA 30033
Phone: 404.320.1472
Website: www.acpe.edu

Graduate Programs in Social Work:
Council on Social Work Education
1701 Duke St., Suite 200
Alexandria, VA 22314
Phone: 703.683.8080
Website: www.cswe.org/Accreditation.aspx

Graduate Programs in Art Therapy:
American Art Therapy Association
4875 Eisenhower Avenue, Suite 240
Alexandria, VA 22304
Phone: 888.290.0878
Website: www.arttherapy.org/aata-educational-programs.html

Appendix F

Undergraduate Programs in Human Services

Human Service Programs Accredited by CSHSE

Council for Standards in Human Service Education (CSHSE)
3337 Duke Street
Alexandria, VA 22314
Phone: 571-257-3959
Website: www.cshse.org
Email: info@cshse.org

Select Online Programs in Human Services

Guide to Online Schools
Website: www.guidetoonlineschools.com/degrees/human-services

"Most Affordable"
Website: www.onlineu.org/most-affordable-colleges/human-services-degrees

College Board Search of Human Services Programs

Type in "Human Services" in the Search Tab on top
Website: https://bigfuture.collegeboard.org/

Appendix G

Overview of DSM-5 Diagnostic Categories

The following offers a brief description of these diagnostic categories and is summarized from DSM-5 (APA, 2013a). Please refer to the DSM-5 for an in-depth review of each disorder:

Neurodevelopmental Disorders. This group of disorders typically refers to those that manifest during early development, although diagnoses are sometimes not assigned until adulthood. Examples of neurodevelopmental disorders include intellectual disabilities, communication disorders, autism spectrum disorders (incorporating the former categories of autistic disorder, Asperger's disorder, childhood disintegrative disorder, and pervasive developmental disorder), ADHD, specific learning disorders, motor disorders, and other neurodevelopmental disorders.

Schizophrenia Spectrum and Other Psychotic Disorders. The disorders that belong to this section all have one feature in common: psychotic symptoms; that is, delusions, hallucinations, grossly disorganized or abnormal motor behavior, and/or negative symptoms. The disorders include schizotypal personality disorder (which is listed again, and explained more comprehensively, in the category of Personality Disorders in the DSM-5), delusional disorder, brief psychotic disorder, schizophreniform disorder, schizophrenia, schizoaffective disorder, substance/medication-induced psychotic disorders, psychotic disorders due to another medical condition, and catatonic disorders.

Bipolar and Related Disorders. The disorders in this category refer to disturbances in mood in which the client cycles through stages of mania or mania and depression. Both children and adults can be diagnosed with bipolar disorder, and the clinician can work to identify the pattern of mood presentation, such as rapid-cycling, which is more often observed in children. These disorders include bipolar I, bipolar II, cyclothymic disorder, substance/medication-induced, bipolar and related disorder due to another medical condition, and other specified or unspecified bipolar and related disorders.

Depressive Disorders. Previously grouped into the broader category of "mood disorders" in the DSM-IV-TR, these disorders describe conditions where depressed mood is the overarching concern. They include disruptive mood* dysregulation disorder, major depressive disorder, persistent depressive disorder (also known as dysthymia), and premenstrual dysphoric disorder.

Anxiety Disorders. There are a wide range of anxiety disorders, which can be diagnosed by identifying a general or specific cause of unease or fear. This anxiety or fear is considered clinically significant when it is excessive and persistent over time. Examples of anxiety disorders that typically manifest earlier in development include separation anxiety and selective mutism. Other examples of anxiety disorders are specific phobia, social anxiety disorder (also known as social phobia), panic disorder, and generalized anxiety disorder.

Obsessive-Compulsive and Related Disorders. Disorders in this category all involve obsessive thoughts and compulsive behaviors that are uncontrollable and the client feels compelled to perform them. Diagnoses in this category include obsessive-compulsive disorder, body dysmorphic disorder, hoarding disorder, trichotillomania (or hair-pulling disorder), and excoriation (or skin-picking) disorder.

Trauma- and Stressor-Related Disorders. A new category for DSM-5, trauma and stress disorders emphasize the pervasive impact that life events can have on an individual's emotional and physical well-being. Diagnoses include reactive attachment disorder, disinhibited social engagement disorder, posttraumatic stress disorder, acute stress disorder, and adjustment disorders.

Dissociative Disorders. These disorders indicate a temporary or prolonged disruption to consciousness that can cause an individual to misinterpret identity, surroundings, and memories. Diagnoses include dissociative identity disorder (formerly known as multiple personality disorder), dissociative amnesia, depersonalization/derealization disorder, and other specified and unspecified dissociative disorders.

Somatic Symptom and Related Disorders. Somatic symptom disorders were previously referred to as "somatoform disorders" and are characterized by the experiencing of a physical symptom without evidence of a physical cause, thus suggesting a psychological cause. Somatic symptom disorders include somatic symptom disorder, illness anxiety disorder (formerly hypochondriasis), conversion (or functional neurological symptom) disorder, psychological factors affecting other medical conditions, and factitious disorder.

Feeding and Eating Disorders. This group of disorders describes clients who have severe concerns about the amount or type of food they eat to the point that serious health problems, or even death, can result from their eating behaviors. Examples include avoidant/restrictive food intake disorder, anorexia nervosa, bulimia nervosa, binge eating disorder, pica, and rumination disorder.

Elimination Disorders. These disorders can manifest at any point in a person's life, although they are typically diagnosed in early childhood or adolescence. They include enuresis, which is the inappropriate elimination of urine, and encopresis, which is the inappropriate elimination of feces. These behaviors may or may not be intentional.

Sleep-Wake Disorders. This category refers to disorders where one's sleep patterns are severely impacted, and they often co-occur with other disorders (e.g., depression or anxiety). Some examples include insomnia disorder, hypersomnolence disorder, restless legs syndrome, narcolepsy, and nightmare Disorder. A number of sleep-wake disorders involve variations in breathing, such as sleep-related hypoventilation, obstructive sleep apnea hypopnea, or central sleep apnea. See the DSM-*5* for the full listing and descriptions of these disorders.

Sexual Dysfunctions. These disorders are related to problems that disrupt sexual functioning or one's ability to experience sexual pleasure. They occur across sexes and include delayed ejaculation, erectile disorder, female orgasmic disorder, and premature (or early) ejaculation disorder, among others.

Gender Dysphoria. Formerly termed, "gender identity disorder," this category includes those individuals who experience significant distress with the sex they were born and with associated gender roles. This diagnosis has been separated from the category of sexual disorders, as it is now accepted that gender dysphoria does not relate to a person's sexual attractions.

Disruptive, Impulse Control, and Conduct Disorders. These disorders are characterized by socially unacceptable or otherwise disruptive and harmful behaviors that are outside of the individual's control. Generally, more common in males than in females, and often first seen in childhood, they include oppositional defiant disorder, conduct disorder, intermittent explosive disorder, antisocial personality disorder (which is also coded in the category of personality disorders), kleptomania, and pyromania.

Substance-Related and Addictive Disorders. Substance use disorders include disruptions in functioning as the result of a craving or strong urge. Often caused by prescribed and illicit drugs or the exposure to toxins, with these disorders the brain's reward system pathways are activated when the substance is taken (or in the case of gambling disorder, when the behavior is being performed). Some common substances include alcohol, caffeine, nicotine, cannabis, opioids, inhalants, amphetamine, phencyclidine (PCP), sedatives, hypnotics or anxiolytics. Substance use disorders are further designated with the following terms: intoxication, withdrawal, induced, or unspecified.

Neurocognitive Disorders. These disorders are diagnosed when one's decline in cognitive functioning is significantly different from the past and is usually the result of a medical condition (e.g., Parkinson's or Alzheimer's disease), the use of a substance/medication, or traumatic brain injury, among other phenomena. Examples of neurocognitive disorders (NCD) include delirium, and several types of major and mild NCDs such as frontotemporal NCD, NCD due to Parkinson's disease, NCD due to HIV infection, NCD due to Alzheimer's disease, substance- or medication-induced NCD, and vascular NCD, among others.

Personality Disorders. The 10 personality disorders in DSM-5 all involve a pattern of experiences and behaviors that are persistent, inflexible, and deviate from one's cultural expectations. Usually, this pattern emerges in adolescence or early adulthood and causes severe distress in one's interpersonal relationships. The personality disorders are grouped into the three following clusters which are based on similar behaviors:

- Cluster A: Paranoid, schizoid, and schizotypal. These individuals seem bizarre or unusual in their behaviors and interpersonal relations.

- Cluster B: Antisocial, borderline, histrionic, and narcissistic. These individuals seem overly emotional, are melodramatic, or unpredictable in their behaviors and interpersonal relations.

- Cluster C: Avoidant, dependent, and obsessive-compulsive (not to be confused with obsessive-compulsive disorder). These individuals tend to appear anxious, worried, or fretful in their behaviors.

Paraphilic Disorders. These disorders are diagnosed when the client is sexual aroused to circumstances that deviate from traditional sexual stimuli *and* when such behaviors result in harm or significant emotional distress. The disorders include exhibitionistic disorder, voyeuristic disorder, frotteurisitc disorder, sexual sadism and sexual masochism disorders, fetishistic disorder, transvestic disorder, pedophilic disorder, and other specified and unspecified paraphilic disorders.

Other Mental Disorders. This diagnostic category includes mental disorders that did not fall within one of the previously mentioned groups and do not have unifying characteristics. Examples include other specified mental disorder due to another medical condition, unspecified mental disorders due to another medical condition, other specified mental disorder, and unspecified mental disorder.

Medication-Induced Movement Disorders and Other Adverse Effects of Medications. These disorders are the result of adverse and severe side effects to medications, although a causal link cannot always be shown. Some of these disorders include neuroleptic-induced parkinsonism, neuroleptic malignant syndrome, medication-induced dystonia, medication-induced acute akathisia, tardive dyskinesia, tardive akathisia, medication-induced postural tremor, other medication-induced movement disorder, antidepressant discontinuation syndrome, and other adverse effect of medication.

Other Conditions That May Be a Focus of Clinical Assessment. Reminiscent of Axis IV of the previous edition of the DSM, this last part of Section II ends with a description of concerns that could be clinically significant, such as abuse/neglect, relational problems, psychosocial, personal, and environmental concerns, educational/occupational problems, housing and economic problems, and problems related to the legal system. These conditions, which are not consider mental disorders, are generally listed as V codes, which correspond to ICD-9, or Z codes, which correspond to ICD-10.

In addition to the above categories, the DSM offers other *specified* and u*nspecified disorders* that can be used when a provider believes an individual's impairment to functioning or distress is clinically significant; however, it does not meet the specific diagnostic criteria in that category. The "other specified" should be used when the clinician wants to communicate specifically why the criteria do not fit. The "unspecified disorder" should be used when he or she does not wish, or is unable to, communicate specifics. For example, if someone appeared to have significant panic attacks but only had three of the four required criteria, the diagnosis could be "Other Specified Panic Disorder—due to insufficient symptoms." Otherwise, the clinician would report "Unspecified Panic Disorder."